ANOTHER JAPAN IS POSSIBLE

ANOTHER JAPAN IS POSSIBLE

New Social Movements and Global Citizenship Education

Edited by Jennifer Chan

Stanford University Press
Stanford, California

Stanford University Press
Stanford, California

The songs on pp. vii and 335 are reprinted by permission of Sugi Goro.

Printed in the United States of America on acid-free, archival-quality paper.

Library of Congress Cataloging-in-Publication Data

Another Japan is possible : new social movements and global citizenship education / edited by Jennifer Chan.
     p. cm.
  Includes bibliographical references and index.
   ISBN 978-0-8047-5781-2 (cloth : alk. paper)--ISBN 978-0-8047-5782-9 (pbk. : alk. paper)
   1. Social movements--Japan. 2. Social problems--Japan. 3. Civics--Study and teaching--Japan. 4. World citizenship. 5. Globalization--Japan. 6. Japan--Social conditions--21st century. 7. Japan--Economic conditions--21st century. I. Chan, Jennifer.

HN723.5A686 2008
303.48'40952--dc22   2007045119

Designed by Bruce Lundquist
Typeset at Stanford University Press in 10/14 Minion Pro

To Claire and Paul—
two global citizens in the making—
and to all "cosmopolitan bricoleurs of resistance,"
who remake the world through their stories

Watashi wa wasurenai [I will not forget]

While I wash my face
While I walk on a street corner
I continue living with the Constitution today
My thoughts on hope for peace, equality, and justice
In the spring night
And in the summer morning
I will not forget

While I cut vegetables
While I write letters
I continue living with the Constitution today
My feelings for peace, equality, and justice
In the fall night
And in the winter morning
I will not forget

Our sky spreads far and wide
Let our voice spread over the world
Our feelings for peace, equality, and justice
Our voice coming from a small town far away

Words by Sugi Goro
Music by Ichino Munehiko
Translation by Hara Hiroko

CONTENTS

TABLES AND FIGURES

Tables

Figures

ACKNOWLEDGMENTS

"**WHY STUDY JAPANESE SOCIAL MOVEMENTS**, and a small segment of it?!" I have often been asked this question. I think it is no longer possible to separate clearly the global and the local. When I first lived in Japan, in the early 1990s, I was a futures trader at a major bank in Tokyo, playing my own part, without the slightest consciousness, in "accelerating the compression of time and space" that globalization theorists talk about. I became interested in Japanese social movements in a rather circuitous fashion by way of UN world conferences. In UN corridors I saw thousands of NGOs from the four corners of the earth working on a wide spectrum of human rights issues. I discovered that Japanese NGOs were no exception. This project, as a sequel of sorts to my first book on gender and human rights politics in Japan, actually began in the idyllic town of Evian in France in June 2003 when I met members of ATTAC Japan during the alternative G8 Summit. The project continued its trajectory through Cancun, Mexico, at the WTO ministerial in September 2003—when the Japanese NGO group Food Action 21, among others, protested against the Agreement on Agriculture—and on the dusty grounds of the World Social Forum in Mumbai in January 2004, where I sat down to lunch next to Yasuda Yukihiro of the Labor Net, who revealed to me a whole subaltern Japanese world. Intellectual curiosity obliges; I attended the first Social Forum in Japan on the beautiful Kyoto University campus in December 2004. Over organic tea and slow food, some four hundred Japanese activists converged and discussed alternatives to free trade and global militarism. I think few people, both within and outside of Japan, know much about these Japanese activists.

I want to go beyond both the predominant Western understanding of local Japanese social movements as weak, without advocacy, and Japanese prejudice against leftist sectarianism to look at the discourses and actions of the nascent alternative globalization movement, revived peace movement, and expanding antidiscrimination movement in Japan.

Citizenship has traditionally been linked to a passport. The realities of transnational issues and the mobilization surrounding these issues, however, make the concept of national citizenship extremely untenable. This book's postnational and postmodern approach to citizenship is intentional. The narratives of the fifty-two activists who have authored the book's chapters demonstrate how citizenship is constantly being performed rather than given. In part to answer the common critiques of postmodernism—that there is nothing outside the text, and the aimless, endless deconstruction—this book bases its postmodern analysis of citizenship on activists' experience, and ties that analysis to a clear political project, that of locating alternatives to neoliberalism, nationalism, and militarism.

I have found the pressures of academia and the demands of parenting to allow very little time for exercising citizenship responsibilities. Editing this book has been a way to assuage my guilt and express my hope to end militarism. (I researched and wrote the book during the Iraq war and the continuing worldwide mobilization against both neoliberal globalization and imperialism.) It has been an extremely rewarding journey. Fieldwork brought me to all kinds of unforgettable places, including to Mumbai for the mega World Social Forum gathering; to the secluded Hōshakuji Temple in Kyoto, where the Advocacy and Monitoring Network on Sustainable Development (AM-Net) organized an activist retreat on the World Trade Organization (WTO) and free trade agreements (FTAs); on a tour of the Sakae area in Nagoya to look at the issue of trafficking firsthand with the founder of the Filipino Migrants Center Nagoya, Ishihara Virgie, and feminist scholar Hanochi Seiko of Chubu University; to Shinjuku Park, adjacent to the towering Tokyo Metropolitan Government buildings, where more than a thousand homeless people waited for their Sunday rice bowl; to Kobe in July 2005 for the provocative seventh International Congress on AIDS in Asia and the Pacific; to the Aichi Expo 2005, where I was a volunteer for the Japan Campaign to Ban Landmines; to the barbed-wired beaches of Henoko in Okinawa; and to spectacular protests at the WTO's ministerial meeting in downtown Wanchai, Hong Kong, in December 2005.

I would like to thank first and foremost the fifty-two trailblazers who have graciously shared their experiences in this volume. I have learned more than I would ever imagine about the Tobin Tax, the Peace Boat, labor restructuring, indirect discrimination, FTAs, trafficking, water privatization, rice politics, military bases, constitutional revision, the landmine ban, nuclear disarmament, HIV / AIDS, racial discrimination, disabled people's rights, the death penalty, and slow food. Each interview was a privileged moment, like an oasis in the Japanese political desert.

I especially want to thank five activists and academics—Yasuda Yukihiro, Hara Yuriko, Uemura Hideaki, Tarui Masayoshi, and Ishihara Mikiko—for their generous recommendations of contacts. Uemura Hideaki and Paul Jobin courageously read through the entire manuscript and provided constructive feedback. I have also been blessed by continuous friendships with Hara Yuriko, Shimada Yoshiko, Nakamura Hayato, Kasuga Sho, Kitagawa Yasuhiro, Uemura Hideaki, and Ishihara Mikiko, who are global citizens par excellence. Thanks to Fukazawa Junko for so kindly arranging accommodations in downtown Tokyo and for introducing me to her circle of feminist friends. This book would not have been completed without the expert assistance of Hiroko Hara, researcher extraordinaire and doctoral student in the Department of Educational Studies at the University of British Columbia (UBC), who worked tirelessly throughout every phase of the project. I am grateful for the funding support of the advanced research fellowship offered by the Program on U.S.-Japan Relations of the Weatherhead Center for International Affairs at Harvard University. My heartfelt thanks go to its director, Professor Susan Pharr; its associate director, Shinju Fujihara; and Shannon Rice and Jason Ri for providing me with the best institutional and intellectual support to undertake this project. Part of the fieldwork was funded by a Humanities and Social Sciences Research Grant from the University of British Columbia. The book was completed during a two-year research leave from my home institution, UBC. I want to thank Dean Rob Tierny and department head Kjell Rubenson for their support. I am also grateful for the visionary support of Muriel Bell and for the editorial help of Kirsten Oster, Joa Suorez, Mariana Raykov, and Alice Rowan of Stanford University Press. Thanks are due as well to the two anonymous reviewers who were brave souls not only to read four hundred pages but also to give constructive feedback.

The majority of the interviews were completed in December 2004. Although I have tried my best to update any information that has changed, the nongovernmental world moves much faster than academia. After each interview, I have added a list of related Web sites and references for readers to turn to for the latest information on each organization and movement referred to in the text. The suggested resources do not necessarily reflect the views or positions of the interviewee or her organization.

Tenure requirements and the dictates of the biological clock made the publication of my first and second books coincide, rather imperfectly, with the tender years of my first and second child. The project often took me away from home. In the eyes of Claire and Paul, each exciting adventure and encounter of Mommy's might mean one less book read together and partial summer vacations. A peripatetic academic career requires children to be flexible and mobile. As the number of manuscript pages increased, Claire attended public elementary school in Cambridge under the shroud of No Child Left Behind while Paul negotiated the three-year waiting lists of Cambridge day care centers. Breaks in the tempo of writing coincided with frequent New England snowstorms, which meant no-school snow days to which Canadian parents were unaccustomed. When Harvard University president Lawrence Summers made his remarks about innate cognitive gender differences, my daughter thought it might be time to return to Canada. I would like to thank Yves, who over the course of the last decade has perfected, more than anyone else, the fine skills of balancing academia and child care. Dual academic careers are not for everyone. Our days are often scheduled by minutes. But the rewards have been gratifying. Not only has Yves' book on corporate restructuring in France, Japan, and Korea been published by Cornell University Press, but for the first time our research agendas crossed paths through labor and food politics.

Now that this book has finally gone to press, I think it is time to live as I preach. One of the most concrete alternatives to neoliberalism and violence is to go slow. While academia remains one of the most progressive institutions, its complicity in breakneck globalization has rarely been challenged. As part and parcel of the alternative globalization movement, we need to believe in and build a new movement for a slow academe!

Vancouver
January 2007

ABBREVIATIONS AND CONVENTIONS

ADB	Asian Development Bank
APEC	Asia-Pacific Economic Cooperation
CAT	Convention Against Torture and Other Cruel, Inhuman, or Degrading Treatment or Punishment
CEDAW	Convention on the Elimination of All Forms of Discrimination Against Women
CPR	Center for Prisoners' Rights, Japan
DPJ	Democratic Party of Japan
ECOSOC	UN Economic and Social Council
EIA	Environmental Impact Assessment
EVSL	Early Voluntary Sector Liberalization
FINRAGE	Feminist International Network Against Reproductive and Genetic Engineering
FOM	Friends of Multifunctionality
GATS	General Agreement on Trade in Services
GMO	Genetically modified organisms
GPPAC	Global Partnership for the Prevention of Armed Conflict
ICC	International Criminal Court
ICERD	International Convention on the Elimination of Racial Discrimination

ICFTU	International Confederation of Free Trade Unions
IFG	International Forum on Globalization
ILO	International Labor Organization
IMADR	International Movement Against All Forms of Discrimination and Racism
IMF	International Monetary Fund
JANIC	Japan NGO Center for International Cooperation
JAR	Japan Association for Refugees
JCLU	Japan Civil Liberties Union
JCP	Japan Communist Party
JDA	Japan Defense Agency
JICA	Japan International Cooperation Agency
JNATIP	Japan Network Against Trafficking in Persons
JNICC	Japan Network for the International Criminal Court
JNNC	Japan NGO Network for CEDAW
JOVC	Japan Overseas Volunteer Corps
KSF	Kyoto Social Forum
LDP	Liberal Democratic Party
LIM	*Liberalization Impacts Monitor*
MAFF	Ministry of Agriculture, Forestry and Fisheries
MDG	Millennium Development Goals
METI	Ministry of Economy, Trade and Industry
MOE	Ministry of Environment
MOFA	Ministry of Foreign Affairs
NAFTA	North American Free Trade Agreement
NAMA	Non-Agriculture Market Access
NGO	Nongovernmental organization
NPO	Nonprofit organization
NPT	Nuclear Non-Proliferation Treaty
NWFZ	Nuclear-weapon-free zone

ODA	Overseas Development Assistance
OECD	Organization for Economic Cooperation and Development
PKO	Peacekeeping Operations
PPSG	People's Plan Study Group
PRI	Penal Reform International
PSI	Public Services International
RENGO	Japan Trade Union Confederation
SDF	Self-Defense Forces
SDP	Social Democratic Party
TRIPS	Trade-Related Aspects of Intellectual Property Rights
UNDP	UN Development Programme
WCAR	World Conference Against Racism, Racial Discrimination, Xenophobia and Related Intolerances
WSF	World Social Forum
WSFJ	World Social Forum Japan
WTO	World Trade Organization
Zenrōkyō	National Trade Union Council, Japan
Zenrōren	National Federation of Trade Unions, Japan

Japanese Names

Japanese names are given in Japanese order: family name first, followed by given name.

ANOTHER JAPAN IS POSSIBLE

INTRODUCTION

Global Governance and Japanese Nongovernmental Advocacy Networks

IN MARCH 2003, nearly forty thousand Japanese swamped Tokyo's Sakuradadori, near the American Embassy, in a peace rally organized by World Peace Now, a coalition of fifty nongovernmental organizations (NGOs), to protest the war in Iraq and, in particular, the dispatch of the Japanese Self-Defense Forces (SDF) to Iraq for "humanitarian" purposes. The gathering was unprecedented in that nothing like it had occurred since the anti–U.S. Japan Security Alliance movement in the 1960s and 1970s. In March of the following year, a few hundred Japanese consumers from the No! GMO (Genetically Modified Organisms) Campaign went to Canada and the United States to protest the imminent approval of genetically modified (GM) wheat by the Canadian federal government and the North Dakota state government. The petition, signed by 414 organizations representing 1.2 million Japanese people who did not want imported GM wheat, seemed to make an impact. Two months later Monsanto announced the suspension of all development of GM wheat. In November 2004, another coalition of fifty-four Japanese NGOs and labor unions, together with fifty-two South Korean counterparts, protested in front of the Japanese Ministry of Foreign Affairs (MOFA) in their campaign against the Japanese-Korean Free Trade Agreement (FTA). The following month, an emergent alternative globalization movement organized the first Social Forum in Japan. More than four hundred Japanese alterglobalization activists converged on Kyoto under the general banner "Another World Is Possible."

This book looks at the new phenomenon of internationally linked Japanese nongovernmental advocacy networks, which since the 1990s have grown in the context of three conjunctural forces: neoliberalism, militarism, and nationalism. The book connects three disparate literatures: on the global justice movement, on Japanese civil society, and on global citizenship education. On the one hand, the literature on the alterglobalization movement that has flourished since the World Trade Organization (WTO) protests in Seattle in 1999 has focused mostly on the Anglo-Saxon neoliberal model and opposition to it by North American as well as European social movements.[1] Japan's role as an economic superpower pushing for a free trade agenda and the role of Japanese social movements in opposition to that agenda remain largely unknown. On the other hand, although Japanese civil society has increasingly attracted scholarly attention, we know little about the internationally oriented advocacy networks that have emerged since the 1990s to monitor a variety of issues in global governance, and about the impact of those networks on Japan.[2] This book raises five questions:

1. Who are the activists and what are the genesis and focus of their groups?
2. What are the activist groups' critiques of and alternatives to neoliberalism, militarism, and nationalism?
3. How are these groups connected regionally, nationally, and internationally?
4. What relationships do these groups have with the Japanese government?
5. How do these groups contribute to global citizenship education?

This book draws on the concept of *global citizenship*, in which people have "access to a variety of political engagement on a continuum from the local to the global, with the local marked by direct and participatory processes while larger domains with significant populations are progressively mediated by representative mechanisms."[3] Despite emergent interest in the concept and practice of global citizenship, its educational foundation and component—that is, how global citizens are actually made—is rarely highlighted. In the case of Japan, most analyses of political change focus on the domestic bureaucracy, on party politics, or on interest-group explanations that assume a national model of citizenship.[4] By examining the concept of global citizenship, this book seeks to understand how new social movements in Japan construct a new identity of the Japanese as global citizens. I argue that Japanese civil society is embedded in global civil society and that it contributes to global citizenship education through participation, knowledge production, and space creation.

Globalization of the Market:
When the Washington Consensus Arrived in Tokyo

Since the early 1980s, the Washington Consensus (a pact among the U.S. Congress, senior members of the U.S. administration, economic agencies of the U.S. government, the Federal Reserve Board, think tanks, and international financial institutions), which emerged in the Thatcher and Reagan era and was based on promarket policies, including financial and trade liberalization, public expenditure cuts, and deregulation, has symbolized a dominant Anglo-Saxon neoliberal economic model worldwide.[5] In Japan, although trade and investment liberalization had begun in the 1980s under *gaiatsu* (foreign, particularly U.S., pressure), deregulation became a key political agenda in the 1990s, after Japan's economy collapsed and entered a long recession. Because gross domestic product growth rates have remained low and even been negative (minus 2.8 percent in 1998, only the second time in the post–World War II period that the economy registered negative growth), Japan has been challenged to find a balance between competitive pressures from globalization and Japan's traditional "people-oriented" economy, that is, to search for "a market economy with a human face."[6] One week after Koizumi Junichiro won the National Diet's lower house elections in April 2001, he announced that he would revisit the employment system centered on lifelong employment and relax the rules for dismissal and for the use of dispatch workers for periods exceeding one year.[7] In 2002, Nikkeiren (the Japan Federation of Employers Association) released a position paper entitled "Promoting Structural Reform to Overcome the Crisis":

For the sake of a bright future for the economy in the 21st century, thorough restructuring is needed to rectify the high domestic cost structure, stimulate creativity in the science and technology field and achieve sustained economic growth based on these changes, which will allow us to contribute to the progress of the global economy. Where global mega-competition is concerned, it is important to clearly define the roles of the government, labor and the private sector and establish a private sector-led economy. Reducing the high cost structure through a private sector-led economy is the most important goal of structural reform. . . . The most desirable labor market for Japan should have the following 4 characteristics: mobility, flexibility, specialization and diversity. In particular, Japan's labor market is highly regulated, and regulatory reform is urgently needed. In the case of temporary worker dispatching agencies, limits on length of employment contracts should be eliminated, a shift made from a permit to a notification basis, and the prohibition on dispatching of manufacturing workers and health care personnel lifted.[8]

In 2003, part-time labor, including contract and dispatch workers, constituted about one-third of the entire labor force, or 12.6 million. In the 2004 mid-term report of the interministerial Deregulation and Privatization Promotion Council, the Koizumi cabinet further laid out fourteen key points in introducing "market testing" and privatization of public services in a variety of sectors, including medical services, child care, education, and social insurance. Among the main targets of privatization are the Narita and Haneda airports, the Japan Highway Public Corporation, the Japan Oil Corporation, the Urban Development Corp, and the Housing Loan Corporation, along with state-run universities and postal services that hold the world's largest pool of savings.

At the level of the WTO, Japan has been under pressure to enact agricultural and service liberalization. Because of the structural and political significance of rice (more than half of all Japanese farm households are engaged in rice farming, and farmers carry disproportionate voting weight and provide disproportionate support for the Liberal Democratic Party), most politicians have thought it "politically dangerous to touch upon rice."[9] When agricultural trade negotiations began under the Uruguay Round in 1986, rice was forced onto the table. In 1990, Keidanren (the Japan Federation of Economic Organizations) issued a letter to the government, urging it to "reduce or eliminate restrictions on agricultural imports, while taking measures to minimize damage to Japan's farmers. . . . Japan should not try to protect any domestic product or service from foreign competition (to successfully conclude the Uruguay Round)."[10] On December 7, 1994, Prime Minister Hosokawa Morihiro, at a midnight press conference, urged Japan to "endure sacrifices in difficult areas such as agriculture for the sake of the future of the world's free-trade system and bringing a successful conclusion to the Uruguay Round."[11] By 1994, when the trade round was concluded, Japan had agreed to a 4 percent "minimum access" to rice imports, a 20 percent reduction in domestic support, tariffication of nontariff barriers, and a 36 percent reduction in export subsidies.[12] Since agricultural trade talks resumed in the Doha Round of WTO negotiations in 2001, Japan has been under pressure to further reduce tariffication, in particular for rice. To counter U.S. domination of the negotiations on the agriculture and service sectors, Japan has been aggressively pushing for investment liberalization, which is considered an "offensive" sector for Japan.[13] In addition, Japan has been concluding or negotiating FTAs with a number of countries, including Singapore, Mexico, South Korea, Thailand, the Philippines, Malaysia, and Indonesia since 2002.

Militarism and Nationalism: Reverting to a "Normal Country" and "International Cooperation"

Neoliberal restructuring has occurred while nationalism and militarism have intensified in Japan, since the late 1990s. Although a nationalist legacy—centered on the ideology of racial purity, restoration of the emperor, and denial of war responsibility—never faded while the conservative Liberal Democratic Party (LDP) predominated, the late 1990s saw the creation of officially sanctioned nationalistic policies. In 1999, despite opposition from local school boards and teachers, the Hinomaru (national flag) and Kimigayo (national anthem) were formally adopted by the Diet, imposing de facto a legal duty on all schools both to display the flag and to sing the hymn during school ceremonies.[14] In 2001 and then 2005, the Ministry of Education, Culture, Sports, Science, and Technology (MEXT) approved a set of changes in middle school history textbooks that diminished the presentation of Japan's wartime aggression. Although the textbook, compiled by the Japanese Society for History Textbook Reform (Atarashii Rekishi Kyōkasho wo Tsukuru Kai) and published by Fuso, is used by less than 1 percent of junior high students, it has aroused significant controversy both within Japan and abroad. In March 2003, the Central Council of Education submitted a report to MEXT recommending the amendment of the 1947 Fundamental Law of Education to restore "the ability of the home to educate children," "respect for tradition and culture, and a sense of love and respect of the country and home and internationalism."[15] Between December 2003 and September 2004, MEXT planted people in five town meetings to present government-authored statements supporting the bill to revise the education law.[16] The revision became a top priority for the new prime minister, Abe Shinzo, and it was passed in November 2006 despite popular protests. The most controversial clause pertains to the nurturing of patriotism as a goal of education. Many also fear that Article 16 of the bill ("free from subjection to unfair control, the administration of education must be conducted in accordance with this law and other education-related laws, with suitable delegation of duties and mutual cooperation between *the central government* and local government organizations" [emphasis added]) opens the door to greater control by the state, which until now has been constrained by Article 10 of the current law ("free from subjection to unfair control, the administration of education should be conducted with responsibility vested directly in all people of the nation").[17]

After September 11, 2001, the Diet passed a series of amendments and special measures that allow more flexibility for the dispatch of Japanese Self-Defense Forces (SDF) in emergency and war situations. In October 2001, the Special Measures Against Terrorism were enacted, allowing the SDF to use arms not only to defend themselves but also to protect those "under their care" such as refugees and wounded foreign troops. In June 2003, a set of three laws was passed, strengthening the power of the SDF in the event that Japan comes under attack. The Diet also passed the Iraqi Reconstruction Special Measures Law to allow the dispatch of the SDF to Iraq for reconstruction efforts. Six months later, the Koizumi cabinet approved the dispatch of the SDF to southeastern Iraq, the first time in postwar history that heavily armed Japanese troops were sent to a "noncombat" area.[18] In June 2004, another set of seven war-contingency laws (*Yūji-hōsei*) was enacted, allowing, among other things, the U.S. military to use private land at the approval of the prime minister. A movement to revise the 1947 Japanese constitution, including Article 9, on war renunciation, is currently gathering steam within the LDP. Although the current Article 9 states that "the Japanese people forever renounce war as a sovereign right of the nation and the threat or use of force as a means of settling international disputes," the November 2005 draft of the LDP revised constitution puts the emphasis on Japan's self-defense army. The emergence of North Korea's nuclear weapons capability has also put Japan's nuclear taboo front and center in its politics. After Prime Minister Abe Shinzo's cabinet was formed, Foreign Minister Aso Taro and the LDP's research chief Nakagawa Shoichi repeatedly argued that Japan should discuss the nuclear issue.[19]

The demise of the Japanese left since the early 1990s means that there is little powerful opposition to the resurgence of right-wing nationalism. In the 1993 lower-house elections, the number of seats held by the Social Democratic Party of Japan (SDPJ) fell from 136 to 70, due to increasing numbers of people being attracted into new parties. The real kiss of death came in the 1996 lower-house election, when the seats of the SDPJ further decreased from 70 to 15 due to the introduction of new electoral rules that squeezed smaller parties such as the SDPJ, because of the anger of traditional socialist voters toward their leadership in the wake of the LDP-SDPJ government of Murayama Tomiichi (1994–1996), and due to the absorption of some SDPJ members into the newly created Democratic Party of Japan (DPJ) just before the election. Meanwhile, the Japan Communist Party (JCP) did well at first in 1996, increasing its Diet representation from fifteen to twenty-six as it picked up discontented SDPJ voters. But this increase proved short-lived, and the new electoral rules squeezed the JCP's presence in the 2000, 2003, and 2005 elections.

Not all concerned Japanese citizens identify with the Japanese left. But many consider nationalistic and militaristic developments at odds with the country's constitution. Japan's neighbors in Asia have also watched these trends closely. The renewed nationalism and militarism, the longstanding issues of Japan's war responsibility, and the presence of American military bases in Japanese territory, particularly in Okinawa, have revived a broad-based peace movement connected to the global antiwar protest movement. Networks such as Children and Textbooks Japan Net 21, No to Constitutional Revision! Citizens' Network, Grassroots Movement to Remove U.S. Bases from Okinawa and the World, World Peace Now, Asia Peace Alliance, and Asia Pacific Peace Forum have developed. These new networks emphasize youth participation, new movement styles and tactics, and regional and international peace building.

Globalization of Human Rights Norms: Japanese Citizens and Residents Strategically Using the UN System

The globalization of the market and the development of militarism and nationalism in Japan have been accompanied by a parallel globalization of human rights standards, or what some scholars have called "globalization from below."[20] A deterministic reading of the globalization of the market would have missed the emergence of global resistance. Like their counterparts elsewhere in the world, women, minorities, indigenous peoples, ecologists, peace activists, farmers, and consumers in Japan, blocked by domestic political institutions, have been claiming their rights at the level of the United Nations (UN). These substate actors practice "boomerang" politics; that is, they bypass Japanese state institutions to lobby international organizations, which then exert pressure on Japan from above.[21] As illustrated by the Convention on the Rights of the Child, the newly adopted 2006 UN Declaration on the Rights of Indigenous Peoples, and the UN Convention on the Rights of Persons with

Disabilities, Japanese NGO networks have been part and parcel of a global civil society that constructs norms around peace, human rights, and ecology.

In the past decade, many scholars have noted a boom in nonprofit organizations (NPOs) in Japan within the larger context of a worldwide "associational revolution."[22] It is often argued that the Kobe earthquake and the subsequent outpouring of volunteer activities in relief work increased public interest in and government attention to the development of the third sector. Since the NPO law was enacted in 1998, more than twenty thousand organizations have obtained legal NPO status. The NPO law was revised in 2001, making donations tax deductible (when certain requirements are met) and extending the number of fields of NPO activities to seventeen: medical welfare; education; city planning; environment; disaster relief; safety; human rights protection and peace; international cooperation; gender; child health; information technology; science and technology; economic promotion; occupational training and job creation; consumer protection; advice; and science, culture, art, and sports.

The literature on Japanese civil society tends to converge on three arguments. A common position locates overwhelming power in the Japanese bureaucracy. Hence, civil society, whether in the Meiji era, the Taisho Democracy, or the postwar period, is no more than part of the state in its larger project of nationalism and developmentalism.[23] A second argument, often based on explicit comparisons with civil society in the United States, concludes that Japanese civil society is small and local and has a close symbiotic relationship with the state.[24] Finally, Japanese civil society has often been characterized as "social capital without advocacy."[25] The existing literature has largely failed to notice the emergence of Japanese advocacy NGOs and networks that have mobilized around a UN human rights system of conventions and norms as early as 1975 and particularly since the 1990s.

One of the earliest NGO advocacy networks that specifically target the UN human rights system was the Liaison Group of International Women's Year, a network of fifty-two Japanese NGOs formed to follow up on the 1975 First World Conference on Women in Mexico and lobby for Japan's signature (in 1980) and subsequent ratification (in 1985) of the UN Convention on the Elimination of All Forms of Discrimination Against Women (CEDAW).[26] Further, in 1986, Nikkyōso (the Japanese Teachers Union) helped form Kodomo no Jinken Ren (Federation for the Protection of Children's Human Rights Japan), a network of more than sixty NGOs today, to lobby for Japan's signature of the UN Convention on the Rights of the Child (CRC), which it did in 1994. Since 1987, groups of Ainu, an indigenous population in Hokkaido, have been attending the UN Working Group on Indigenous Populations (WGIP) in Geneva, and they continue to lobby for adoption of the UN Declaration on the Rights of Indigenous Peoples.

Throughout the 1990s, many Japanese advocacy NGOs and networks were formed to focus on a wide spectrum of human rights and environmental issues. In 1991, A SEED Japan was established as part of an international youth mobilization on environment and social justice issues. It aimed to include youth voices at the 1992 UN Conference on Environment and Development (also known as the Rio Earth Summit). In 1992, an NGO liaison group for the World Conference on Human Rights was founded by six Japanese human rights NGOs, including Korean resident, Buraku, women, and AIDS groups, to prepare for the 1993 World Conference on Human Rights in Vienna. Similar to the International Women's Year Liaison Group on the CEDAW and the Federation for the Protection of Children's Human Rights Japan on the CRC, the NGO Liaison Group for the World Conference on Human Rights was the major advocacy network behind Japan's ratification of the International Convention on the Elimination of Racial Discrimination (ICERD) in 1995. The group has since been renamed the International Human Rights NGO Network and has become a major watchdog on Japan's obligations to international human rights conventions. In 1992, End Child Prostitution in Asian Tourism (ECPAT) Japan was also created as part of a global network to lobby against the commercial sexual exploitation of children. At the First World Congress Against Commercial Sexual Exploitation of Children, held in Stockholm in 1996, the Japanese government was heavily criticized for its inattention to child prostitution and pornography. Largely as a result of the lobbying of ECPAT Japan, Japan passed the Child Prostitution and Pornography Prohibition Law in 1999.[27] In 1992, the Japan Citizens' Coalition for the UN International Decade of the World's Indigenous People was formed. Then, in 1994, Japan's Network for Women and Health was founded by eleven feminist scholars, activists, and politicians. It became a national network of more than forty NGOs that attended the International Conference on Population and Development in Cairo and continues to lobby for women's reproductive rights in Japan. After a long debate, Japan finally legalized the birth control pill for women in 1999, largely as a result of mobilization by this feminist network.[28]

The rest of the decade saw the rise of advocacy NGOs and networks working on a variety of global issues: military sexual slavery (Violence Against Women in War—Network Japan); the UN Convention Against Torture and Other Cruel, Inhuman, or Degrading Treatment or Punishment, which Japan ratified in 1996 (Center for Prisoners' Rights, Japan); the Kyoto Protocol to the UN Framework Convention on Climate Change (Kiko Forum) and the Convention on the Prohibition of the Use, Stockpiling, Production, and Transfer of Anti-Personnel Mines and on Their Destruction (Japan Campaign to Ban Landmines) in 1997; the UN Convention on the Rights of Migrants (Solidarity Network with Migrants Japan, a network of eighty-seven NGOs formed in 1997); and the International Criminal Court in 1998 (Japan Network for the International Criminal Court). The trend continues in the new millennium. The Beijing-Plus-Five Alternative Report Group, a coalition of fifty-two NGOs, including several networks addressing issues of environment, minorities, disabilities, and migrants, was formed to attend the UN Beijing-Plus-Five Conference on women in 2000. Similarly, Durban 2001 Japan, an NGO coalition of minority rights groups, was established to lobby at the World Conference Against Racism in Durban.[29] In 2003, when CEDAW reviewed Japan's Fourth and Fifth Periodic Reports, forty-three women's groups came together to form the Japan NGO Network for CEDAW (JNNC). In December of the same year, the Japan Network Against Trafficking in Persons (JNATIP) was also created to lobby for Japan's ratification of the Protocol to Prevent, Suppress and Punish Trafficking in Persons, which supplemented the UN Convention Against Transnational Organized Crime. Table 1 summarizes the development of Japanese alterglobalization, antiwar, and antidiscrimination NGO networks in the past three decades.

Performativity and Conversability: A Postmodern Conception of Global Citizenship

The large body of literature on globalization, as some critics charge, is "almost entirely based on statements raised occasionally almost to the status of axioms about the way in which citizens are reacting to the processes which are taking place. It seems to believe that citizens—and even states—have no alternative but to accept globalization as a fact."[30] Despite groundbreaking work by multiculturalists such as Charles Taylor and Will Kymlicka as well as feminists such as Iris Marion Young and Nira Yuval-Davis that shifts the focus of citizenship theories from equality or equal rights to difference or access to minority rights, most of this research surprisingly remains national.[31] Studies that attempt to formulate a theory of postnational citizenship remain nonetheless confined to the predominant national juridical framework; that is, for example, how migrant workers may be granted minimal human rights by their host countries but nonetheless be treated as noncitizens,[32] or how transnational elites strategically and flexibly exploit multiple national citizenships.[33]

In the past decade, two bodies of citizenship research that emphasize cosmopolitan and postmodern approaches have emerged. The first, led by political theorists, focuses on an expanded continuum of political responsibility tied to membership in the human race and planet. Heater, for example, defines world citizenship as citizenship that "embraces the need for some effective form(s) of supra-national political authority and for political action beyond the nation-state."[34] Held argues for a model of multiple cosmopolitan citizenships in which people would have access to a variety of political engagement on a continuum from the local to the global.[35] The second approach, a product of a cultural turn within social movement studies, emphasizes how social movement practices produce new cultural identity.[36] According to Melluci, "collective identity is an interactive, shared definition produced by several individuals (or groups at a more complex level) . . . that must be conceived as a process because it is constructed and negotiated by repeated activation of the relationships that link individuals (or groups) [to the movement]."[37] Castells argues that citizens are actors within networks and social movements with the traditional concept of national society playing a decreasing role in shaping identity.[38]

This book links political and social movement theories on global citizenship to the field of Japanese studies. Scholars on Japanese citizenship have noted a conceptual shift away from the cultural margins toward redefining Japanese national identity as "more accepting of heterogeneity, diversity, and hybridity."[39] They point to a "citizenship gap" between the predominant state narrative of a homogenous Japan on the one hand and the historical making of modern Japan as well as the contemporary realities of migration on the other.[40,41] For example, despite the fact that many second- and third-generation Korean residents were born in Japan and, in many cases, speak only Japanese, they continue to be treated as permanent residents, unable to exercise basic citizenship rights. Ainu and Okinawans, while having Japanese citizenship, are denied their status as indigenous peoples of Japan. Meanwhile, the Buraku, despite their Japanese nationality, are treated as second-class citizens.[42] In his 2006 Mission to Japan report, Doudou Diène, Special Rapporteur on

TABLE 1. Development of Japanese Nongovernmental Advocacy Networks 1975–2005

Year	Japanese Nongovernmental Group or Network (Number of Organizational Members)	Trigger (UN Conference, Convention, Decade, Year, or Report; Other Summit; or Local Event) (Year)	Targeted Treaty, Conference, or Organization (Year Ratified by Japan); Domestic Legislation; or Other Actions
1975	Liaison Group of International Women's Year (52)	International Women's Year (1975)	Convention on the Elimination of All Forms of Discrimination Against Women (CEDAW) (1985)
1982	Soshiren	Revision of the Eugenic Protection Law (1982)	Stopped revision of the Eugenic Protection Law
1986	Federation for the Protection of Children's Human Rights, Japan (60)	Convention on the Rights of the Child (CRC) (1990)	CRC (1994)
1987	Japanese Association of International Women's Rights	CEDAW (1979)	CEDAW (1985)
1987	Ainu Association of Hokkaido and Shimin Gaikō Centre began attending Working Group on Indigenous Populations (WGIP)	WGIP (1982)	UN Declaration on the Rights of Indigenous Peoples
1991	A SEED Japan; People's Forum 2001	UN Conference on Environment and Development (1992)	Agenda 21; Rio+10
1992	Japanese Citizens' Coalition for the UN International Year of the World's Indigenous People (IYWIP)	IYWIP (1993)	UN Declaration on the Rights of Indigenous Peoples
1992	NGO Liaison Group for the World Conference on Human Rights (WCHR)/International Human Rights NGO Network (15)	WCHR (1993)	Extensive review of the UN human rights system, including establishment of the UN High Commissioner for Human Rights
1992	End Child Prostitution in Asian Tourism (ECPAT) Japan	First World Congress on Commercial Sexual Exploitation of Children (1996)	Child Prostitution and Pornography Prohibition Law (1999)
1993	Japan Citizens' Coalition for International Decade of the World's Indigenous People (IDWIP) and Ainu Association of Hokkaido and Shimin Gaikō Centre began attending Working Group on the Draft Declaration (WGDD) on the Rights of Indigenous Peoples	IDWIP and WGDD (1995)	UN Declaration on the Rights of Indigenous Peoples (in negotiation)
1994	Japan Network for Women and Health (40)	International Conference on Population and Development (ICPD) (1994)	ICPD; legalization of the birth control pill for women (1999)
1995	Association to Call for the Ratification of the Convention Against Torture (CAT)	CAT (1984)	CAT (1999)
1995	Japan NGO Forum for Social Development	World Summit on Social Development (1995)	Copenhagen Declaration and Programme of Action
1995	Beijing Japan Accountability Caucus	Fourth World Conference on Women (1995)	Beijing Platform for Action

1995	Asia Pacific Economic Cooperation (APEC) Monitor NGO Network (AM-Net)	APEC Meeting in Osaka (1995)	APEC and World Trade Organization (WTO)
1996	Japan NGO Forum for Habitat	Second UN Conference on Human Settlements (Habitat II) (1996)	Habitat Agenda
1996	Kikō Forum	Kyoto Protocol (1997)	Kyoto Protocol (2002)
1997	Japan Campaign to Ban Landmines (50)	Convention on the Prohibition of the Use, Stockpiling, Production and Transfer of Anti-Personnel Mines and on Their Destruction (1997)	Landmine Ban (1998)
1997	Solidarity Network with Migrants Japan (87)	Convention on the Rights of Migrants (2003)	Convention on the Rights of Migrants
1998	Violence Against Women in War Network—Japan	Report of the UN Special Rapporteur on Violence Against Women (1994)	[UN human rights system does not deal with past military sexual slavery]
1998	Japan Network for the International Criminal Court (ICC)	ICC (1998)	Statute of the ICC
1999	No to Constitutional Revision! Citizens' Network	Movement to revise the Constitution (1999)	To stop Article 9 revision
2001	Japanese NGO Coalition on HIV/AIDS	International Conference on HIV/AIDS, Durban, South Africa (2001)	Access for all
2001	Durban 2001 Japan (12)	World Conference Against Racism	International Convention on the Elimination of Racial Discrimination
2002	Ainu Association of Hokkaido, Association of Indigenous Persons in the Ryūkūs, and Shimin Gaikō Centre began attending the Permanent Forum on Indigenous Issues (PFII)	PFII (2002)	UN Declaration on the Rights of Indigenous Peoples
2003	Beijing-Plus-Five Alternative Report Group (52)	Beijing-Plus-Five Conference (2000)	Beijing Platform for Action and CEDAW
2003	Japan Network Against Trafficking in Persons (25)	Protocol to Prevent Trafficking in Persons (2002)	Protocol to Prevent Trafficking in Persons (not yet ratified by Japan)
2003	World Peace Now (42)	War in Iraq (2003)	Stop war in Iraq and end dispatch of Self-Defense Forces
2003	Japan NGO Network for CEDAW (43)	CEDAW Review of Japan's 4th and 5th Periodic Reports (2003)	CEDAW
2004	Refugee Council Japan (10)	Convention on Refugees (1951)	Convention on Refugees (1981)
2004	World Social Forum (WSF) Japan listserv	Fourth World Social Forum (2004)	WTO
2004	Japan Disability Forum	Convention on the Rights of Persons with Disabilities (2004)	Convention on the Rights of Persons with Disabilities (2006)
2005	Millennium Development Goals (MDG) Campaign Japan Network	MDG (2000)	MDG

contemporary forms of racism, racial discrimination, xenophobia, and related intolerance, highlights three circles of discriminated groups: the national minorities—the Buraku people, the Ainu, and the people of Okinawa; the people and descendants of former Japanese colonies—Koreans and Chinese; and foreigners and migrants from other Asian countries and from the rest of the world. Diène discusses the historical, cultural, social, economic, and political nature of the discrimination and concludes that "the national minorities are invisible in state institutions."[43] Women in Japan—particularly, Buraku, Korean, Ainu, and Okinawan women as well as non-Japanese women married to Japanese men—continue to struggle for their citizenship rights in health, education, employment, public office, and so on.[44] People living with HIV / AIDS—in particular, illegal migrants who do not have access to national medical insurance—demand their basic right to accessible AIDS treatment. In the context of agricultural liberalization, corporate restructuring, and militarism, consumers lobby for their right to food self-sufficiency and safety, and workers claim their basic right to decent work and livelihood. In the post–September 11 context, regular citizens claim their right to peace and physical security.

The research presented in this book builds on this new body of citizenship theorizing in Japan but adds two important dimensions: it focuses first on *global* citizenship and then on global citizenship *education*. I argue that the predominant sovereign conception of citizenship has been increasingly challenged not only by racial, ethnic, and sexual minorities, but also by anyone on the economic, social, political, and cultural margins who takes issue with the metanarratives of the state and the market. A postmodern conception of citizenship emphasizes deconstruction, performativity, and conversability.[45] Examining Japanese citizenship in a postmodern way requires first and foremost deconstructing or undoing the claim by the Japanese state to unequivocal domination of one mode of signifying sovereignty and citizenship over others. A postmodern approach does not end with the deconstruction of the networks of power behind existing metanarratives. It is centered on the production of alternatives, performed in the daily acts of activism. Citizenship in this light "is a term in process, a becoming, a constructing that cannot rightfully be said to originate or to end. As an ongoing discursive practice, it is open to intervention and resignification."[46] When activists participate at the World Social Forums and the local Kyoto Social Forum, they "perform" their citizenship through both a critique of the neoliberal, nationalistic, and militaristic ideologies of the Japanese state and the construction of alternatives based on perspectives on people's security, community development, peace, sustainable development, ecology, and slow life.

Critics of postmodernism often point to the danger of a permanent slippery slope of cultural relativism. What is the political project of postmodernism if all we have is narratives? A postmodern conception of citizenship also emphasizes conversability, that is, a multiplicity of narrative knowledges that exist in webs of dialogue. As Benhabib argues,

In deliberative democracy, as distinguished from political liberalism, the official public sphere of representative institutions, which includes the legislature, executive and public bureaucracies, the judiciary, and political parties, is not the only site of political contestation and of opinion and will formation. Deliberative democracy focuses on social movements, and on the civil, cultural, religious, artistic, and political associations of the unofficial public sphere, as well. The public sphere is composed of the anonymous and interlocking conversation and contestation resulting from the activities of these various groups.[47]

The narratives in this book have emerged out of many cross-border conversations. According to Rorty, "narrative means telling a story about something . . . in which you can place your own story," to give sense to your existence and partake in ongoing dialogues.[48] A postmodern approach to citizenship and democracy insistently asks "whether there are new ways of describing and redescribing the world that better serve our variety of goals, with the understanding that 'hope of agreement is never lost so long as the conversation lasts.'"[49] These narratives not only become new bodies of knowledge, but also constitute new subjectivities, redefining "who we are, how we view the world, how we interact with each other."[50] Recognizing and providing space for the "right to narrate," to "tell stories that will bind us together," is a central task in global citizenship education.[51] Through the narratives of activists belonging to fifty networks, this book explores how new social movements in Japan construct a new identity of the Japanese as global citizens.

Methodology

Social movement and international relations scholars have been, in the words of Khagram, Riker, and Sikkink, "myopically domestic" and "myopically state-centric."[52] On the one hand, studies of global civil society continue to be constrained by "methodological nationalism" that has prevented us from grasping the complexity and significance of the multifaceted and multi-leveled phenomenon of grassroots globalism.[53] On the other hand, studies of Japanese civil society continue to be framed largely in a national context and, in particular, to focus on its limited impact on the Japanese state. This book attempts to go beyond a domestic and state-centric approach to look at the connections between the global justice, antiwar, and antidiscrimination movements and civil society in Japan. Like others who have privileged the "voiceless voices" within Japanese social movements,[54] I employ the method of writing "marginal experience narratives."[55] The narratives in this volume represent counterdiscourses to state and media metanarratives. The aim of marginal-experience narratives is to grasp how activism is lived and how in turn participation in grassroots globalism contributes to the construction of new ideas and subjectivities, and an alternative Japan.

The findings in this book are based on fifty semistructured interviews with members of Japanese nongovernmental networks, including labor unions, in the alterglobalization, antiwar, and antidiscrimination movements in Japan. Scholars from a wide range of disciplines have increasingly turned to interviews as a powerful academic tool. According to Mendieta, the fundamental inspiration of interviews is public dialogue and public debate:

The interview is invariably conducted by a servant of open discussion and its audience is a broad public. Its role is not just to translate an arcane or potentially obtuse area of research. Its role is to register the zeitgeist and to instigate public debate. The interview is a barometer of the cultural life of a discipline and a nation. By agreeing to be interviewed the interviewee agrees to step outside his other role as an expert and to speak as a citizen, outside an official role.[56]

I conducted these interviews, which lasted between one and a half to four hours each, in Tokyo, Nagoya, Kyoto, and San Francisco between November 2004 and September 2005. Interview questions clustered around (1) personal background; (2) founding and activities of an NGO or network; (3) relationships with the government, other NGOs, and international organizations; and (4) issues, concerns, and challenges. The groups were carefully chosen to allow comparisons across time, issue, size, gender, race, and youth representation, and the degree of national, regional, and international networking. With the exception of five groups that can be considered local chapters of international networks, in which international linkages are expected (A SEED Japan, ATTAC Kyoto, Japan Campaign to Ban Landmines, Disabled Peoples' International, and Japan Civil Liberties Union), the focus of this book is homegrown advocacy networks.[57] The interview data are further supplemented by primary research materials and by my participant observation at local peace parades in Tokyo and Okinawa, as well as at fourteen international conferences and summits between 2000 and 2005 where Japanese NGO networks were present: the Asia-Pacific Symposium on Trafficking in Persons, organized by the Japanese Ministry of Foreign Affairs, Tokyo, January 2000; the UN Beijing-Plus-Five Conference, New York, June 2000; the Women's International War Crimes Tribunal on Japan's Military Sexual Slavery, Tokyo, December 2000; the World Conference Against Racism, Racial Discrimination, Xenophobia, and Related Intolerance, Durban, South Africa, September 2001; the Second World Congress Against Commercial Sexual Exploitation of Children, organized by ECPAT and UNICEF, Yokohama, December 2001; the Anti-G8 Summit, Evian, France, June 2003; the Anti–World Trade Organization meeting, Cancun, Mexico, September 2003; the World Social Forum, Mumbai, India, January 2004; the Kyoto Social Forum, Kyoto, November 2004; the International Symposium on Diaspora and Art, Tokyo, November 2004; the Women's World Congress, Seoul, June 2005; the Seventh International Congress on AIDS in Asia and the Pacific, Kobe, July 2005; Aichi Expo 2005, Nagoya, July 2005; and finally, the fifth WTO ministerial meeting, Hong Kong, December 2005. The interview data are organized around eight overlapping issue areas: global governance, labor, food sovereignty, peace, HIV / AIDS, gender, minority and human rights, and youth. Five recurrent themes from the interviews are identified: (1) activism, the genesis of advocacy NGO networks, and their relationships with new social movements; (2) the critiques of and alternatives to neoliberalism, militarism, and nationalism; (3) global, regional, and national networking; (4) NGOs, NPOs, and government partnerships; and (5) the educational components of activism.

Before I continue, let me provide some definitions and state my caveats. The title of this book, *Another Japan Is Possible*, reflects the slogan and frame of mind of some of the alterglobalization activists in Japan, who are part of a larger global justice movement worldwide that rallies around the belief that another world *is* possible. In this book, I use *alternative globalization movement* and *global justice movement* interchangeably. I have avoided the common usage of *antiglobalization movement* because the movement is not against globalization per se. It aims at alternative models of globalization based on transparency, democracy, and participation. The "new" in the new social movements being discussed refers not only to the age of these networks (thirty-five out of the fifty groups have been created in the decade since 1995); the networks in this book constitute new social movements as they go beyond the politics of the traditional left (represented by the Japan Communist Party and Social Democratic Party of Japan) and the "New Left," often a negative label on splinter groups of the Japanese Communist Party after it abandoned its avowed platform of violent revolution in 1955. Besides going beyond a class focus, these social movements are also new in their ways of exploring new movement tactics. Several activists have pointed out the need to innovate, to be "colorful," and to be "fresh, cool, and natural" in order to be effective and to attract the younger generations (see Chapters 18 and 48).

In the ensuing analysis, *advocacy* means not only the process of using information strategically to change policies, but also the strengthening of structures that foster the empowerment of the disadvantaged. Finally, this book focuses on a specific subset of groups—internationally linked advocacy NGOs—within Japanese civil society and does not argue that they are representative of the entire Japanese civil society or consequential in Japanese politics. The aim of this book is to introduce Japanese new social movements with their perspectives. It will be the scope of a separate study to examine these groups' claims from the perspectives of other actors. The narratives presented here provide a snapshot not only of Japanese civil society as it is experienced by various activists, or of the issues these activists represent within their larger sociopolitical background, but also of the nature of democratic participation in these activists' quest for an alternative Japan and world.

Analytical Overview

I conclude this introductory chapter by providing an analytical overview of the fifty interviews contained in this volume according to four themes: (1) activism and advocacy; (2) critiques of and alternatives to neoliberalism, militarism, and nationalism; (3) NGO-government partnerships; and (4) global, regional, and national networking.

Activism, Advocacy, and Social Movements

The backgrounds of the activists are as diverse as the issues they represent. Some grew up in an activist family environment in which their parents or even grandparents were involved in the local Buraku, Ainu, and Okinawan movements or in peace struggles in general (Mori, Chapter 37; Sakai Mina,

Chapter 39; Taira, Chapter 40; and Hirayama, Chapter 17). Others are more products of their own times, the eras of the vibrant student, antiwar, and women's movements of the 1960s, 1970s, and early 1980s (Sakai Kazuko, Chapter 9; Ohno, Chapter 13; Ōhashi, Chapter 30; and Wakabayashi, Chapter 31). Some dropped out of college or took time off to pursue activities that led to their eventual activism (Sakuma, Chapter 2; Yoshioka, Chapter 47; and Takahashi Kenkichi, Chapter 50) while others narrate a coming of age, an "epiphany" after a mainstream educational or professional background (Hara, Chapter 29; and Morihara, Chapter 36). Many of these "cosmopolitan *bricoleurs* of resistance" seem to share two characteristics: they experience internationalism and world conference participation as catalytic events.[58] For several activists, their living, working, or experiences traveling abroad directly led to their consciousness of a particular issue, whether related to the Multilateral Agreement on Investment, to lesbianism, or to development and education in Cambodia (Sakuma, Chapter 2; Wakabayashi, Chapter 31; and Takahashi Kenkichi, Chapter 50). In four instances, graduate studies or research in human rights, development, and sexuality in Europe and North America seems to have played a key role in the person's activism (Takahashi Kiyotaka, Chapter 6; Nakamura, Chapter 23; Hara, Chapter 29; and Hyōdō, Chapter 26). In addition, several activists suggested that their participation in world conferences was catalytic for their activism (Morihara at the UN Conference on Human Settlements, Istanbul, 1996, Chapter 36; Higashizawa at the Rome Conference on the International Criminal Court, 1998, Chapter 21; and Mitsumoto at the World Conference on Sustainable Development, Johannesburg, 2002, Chapter 48).

The activists interviewed for this book occupy various positions in nongovernmental groups and networks—founder, paid staff member, volunteer, secretariat, board member, coordinator, former executive director, and so on. In the brief space of these interviews, it is difficult to discern, much less generalize, how these people live their lives as activists. However, a generalized problem of lack of funding shapes the day-to-day functioning of their organizations. Almost one-third (seventeen out of fifty) of the groups have no paid staff members. Twenty-two have between one to ten staff members; six have between ten and fifty; and only four well-established labor unions and NGOs (RENGO, Nikkyōso, Japan International Volunteer Center, and Peace Boat) have more than fifty paid staff members. The problem of chronic underfunding is best summarized by Nakamura Keiko of Peace Depot. Despite her research position, 80 percent of her time is spent on administrative tasks. An advocacy

NGO activist in Japan is typically a secretariat, fundraiser, campaign manager, coalition builder, lobbyist, and researcher all in one, while in some cases also holding a full-time job. The scarcity of paid NGO positions and the low wages paid for such positions help to shape a sort of "hourglass" structure in NGO employment, that is, a concentration of the above sixties (retirees) and below thirties (students or young singles who can afford a low income), leaving a gap in the middle age range. As Nakamura Keiko points out, this funding issue has great implications for gender participation. A man in his thirties or forties with a family to support simply cannot afford to work for an NGO in Japan.

TABLE 2. Historical Periodization of Japanese Advocacy NGOs

Before 1945: Taisho Democracy and Total War
1922
First nationwide organization of the Burakumin was founded in 1922 as Zenkoku-Suiheisha (National Levellers Association).

1945–1990: AMPO and Internationalism
1969
Publication of *AMPO: Japan-Asia Quarterly Review* led to subsequent creation of the Pacific Asia Resource Center in 1982.

1980
Japan International Volunteer Center was formed after Japanese activists rushed to Thailand to help solve the Indochina refugee crisis.

1982
Shimin Gaikō Centre was created to support the Second UN Special Session for Disarmament.
Soshiren was founded to halt the movement to revise the 1948 Eugenic Protection Law.

1983
Peace Boat was created by university student activists.

1986
Disabled Peoples' International Japan was formed as the Japan chapter of DPI, created in 1981 at the occasion of the International Year of Disabled Persons.

1988
International Movement Against All Forms of Discrimination and Racism was established in Tokyo.

1990
Japan AIDS and Society Association was created in the midst of the blood contamination scandal.
Forum 90 was formed to network for Japan's ratification of the Second Optional Protocol to the International Covenant on Civil and Political Rights, aimed at abolition of the death penalty.

1991–2000: Global Human Rights
1991
Mirine was created after the coming out of the first Korean "comfort woman," Kim Hak-sun.
A SEED Japan was formed as part of an international youth movement to mobilize at the Earth Summit in Rio.

1992
Japan Center for a Sustainable Environment and Society was formed after the Earth Summit in Rio as a part of a national network to monitor Agenda 21.
International Human Rights NGO Network was formed to lobby at the World Conference on Human Rights in Vienna.
Issho Kikaku was formed in the context of enlarging foreign resident communities in Japan.

1994
Africa-Japan Forum was formed after the First Tokyo International Conference on African Development in 1993.
Shinjuku Homeless Support Center was established.
Food Action 21 was created when the Basic Law on Food, Agriculture, and Rural Areas, established in 1961, was amended in response to the World Trade Organization (WTO) Agreement on Agriculture.

The groups represented in this volume span more than half a century. The oldest, the Buraku Liberation League, was created in 1922 and the newest, the Japan Network Against Trafficking in Persons, was formed in 2003. The fifty groups and networks could be broadly divided into four periods: (1) before 1945; (2) from 1945 to 1989; (3) from 1990 to 2000; and (4) after 2001 (see Table 2).

Because this study focuses on Japanese advocacy networks that have sprung up in the past two decades, only one group from the interwar period—the Buraku Liberation League—has been included. The interwar period, commonly known as the Taisho Democracy, was an important time for diverse

---

1995
Advocacy and Monitoring Network on Sustainable Development was formed after its founders organized the NGO Forum on APEC in Osaka.

1996
No! GMO Campaign Japan was created to protest the import of genetically modified soybeans and corn by the Japanese government.

1997
Japan Campaign to Ban Landmines was formed with more than forty NGOs to lobby for Japan's participation in the Ottawa Process and the signing of the Mine Ban Treaty.

1998
The Association of Indigenous Peoples in the Ryūkyūs was formed after Okinawans began to attend the UN Working Group on Indigenous Populations in 1996.

1999
No to Constitutional Revision! Citizens' Network was established.
Sex Work and Sexual Health was created after a sex worker's arrest.
Japan Association for Refugees was founded to coordinate work on refugees.

2000
Equality Action 21 coalition was formed to support the International Labour Organization principle of "equal pay for equal work."
Filipino Migrants Center was founded.

From 2001: Post–September 11

2001
Labor Net, a cross-company and cross-industry coalition of labor activists, was created and connected to Labor Net UK and Labor Net US, and to Nodong in South Korea.

2002
Association for Taxation of Transactions to Aid Citizens Kyoto was formed.
Japan Campaign for a Basic Law on Water was established as part of the international Quality Public Service Campaign of Public Services International.
Body and Soul, a youth-based ecology and slow movement group, was founded at Meijigakuin University.

2003
World Peace Now and Feminist Art Action Brigade were formed to protest the war in Iraq.
Japan NGO Network for the Convention on the Elimination of All Forms of Discrimination Against Women (CEDAW) was founded to lobby the CEDAW review of Japan's Fourth and Fifth Periodic Reports.
Japan Network Against Trafficking in Persons was created after an Asia Foundation symposium on trafficking.

2005
Japan Campaign for the Global Call to Action Against Poverty, a coalition of sixty Japanese NGOs, including those in this volume, was established.
Japan Citizens' NGO Network on the WTO met in Hong Kong to lobby at the WTO Ministerial Conference.

movements, from basic social rights to Korean minority rights, women's rights, Buraku liberation, universal suffrage, and labor rights.[59] The second period, covering four postwar decades, saw the establishment of development groups (the Pacific Asia Resource Center and the Japan International Volunteer Center), human rights NGOs (the Shimin Gaikō Centre, Disabled Peoples' International Japan, the International Movement Against All Forms of Discrimination and Racism, the Japan AIDS and Society Association, and Forum 90), women's organizations (Soshiren), and peace groups (Peace Boat). The turbulent period of the 1960s and 1970s was marked by coalition and conflict among students, trade unionists, farmers, and feminists against militarism, nuclear power, industrialization, and absolute state power. The mobilization of several million people, including many nonradical students and housewives, against AMPO in 1960 became a turning point in Japanese protest movements when the New Left entered mainstream politics. (Eisenhower had to abandon his trip to Japan due to massive street protests.) Coalitions of Sōhyō (the General Council of Trade Unions of Japan, affiliated with the Socialist Party of Japan), Zengakuren (the All Japan Student League, which originally formed under but then broke away from the JCP), Beheiren (the Anti–Vietnam War Alliance), and women's groups mobilized against a series of issues: nuclear testing after 1961, the bombing of North Vietnam in 1965, the construction of Narita Airport from 1966 well into the 1980s (famously known as the Sanrizuka struggle), industrial pollution (notably the Minamata mercury poison case) in 1967, and AMPO revision in 1970.

The Japanese student movement, like its counterparts elsewhere in the world, peaked in 1968, emblematized by the students' control of Tokyo University. Cross-killings within some New Left sects, such as the Kakumaru-ha and the Chūkaku-ha of Zengakuren and Kaihō (Liberation), not only led to the fragmentation of the New Left but also gave perfect grounds for state repression and left a permanently tarnished image of the Left in the eyes of the general public. Indeed, activists often feel that the Japanese left has suffered an unstoppable decline since the late 1970s and early 1980s, even though many NGO networks since the 1990s find their seeds in the earlier AMPO precursors.[60] Founders and board members of groups such as the People's Plan Study Group, Equality Action 21, No WTO—Voices from the Grassroots group, and Peace Boat, for example, were involved in the student, antiwar, and women's movements of the 1960s and 1970s.

From the early 1970s, the women's liberation movement was in full swing, beginning with the fight against the anti-abortion backlash (abortion, under specified conditions, had been legal in Japan since 1948). The first women's liberation center was created in Shinjuku in 1972. The movement's focus was diverse, ranging from reproductive rights (with groups such as Chupiren and the Women's Coalition for Abortion Rights and Contraceptive Pills) to Asian sex tours by Japanese men in the 1970s, and from the migration of *Japayuki san* (women migrant workers from Asia and other regions, ending in Japan's multibillion-dollar entertainment "ejaculation businesses," or *shasei sangyō*) since the 1980s to the Equal Employment Opportunity Law passed in 1985 (a victory for the International Women's Year Liaison Group Japan, made up of fifty-one women's organizations). The latter success is important to note because it ushered Japanese civil society into a new international era in which domestic nongovernmental groups began to use the UN human rights mechanisms to gain leverage for their claims at home. The decade of the 1980s was also marked by international development cooperation and cultural exchanges in the broader context of internationalization encouraged by the state. With Vietnamese refugees beginning to arrive in Japan in the late 1970s, refugee-focused NGOs were established to help asylum seekers, on the one hand, and to lobby, with little success, for changes in immigration law, on the other. Despite an increasing number of applications and Japan's ratification of the Refugee Convention in 1981, the number of applicants being granted refugee status is dismally low: for example, two in 1989 and eight in 2003. Many international development organizations were established during this period to fund and participate in overseas projects on poverty reduction, education, health care, emergency relief, and environmental protection. Some of the pioneer internationally linked human rights NGOs—such as Japan Shimin Gaikō Centre, which has consistently targeted the UN Working Group on Indigenous Populations, the ICERD, and the International Covenant on Civil and Political Rights to monitor minority rights protection in Japan—were also formed in the 1980s.

The third period, from 1991 to 2000, was characterized by the emergence of global human rights norms. This period represents significant transformations in the nature and extent of Japanese civil society's activities, its connections to other global movements, and its impact on the state. The passage in 1998 of the Non-Profit Organization Incorporation Law, which recognizes twelve categories of activities (health and welfare, social education, community development, arts and sports, environment, disaster relief, neighborhood safety, human rights protection, international cooperation, gender equality, children, and others), has legitimated the existence of the nonprofit and nongovernmental sector in Japan. Further, more advocacy rather than self-interest or service delivery NGOs have been formed to monitor a variety of global governance issues and to lobby for Japan's ratification of international human rights treaties. This is true not only in the women's movement, but also in the youth, environmental, indigenous peoples, disability rights, and migrant workers' movements. A SEED Japan, for example, was created in 1991 to add youth voices to the 1992 UN Conference on Environment and Development. The Japan Center for a Sustainable Development and Society was formed right after the Rio Summit. AM-Net was formed after the counter-APEC Osaka summit in 1995.

Finally, the last period, from September 11, 2001, till today, has seen the merging of antidiscrimination and alterglobalization networks with a renewed antiwar movement. Lobbying activities at the UN or at world and regional summits continue to provide the impetus for many groups and networks to be formed. No WTO—Voices from the Grassroots group was created to lobby at the WTO ministerial meeting in Cancun in 2003. Similarly, JNNC was created in 2003 to lobby CEDAW during its review of Japan's Fourth and Fifth Periodic Reports, while the JNATIP was formed in December of that year to lobby for Japan's ratification of the Protocol to Prevent, Suppress and Punish Trafficking in Persons, which supplemented the UN Convention Against Transnational Organized Crime. Further, this last period saw the emergence of several coalitions—World Peace Now, No to Constitutional Revision! Citizens' Network, and Asia Pacific Peace Forum—that involve partnerships between veteran peace activists and young leaders to renew a peace movement in Japan.

Critiques of and Alternatives to Neoliberalism, Militarism, and Nationalism

The critiques of the alterglobalization, antiwar, and antidiscrimination movements in Japan are multifaceted and interrelated. For a college student like Mitsumoto Yuko who is involved in the youth and environmental movement, neoliberal globalization has increased poverty and the wealth gap and brought about insecurity and human rights violations such as lack of access to water in countries such as South Africa, which Mitsumoto Yuko witnessed, or increasing privatization of water services in countries such as Japan (see Chapter 48). According to the leader in the national anti-GMO campaign, Amagasa Keisuke, the WTO is dominated by multinational corporations such as Monsanto (see Chapter 15). Other food activists, including Yamaura Yasuaki, believe that agricultural liberalization under the WTO has brought profits and

benefits only to developed exporting countries, multinational agricultural industries, and consumers in developed countries such as Japan, while almost
all importing countries have suffered (see Chapter 14). For environmental-
ist Kawakami Toyoyuki, the WTO rules are based on market mechanisms
that cannot properly deal with externalities such as environmental issues (see
Chapter 1). In short, as the slogan of the global justice movement goes, these
activists believe that "our world is not for sale."

These activists' critiques of neoliberal ideology are aimed not only at the
global level. Several interviewees point out the role of Japanese multinational
corporations as well as the Japanese government as actors in neoliberal globalization. Mitsumoto Yuko highlights the responsibility of Japanese corporations in environmental destruction through "development" projects (Chapter
48). Shikita Kiyoshi points out the "huge gap" between the Japanese economy
and the environment (Chapter 49). Above all, labor activists, homeless support activists, and migrant workers' groups have all pinpointed the detri-
mental effect on labor conditions of *kōzō kaikaku* (restructuring) under the
shinjiyūshugi (neoliberalism) of Japan's Koizumi administration. They have
argued that, if unchecked, neoliberal globalization will further increase nonregular employment, homelessness, liberalization and privatization of public
services, decreases in average wage levels, and the disappearance of the social
safety net that used to be provided by the corporate system (Yasuda, Chapter
11; Sakai Kazuko, Chapter 9). From a migrant worker's perspective, Ishihara
Virgie reminds us that the structural employment crises caused by neoliberal
globalization in countries such as the Philippines are a direct cause of migration and trafficking into Japan (Chapter 10).

For many Japanese who are involved in the opposition movements, neoliberalism and militarism have been developing in tandem in Japan to support
globalization and militarism led by the United States.[61] Within Japan, no place
represents that development in a more poignant way than Okinawa. If the
United States' economic power depends on its military muscles, Okinawa has
been crucial to U.S. dominance. More than one-fourth (about twenty-eight
thousand out of a hundred thousand) of all U.S. troops stationed in the Asia
Pacific are located in Okinawa. Several antiwar activists (Hirayama, Chapter 17; Hanawa, Chapter 18; and Taira, Chapter 40) have suggested that the
Japanese media are blatantly racist. One of the reasons that the anti-U.S. military base movement in Okinawa has not developed into a national antiwar
movement is the lack of national media coverage and public attention. For

Okinawans, the critiques against militarism are loud and clear. Their land has been confiscated with little compensation. They live under the constant threat of military accidents. Women worry about rapes. Residents have to bear with the noise and pollution, not counting the psychological impact of "contributing" to war when troops are sent from bases in Okinawa. Since September 11, 2001, militarism has manifested in Japan in many ways. The antiwar coalition, World Peace Now, for example, clearly states their critiques of increasing militarism in Japan in four principles: no more war, opposition to the attack on Iraq, opposition to the Japanese government's cooperation in the occupation of Iraq, and nonviolent action. This coalition and others, such as the No to Constitutional Revision! Citizens' Network, also oppose the conservative movement to revise Article 9 of the constitution to give more "flexibility" to the Japanese military to participate in "international cooperation" as a "normal country." Despite these personal networks and overlapping memberships, it remains unclear whether the anti-military-base movements in Okinawa and the new peace coalitions in Japan proper are connected as a large antiwar movement in Japan (Fukawa, Chapter 5).

The developments of neoliberalism and militarism since the late 1990s coincide with a resurgence of nationalism. As Nishihara Nobuaki of Nikkyōso reminds us, the movement to amend the Fundamental Law of Education dated back to the early 1950s (see Chapter 20). For him, to legally mandate a respect for tradition and culture, and a sense of love and respect of the country in this law, contravenes the freedom of thought and conscience stipulated in the constitution as well as in the UN Convention on the Rights of the Child (Article 14). This wider conservative movement has also targeted women's bodies as a site of control. As Ōhashi Yukako of Soshiren points out, the backlash against the movement to legalize abortion, promote sex education, and provide gender-equal education is synchronized with a wider movement within Japan to revise the constitution and restore the state and the "standard family" as the basic unit at the expense of individual freedoms (Chapter 30). Further, nationalism is manifested in a nationwide campaign by the police against "foreigner crime" as well as in an Internet system for reporting suspected illegal migrants, operated by the Immigration Control Bureau of the Ministry of Justice since 2004. The latter has been regarded by the UN Special Rapporteur on contemporary forms of racism, racial discrimination, xenophobia, and related intolerance as an "incitement to racism, racial discrimination and xenophobia . . . based on the criminalization of foreigners and promotes a climate of suspicion and rejection towards foreigners."[62] Despite Japan's ratification of the ICERD, for various minority groups in Japan, including the Buraku, Ainu, Okinawans, Koreans, Taiwanese, Chinese, migrant workers, and other foreign residents, the lack of a legal framework to prohibit racial discrimination, including utterances and incitement by high-level politicians such as Ishihara Shintarō, remains problematic.

A common critique against the global justice movement is the lack of concrete alternatives.[63] What do the alterglobalization, antiwar, and antidiscrimination movements in Japan propose? A sample of their mission statements gives an idea of the variety of alternatives they advocate (see Table 3).

For example, the Pacific Asia Resource Center aims at "creating an alternative society where both people of the North and those of the South can live equally." World Peace Now "encourages individuals to express themselves and respect the diversity of expressions for peace." Place Tokyo tries to "build up a community where people living with HIV / AIDS are empowered to live positively." Beyond their mission statements, these movements' varied responses can be grouped into five categories. The first type of response represents a reformist approach to existing international institutions. For example, Kumagai Ken'ichi of RENGO advocates the inclusion of "social dimensions in existing international economic and trade institutions including the WTO" (see Chapter 7). Similarly, the Japanese and Korean NGO networks that protested in front of the Japanese Ministry of Foreign Affairs against the Japanese-Korean FTA in November 2004 demanded recognition of the basic human rights of Japanese and Korean workers, information disclosure, and the participation in the agreement of Japanese and Korean civil society, especially in the affected sectors of labor, human rights, environment, and food. Nikkyōso advocates the outright exclusion of education from the WTO's General Agreement on Trade in Services. Most Japanese NGOs involved in global governance, including the No WTO—Voices from the Grassroots in Japan and the No! GMO Campaign, fight for the strengthening of a citizens' movement to monitor rather than eliminate the WTO.

A second approach focuses on legal changes at the national level. Food Action 21 successfully lobbied for the Basic Law on Food, Agriculture and Rural Areas, which was passed in 1999. The All-Japan Water Supply Workers' Union has proposed the Basic Law on Water. Currently, an antidiscrimination movement is pushing for the Law to Eliminate Racial Discrimination, while the JNATIP is lobbying for domestic legislation to prohibit trafficking as well as to protect victims.

TABLE 3. Examples of Japanese Advocacy NGO Mission Statements

Africa Japan Forum
Realize the importance of forming ties with people in Africa. Intend to establish equal partnerships with the people of Africa. Organize networks of those involved in Africa-related activities. Promote activities related to Africa and raise awareness of Africa. Propose policies to alleviate the difficulties of the people of Africa.

AM-Net
Advocate policy proposals on the basis of our activities to monitor the impact of trade liberalization and investment promoted by Asia-Pacific Economic Cooperation (APEC) and the World Trade Organization (WTO) on the lives and labor conditions of global citizens, on human rights, and on the environment.

A SEED Japan
Realize that environmental issues and North-South problems result from economic and social structures. Provide comprehensive information about environmental issues from the viewpoint of youth. Clarify the close connection between environmental issues and people's lifestyles. Intend to change society with a long-term view.

Asia Pacific Peace Forum
Sustain solidarity with Japanese NGO groups and individuals pursuing peace, as well as those of other nations. Diffuse a campaign advocating the importance of peace. Research and offer information to promote peace and demilitarization.

Association for Taxation of Transactions to Aid Citizens (ATTAC) Kyoto
Campaign for Tobin tax. Lobby against WTO and free trade agreements (FTAs). Focus on issues related to privatization of public services such as the former Japanese National Railway and the postal service. Mediate among social movements such as environment protection movements, labor movements, homeless movements, and farmers' movements. Participate in antiwar movements.

BeGood Cafe
Pay attention to issues of war and conflict, the destruction of the environment, and widening disparity in wealth around the world, as well as to issues of social injustice in Japan. Promote happiness for people in the world. Seek to extend peaceful networks dealing with these issues.

Body and Soul
Advocate for the importance of nature and food through agricultural experience. Promote the construction of a peaceful Northeast Asia through cultural exchange between Japanese and Korean youths. Seek to establish a space where young people can participate in carrying out social activities focused on environmental and peace issues.

Center for Prisoners' Rights Japan
Advocate for the improvement of detention facilities and immigration-control facilities to meet international standards. Investigate cases of human rights violation inside detention facilities. Provide relief to prisoners through consultations with lawyers and lawsuits. Support Japan's ratification of human rights conventions.

Disabled Peoples' International Japan
Mobilize to combat challenges that all persons with disabilities are facing. Advocate for the human rights of persons with disabilities and for equal opportunity to make it possible for everyone to have access to housing, transportation, social aid, health services, education, employment, and recreation. Create a coalition with other disability-related organizations.

Equality Action 21
Aim at the practice of equal treatment among employees. Fight for equal pay for equal work. Create favorable work conditions for women. Campaign against indirect discrimination. Advocate for a law on the prohibition of indirect discrimination.

Forum 90
Foster public opinion in support of abolition of the death penalty in Japan. Create a space where abolitionists can meet and develop broader relationships. Appeal to society and the government for the ratification of the Second Optional Protocol to the International Covenant on Civil and Political Rights.

Grassroots Movement to Remove U.S. Bases from Okinawa and the World
Mobilize to prohibit a new base from being established in Okinawa. Search for ways to prevent damages such as noise from military planes and pollution from the bases. Advocate removing the U.S. bases from Japan, including Okinawa. Maintain solidarity with movements against the U.S. bases outside the border of the United States.

International Movement Against All Forms of Discrimination and Racism
Through solidarity among peoples and groups, promote the elimination of all forms of racial discrimination and racism as well as protect the rights of minorities and indigenous peoples in different regions, as laid down in the Universal Declaration of Human Rights and other internationally recognized human rights instruments.

Issho Kikaku
Aim for the coexistence of Japanese people and foreigners. Present discrimination issues around the world, including issues of discrimination against foreigners in Japan. Conduct research on culture, language, race, ethnicity, and diversity.

Japan AIDS and Society Association
Realize the importance of preventing the spread of HIV infection and removing prejudice against the disease. Based on the idea that the best way to prevent the disease is to promote better understanding of the disease and to support people living with HIV, conduct research, practice education, and exchange information on HIV.

Japan Association for Refugees
Facilitate the provision of relevant legal and social assistance to meet the needs of refugees and asylum seekers. Advocate for the rights of refugees and asylum seekers through government bodies, local authorities, and media relations. Exchange information on refugee issues and seek to build active and effective networks with concerned parties and NGOs.

Japan Campaign to Ban Landmines
Consider landmines to be humanitarian as well as environmental issues preventing social reconstruction and development. Appeal to the international society to search for and remove landmines in order to achieve the complete abolition of landmines, support victims of landmines, and expand landmine education to minimize damage by landmines.

Japan Center for a Sustainable Environment and Society
Realize a sustainable environment and society in Japan and around the world through broad participation and cooperation of citizens and professionals. Analyze and evaluate Japanese environmental policy and provide information on the environment and relevant policy movements in Japan. Monitor and assess Japanese official development assistance (ODA) and international financial institutions (IFIs) in terms of their environmental and social impacts. Monitor decision-making procedures at the Earth Summit (UN Conference on Environment and Development, or UNCED) in 1992 and encourage the participation and cooperation of citizens and citizen groups in the process of UNCED follow-up.

Japan International Volunteer Center
Realize a world in which all people can live in harmony with one another and with nature. Aim to achieve community-based sustainable development. Search for ways to accomplish postconflict reconstruction and reconciliation. Get involved in disaster relief and reconstruction, and extend grassroots networking.

Labor Net
Aim at establishing an international coalition of workers around the world. Link the tradition of organization and solidarity of labor movements to the information technology era. Cooperate with other social movements to advocate for the protection of the environment, for peace, and for women's rights.

Japan Network Against Trafficking in Persons
Aim to formulate effective laws on the prevention of trafficking in persons, on victim relief, and on the punishment of perpetrators. Compile data clarifying the situation of human trafficking in Japan. Propose a draft bill that will prevent human trafficking and relieve victims of trafficking. Campaign to build constituency to formulate the laws.

Japan NGO Network for CEDAW
Work on the consideration of the Fourth and Fifth Periodic Reports of Japan at the twenty-ninth session of the Committee on the Elimination of Discrimination Against Women (CEDAW), in collaboration with other Japanese NGOs. Generate the NGO alternative answers to the list of issues and questions for the consideration of the Japan reports by CEDAW.

No! GMO Campaign
Advocate for the suspension of the purchase, sale, production, and consumption of genetically modified organism (GMO) products. Appeal to mandate the labeling of GMO products. Seek to accomplish self-sustenance in food and to revive agriculture. Search for ways to preserve seeds.

No to Constitutional Revision! Citizens' Network
Mobilize to prevent the Guidelines for U.S.-Japan Defense Cooperation from being passed and to stop establishing the Constitution Research Committee in the Diet. Seek to conduct a powerful movement in cooperation with other people in Asia to admit no path to war. Extend a network among individuals and civil groups.

No WTO—Voices from the Grassroots in Japan
Send the message gathered at the local and workplace levels to the outer world. At the grassroots level, build a connection with civil movements against globalization and the WTO around the world. Seek to establish a system of economy and trade that makes it possible for people to participate in decision making and operation beyond the WTO.

(Continued on next page)

TABLE 3. (continued)

Pacific Asia Resource Center
Aim to create an alternative society in which people of both the North and the South can live equally. Mediate to widen networks in which people from different nations can meet and be empowered to broaden their views.

Peace Boat
Promote peace, human rights, equal and sustainable development, and respect for the environment. Organize and carry out global education programs, responsible travel, cooperative projects, and advocacy activities on a partnership basis with other civil society organizations and communities in Japan, Northeast Asia, and around the world.

Peace Depot
Promote activities consistent with the understanding that Japanese people may play a role in advancing world peace, based on Japan's pacifist constitution, its experience of atomic bombings, and its reflection with regret on its aggressive wartime role. Develop new cooperative relations between grassroots movements and scientific communities.

People's Plan Study Group
Search for alternative social, economic, and cultural systems controlled by the people that will eventually take over global capitalism, with all of its destructive consequences. Intend to go beyond the borders of gender, generation, nation, and culture while respecting differences in positions and approaches.

Place Tokyo
Aim to build a community where people living with HIV/AIDS are empowered to live positively. Provide information about the prevention of HIV. Offer consulting services to HIV-positive people and those who might be HIV positive. Distribute pamphlets and newsletters on sexual health for teens and gay men.

Regumi Studio Tokyo
Mobilize to change male-centered heterosexual society and to create a society where lesbians can live more easily and women can lead abundant lives, economically and mentally, without marriage. Aim to establish a broad network of women and remove prejudice and discrimination against lesbians from the perspective of women's liberation.

Sex Work and Sexual Health
Promote an environment in which sex workers can work safely without anxiety. Focus on the prevention of sexually transmitted infections, including HIV, and on sexual health. Distribute pamphlets providing essential knowledge about sexually transmitted diseases and how to protect oneself from getting them.

Shimin Gaikō Centre
Take account of peace, human rights, environment, and development issues internationally. Support indigenous peoples and NGOs. Develop programs with the Ainu people and the small island-nations in the South Pacific. Maintain close communication with concerned people and NGOs all over the world.

Shinjuku Homeless Support Center
Advocate for the improvement of the status of the homeless in Tokyo. Pay attention to the actual conditions of the homeless. Help the homeless support themselves by providing the opportunity for employment and a place to live.

Soshiren
Promote women's reproductive freedoms. Aim for a complete decriminalization of abortion in Japan. Realize the importance of protecting women's bodies from being used as tools by reproductive technology. Empower women to choose whether to have a baby or not by themselves.

Women's Active Museum on War and Peace
Focus on sexual violence during wartime from the point of view of gender justice. Clarify the responsibility for crimes. Preserve and exhibit the past, creating a base for future activities. Operate the museum as people's activity unrelated to state authority. Dispatch information to the outer world, promoting cross-border solidarity.

World Peace Now
Encourage individuals to express themselves and to respect the diversity of expressions for peace. Create a broad coalition of various groups of people who agree on four principles: no more war, opposition to the attack on Iraq, opposition to the Japanese government's cooperation in the occupation of Iraq, and nonviolent action.

SOURCE: NGO homepages.

In addition to these two classic responses focused on legal and institutional reforms, a third alternative proposed by various advocacy movements in Japan emphasizes the construction of people's networks, whether related to self-governance and people's security (Ogura, Chapter 3), community development (Takahashi Kiyotaka, Chapter 6), peace (Nakamura, Chapter 23; Ōtsuka, Chapter 24; and Yoshioka, Chapter 47), sustainable development (Shikita, Chapter 49), ecology, or slow life (Takahashi Kenkichi, Chapter 50), not only in Japan but also regionally and internationally. This is particularly the case when both international and national legal and political changes seem to be out of reach. Hirayama Motoh of the Grassroots Movement to Remove U.S. Bases from Okinawa and the World, for example, aims at building a broad national and international citizens' movement against U.S. militarism (Chapter 17). Nakamura Keiko of Peace Depot emphasizes the importance of citizens' initiatives in creating a Northeast Asia nuclear weapon-free zone (Chapter 23).

A fourth related approach focuses on alternative agriculture, lifestyle, and economy. Since 1998, Food Action 21 has engaged in a nationwide Soybean Field Trust movement with thirty-nine local production areas to increase the self-sufficiency of soybean production through the growth of organic crops in Japan as part of the broader movement on local production and local consumption (*chisan chishō*). BeGood Cafe works to promote permaculture and ecovillages. A SEED Japan runs projects on ecosaving and youth NPO banking.

Finally, a fifth alternative centers around self-expression. This is the case not only for minority members such as Hwangbo Kangja, who uses family photos to narrate an alternative history of Japan and Koreans in Japan (see Chapter 41); for Jewong and Liyoon of the KP group, who use hip-hop to express their Korean cultural identity and issues of multiethnicity in Japan (see Chapter 50); or for Sakai Mina, who insists on her right to an education in Ainu (see Chapter 39); but also for peace activists who use Samba music, Korean drums, traditional Okinawan dance (*eisā*), and color (Momoiro Gerira—Pink Guerrilla—and Women in Black Tokyo) (see Chapters 18 and 34). Indeed, the question of the role of self-expression, art, activism, and resistance in the larger context of neoliberalism, militarism, and nationalism has emerged as a critical one posed by intellectuals and activists in Japan. In the inaugural issue of the quarterly *Zenya* [The Eve], Kō articulates the importance of individual resistance, of resistance becoming a culture, of culture becoming resistance, and of connections with past resistance,[64] with culture being broadly defined across genres and oppressions being understood from multiple perspectives, including those of gender and minority.[65]

NGO, NPO and Government Partnerships

One of the most contentious issues related to networking is the relationship of NGOs and NPOs with the government. Many scholars of Japanese civil society have pointed out the traditional and continuing close relationship between voluntary associations and the central and local governments.[66] In particular, since the NPO Law was enacted in 1998, the Japanese government has taken an active role in managing various aspects of NPO activities, from providing the overall regulatory framework to funding and, in some cases, soliciting NPO participation in international cooperation. Ogawa argues that the Japanese government has engaged in constructing a "volunteer subjectivity" to promote "civil society" that provides service in the context of a retrenching Japanese state.[67] Through the investigation of a specific case involving Nihon Iraku Igaku Kyōkai (Japan Iraq Medical Association)—an NPO that allegedly shares its founder and office with a for-profit medical consulting company—which delivered medical equipment worth 3.56 billion yen (about $356,000) to hospitals in Iraq as part of Japanese official development assistance (ODA) in February 2004, Ogura argues that some NPOs have actually become vehicles by which the MOFA promotes Japanese business interests in the name of "humanitarian reconstruction."[68]

Regardless of whether this is a widespread phenomenon, the issue of the service provider role of Japanese nonprofit organizations has aroused heated debates within the nongovernmental as well as scholarly communities.[69] In addition to the contentious gap in funding—NPOs that receive support from MOFA have big offices and full-time staff members and are run like businesses, according to some activists—there is the more fundamental issue of independence. On the one hand, many Japanese NPOs do not see any conflict of interest in accepting grants from MOFA, but many do and have been implementing projects in education, infrastructure, medical services, and community development, particularly in Afghanistan and Iraq, where most of Japanese ODA has been channeled in the past few years. In particular, twenty NGOs have signed up for Japan Platform, a network involving the Ministry of Foreign Affairs, foundations, the One Percent Club of Nikkeiren, and NPO and NGOs for emergency relief (see Appendix 3). On the other hand, many NGOs are critical of the close relationship between these service delivery NPOs and the government. Uemura Hideaki of Shimin Gaikō Centre argues that these groups have lost the raison d'être of NGOs, that is, critical independence from the authorities and support from the citizens. For instance, NPOs and NGOs that have received money from the government might not be able to convey antiwar comments to the Japanese government (see Chapter 38). Kawakami Toyoyuki of AM-Net emphasizes that real partnerships with the government depend on some minimum common ground; NGOs must be able to participate in the entire process from planning to objective analysis, from decision making to implementation, rather than being only on the delivery end (see Chapter 1).

Beyond the issue of independence lies the broader question that feminists, for instance, have raised about the state as the site of engagement.[70] For three decades, since the International Year on Women in 1975, the women's movement in Japan has focused on legal and political change as one of its main objectives. The last decade has been particularly significant in terms of the institutionalization of gender equality in diverse areas from employment to violence against women, from political participation to state feminism.[71] The legal changes as well as the strengthening of the Council for Gender Equality (beyond being merely an interagency liaison body) can be interpreted as evidence of the success of the women's movement in Japan. Yet feminist activists and scholars have begun to question the co-optation of women's participation by the Japanese government to serve its own agenda in combating aging and surviving global competition.[72] Kanai, for example, critiques a perverted shift from a focus on women's human rights by the women's movement in the Law on Gender Equal Participation in 1999 to subsequent government policies that focus on the strategic use of women's labor in what she calls a "total mobilization."[73] Kanai as well as two interviewees in this volume (Watanabe Miho, Chapter 28; and Ōhashi Yukako, Chapter 30) are highly critical of the disciplinary power of the state in controlling women's bodies. On the one hand, a backlash is eroding both the institutional support and individual freedoms that the women's movement has won (for example, the future of the public National Women's Education Center is in question and textbooks using a reproductive rights approach were scrapped). On the other hand, the Koizumi administration has been actively managing women's reproductive and productive capacities, for example, through the 2002 *Josei charenji shiensaku* (Women Challenge Support Policy). On this delicate issue of women's engagement and disengagement with the state, Kanai advocates both participation and resistance, that is, participation in order to resist. In particular, she urges a return to the spirit of radical feminism that was present during the women's liberation movement's opposition to the encroachment of the state in women's lives.

A similar critique of state co-optation has been made by the minority rights movement in Japan. Although this movement of movements on various minority groups, from Okinawans to foreign residents, continues to focus on domestic legal change (for example, an antiracial discrimination or migrant protection law), some have raised concerns about the official multiculturalism practiced by the Japanese government. Uemura Hideaki of Shimin Gaikō Centre, who advocates on behalf of indigenous groups in Japan, calls the governmental approach "cosmetic multiculturalism" (see Chapter 38). The Ainu Culture Promotion Act, for instance, does not recognize the basic human rights of the Ainu people: land rights, fishing rights, and right to education in one's own culture and language, as stipulated in the Convention of the Rights of the Child (Sakai Mina, Chapter 39).

More basic than these questions of independence and extent of engagement is the possibility of dialogue with the Japanese government. It is important to disaggregate the "state." Depending on the issue, NGOs deal with various organs of the Japanese state, from the bureaucracy that includes the Ministry of Foreign Affairs; the Ministry of Health, Labor, and Welfare; the Ministry of Agriculture, Forestry, and Fisheries; the Ministry of Economy, Trade, and Industry; and the Ministry of Environment to political parties and politicians. Several interviewees have lamented the "high wall" that the Japanese political system represents and the lack of recognition not only by the Japanese government but also by the general public (Uemura, Chapter 38; Sakuma, Chapter 2; and Takahashi Kenkichi, Chapter 50). Here strategies among Japanese NGOs diverge. Groups such as the Asia Pacific Peace Forum, cognizant of the gap between social movements and the political process within the National Diet, aim at creating a better connection between citizen groups, Diet members, and international NGOs. Other groups such as the People's Plan Study Group and the Asia Peace Alliance move beyond only responding to the state and focus instead on grassroots empowerment and people's networks. The question of dialogue and partnership with the state remains one of the biggest challenges that Japanese advocacy NGO networks face today.

Global, Regional, and National Networking

Traditionally, "advocacy" has focused on various forms of collective action to bring about political change. In our post–Cold War, post–September 11 context, the target of collective action has become much broader and diffused, so one might argue that the idea of advocacy has become much more fluid.

As Shimada Yoshiko of Feminist Art Action Brigade succinctly puts it, "In Japan in 2005, we do not have a clear enemy. I think having a clear enemy itself is a false notion. We are not in the 1960s anymore. Our lives and world politics have become much more complicated" (see Chapter 34). Several other interviewees (Ogura, Chapter 3; Hyōdō, Chapter 26; Morihara, Chaper 36; and Hwangbo, Chapter 41) have suggested a stronger emphasis on people's empowerment through their own participation and expression, in addition to or even away from the predominant state-focused advocacy work.

The shift away from the traditional emphasis on political outcomes, for some NGOs at least, opens up the question about the relationship between advocacy NGO networks and social movements in Japan. As Keck and Sikkink argue, networks are sets of actors linked by shared values, dense exchanges of information, and common discourses; some networks are formalized while others are based on informal contacts.[74] But having many networks does not equal a social movement.[75] Nongovernmental advocacy networks vary in their degrees of connection and mobilization. A network can be identified expansively to include all relevant actors working to influence social change in an issue area. For example, the Refugee Council of Japan has ten NGO members in social work, legal aid, and refugee support, and the Japan Disability Forum has nine NGO members dedicated to various disability-related issues. For a movement to occur, there needs to be some form of joint mobilization. Hence one might say that there has been a relatively strong women's movement in Japan since the 1990s to hold the Japanese government accountable to its treaty commitments on CEDAW and to implement the Beijing Platform for Action. Both the JNNC and the JNATIP are evidence of this movement that remains despite the increasing backlash that some activists have mentioned. Similarly, there has been a movement against racial discrimination, although it has been less successful in terms of effecting political change. The discussion by Fujimoto of the Japan Civil Liberties Union of the proposal on the Law to Eliminate Racial Discrimination, as well as the organization by Shimin Gaikō Centre, International Movement Against Discrimination and Racism, Buraku Liberation League, Issho, and others of the NGO coalition to attend the World Conference Against Racism, Durban 2001 Japan, are signs of a concerted mobilization effort supporting minority rights in Japan (see Chapters 35, 36, 37, and 42). Other movements are also represented in this book: for the landmine ban in 1997, against the war in Iraq and the dispatch of Japanese troops there since 2003, against the approval of Monsanto's genetically modified wheat by the Canadian federal and North Dakota state governments in 2004, and so on. When one looks, however, at the multiple networks targeting the WTO or FTAs, whether from the perspective of farmers, labor, food, the environment, or development, joint mobilization seems to have just begun. A community of about forty alter-globalization groups and networks has been attending the annual NGO Forum on the WTO's FTA that AM-Net has organized since 2003. A cross-issue Japan Citizens' NGO Network on the WTO in Hong Kong was also formed by more than fifty NGOs, unions, and networks. Regarding the emerging youth-based activities surrounding peace and slow food, however, some activists have raised

TABLE 4. A Protestography of Japanese Advocacy NGOs Since the Early 1990s

1992	Earth Summit, Rio de Janeiro. Attended by members of the Japan Center for a Sustainable Environment and Society, and A SEED Japan.
1993	World Conference on Human Rights, Vienna. The founder of Shimin Gaikō Centre, Uemura Hideaki, organized the first human rights NGO network in Japan to attend the conference.
1994	International Conference on Population and Development, Cairo. Attended by members of Place Tokyo. International Conference on AIDS, Yokohama. Place Tokyo formed afterward.
1995	Fourth World Conference on Women, Beijing. Attended by members of Japan NGO Network for CEDAW, Japan Network Against Trafficking in Persons, Soshiren, Regumi Studio Tokyo, and Women's Museum of War and Peace. Seventh Ministerial of APEC, Osaka. Founders of the Advocacy and Monitoring Network on Sustainable Development (AM-Net) organized NGO Forum on APEC. Peace Depot (formally established in 1997) published bimonthly bulletin, Nuclear Weapons Nonproliferation and Testing Monitor. Okinawan Citizens' Forum, Naha, organized after the schoolgirl rape incident. Association of Indigenous Peoples in the Ryūkyūs formed afterward.
1996	Habitat II, Istanbul. Attended by members of the Japan NGO Forum for Habitat (Morihara Hideki of the International Movement Against All Forms of Discrimination and Racism was a secretariat member of this network). Protests against eviction of homeless people in Shinjuku by Shinjuku Homeless Support Center. First Ministerial of World Trade Organization, Singapore. Attended by Sakuma Tomoko, member of People's Forum 2001.
1997	Thirtieth Asian Development Bank annual meeting in Fukuoka. Protests by members of Watch out for WTO! Japan campaign against the Multilateral Agreement on Investment by an NGO network, including AM-Net, Pacific Asia Resource Center, and People's Forum 2001. Japan Campaign to Ban Landmines. Signature petition (35,000) submitted to Prime Minister Obuchi Keizō to urge Japanese participation in the Ottawa Process.
1998	Ministerial Conference of WTO, Geneva. Attended by Sakuma Tomoko, member of People's Forum 2001. International Labor Video Festival, Seoul. Attended by Yasuda Yukihiro, member of Labor Net, formed in 2001. Rome Conference on the International Criminal Court. Attended by Higashizawa Yasushi, who later became a board member of the International Criminal Bar, formed in 2002, just before the Rome Statute came into effect.
1999	Ministerial Conference of WTO, Seattle. Attended by members of AM-Net, No WTO—Voices from the Grassroots group, Food Action 21, and so on.

doubts about whether this lifestyle-based movement constitutes or will become a social movement beyond a mere commodification of peace-and-ecology thinking (see Sakuma, Chapter 2; and Fukawa, Chapter 5).

How are Japanese NGO networks connected globally, regionally, and nationally? Studies on the diffusion of international norms have tended to focus on formal features of international linkages such as state ratification of international conventions and NGO participation in international conferences.[76] A brief protestography in Table 4 demonstrates the astonishing global reach of Japanese advocacy NGO networks.

2000	Protests at G8 Summit in Okinawa. Attended by members of AM-Net, People's Plan Study Group, Pacific Asia Resource Center, Grassroots Movement to Remove U.S. Bases from Okinawa and the World, and so on.
	Women's International War Crimes Tribunal on Japan's Military Sexual Slavery, Tokyo. Led to the formation of the Women's Active Museum on War and Peace in 2005.
2001	Thirteenth International AIDS Conference, Durban, South Africa. Direct action by members of the Japanese NGO Coalition on HIV/AIDS.
	World Conference Against Racism, Durban, South Africa. Durban 2001 Japan went as NGO coalition.
2002	Sixth Disabled Peoples' International (DPI) World Assembly, Sapporo. Co-organized by DPI Japan.
	World Summit on Social Development, Johannesburg, South Africa. Direct action by members of A SEED Japan.
	"For Whom Is the WTO?" campaign, organized by A SEED Japan prior to WTO ministerial in Cancun, Mexico.
	Asia Pacific Peace Forum invited Congresswoman Barbara Lee and activist Richard Becker of the U.S.-based antiwar coalition ANSWER to Japan.
2003	Third World Water Forum, Kyoto. Sakuma Tomoko of the Japan Center for a Sustainable Environment and Society wrote "Third World Water Forum: Concerned Citizen's Perspective on Water Privatization."
	Japan NGO Report on CEDAW, submitted by the Japan NGO Network for CEDAW.
	Proposal for the Northeast Asia Nuclear Weapon Free Zone, presented by Peace Depot at the preparatory committee of the Nuclear Nonproliferation Treaty Review Conference.
	Fifteenth International AIDS Conference, Bangkok. Attended by members of the AIDS and Society Research Association, Place Tokyo, and the Africa Japan Forum.
2004	Global Call to Action Against Poverty Japan Campaign, launched by a network of sixty Japanese NGOs, including Peace Boat, Japan International Volunteer Center, Africa Japan Forum, and Body and Soul (http://www.hottokenai.jp/english/index.html).
	A SEED Japan published Guide to Globalization.
	Sakuma Tomoko of the Japan Center for a Sustainable and Environmental Society translated The Water Barons into Japanese.
	Board member of Africa Japan Forum Inaba Masaki attended board meeting of the Global Fund.
	Nairobi Summit on a Mine-Free World, attended by members of the Japan Campaign to Ban Landmines.
2005	Mayors for Peace and Abolition 2000 held demonstrations at the Nuclear Nonproliferation Treaty Review Conference, New York.
	Seventh International Conference on AIDS in the Asia Pacific, Kobe. Tarui Masayoshi of the AIDS and Society Research Association was the undersecretary-general.
	Sixth Ministerial Conference of the WTO, Hong Kong. The Japan Citizens' NGO Network on the WTO in Hong Kong was created to lobby at the Ministerial.

NOTE: The idea for this list is borrowed from Collins 2004. The list is by no means exhaustive. It largely summarizes the events mentioned by the interviewees.

The founder and representative of Issho, an NGO on the rights of foreign residents in Japan, for example, went to Geneva in 1999 to submit to the ICERD Committee two reports on discrimination and multiple discrimination at the occasion of the ICERD review of Japan's First and Second Periodic Reports. Similarly, other Japanese NGOs (such as the Center for Prisoners' Rights) have addressed their concerns (about torture, for example) directly to the UN Human Rights Committee or published findings that subsequently appeared in the committee's recommendations (such as the Immigrant Review Task Force's findings on the deportation process in Japan). The JNNC, a coalition of forty-three women's groups, for example, was set up in 2003 specifically to lobby CEDAW about Japan's treaty obligations through NGO alternative reports and personal informal meetings with CEDAW members.

Yet another way in which NGO networks are connected is by organizing a dialogue with UN human rights officials during their visits to Japan or by inviting them directly. In November 2004, twenty-eight Japanese human rights NGOs met with and submitted a report to the new UN High Commissioner for Human Rights, Louise Arbour. In 2003, after a torture scandal in a Nagoya prison the previous year, the Center for Prisoners' Right invited a member of the UN Committee Against Torture, Ole Vedel Rasmussen, to Japan as part of a campaign against torture in Japan. Leather handcuffs subsequently became forbidden in Japanese prisons after the campaign. Besides these formal linkages, outcome documents of world conferences, though not binding, can also exert a strong normative influence. As Taira Satoko narrates, seventy-five Okinawan women attended the Fourth Conference on Women in Beijing in September 1995, and although rape had always been around the U.S. military bases, the Beijing Platform for Action provided an international definition and standard that rape constituted a violation of women's human rights, a definition that Okinawan women's groups have strategically used since the 1995 rape incident.

However, to focus only on the formal aspects of the UN human rights system (conventions, committees, world conferences, rapporteur systems, and so on) would have missed the myriad ways in which international norms travel. When one looks at the brochures and Web sites of Japanese advocacy NGOs or asks these activists directly whether their groups are connected internationally, one might get the impression that, in terms of organizational linkages, few are, with the exception of those that are part of international campaigns such as the Japan Campaign to Ban Landmines and the Japan Network for the International Criminal Court. Yet throughout the interview data are connections between Japanese NGOs and international NGOs (INGOs) on specific issue areas. In 1993, before the Center for Prisoners' Rights was formed (in 1995), the founder visited the U.K.-based NGO Penal Reform International. At the same time, members of Human Rights Watch went to Japan, researched prisoners' conditions, and wanted support from Japanese NGOs on penal reforms. Similarly, in 1997 Sakuma Tomoko of the Japan Center for a Sustainable Environment and Society helped several other NGOs in Japan start a national campaign against the Multilateral Agreement on Investment after visiting Public Citizen in the United States. On the issue of timber liberalization, AM-Net was contacted by U.S.-based NGO Pacific Environment to organize opposition prior to the APEC meeting in Vancouver in 1997. Then, in 2001, AM-Net formed a research group after inviting participation by a member of an Indonesian NGO, Telapak Indonesia, which focuses on the illegal logging and trade of ramin, a tropical hardwood tree, and found that more than half of five hundred Japanese companies imported rare species of ramin that are registered with Appendix II of the Convention on International Trade in Endangered Species of Wild Flora and Fauna. On the issue of genetically modified foods, No! GMO Campaign in Japan, begun in 1996, invited the participation of Canadian farmer Percy Schmeiser, who was sued by Monsanto for pirating canola seed to Japan in 2003. As a result, No! GMO Campaign in Japan became connected to Canadian NGO Council of Canadians and subsequently went to Ottawa to oppose, successfully, the imminent approval of GM wheat developed by Monsanto.

Japanese advocacy networks are connected not only internationally through intergovernmental organizations and INGOs; many alternative globalization, peace, and human rights activists also emphasize the importance of regional networking in Asia, and in many cases have already been doing networking and grassroots empowerment activities.[77] The Japan International Volunteer Center, an NGO addressing community development, peace exchange, emergency relief, and advocacy since 1980, has been doing projects in agriculture, water provision, forest preservation, children's education, and peace building in six Asian countries—Cambodia, Vietnam, Laos, Thailand, Afghanistan, and North Korea. Regumi, a lesbian NGO in Japan since 1987, was part of the first Asian Lesbian Network conference in Bangkok in 1990. The vision of People's Plan Study Group, a researcher-activist network founded in 1995, is to create alternatives to nation-state construction in Asia. Together with NGOs such as Focus on Global South and the Asian Regional Exchange for Alternatives, People's Plan created the Asian Peace Alliance in 2003 to construct a people-based (as opposed to state-based) peace movement in Asia. The International Movement Against All Forms of Discrimination and Racism, a Tokyo-based international human rights group, has been doing projects with women migrant workers in Sri Lanka and with Dalits (untouchables) in India. Body and Soul, a youth and ecology group around since 2002, has organized student exchanges between Japan and Korea. Since 2003, Pacific Asia Resource Center has also been engaged in a farmer cooperative project in collaboration with local NGOs and cooperatives in Sri Lanka and East Timor to focus on grassroots capacity building. Peace activists Hirayama, Nakamura, and Ōtsuka, among others, have all emphasized a people-based peace movement within Asia, while labor activists, including Yasuda and Mizukoshi, have highlighted the importance of joining hands with Korean labor unions in their fight against neoliberalism.

Although international and regional networking exists, most networking activities of Japanese advocacy NGOs remain at the national level. The fifty portraits in this book represent networks in at least twenty-five issue areas: women, minority women, sexuality, sex work, violence against women, disability, indigenous peoples, caste, minority and foreign residents, labor, migrant workers, trafficking, HIV/AIDS, prisoners, refugees, environment, WTO, food, the war in Iraq, constitutional revision, Okinawa, nuclear disarmament, art and resistance, youth, and peace education. The size of each network varies, from more than two hundred members (such as the No to Constitutional Revision! Citizens' Network) to nine NGO group members (such as the Japan Disability Forum, of which Disability Peoples' International Japan is a member) (see other examples in Appendix 1). The existence of networks, however, suggests neither the extent of their activity nor their effectiveness. As Ōtsuka Teruyo of the Asia Pacific Peace Forum has mentioned, the breadth and depth of Japanese NGO networks remains an issue. Like any networks, in particular, nongovernmental ones, Japanese NGOs face several concerns. A main one is the lack of resources for network building. For a while the JNATIP had neither an office nor a staff member and had to rely on the resources of the secretariat of the International Movement Against All Forms of Racism. The JNNC, despite its networking skills and relative success in lobbying CEDAW about Japan's Fourth and Fifth Periodic Reports, almost broke up after review because "no one wanted to pick up the extra work" (see Chapter 29). In addition to these pragmatic issues of funding, staff, postcampaign follow-up work, and capacity in general, networks are also plagued by ideological as well as gender divisions. As Sakuma Tomoko of the Japan Center for Sustainable Environment and Society has pointed out, the potential of developing networks is hampered by "ownership" and "identity" issues and an implicit gender division of labor (see Chapter 2). According to Sakuma, the movement against agricultural liberalization in Japan is dominated by men and has not been successful in attracting mothers who are concerned about food safety or self-sufficiency. Tony László of Issho further pinpoints the fact that in Japan NGOs that are divided along political party lines do not mix well (see Chapter 42). The challenge remains to find actual points of agreement so that NGO networking can better serve the public. Networks work best when there is some minimum of common ground without eliminating the diversity among network members. Hyōdō Chika of Place Tokyo explains that in her coalition-building work she tries to build solidarity without much debate on the definition of sex work, because there would be no more solidarity if there were too much discussion (see Chapter 26). Similarly, Takada Ken, a secretariat member of a national and local association of networks supporting the preservation of Article 9, on war renunciation, of the 1947 Japanese constitution, emphasizes the common desire of the nine intellectuals and prominent individuals who make up the association to preserve Article 9 despite their different political leanings (see Chapter 19).

THE FIFTY INTERVIEWS that constitute the rest of this book are organized into eight issue sections followed by a concluding discussion on a postmodern conception of citizenship and suggestions for future research on the role of media, academia, and regional social movements in Asia.

Notes

1. Mertes 2004; Fisher and Ponniah 2003; Stiglitz 2002; Bove and Dufour 2001; Shiva 2000.
2. Schwartz and Pharr 2003; Osborne 2003; Pekkanen 2006; Yamamoto 1999.
3. Held 2003, 175.
4. Chan-Tiberghien 2004a.
5. Williamson 1993.
6. Nikkeiren 1999, 2000.
7. Shimamoto 2004.
8. Nikkeiren 2002.
9. Davis 2003.
10. Davis 2003, 189.

11. Akao 1994, quoted in Davis 2003, 196.

12. Ohno 2004.

13. Interview with former executive director of AM-Net, March 21, 2005.

14. Ukai 2000.

15. Interview with the director of the Education and Culture Bureau, Japan Teachers Union (Nikkyōso), December 14, 2004.

16. Nakata 2006.

17. Prideaux and Nakamura 2006.

18. Japan Civil Liberties Union 2005.

19. "Japan Discussing, Not Developing, Nukes" 2006.

20. Brecher, Costello, and Smith 2000; Falk 1999.

21. Keck and Sikkink 1998.

22. Schwarz and Pharr 2003; Yamamoto 1999; Salamon 1994.

23. Garon 1997.

24. Pharr (2003) concludes that there are eight distinct features of Japanese postwar civil society: (1) the domination of producer groups; (2) weak labor and consumer organizations; (3) weak religious organizations; (4) underrepresentation of political advocacy groups; (5) comparatively few "new social movements"; (6) non-independent mass media; (7) small number of international NGOs; and (8) a close symbiotic relationship between an activist state and civil society.

25. Pekkanen 2006.

26. Chan-Tiberghien 2004a.

27. Ibid.

28. Ibid.

29. For an analysis, see Chan-Tiberghien 2004a.

30. Blondel and Inoguchi 2002, 155–156.

31. See Taylor 1992; Kymlicka 1996, 2000; Young 2000; Yuval-Davis 1999.

32. Soysal 1994.

33. Ong 1999.

34. Heater 2002, 11–12.

35. Held 2003.

36. See Johnston and Klandermans 1995; and Alvarez, Dagnino, and Escobar, 1998.

37. Melucci 1995.

38. Castells 1997.

39. Hein and Selden 2003, 2.

40. Brysk 2002.

41. Murphy-Shigematsu 2002; Douglass and Roberts 2002; Ryang 2001; Lie 2001; Morris-Suzuki 1998; Weiner 1997; Siddle 1996; Denoon, McCormack, Hudson, and Morris-Suzuki, 1996.

42. Miyazaki 1999; Tomonaga 1999; Neary 1989, 1997.

43. http://www.crnjapan.com/articles/2006/en/20060124-doudoudienereport.html

44. Japan NGO Network for CEDAW 2004.

45. I draw on the ideas of Derrida as presented by Sallis 1987, Butler 1999, and Rorty 1997, respectively.

46. Butler 1999, 40.

47. Benhabib 2002, 21.

48. Rorty 2006, 43.

49. Rorty 2006, 8.

50. Hardt and Negri 2004, 66.

51. Bhabha 2003; Appiah 2003.

52. Khagram, Riker, and Sikkink 2002, 6.

53. Ezzat 2005, 40.

54. Sasaki-Uemura 2001.

55. Stone-Mediatore 2003.

56. Mendieta 2006, xxviii.

57. All groups and networks are based in Japan except one—the International Criminal Bar (ICB), which is based in The Hague, the Netherlands. The Japanese activist involved is a board member of the ICB as well as a member of the local Japan Network for the International Criminal Court. It is included in this collection to demonstrate increasing Japanese participation in global civil society.

58. Hardt and Negri 2004, 50.

59. Chan 2005.

60. Sasaki-Uemura 2001.

61. Shirakawa 2004.

62. http://www.crnjapan.com/articles/2006/en/20060124-doudoudienereport.html

63. See Cavanagh and Mander 2004 for a response to this criticism.

64. Ko 2004.

65. Ko 2004.

66. Garon 1997; Pharr 2003.

67. Ogawa 2004.

68. Ogura 2004.

69. Shirakawa 2002, 2004.

70. Stetson and Mazur 1995.

71. Chan-Tiberghien 2004a.

72. Kanai 2004.

73. Kanai 2004, 17.

74. Keck and Sikkink 1998.

75. Khagram, Riker, and Sikkink 2002.

76. Boli and Thomas 1997.

77. Fan, Arasaki, Tsushima, Ito, Nakazawa, and Yoon 2004.

PART I

GLOBAL GOVERNANCE

FIGURE 1. Kyoto Social Forum, "Another World Is Possible," December 11–12, 2004

INTRODUCTION TO PART I

A COHERENT INTERNATIONAL ECONOMIC POLICY FRAMEWORK emerged after World War II to prevent economic collapse by avoiding balance-of-payment problems (through the efforts of the International Monetary Fund, or IMF), promoting economic development through international lending (through the World Bank), and facilitating international trade through tariff reduction (through the General Agreement on Tariffs and Trade).[1] Many factors, however, have dramatically changed the social, economic, and political landscapes in which this postwar multilateral policy framework finds itself today: the end of a fixed exchange rate system, the availability and rapid growth of international capital flows, debt and financial crises, the scope and patterns of international trade, institutionalization of international human rights norms, and transnationalization of social movements. The postwar multilateral institutions have either not evolved fast enough, in matters such as debt relief or human rights, or gone beyond their original mandates, in international lending for national institutional reforms, for example.

Embodied in the policies of the World Bank and IMF, as well as in trade agreements of the World Trade Organization (WTO), the Washington Consensus has come increasingly under attack not only from diverse social movements but also from UN agencies and the World Bank's inner circles.[2, 3] The discontents generated by neoliberal globalization have come to the political fore in the past decade, whether visible in antisummit protests in Seattle or Cancun; in local, regional, and world social forums in Porto Alegré; or in the growing literature on resistance to globalization.[4] The multiple critiques that have been made against an inherited global governance structure that supports a neoliberal agenda can be summarized in two interrelated concerns: democratic deficits and market fundamentalism (ignoring human development and the environment).[5] From the perspectives of diverse social movements that constitute the alternative globalization movement, what is needed is more than more funds through multilateral and bilateral overseas development assistance (ODA); what is needed is a fundamental reconfiguration and practice of multilateralism and global democracy according to principles of subsidiarity, ecological sustainability, common heritage, economic and cultural diversity, human rights, and food sovereignty.[6]

The literature on alternative globalization and global governance reforms has focused almost exclusively on the United States and the European Union in pushing for a free trade agenda, and on opposition movements in the North (North America and Europe) and the South (in particular, Latin America). Hence we know about Public Citizen, a U.S.-based group that played a pivotal role in bringing down the 1998 Multilateral Agreement on Investment;[7] the Association for Taxation of Transactions to Aid Citizens (ATTAC), a Paris-based international network that lobbies for the Tobin Tax on currency transactions;[8] and the Sam Terra (landless) movement in Brazil, among other organizations.[9] What is much less known are social movements across Asia, despite the fact that the Asian financial crises in 1997, subsequent austerity measures imposed by the IMF, as well as active negotiations on free trade agreements (FTAs) in the region have ignited strong national and regional alterglobalization movements. In South Korea, for example, NGO networks such as the Korean People's Action Against FTA and WTO, have begun to connect with alterglobalization NGOs in Japan.

A common perception of Japanese nongovernmental groups is that they are predominantly local in terms of activities and issue focus. The transnationalization of social movements and the institutionalization of an international human rights regime in the 1990s, however, have helped bring the issue of the democratic deficit of the current global governance structure to the forefront. International summits hosted by the Japanese government, such as the Tenth International Conference on AIDS in Yokohama in 1994, the APEC summit in Osaka in 1995, and the Third World Water Forum in Kyoto in 2003, became catalytic events for domestic NGO networking. Above all, mobilization against summits of international financial and trade institutions has provided the opportunity for various Japanese NGO networks to coalesce into a loose alternative globalization movement within Japan since the early 2000s. Twenty-four, forty-one, and forty-eight Japanese NGOs attended the WTO ministerial meetings in, respectively, Seattle in 1999, Cancun in 2003, and Hong Kong in 2005 (see Appendix 2). After the fourth World Social Forum (WSF)—the annual gathering of the global justice movement—in Mumbai in January 2004, where a few hundred members of Japanese NGOs participated in workshops and demonstrations, the co-president of People's Plan Study Group, Ogura Toshimaru, started the WSF Japan listserv so that members of the emerging alterglobalization movement in Japan could connect and organize. In December that same year, ATTAC Kyoto—a local chapter of ATTAC International—organized the Kyoto Social Forum to create a space for various resistance movements within Japan to come together. Environmental, labor, development, food, peace, and other groups monitor international as well as regional intergovernmental bodies such as the WTO, the World Bank, the IMF, the G8, and APEC. Similar to their counterparts elsewhere in the world, Japanese NGOs within this emergent alternative globalization movement share not a singular ideology but the same concerns about the lack of transparency and democracy in the inherited postwar global governance structure.

The six chapters in Part I of this book contain interviews of people from two environmental groups, one global governance research center, the Japan chapter of an international NGO network, and two established development NGOs formed in the early 1980s. Several themes emerge from the conversations. The alterglobalization movement in Japan is only slowly emerging. It hangs together loosely among labor unionists, farmers, environmentalists, youth, feminists, and so on. Although together they might attend events such as the WSF, issues of ownership and identity make coalition among the networks or with the antiwar and antidiscrimination movements challenging. One of these networks' main critiques of the WTO is that by focusing uniquely on market mechanisms, it ignores externalities such as the environment and the increasing income gap between the North and the South. Many of these advocacy groups are careful about maintaining their independence from the Japanese government and are critical of the booming NPO sector, which often receives funding from the government and serves as a service "subcontractor." Although a rights-based approach could be used as a common platform for the antiwar, antidiscrimination, and alterglobalization movements in Japan, activists realize that far more public educational work needs to be done to make explicit the myriad connections between the global economy and war. Finally, many recognize the urgency in scaling up their work in terms of funding, professionalization, and public support.

Notes

1. Vines and Gilbert 2004.

2. O'Brien, Goetz, Scholte, and Williams 2001; Danaher 1994.

3. United Nations Development Programme 1992; Stiglitz 2002.

4. Sholte 2003; Teivainen 2002; Bello 2002; Falk 1999.

5. United Nations Development Programme 1999, 2002; Charter 99 2000; Group of 77 1997; South Centre 1996; Commission on Global Governance 1995; Childers and Urquhart 1994.

6. Cavanagh and Mander 2004. "Accountability is central to living democracy.... The principle of new democracy means creating governance systems that give those who will bear the costs the vote when decisions are being made" (79–80). Subsidiarity "respects the notion that sovereignty resides in people . . . whatever power can reside at the local level should reside there" (84). "We believe that there are three categories of common heritage resources. The first category includes water, land, air, forests, and fisheries on which everyone's life depends. The second includes culture and knowledge that are collective creations of our species. Finally, more modern common resources are those public services that governments perform on behalf of all people to address such basic needs as public health, education, public safety, and social security, among others" (87–88).

7. Naim 2000.

8. Cassen 2003.

9. Mertes 2004.

GLOBAL GOVERNANCE MONITORING AND JAPAN

Kawakami Toyoyuki

KAWAKAMI TOYOYUKI is a board member of the Advocacy and Monitoring Network on Sustainable Development (AM-Net). He is also a staff member of the Rainforest Action Network's Japan Representative in Tokyo. Born in Okayama Prefecture in 1967, he earned a master's degree in economics from the Graduate School of International Cooperation at Kobe University in 1995. He has been involved in globalization, development, and environment issues since the 1995 APEC meeting in Osaka. In 2005 he was a fellow at the International Forum on Globalization in San Francisco.

How did you become involved in the alternative globalization movement?

It all began with social movement mobilization on the Asia-Pacific Economic Cooperation (APEC) meeting in Osaka in 1995. When the founder of AM-Net, Kanda Hiroshi, knew that the APEC meeting was going to be held in Osaka in 1995, he took the initiative to organize the NGO forum on APEC as a coalition of Japanese NGOs, citizen movements, and labor unions. He participated in a strategic premeeting in New Zealand. Despite the fact that the Kobe earthquake in January 1995 took up most media and public attention, some one hundred NGOs from Japan and Asia in the areas of social development (such as the Japan International Volunteer Center), labor (such as the Asian Pacific Workers Solidarity Links Japan Committee), environment (such as the Peoples' Forum 2001), food, and human rights gathered in Osaka in December 1995. After the meeting, members of the secretariat of the NGO Forum on APEC, including myself, decided to create our group to continue monitoring liberalization trends of regional as well as world economic and trade bodies.

What are the goals of AM-Net?

Our first goal was to monitor trends in liberalization. We issued a quarterly newsletter called *Liberalization Impacts Monitor* (*LIM*). We acted more as a focal point for existing NGOs in different sectors from labor to environment, social development, and north-south issues to come together. In 1996, for example, a member of the environmental group Peoples' Forum 2001, Sakuma Tomoko, alerted us about the international campaign on the Multilateral Agreement on Investment (MAI) after she attended a World Trade Organization (WTO) meeting in Singapore where the problems of MAI were discussed. In 1997, several NGOs, including AM-Net, organized a nationwide campaign against MAI in Japan. We prepared a pamphlet and also organized a caravan that covered Osaka, Kyoto, Nagoya, Nagano, Yamanashi, Kanagawa, and Tokyo. As you know, the MAI was defeated in 1998 because of coordinated NGO mobilization in many countries.

What is the relationship between AM-Net and the Japanese government?

The main focus of AM-Net had been NGO-society rather than NGO-government relations. When we began to work on forestry liberalization issues in 1997–1998, we still did not have much dialogue with the government and were not entirely sure what the Japanese government's position was. When negotiations were under way on Early Voluntary Sectoral Liberalization (EVSL) of forest products prior to the APEC meeting in Vancouver in 1997, we were contacted by David Korten, an activist from the U.S.-based NGO Pacific Environment, who came to Japan to look for Japanese NGOs in order to organize opposition to timber liberalization. The Japanese government had consistently opposed liberalization, for example, through tariff elimination of forest products. In 1998–1999, when we learned that the position of the Japanese government was close to ours concerning the liberalization of fisheries and forestry products, we began to dialogue with them. Before and at the WTO ministerial meeting in Seattle in November 1999, we met with officials from the Ministry of Foreign Affairs and the Forestry Agency, and handed them our appeal against liberalization of fisheries and forestry products. To the extent that the basic position of the government on fisheries and forestry was close to ours, it was relatively easy to have dialogue in that sector. At an NGO-government dialogue meeting in Cancun, when we used the concept of "food sovereignty" (*shokuryō shuken*), a concept that has been debated even within the UN Food and Agricultural Organization, an official from the Ministry of Agriculture,

Fisheries, and Forestry (MAFF) said, at an NGO-government meeting, that he did not understand the concept of food sovereignty. For us, lobbying the Japanese government on WTO issues involves dealing with many ministries and agencies. From our perspective, we would like a stronger authority for the Ministry of the Environment. Now, the Ministry of Economy, Trade, and Industry and the MAFF have more power according to the influence of the committee on agricultural issues within the ruling Liberal Democratic Party. Ultimately, Prime Minister Koizumi and his cabinet office may have overarching power on trade negotiations on these issues.

What are the stakes for the Japanese government and Japanese NGOs in the WTO ministerial meeting in December 2005 in Hong Kong?

I think the ministerial in Hong Kong will focus on agriculture (as you know, negotiations broke down in Cancun due to opposition from the emergent developing countries bloc, G21), service, nonagricultural market access (NAMA) goods, environment issues, and rules issues (antidumping, subsidies, and regional trade agreements). Both Japan and the European Union have been actively pushing for investment liberalization, because it is an "offensive sector" for them. Liberalization in agriculture (under the Agreement of Agriculture) and services (under the General Agreement on Trade in Services), both aggressively pushed by the U.S. government, are considered "defensive sectors" by the Japanese government. For us Japanese NGOs, we have similar concerns as other international NGOs concerning the Singapore issues (investment, competition policy, transparency in government procurement, and trade facilitation). We think the Singapore issues should be stopped. Of course all issues are important, but NAMA and agricultural issues are the hottest. We urge the WTO members not to agree on trade liberalization in haste, without full consideration of development or poverty and environment concern.

What are your criticisms of the WTO or trade liberalization in general?

I was an economics major in college. I know that market mechanisms cannot properly deal with externalities such as environmental problems and income and assets transfer for social stability, and they make universal service difficult, that is, only the rich can afford it. Besides these structural issues, there are also labor concerns, because labor cannot move freely as capital does. The principle of the WTO rules is that they are based on market mechanisms.

However, market "solution" by liberalization cannot solve those problems, but rather deepens the problems. In addition to that, the WTO does not have a democratic decision-making system. That is one of the biggest problems of it. I think that you can see the problems of the WTO through the statement "Our World Is Not for Sale: Sink or Shrink," which many NGOs have signed. I have been involved in forest issues. Domestic forest degradation in Japan is related to illegal commercial logging, deforestation, and unsustainability overseas. Illegal logging is actually a difficult issue. Japanese companies would often say that they don't know that what they buy is from illegal logging. We NGOs do not always have proof either. But we invited a staff member of an Indonesian NGO, Telapak Indonesia, which focuses on the illegal logging and trade of ramin. Then, in February 2001, AM-Net and other forest groups in Kansai, like Hutan Group and Tropical Forest–Kyoto, formed a ramin research group. We did some investigation and found that more than half of five hundred Japanese companies imported rare species of ramin that are registered with Appendix II of the Convention on International Trade in Endangered Species of Wild Flora and Fauna (CITES). After our campaign, many of them, except really bad companies, did stop. I think that the world needs fairer, socially responsible, and environmentally sustainable rules for international trade and investment. In practice, we need more rules or agreements such as the CITES to contain the WTO rules. For example, AM-Net has lobbied for the enactment of laws for the assessment of the social and environmental impacts of trade and investment liberalization, and laws or bilateral agreements to stop the import of illegal forest products.

What does AM-Net do in terms of educating the Japanese public about these issues?

We work on a whole range of issues under the WTO, from the liberalization of forestry products to water privatization. I would categorize our work into four main areas: participation, research-analysis, public education, and advocacy-lobbying. For example, during the Osaka APEC summit, together with other organizations, we organized citizens' public meetings both in Tokyo and in Kansai. Similarly, at the World Water Forum in Kyoto in 2003, we organized and participated in many public education workshops. We conduct research on the WTO and various free trade agreements (FTAs) or economic partnership agreements, which include service sector liberalization, investment liberalization, intellectual property, government procurement, business environment improvement, and so on, between Japan and other countries. Lately we have also focused on these problems from the perspectives of migrant workers' rights. Public education about these issues is actually difficult because they appear abstract in the minds of most Japanese. We try to use a variety of ways, from radio programs to Internet homepages, e-mail magazines, introductory courses, and newsletters. The trick is how to translate these issues into easy terms. In general, most people associate the WTO with agricultural negotiations, because food concerns are direct, simple, and high on people's minds. We also use our meetings with the government as a public education opportunity. We think education of the general public, mass media, and opinion leaders is very important in confronting neoliberal globalization, and we have to do more.

In what ways is AM-Net connected to other Japanese NGOs and social movements? Could you give me some examples?

It really depends on the issue. After Seattle, we have been working closely with Friends of the Earth Japan on forestry issues and environmental impact assessment. On other issues, we do not have enough capacity (we have only one part-time paid staff in our office because of limited financial resources), so it works often through networking linkages, when our members have different sectoral interests or know of friends working on similar issues at other NGOs. As you know, a Japanese NGO network emerged to prepare for the WTO ministerial in Hong Kong in December 2005. AM-Net is an active member of that network.

Do you think a loosely formed alternative globalization movement has begun to emerge in Japan?

If you look at the NGO Forum on the WTO / FTA that AM-Net has been organizing since 2004, and at the thirty to forty NGO networks that attend, yes, we do seem to have an emergent movement. As you know, the first Social Forum in Japan, a sort of local version of the World Social Forum, was organized in Kyoto in December 2004. More than three hundred participants from various Japanese NGO networks were involved in the alternative globalization movement. Now, as I already mentioned, a cross-issue Japan Citizen NGO Network on the WTO in Hong Kong was formed with more than fifty NGOs, unions, and networks.

Could you comment on the evolving relationship between Japanese civil society and the Japanese government?

The number one problem is independence, that is, how we can have partnership with the government. Real partnership with governments depends on some kind of minimum common ground or common goals. If governments have the intention to make real partnerships with NGOs, NGOs should be ensured participation in the entire process from planning to objective analysis, and decision making, especially in the early stages, as partners, rather than being only in the delivery end of implementation as subcontractors.

In what ways are alterglobalization groups related to antiwar groups in Japan? In other words, how do you see the relationship between neoliberal globalization and militarism in Japan?

First of all, personally, I think the Iraq war is an invasion. There was no evidence of threat to the United States. In this sense, George W. Bush can be accused as a war criminal. I do not understand why Prime Minister Koizumi follows Bush (I suppose it is for the strategic relationship with the United States); I think it is a misjudgment. The decision to dispatch the Japanese Self-Defense Forces to Iraq was wrong because it substantively assisted the U.S. invasion of Iraq. Japan could have done many things in other ways. But on whether the dispatch of Japanese Self-Defense Forces to Iraq is anticonstitutional, I am not sure. I am not an expert on the constitution. As for the relationship between alterglobalization and antiwar groups, one issue that has been picked up by international NGOs concerns Iraq as a market for U.S. corporations; that is, they expose the illegitimacy of the Iraq war through unveiling American economic interests behind the invasion. One Japanese NGO network called the No WTO—Voices from the Grassroots group does work on this. If you extend the concept of peace to include the absence of poverty, yes, alterglobalization and antiwar groups are related.

Why did you decide to spend a year at the San Francisco-based NGO International Forum on Globalization (IFG)? What are your activities here?

I have known Victor Menotti, environmental director at the IFG, since Seattle. I wanted to improve my English. Also, here I learn project development, nonprofit management, and fundraising. In Japan we thought we needed to raise funds before starting any project because of the risks involved. But here they can start projects first and then try to raise funds. It is more difficult for nonprofit organizations involved in globalization issues in Japan to raise funds. In Japan, now we have only one part-time staff person. Others are all volunteers. So AM-Net is really a voluntary group, though I would like to change it somehow. I have been focusing on the discussions on the impact of globalization on human rights within the UN Sub-Commission on the Promotion and Protection of Human Rights.

Related Web Sites

Advocacy and Monitoring Network on Sustainable Development (AM-Net) (including quarterly newsletter, *Liberalization Impacts Monitor*): http://www1m.mesh .ne.jp/apec-ngo/english/index_en.htm

International Centre for Trade and Sustainable Development, Bridges: Weekly Trade News Digest: http://www.ictsd.org/weekly

International Forum on Globalization: http://www.ifg.org

NGO Forum on APEC Osaka Summit, November 1995: http://amnetngo.hp.infoseek .co.jp/apec/Welcome_E.html

NO! to MAI Japan Campaign, 1997: http://www.jca.apc.org/pf2001jp/contents-e .html

On NAMA negotiations, see http://www.wto.org/english/tratop_e/markacc_e/ markacc _negoti_e.htm and http://www.ifg.org/analysis/wto/NAMAenv.html

"Our World Is Not for Sale: Sink or Shrink," NGO statement: http://www .ourworldisnotforsale.org

Radio educational program by AM-Net at the Kyoto Sanjō Radio Café: http://www .radiocafe.jp/b_syoukai/amnet.php

Statement by Japanese Citizens and NGOs on the Multilateral Agreement on Investment, October 1997: http://www.jca.apc.org/pf2001jp/english/ngostatement.htm

Related References

Cavanagh, John, and Jerry Mander, eds. 2004. *Alternatives to Economic Globalization: A Better World Is Possible*. San Francisco: Berrett-Koehler.

Eschle, Catherine, and Bice Maiguashca. 2005. *Critical Theories, International Relations and 'the Anti-Globalisation Movement': The Politics of Global Resistance*. London and New York: Routledge.

Gallagher, Kevin. 2004. *Free Trade and the Environment: Mexico, NAFTA, and Beyond*. Stanford, CA: Stanford University Press.

Kitazawa, Yoko. 2003. *Rijun ka jinken ka: Gurōbaruka no jittai to atarashii shakai undō* [Profits or humanity? The reality of globalization and new social movements]. Tokyo: Commons.

Sandbrook, Richard, ed. 2003. *Civilizing Globalization: A Survival Guide.* Albany: State University of New York Press.

Wallach, Lori, and Michelle Sforza. 1999. *The WTO: Five Years of Reasons to Resist Corporate Globalization.* New York: Seven Stories Press.

2

EDUCATION, EMPOWERMENT, AND ALTERNATIVES TO NEOLIBERALISM

Sakuma Tomoko

SAKUMA TOMOKO is director and part-time staff member of the Japan Center for a Sustainable Environment and Society. She was a full-time staff member of People's Forum 2001 from 1994 to 2001, serving as secretary-general from 1996 to 2001. Currently she is a part-time instructor at Joshi Eiyō University, a researcher in the Peace Research Institute at Meiji Gakuin University, and a councilor in the Development Education Association and Resource Center. She is involved in research and education on the social impact of economic globalization, with a focus on food.

How did you become an alterglobalization activist?

I attended college during the "bubble" years (a period in which land and stock prices skyrocketed) in the 1980s. Studying in college was not exciting for me then. Eventually I left and attended a glassblowing school before working as an assistant at an art gallery. I wanted to use my five senses, so I was naturally attracted to fine arts. But as I worked at the art gallery, I realized that artworks that did not have a social dimension bored me. Then I worked at a translation firm between 1992 and 1994. It was there that I first learned about labor union and environmental activism against the North American Free Trade Agreement. In 1994 I became a staff member of People's Forum 2001, a network of environment groups that was started in Japan to follow up on the Earth Summit in Rio in 1992. In preparation for the counter-APEC Osaka summit in Kyoto in 1995, I organized monthly seminars and an international symposium in Tokyo, as well as took part in the NGO Forum on APEC in Kyoto. In

1995 and 1996 I went to follow-up meetings of the Rio summit, where many NGOs realized that one of the biggest challenges to implementing Agenda 21 and the Declaration and Plan of Action on Environment and Development was the World Trade Organization (WTO). So I attended the WTO ministerial meeting in Singapore in December 1996 as an NGO observer. As I noticed the danger of an investment agreement under negotiation at the OECD, I took advantage of my one-month visit to the United States to meet with activists from Public Citizen and Friends of the Earth and so on to learn more about it. Upon returning to Japan, I started a national campaign against the Multilateral Agreement on Investment with several Japanese NGOs in 1997. I also went to the WTO ministerial in Geneva in 1998 and in Seattle in 1999. The Japanese media did not even report much about it.

Could you tell me more about the Japan Center for a Sustainable Environment and Society (JACSES)?

JACSES was created right after the Rio summit in 1992. It was one of the NGOs in the Japanese campaign network on Rio, focusing on survey, research, and advocacy. Our funding mainly comes from various foundations, including the Japan Fund for the Global Environment and the Mott Foundation in the United States. We have three full-time paid staff members since 2001. My responsibility is in trade and globalization. I mostly do research, write articles and books, and do quite a bit of public speaking and education. I do not really do campaign work now. My motivation to work for JACSES is to find an alternative to neoliberalism in the North from the perspective of the Global South. This latter is not necessarily identical to the New Left in Japan. It is unfortunately true that it is not advantageous to be seen as part of the New Left in Japan.

What is problematic with the New Left in Japan?

I think the biggest issue is that the discussions and the direction within the New Left seem to be focused too much on international politics and social minorities, and thus it is not successful in attracting the attention of emerging new economic minorities and others who are rather conservative but who question the current model of globalization and its consequences. If an important part of any movement is to *move*, I think discussions need to be extended and new thoughts need to be implanted. Otherwise, I don't see how the New Left can renew itself. We probably do not agree on everything, but we may agree on something. The critical thing is to identify at what level we can have innovation. Take the movement against agricultural liberalization in Japan, for instance. It is completely dominated by men and has not been quite successful in attracting mothers who are concerned about food safety or food self-sufficiency.

How would you characterize the alterglobalization movement in Japan?

First, it is made up of leftists who are against privatization and neoliberal globalization. Then there are those who are involved in unions directly affected by neoliberal globalization. Concerns are also shared among organic farmers, consumer cooperatives, fair trade organizations, and local activists, including those involved in local currency experiments. In a world dominated by market relations between firms and labor where the main concern seems to be augmenting one's market value, an alternative lifestyle is tantamount to a market boycott. The affirmation that "I grow my own foods and I live in accordance to nature" is really a retreat from the predominant market principles, which can be quite empowering. The problem with the slow life movement, however, is that, how about those who cannot afford to go slow? Does the movement have a class bias? Nonetheless, people should be able to claim this right. It is about participation and grassroots governance. The key to the alterglobalization movement is human rights education. People should know what their rights and responsibilities are. Many people take current policies as given. They think that they are created by our government, and it is the government that has negotiation power. But the Japanese government does not always take care of our needs. We need to begin from the local levels and empower individuals to examine the linkages between WTO policies and their own lives.

What are some of the issues that the alterglobalization movement in Japan faces?

Left intellectuals and social movements do not always go together. If you are an academic who also becomes an activist, you can be discredited in your academic circles. I think the strict objectivity required by academism is misunderstood as *neutrality* rather than *impartiality*. Academic language can also be difficult for social movement activists. The connections between left intellectuals, the labor movement, and other social movements are weak, so it is easy for the government to control. Then of course there is the perennial problem of funding. NGO work means part-time or unpaid work. It is also sensitive to receive money from the government or private corporations, as your activities might be affected. I believe that a diverse funding source is important.

What do you think of the statement made by some Japanese government officials that Japanese NGOs are not credible?

The government has established a huge nonprofit sector, or the so-called public interest corporations, within and under the bureaucracy that has strong ties with the business sector. Given that the traditional nonprofits such as hospitals and social welfare corporations rarely identify themselves with NGOs, NGOs in Japan represent a very limited sector of the society. Thus it is difficult to expect not only bureaucrats but also the general public to understand and trust the NGO sector as a whole. In fact, some NGOs are like consultants, who often prioritize growth of the organization over social objectives. With respect to the social movement against the WTO, there is an essential difference between the movement and the government in value and priority, and it impels the government officials to discredit the NGOs.

You have served as a guest lecturer on Peace Boat four times. Could you tell me about your experience?

Typically, each boat tour around the world lasts for about three months, with between five hundred and fifteen hundred passengers, and fifty staff members, volunteers, and of course crew members. In addition to English and French classes by native instructors, various courses are offered. I taught Introduction to Globalization, American Food Strategy, and so on. The participants, usually 50 percent young people and 50 percent retirees, also do group work. It is extremely interesting to observe. It is like a floating Japanese village, a mini-Japan. I enjoy going on the Peace Boat time and again, because I think it is an outstanding educational example. First, it aims at the empowerment of Peace Boat staff members. The cruise director of this last boat I was on, for example, was only twenty-three years old. It does not matter how old you are, but you are fully involved in the planning, organization, and implementation of the various programs. It is very democratic. I have never seen anything like this in other NGOs. Then it is interesting to see how the passengers change during the course of the trip. Many join to have fun. But often it becomes an eye-opening experience for them, and in some cases the tour changes their lives. It is hard to summarize the impact of education offered by Peace Boat.

I know, for instance, that a young participant of Global University, one of the group programs on the boat, later became a UN volunteer in Eritrea.

How about the relationship between the alterglobalization, antidiscrimination, and antiwar movements in Japan? Any possibility of networking among them?

I think the three movements share some influence even though they might not realize it. Networks are possible for sure, but I think this possibility has been plagued by *ownership* and *identity* issues. Each of the three movements is made up of small groups with small owners. It is difficult to find time to network. Of course we do it sometimes, but movement-wise, this has yet to happen. The groups are marked by difference as well, which is often seen as a group's identity and which yields to the tendency of separation rather than unity.

Related Web Sites

Agenda 21: http://habitat.igc.org/agenda21/index.htm

Development Education Association and Resource Center (DEAR): http://www.dear
.or.jp

International Center for Trade and Sustainable Development: http://www.ictsd.org

Japan Center for a Sustainable Environment and Society (JACSES): http://www
.jacses.org/en/index.html

Peace Boat: http://www.peaceboat.org/index_j.html

People's Forum 2001: http://www.jca.apc.org/pf2001jp

Public Citizen, Global Trade Watch: http://www.citizen.org/trade/wto/articles.cfm
?ID=5477

Related References

Hasegawa, Koichi. 2004. *Constructing Civil Society in Japan: Voices of Environmental Movements*. Melbourne, Australia: Trans Pacific Press.

Jawara, Fatoumata, and Aileen Kwa. 2003. *Behind the Scenes: Power Politics in the WTO*. New York: Zed Books.

Lal Das, Bhagirath. 1999. *The World Trade Organization: A Guide to the Framework for International Trade*. Penang, Malaysia: Third World Network.

Rajagopal, Balakrishnan. 2003. *International Law from Below: Development, Social Movements and Third World Resistance*. Cambridge, UK: Cambridge University Press.

3

BUILDING A PEOPLE-BASED PEACE AND DEMOCRACY MOVEMENT IN ASIA

Ogura Toshimaru

OGURA TOSHIMARU is co-president of the People's Plan Study Group (PPSG), an independent research organization of activists and intellectuals, and also professor in the Department of Economics at the University of Toyama in Toyama, Japan. He teaches political economy and modern capitalism, and works as an activist in the antiglobalization and civil liberties movements in Japan. He has written many books and articles about alternatives to neoliberal globalization, including his most recent book, *Tayousei no zentaishugi t• minshushugi no zankoku* [Totalitarianism of diversity and the cruelty of democracy].

How did you become involved in the alternative globalization movement?

I was involved in the student movement in the 1960s during the Vietnam War, when I was in high school. Now I have become an academic and have often felt that there is little connection between academia and activism. I have participated in the People's Plan Study Group (PPSG; we call it PP Ken in Japanese) since it was established in 1998 and have now become a board member. My main concern is how to construct an alterglobalization movement in Japan through a research-activism connection.

Could you tell me about the activities of PP Ken?

We organize a few study groups (*kenkyūkai*) on alterglobalization, post–World War II social movements, people's security against national security, and post-1945 political thoughts. We are having a new study group on constitutional revision (*kenpō kaisei*). Once every three months we also organize a roundtable with guest speakers. For example, two recent themes were gender backlash and grassroots fascism, that is, backlash and fascism from below. There has been a strong backlash against gender-equal education, including sex education, from the right wing. Besides study groups and roundtables, we hold an annual symposium. The theme this year (2004) is on the war in Iraq and constitutional revision. In addition, we also publish an online journal in English called *Japonesia*.

You have been the coordinator of the World Social Forum Japan (WSFJ) listserv. Could you tell me more about WSFJ?

WSFJ was created before the fourth World Social Forum (WSF) in Mumbai, India, in January 2004, for information exchange. Our vision was threefold: first, to translate the WSF process into a Japanese WSF; second, to translate what we do in Japan into English; and third, to act as a discussion place for the various movements within Japan, because we have different views, depending on the issue focus. As you know, there was even opposition to the WSF in Mumbai, called the Mumbai resistance. It is difficult to connect the various kinds of resistance within Japan. Right now there is not much beyond the mailing list. In Mumbai, Japanese NGOs and social movements had an information booth and also a networking meeting among them. Individual NGOs held some workshops. At the 2005 WSF back in Porto Alegré, Brazil, Japanese groups, including ATTAC Japan and the Japan Council Against Atomic and Hydrogen Bombs (Gensuikyō), organized several workshops. Closer to home, members of WSFJ, including NGOs and labor unions, demonstrated against the Japan-Korean Free Trade Agreement in early November 2004. Now we have more connections with Korean labor unions and NGOs. I always talk about networks, but first, we don't even have a place to talk about policy and strategy, so WSFJ was created to facilitate this discussion. The WSF is too big and there are transparency issues (for example, who gets to be included in the International Organizing Committee?) and funding issues (should WSF accept money from the Ford Foundation?). Although WSF is a space for resistance, we need to deal with issues of democracy within it.

What are some of the problems you face in organizing resistance in Japan?

One of the biggest issues facing the alterglobalization movement, I think, is the need to make explicit the connection between economy and war. For example, we have to analyze how Japanese multinational corporations and the Japanese government are intimately related when it comes to the war in Iraq. I am not sure the alterglobalization movement and the peace movement in Japan are tightly connected. More generally speaking, the problems we face now are common to the postwar new social movements in Japan, including the labor movement and various kinds of grassroots movements of the Left. There have been a lot of single-issue community-based movements, but we were unable to have a major powerful social movement. Politically speaking, we still do not have a kind of oppositional culture-environment. We certainly can talk about things, but we cannot go much further than just talking. It is difficult to frame the issues as political, economic, and global problems. Then there is the issue of movement organization. Take the labor movement, for instance. Most Japanese labor unions are attached to national parties such as the Social Democratic Party and the Communist Party. There has not been much change in the tactics of the labor movement, and I am not sure whether they are adequate in responding to the labor market situation today. Organizationally speaking, Japanese labor unions cannot handle the issue of *freeta* (nonregular employment), for example. There is little social consciousness in Japan about issues of alterglobalization as economic problems. In the United States there are alternative economic views. Researchers work together with activists. In Japan, Marxist economics is actually mainstream within academia (even though it is getting more marginalized now). But the problem is that very few researchers are involved in activism, so it does not really become a movement. I would also like to see the consciousness of Japanese activists themselves becoming more global, in the sense that they can tie the local to the global in their community movements. Last but not least, I think it is important that we look at issues of globalization from the viewpoints of gender and minority.

How about NGO relationships with the Japanese government?

It has become a new Japanese government management thing, that is, relying on NGOs to provide services on the ground, for example, in senior care. The government budgets the expense in their administrative plan and gives it to the NGOs, and they call it *partnership*. You can see this in the reconstruction work in Afghanistan and Iraq, where NGOs become part of the Japanese government. The Japanese government talks about *shimin shakai* (civil society), but in reality there is no space for *shimin shakai*. The government controls the civic functions of Japanese civil society.

What is the focus of your peace activities?

Right now there are many issues. First and foremost is the concern about constitutional revision. Then we want to bring the Japanese Self-Defense Forces back home. U.S. military bases in Japan continue to be a big problem. Regionally speaking, peace in East Asia is a big concern. North Korea is a hot spot. Then there is the Taiwan-China debacle. Since we have a significant Korean and Chinese population in Japan, these issues are sensitive, because racism and social exclusion are still strong among the Japanese population. Solutions at the national level seem very difficult. What we strive for are people's networks beyond borders, emphasizing the basic right to livelihood. In 2000, for example, at the G8 Okinawa summit, Japanese and Asian NGOs organized a counter forum that focused on people's security rather than on national security. The traditional national security framework focuses on interests of the nation-state. A people's security framework emphasizes gender and people security.

What is your vision of building people-centric democracy within Asia?

I want more general citizens to be involved, that is, giving priority to people's plans rather than government plans. Democracy has to be built from the bottom up. I have the feeling that dialogue is possible in Europe. In Asia it is still difficult unless we change the fundamental political systems and construct alternative space by and for the grassroots. We want to draw a line from the Japanese government to emphasize people's autonomy. It is about asserting our rights. Among young Japanese, fighting against the government is like a taboo; rights consciousness is thin. We keep asking ourselves the question, is civil society possible in Asia? Part of PP Ken's vision is to create alternatives in Asia, different from nation-state construction. The difficult issue is how to construct democracy that is divorced from the government. One concrete initiative is the Asian Peace Alliance, begun in 2003, to create a people-based peace movement in Asia. Besides PPSG, Focus on Global South and the Asian Regional Exchange for Alternatives, among others, are members of this alliance.

Related Web Sites

ARENA Online, Inauguration of Asian Peace Alliance: http://www.arenaonline.org/details/103816730831637.shtml

Focus on the Global South: http://www.focusweb.org/main/html/index.php

People's Plan Japonesia, electronic journal of PPSG: http://www.ppjaponesia.org

People's Plan Study Group: http://www.jca.apc.org/ppsg
Third World Network: http://www.twnside.org.sg

Related References

Mutō, Ichiyo. 2004."Asian Peace Movements and Empire." Presentation at the Con-
    ference on the Question of Asia in the New Global Order, Asia/Pacific Studies
    Institute, Duke University, October 1–2. Available at http://multitudes.samizdat.
    net/article1254.html
Ogura, Toshimaru. 2004a. "Making an Issue of the Alternative World." *People's Plan
    Japonesia*. Available at http://www.ppjaponesia.org/modules/tinycontent0/index
    .php?id=3
Ogura, Toshimaru. 2004b. "Kokka to shihon ni nomikomareru 'shimin shakai'"
    [Civil society that is swallowed by the state and capital]. *People's Plan*, 28(Special
    Issue: NGO, NPO wa ima, doko ni iruka: teikō ka sanka ka [Where are the NGOs
    and NPOs? Resist or participate]), 6–15.

4

TOBIN TAX, KYOTO SOCIAL FORUM, AND PLURALISM

Komori Masataka

KOMORI MASATAKA is a member of the Association for the Taxation of Financial Transactions to Aid Citizens (ATTAC), Kyoto, and an organizing member of the Kyoto Social Forum. He is a student in the Graduate School of Agriculture at Kyoto University. Born in Gifu, Japan, in 1981, he has been involved in social movements in Kyoto since he entered Kyoto University. He is now studying in the field of ecology and participating in ATTAC and in a labor union in Kyoto.

How did you become an alterglobalization activist?

Between 1999 and 2002, after I entered Kyoto University, I joined a small political group that is an offshoot of Marxism. While I was in that group, I learned about the global economic structure and various other social issues and became a leftist activist. However, despite the small number of members in the group (about fifty or sixty), the group was unnecessarily centralized and secretive. In addition, their primary activities were to persuade people to become members and force dogmatic theory on them. Members of the executive committee told me that it was Leninism. I was disappointed with the group. I was dismissed as a result of criticizing the executive committee. After that experience, I joined a meeting held by ATTAC Kansai, established in November 2001. I learned about the principles of the ATTAC movement. On the basis of a common agreement to oppose neoliberalism, activists from various ideological backgrounds and movements gather together, discuss, and take action. Another thing that appealed to me was that no single person could appropriate the name and movement of ATTAC. This was opposite to the demands of the political group to which I used to belong. I knew that movements around the world already work together on the basis of pluralism and diversity, and they become a big power, as seen in Seattle and the World Social Forum (WSF). This was astonishing to me because I had only known about a subgroup of Marxism. I became a member of ATTAC Kansai.

Could you tell me about ATTAC Kyoto?

ATTAC Kyoto was established on May 9, 2002, when we held an inaugural meeting. From among the members in ATTAC Kansai, about ten members living in Kyoto appealed to people involved in social movements in Kyoto. In my opinion, leftist (particularly new leftist) movements split many times in the last thirty years, and broke public movements. Therefore, Japanese social movements on the whole were subdivided and declined. It became especially unattractive to young people. I thought that in order to change such a situation, ATTAC and the anti-neoliberal movement in general should focus on pluralism within Japanese social movements. Anybody, from experienced activists to young people, individuals, and groups that start their activity, can join the movement of ATTAC. Therefore, I accepted the position of being the first secretary-general of ATTAC Kyoto. Currently we have about thirty members and half of them are under the age of thirty. One third of the members are academics. Half of the members are activists. There is no paid staff member. Our funding comes from membership dues of three thousand yen per year, as well as from event participation fees. I would group our main activities into five areas: campaign for a Tobin tax; movement against the WTO / FTA; issues of privatization of public services such as the former Japanese National Railway and postal services; mediating among social movements such as the environmental, labor, homeless, and farmers' movements; and finally the anti-war movement.

What do you think are the major issues concerning neoliberal globalization in Japan?

The manufacturing industry as well as agriculture in Japan have been severely hit by Japanese corporations moving abroad since the 1980s. Japan imported a large quantity of foodstuffs except rice (even though rice is also in danger because of the aging of farmers and lack of profitability). If we leave the WTO / FTA as they are, it will bring death to small businesses and agriculture in Japan. At the same time, due to economic globalization, industries in Japan try to maintain their competitive power by controlling labor costs. This is particularly clear in subcontract corporations. As a result, middle-aged workers are laid off, working conditions deteriorate, and young people are employed as nonregular workers. In particular, the average income of the younger group has rapidly declined, and it is getting worse. These people are not receiving effective assistance because of weakened labor movements and a general cooperative stance between capital and labor in Japan. Another issue concerns care for the old people. The cost is now charged to the user under the Nursing Care Insurance Law. In terms of care for people with disability, there is also a trend in charging the expenses to the user. Furthermore, the low wage of workers in the welfare sector is a problem. This results from the government cutting down the welfare budget. Finally, after the division and privatization of the Japanese National Railway in the latter half of the 1980s, many public services are being privatized. The postal service agency is going to be turned into a private corporation. National universities are already incorporated. In addition, the privatization of public facilities such as nursery schools has been promoted through a "designated warden system" which private corporations are commissioned to operate. This increases the economic burden of users, lowers the service quality, and reduces workers' wages. These are all important issues, but so far no social movements have been successful in launching an effective counterattack.

Why is a Tobin tax important in countering neoliberalism in Japan? Could you describe your campaign work for it in Japan?

The Tobin tax is a symbol of our possibility in making a counterproposal against globalization propelled by multinational capital and the government. In order to implement it, various social movements need to work in closer cooperation to oppose neoliberalism and expand each movement, and civil society should gain power through that. In addition, social movements need to have power not only in Japan but also in other Asian countries. However, up till now, Japan is one of the weakest nations in Asia in terms of the power of social movements. ATTAC Kyoto works to let Japanese civil society know widely the bad influence of limitless activities of multinational corporations on people's lives. We publicize the Tobin tax as a counterproposal presented by civil society regarding this situation. In addition, we hold meetings to study international financial business and make educational booklets.

Do you see an alternative globalization movement emerging in Japan? What role does ATTAC Kyoto play in this movement?

Since September 11, 2001, two major changes have occurred in social movements in Japan. First, those who used to take active but separate roles (people joining the Japanese Communist Party, the Social Democratic Party, the New Socialist Party, and new leftist groups) have increasingly worked together in the antiwar movement. They were against the wars in Afghanistan and Iraq, and also against the Japanese government expanding military activities in cooperation with the United States. They held meetings and demonstrations together, and organized a signature-collection campaign. Some Christian and Buddhist groups also played an important role. Second, the younger generation has increasingly participated in antiwar movements even though the number is much smaller compared to those in other countries. It reached its peak during the outbreak of the war in Iraq in 2003. These people did not know the culture of previous social movements. Because of these two new trends, various groups that had never met each other before were able to gain knowledge of other social movements and discuss with people of various opinions. Currently, the party in power and the Japanese government are preparing to revise the Constitution of Japan in order to make it possible for the Japanese Self-Defense Forces to use military strength in foreign countries. Those who are on the side of social movements are making efforts to organize a massive movement against that. The foundation of this movement was made in the collaborative antiwar action after September 11, 2001. We can say that ATTAC Kyoto is in such a stream since it is composed of people with various thoughts, such as communism, anarchism, and ecology. Each member has his or her own specialization and is active in the environmental, farmers', labor, and small business owners' movements. In addition, we organize meetings and actions that make these collaborative actions among movements possible. Although ATTAC Kyoto has only thirty members, we have connections with many movement groups.

With other members of ATTAC Kyoto you helped organize the first Social Forum in Japan at Kyoto University in December 2004. Why was the Kyoto Social Forum (KSF) held? Could you tell me about that experience?

In Kyoto as well as other areas there was friction and breakup among the social movements in the past. As I mentioned, since September 11, 2001, the social movements have increasingly cooperated in almost all the areas. Kyoto was one of the areas where cooperation advanced. In my opinion, compared to other areas in Japan, the cooperation among leftist groups, except the Japanese Communist Party, advanced further in Kyoto. After September 11, 2001, it took little time for the Japanese Communist Party and other groups to come to an agreement concerning cooperation. It was also important that there were distinguished people who were willing to make this cooperation happen among the Communist Party, new leftists, and religious people. ATTAC Kyoto, established in May 2002, accelerated this trend. When we announced the organization of the KSF at the end of 2003, we had already gained many friends in various social movement groups through the activities we did. Those who were in leadership positions in other social movement groups signed their names on an appeal of the KSF. Although the members of ATTAC Kyoto belonged to various movements and political groups, we were not affected by any one particular group. Because of that, I think we were able to play a role in mediating between groups that had been confronting each other.

What are some of the issues and problems that came out of the KSF process?

The number of staff members preparing for the forum was too small. The majority of the staff members in the organizing secretariat were from ATTAC Kyoto. Others were volunteers. The secretariat shouldered a huge burden, because social movement groups did not provide human resources even though they shared the expenses. When we plan for the second KSF, it is important to recognize that the social forum is a project by social movement groups as a whole.

I know that ATTAC Japan has been participating in and organizing workshops at the WSF since 2002. Could you tell me more about your activities at WSF? In what ways are you connected to the global justice movement?

I participated in the WSF in India in 2004. In addition, members of ATTAC Kyoto joined the Asian Social Forum in 2003 and the WSF in Porto Alegré in 2005. I personally have not taken an active part in the WSF. When WSF was held in India, Mumbai resistance against the WSF was also held. I participated in both of them. After I returned to Japan I analyzed differences of the claims between the two forums and explained to activists in Japan. In Japan it was said that extreme Maoists held the Mumbai resistance. I thought that such a stigmatization was harmful to the WSF. In terms of the connection with movements in the world, we mostly depend on ATTAC Japan. So far we exchanged information on social movements with them and also introduced Kyoto to activists from the United States, Indonesia, the Philippines, Germany, India, and Thailand.

More generally speaking, what are some of the problems ATTAC Kyoto confronts in organizing resistance to neoliberal globalization in Japan?

In the last several years the number of people who know terms such as *neoliberalism* and *globalism* has increased considerably, but it is not enough. The media always sides with neoliberalism. Even among those who are engaged in social movements, anti-neoliberalism is not their slogan. The Communist Party in Japan, the biggest group of the left wing, considers issues of neoliberal globalism to be issues of the Japanese government following the United States rather than issues of activities by multinational corporations. In addition, it seems that a better understanding of issues of neoliberalism is not promoted in the environmental movement that is popular among youth. Another main issue is that young people participating in the antiwar movement do not understand enough the cause of war. Therefore, an upsurge in antiwar movements is not connected directly to the anti-neoliberal globalization movement. Generally speaking, issues of neoliberalism are still difficult to comprehend. So ATTAC Kyoto is having a hard time attracting new members.

The Tobin tax and other globalization issues that ATTAC Kyoto focuses on are complex issues. How do you make them understandable to the average Japanese?

This is the most important task for ATTAC Kyoto. Frankly speaking, we are not successful in explaining issues of globalization so that people can understand them. We have been trying to use actual examples (such as Japanese farmers under the pressure of imported crops and the reduced wage of young workers due to international competition) as much as we can.

Do you consider yourself a global citizen? What is your vision of a just Japanese society?

I want to be a global citizen. However, in Japanese society, many people still discriminate against Koreans in Japan and look down on China. In addition, Asians who suffered from the Japanese army in World War II are not getting enough compensation. Therefore I have not fulfilled my responsibility as a global citizen. In the last thirty years, Japanese social movements have declined. Predominant public opinion is Japan centered. Under neoliberal policies, people are trying to help only themselves rather than helping each other. I don't have good prospects, but I am working hard on it. It is my hope that I will have many friends who continue their activities without giving up.

Related Web Sites

ATTAC International: http://www.attac.org/?lang=en
ATTAC Japan: http://www.jca.apc.org/attac-jp
ATTAC Kyoto: http://kattac.talktank.net

Related References

Cassen, Bernard. 2003. "On the Attack." *New Left Review*, Jan.–Feb., 41–60.
Halifax Initiative. 2001. "Taxing Currency Transactions: From Feasibility to Implementation." Ottawa, Canada: Halifax Initiative. Accessed February 25, 2005, at http://www.halifaxinitiative.org/updir/Conference_Papers.pdf
Kennedy, Joy. 2003. "Currency Transaction Tax: Curbing Speculation, Funding Social Development." In *Civilizing Globalization: A Survival Guide*, edited by Richard Sanbrook. Albany: State University of New York Press.

5

EDUCATION FOR CIVIL SOCIETY CAPACITY BUILDING

Fukawa Yoko

FUKAWA YOKO is a director of the Pacific Asia Resource Center (PARC) after serving as its secretary-general. Born in 1972 and graduated from Hitotsubashi University and the University of East Anglia, she participated in "Jubilee 2000," an international campaign advocating for debt forgiveness. She has been engaged in subjects such as debt issues, ODA, and trade.

How was Pacific Asia Resource Center (PARC) created?

It began with the publication of our English quarterly, *AMPO*, in 1969 at the height of the students', farmers', and environmental movements in Japan. On the one hand, we wanted to connect the various movements within Japan into networks. On the other, we tried to connect social movements in Japan with those in Asia. Even thirty years ago, people at PARC thought very much about "networking." PARC was created in Tokyo in 1973. Our motto since the early 1980s has been, "We are a catalyst."

Could you tell me more about the organization and activities of PARC?

Currently we have sixteen board members, six full-time paid staff, two part-time staff, and about seven hundred members. In terms of activities, we publish a monthly magazine and booklets, and make educational videos, including translating foreign language ones on global justice issues such as debt, water, trade, and so on, which we sell to universities both for educational and fundraising purposes. We also organize international conferences and symposia. For example, in 2003, to commemorate our thirtieth anniversary, we held an international symposium called Another World Is Possible. In 2003 we started a farmer cooperative project in collaboration with local NGOs and cooperatives in Sri Lanka and East Timor.

PARC is much noted among Japanese NGOs for its Freedom School? Could you tell me more about it?

We started Freedom School (Jiyū Gakkō) in 1982, so we celebrated our twenty-third anniversary in 2004. The idea was to encourage individuals to be able to read various materials and communicate with people in English by themselves. It is about education on a small scale. Freedom Schools have spread throughout Japan since the mid-1980s. Our year typically runs from May till February, with a cohort of about three to four hundred students, including "salarywomen," "salarymen," housewives, retirees, students, and activists. We offer about thirty courses on different topics, from English language to the World Trade Organization (WTO). We cater to the general public. Other NGOs, like the Japan NGO Center for International Cooperation (JANIC), offer training of trainers, that is, courses catered to activists and NPO staff members.

What are some of the issues that you face in doing this kind of adult education work?

In contrast to lifelong education in general, Jiyū Gakkō is for civil society capacity building. Despite our aim, it is not always easy to stimulate discussions in class. Many participants are used to passive learning. For example, in a course on trade there was a huge gap between half of the class who had high consciousness of trade issues and the other half who knew little about it. Sometimes it made me wonder how far this kind of education could go. Another issue is that there is increasing competition in this kind of course offerings. During the bubble period in the 1980s we were rich; I mean we had the budget to do things. But now local city governments offer courses that are modeled on our Freedom School. Many other NPOs and open colleges and so on are doing a similar thing. So we have to rethink in a fundamental way what it is that distinguishes us from them. For PARC, to educate is to connect with the South, as citizens.

PARC produces an alternative magazine, booklets, and videos. Could you tell me more about the alternative media in Japan?

In my opinion there are two kinds of alternative media in Japan. The first one, including *Zenya, Impaction*, and *Sekai*, caters to left intellectuals. It does have an alternative vision, but it fails to change Japanese society and politics. For the postwar generations educated under the Cold War framework, the Left has a bad image in Japan. Like in the United States, liberalism and neoliberalism have been the dominant political ideologies. For Japanese who do not identify themselves with the extreme Right but also find the extreme Left problematic, the default becomes center-right. I think this is an important educational issue, that is, how this first type of alternative media tries to reach out to the Japanese public. If you take a look at these journals and magazines, they are wordy and difficult. A second type of alternative media is more recent. Magazines like *Eco* that focus on ecology, slow life, and natural goods are close to commercial magazines in style and appeal a great deal to young people and the general public. They have become popular in the past few years. Of course, whether these really constitute alternative media is subject to debate.

What do you think of the slow life movement in Japan?

People like Tsuji Shin'ichi, who wrote the book *Slow Is Beautiful*, understand the linkage between structural issues and slow life. I am not sure the same can be said for those who have taken slow life as a fashionable way of life. Surely many Japanese have become interested in the idea; many find it good for their health. But whether it becomes a social movement is questionable. I wonder how many of the slow-life followers go to demonstrations, for example.

How about the recent peace coalitions against the war in Iraq? They seem to be reviving a movement that had become dormant since the AMPO protests in the 1960s and 1970s. How do you feel about this?

I think there is a huge generation gap. In the 1960s and 1970s, hundreds of thousands of Japanese participated in social movement protests, something that is unimaginable today. There was a gap of twenty to thirty years when there was not much activism at all. I do think the recent peace coalitions like World Peace Now, where the older and younger peace activists come together, is a good thing. But I find myself somewhat in the middle. I feel alienated by the old ideological approach of the so-called AMPO generation and at the same time do not quite share the rather lighthearted approach of some young activists. Many young Japanese who participated in recent antiwar parades may think that "peace is good and peace is fashionable," but why don't they care about Okinawa? They do not make the connection between the war in Iraq and the U.S. military bases in Okinawa.

And the alterglobalization movement in Japan?

Yes, there are quite a few NGOs involved in this, including PARC and ATTAC Japan, and we do various campaigns together, such as the current Millennium Development Goals Japan campaign. But I am not sure it has become a social movement yet. Antiglobalism is still weak in Japan; unlike in some other countries, such as France, it does not receive general public support. Social movements in Japan are split about alterglobalization as well. Prior to Cancun, we had a meeting in Japan to organize a sort of NGO alliance to stop the WTO ministerial meeting. But many development NGOs were hesitant to join the alliance because they equated Seattle with violence. Many Japanese NGOs have been going to the WSF, but they are only a subset of all NGOs. If you were to chart them along a political left-right continuum, you would see ATTAC Japan on the left, close to the labor left, then PARC, and most development-oriented NGOs, including JANIC and other younger, nonpolitical NGOs, more on the center and right. These latter tend to be single-issue focused. So there seems to be a generational-cum-ideological divide, with some of the older NGOs being involved in the alterglobalization movement in Japan and the newer ones not tightly connected. At times this can become a source of tension in alliance building. Another issue is the role of academics. Among the alterglobalization groups there are few academics. Academic associations in Japan are removed from the people's movement, but some of them, such as the Peace Studies Association of Japan, as a policy include some activists.

What is the relationship between PARC and the Japanese government?

PARC has traditionally been critical of the Japanese government, such as the Ministry of Foreign Affairs on official development assistance (ODA) issues. But for our project in East Timor we had discussions among us and finally decided to receive ODA money. Our stand remains that, despite government funds, we continue to be critical of government policy. Our grant, which totals fifteen million yen, covers a three-year period, after which we will have to think about the funding issue again.

Related Web Sites

Alter Trade Japan: http://www.altertrade.co.jp
Minamata Declaration, Alliance of Hope (1989): http://www.jca.apc.org/ppsg/Doc/
    minamata.htm
Pacific Asia Resource Center: http://www.parc-jp.org/parc_e/About_PARC/About_
    us.html

Related References

Kitazawa, Yōko, Reiko Inoue, and Tomoko Sakuma. 2003. *Jiyū bōeki wa naze machi-gatte iru no ka? Shimin ni totte no WTO* [What is wrong with free trade? WTO for citizens]. Booklet 12. Tokyo: Pacific Asia Resource Center.

Pacific Asia Resource Center. 1969–2000. *Japan Asia Quarterly Review*. CD-ROM. Tokyo: Pacific Asia Resource Center.

Pacific Asia Resource Center. 1995. *The Debt Crisis: The Unnatural Disaster*. Video. Tokyo: Pacific Asia Resource Center.

6

COMMUNITY DEVELOPMENT, PEACE, AND GLOBAL CITIZENSHIP

Takahashi Kiyotaka

TAKAHASHI KIYOTAKA is research and policy advisor at Japan International Volunteer Centre (JVC). Born in 1960, he graduated in physics from Sophia University and earned a master's degree in social anthropology from Manchester University. He was a research fellow in the Refugee Studies Program at Oxford University, and has served with the Japanese Peace Corps in the Philippines and as a development consultant in Indonesia and Pakistan. He has been working at JVC since 1996, focusing on official development assistance (ODA) reform, microfinance initiatives, farmers' indebtedness, and Japan's role in peace building, poverty reduction, and UN reform.

How did you become involved in community development and peace building?

After I graduated from college, I went to the Philippines and taught science at the Technical University of the Philippines as part of Japan Overseas Cooperation Volunteers from 1992 to 1994. I enjoyed my stay there very much and loved the Filipino people. It was my first opportunity to realize North-South issues. I wanted to work for international cooperation. I joined a private consulting company that worked for the governmental Japan International Cooperation Agency. I stayed there for six years. My main field was health care and I spent most of my time in Indonesia. Indonesia was under Suharto at the time and I had to spend a lot of money on bribes. It was a bad experience and I had a sort of epiphany that I wanted to do advocacy work, so I quit. I went to Manchester University and began my graduate work in social anthropology. My supervisor was an Africanist and he was very critical about development.

I used discourse analysis to deconstruct development in my master's thesis. Then I received a fellowship from both the U.K. government and a private sponsor to begin doctoral work. I wanted to work on NGO civil society discourse, so I went back to Japan to do fieldwork and did participatory observation at the JVC. Unfortunately my private sponsor passed away and I had to stop my studies. I was offered a staff position at JVC.

Could you tell me about JVC?

JVC is an international NGO on community development, peace exchange, humanitarian assistance, emergency relief, and advocacy. It was established in 1980 by young Japanese volunteers who rushed to Thailand to save displaced people in Indochina. Later our activities were developed from refugee relief to rural development for a safe and stable life, which JVC thought was the ultimate solution to prevent refugees. Currently we have projects in agriculture, water provision, forest preservation, children's education, and peace building in nine countries in Asia and Africa: Cambodia, Vietnam, Laos, Thailand, South Africa, Palestine, Afghanistan, Iraq, and North Korea. We emphasize empowering people and building grassroots capacity through the use of local resources and culture. In Japan we are mainly engaged in advocacy and educational activities to realize a fair and just world with global citizens. Instead of sending project money, we send experts and volunteers to work on, for example, sustainable agriculture and community development in Cambodia. We have eighty staff members worldwide and twenty-two in Japan.

How would you describe JVC as an NGO?

I would describe it as a *colorful* NGO. A good image to describe our work might be a "broken mirror," with each piece reflecting something different from the other pieces. I think in this date and age we have to be flexible. I like to experiment with new ways of doing things. But this can be our weakness as well. I am not sure that the Japanese government likes colorful NGOs!

How have the activities of JVC changed over time?

For the first twenty years, with some exceptions (such as on Cambodia in the 1980s), JVC had not engaged in much advocacy work. Now we have shifted to do more of that. After September 11, for instance, we issued a statement against the war in Afghanistan, another one before the war in Iraq began, and yet another one before Japanese Self-Defense Forces (SDF) were sent to Iraq.

We find problematic the position of the Japanese government that the SDF are sent to Iraq for "humanitarian" work. If you look at our homepage, we do put peace building as one of our main goals. We were contacted by NHK Special (a program of the Japan Broadcasting Corporation) for a television program on constitutional revision, scheduled to be aired on January 23, 2005. Of course this is a very sensitive issue. We had a senior staff meeting in which we discussed whether JVC should have a position on the issue, and if yes, what that might be. We decided that we would participate. We think it is important to draw the distinction between civilian and military activities. In that sense, we are concerned about the revision of Article 9. As a humanitarian NGO, we have to say something. I think Japanese SDF can have some role in peacekeeping but not in humanitarian functions. What has happened in Iraq is that the humanitarian corridor has narrowed down and it has become extremely dangerous for NGOs to do humanitarian work.

What issues concern you right now as an activist and researcher?

I see four main issues: neoliberalism or expansion of free trade, debt, ODA policy, and Japanese SDF and war. JVC mainly focuses on the latter two because of limitation in our capacity. Some JVC board members, including Ohno Kazuoki, are personally involved in the first two issues. Other NGOs, such as Pacific Asia Resource Center, are part of the international Jubilee debt cancellation. But in terms of the first issue area, concerning neoliberalism, I think Japanese NGOs are still weak. We have a few groups, such as ATTAC Japan. After September 11, the world has focused much more on security at the expense of poverty issues. This is clearly reflected in Japan's ODA policy; much of Japanese ODA in 2004 is earmarked for Iraq. ODA disbursements are supposed to be decided by an independent development agency body in consultation with local people on the ground, but right now the Ministry of Foreign Affairs has become dominant. This is the reason I am working hard on the UN Millennium Development Goals Campaign in Japan, to refocus public and governmental attention on poverty issues.

Do you see any connections between the antiwar, antidiscrimination, and alterglobalization movements in Japan?

I think the overlapping element in these three movements is human rights. The antiwar movement focuses on the right to life and security. The antidiscrimination movement looks at a range of social, economic, and political rights.

The alterglobalization movement demands the basic right to livelihood. The work at JVC is guided by a rights-based approach. Our work, like that of many alterglobalization groups, concerns the right to livelihood.

What is your vision for JVC?

JVC is celebrating its twenty-fifth anniversary in 2005. One of the main tasks is to think of how to go forward from where we are. I would like to see us scale up our efforts. I think scaling up has become a main issue for a lot of operation-type NGOs in Japan. Many development NGOs are country and issue focused, or if you will, they see the trees and lose the forest. I also think we have to develop more external relations, with young people and media and so on, to have a more comprehensive vision.

Related Web Sites

Japan International Cooperation Agency and Japan Overseas Cooperation Volunteers: http://www.jica.go.jp/english

Japan International Volunteer Centre: www.ngo-jvc.net

Japan NGO Center for International Cooperation: http://www.janic.org/en/en-index.html

UN Millennium Development Goals: http://www.un.org/millenniumgoals

Related References

Japan International Volunteer Centre. 2000. *NGO no jidai: Heiwa, kyōsei, jiritsu* [The NGO era: Peace, coexistence, and independence]. Tokyo: Mekon.

Japan International Volunteer Centre. 2003. *Kodomotachi no Iraku* [The children's Iraq]. Tokyo: Iwanami Shoten.

Japan NGO Center for International Cooperation. 2004. *Directory of Japanese NGOs Concerned with International Cooperation.* Tokyo: JANIC.

PART II

LABOR

FIGURE 2. Nonregular Employment Forum Inaugural Symposium, Tokyo, December 15, 2004

INTRODUCTION TO PART II

UNTIL THE 1990s, Japan was held in high regard throughout the world as an economic model. For almost four postwar decades, economic development in Japan had been characterized by high growth rates, full employment, technological innovation, and market leadership. In particular, its "developmental state model," marked by direct state guidance in setting economic priorities, created an illusion that somehow Japan might be immune from the adverse impact of economic globalization.[1] With an economic recession continuing beyond the 1990s, corporate and labor restructuring has led to a record unemployment rate of around 5 percent, and widespread angst among the working populace.

If corporate and labor restructuring has been happening across the developed world and is painful everywhere, the phenomenon seems to hit particularly hard in Japan due to four factors. First, it is often argued that Japan practices a kind of capitalism that is different from either the neoliberal Anglo-Saxon model or the European social democratic model.[2] The traditional social safety net has largely been provided by corporate Japan rather than public social welfare. When corporate restructuring occurs, not only employment issues but also the general social fabric, if not national identity, are affected.

Second, the corporate-based structure of Japanese unions, with their basic stance of "cooperationism," makes it difficult for the Japan Trade Union Confederation (RENGO) to have an effective response. RENGO, for example, has traditionally focused exclusively on large Japanese companies (roughly 40 percent of the labor market), where lifelong employment is the norm. It is now forced to articulate a response to the labor crisis both in the small and medium-size enterprises and in the ever-increasing nonregular labor market, because the trend of using nonregular workers constitutes a direct threat to full-time workers.[3] Further, compared to its Western counterparts, RENGO takes a much more conciliatory approach to trade liberalization under the World Trade Organization (WTO) and bilateral free trade agreements (FTAs) between Japan and a number of countries, including Singapore and Mexico, since 2002, and under those being negotiated or in preparation with Korea, Thailand, the Philippines, Malaysia, and Indonesia. According to a 2004 RENGO position paper on the FTAs and economic partnership agreements (EPAs),

RENGO has judged that Japan's efforts to conclude FTAs and EPAs are unavoidable for Japan not to be isolated and to play an active role in establishing rules for fair dealings, taking into account slow progress at the General Agreement on Tariffs and Trade / WTO and a reality that conclusions of FTAs and EPAs have been expanded in most parts of the world. RENGO makes the argument to avoid disadvantages of FTAs and EPAs, such as harmful impact on employment and environment. . . . RENGO will request that the government work to shape a web of quality FTAs and EPAs.

Although it emphasizes that International Labour Organization core labor standards and Organisation for Economic Co-operation and Development Guidelines for Multinational Enterprises should be incorporated into trade and investment rules and that there should be mechanisms for information disclosure and public consultation, RENGO, unlike smaller community unions and other social movements, focuses more on increasing its "negotiation power" rather than challenging the trade liberalization policies of the Japanese government.[4]

Third, women have traditionally dominated the part-time labor market. Recent waves of corporate restructuring have ushered men into this domain, further complicating existing gender labor dynamics. The gender wage gap in the dispatch labor market, for example, is 53 percent (that is, women earn fifty-three yen when men earn one hundred yen), almost 14 percent below that in the full-time labor market.[5] Although the unemployment rate for women stands at 5.1 percent (2002) compared to that of men (5.5 percent), the majority of the homeless are men, with the average in their late fifties, joined by an increasing number of young men in their late twenties and early thirties.[6]

Finally, unlike in many other developed countries where a significant migrant worker population is present, Japan has an extremely restrictive immigration policy vis-à-vis migrant labor. The 1990 Immigration Control Act made it illegal to import unskilled labor while allowing South Americans of Japanese descent to live and work in Japan. The latest revision of the Immigration Control Act in 2003 increased the penalties of illegal migrant workers from three hundred thousand to three million yen, and a period of ten years before deported migrant workers can reenter Japan. The tensions between Nikkeiren (the Japan Federation of Employers Associations, which desires to introduce a more flexible migrant labor policy) and RENGO, whose policy is to protect Japanese workers) add an extra unresolved dimension to the labor crisis in Japan.[7]

The ineffective response of Japanese unions has not only galvanized the labor left but also posed some hard questions about the traditional corporate union structure and strategy in Japan. In view of the characteristics—continuing trend of structural reforms, limited effectiveness of RENGO, gender gap, and the controversy of migrant labor—community unions and other members of an emerging alternative globalization movement in Japan have opted for a continuum of methods, from the local to the international, to counter the deteriorating labor situation in Japan. Existing unions have taken on the issue of nonregular employment. For example, Tokyo Union set up the Haken Rōdōsha Union.[8] New networks have been formed, such as the Haken Rōdō (Dispatch Workers) Network in 1991;[9] Kintō Taigū (Equality Action) 21, which focuses on the equal treatment of male and female workers, on the one hand, and that of full-time and part-time workers, on the other, in 1999; the Human Rights Center for Working Women in Osaka in 2004; and the Hiseiki Koyō (Nonregular Employment) Forum, which organizes study groups and symposia, raises consciousness, advocates, and connects internationally, in 2004.[10]

The six interviews included in this section begin with the official positions of RENGO on the liberalization polices of the WTO and Japanese bilateral FTAs, and then move on to examine labor discontent from the perspective of five groups: the homeless, women, migrant workers, a labor NGO, and a public service union. Several themes emerge from the discussion. Many unionists and activists realize that labor restructuring and the privatization of public services are problems beyond Japan and have been networking with their counterparts in Asia. Nonformal work has increased dramatically in Japan since 1995, creating an economic underclass and the homeless (average age fifty-six). Women suffer disproportionately in terms of wage differentials (even among part-timers), job segregation, and indirect discrimination. Migrant workers face a unique set of issues, including immigration controls, antiforeigner sentiments, and lack of access to medical insurance if they overstay their visa. Traditional labor union structures largely fail to provide answers to these complex labor issues in Japan. Activists pursue a spectrum of strategies, from international lobbying (for example, through the International Confederation of Free Trade Unions) to regional labor activist community building and domestic legal reforms in homeless support, equal treatment for equal work, immigration, trafficking, and public services.

Notes

1. Johnson 1982.

2. Hall and Soskice 2001.

3. Interview with the director of the International Division of the Department of International Affairs, Japanese Trade Union Confederation, December 14, 2004.

4. Ibid.

5. Nakano 2004.

6. Interview with the executive director of the Shinjuku Homeless Support Center, November 28, 2004.

7. RENGO's stance on migrant workers can be summarized as follows (from its 2004 position paper on FTAs and EPAs): "It should be taken into account that receiving foreign workers may adversely affect national employment conditions and have possible risks of vast costs over the future, including nonfinancial ones in terms of medical and housing services, education, cultural friction, and security. Consequently, foreign workers should be limited to those engaged in jobs requiring professional knowledge, techniques, and skills in conformity with the national employment situation, based on national consensus. . . . Nonskilled foreign workers should not be admitted to work in Japan. . . . Foreign workers who have already been admitted to the country should be guaranteed fair labor standards."

8. http://www.t-union.or.jp, accessed March 21, 2005.

9. http://www.union-net.or.jp/haken, accessed March 21, 2005.

10. Haken Rodō Nettowāku 2004.

7

GLOBALIZATION AND LABOR RESTRUCTURING

Kumagai Ken'ichi

KUMAGAI KEN'ICHI has been director of the International Division of the Japanese Trade Union Confederation (RENGO) since 2003. Born in Tokyo in 1949, he graduated from National Saitama University in 1974 with a bachelor of science degree. He got an engineering job at an automobile factory in Japan and was elected its union officer. Since being transferred to the national trade union center in 1976, he has participated in education, organization, labor policy, and international activities. In 2001, the National Labor College in Washington, D.C., granted him a diploma.

Could you tell me a little bit about RENGO?

RENGO, the Japanese Trade Union Confederation, is the national center of Japan's trade unions. It has a membership of around seven million people, accounting for 67 percent of all trade union members in Japan. RENGO was established in 1989 as a merger of private and public sector unions into the new national Trade Union Confederation. RENGO's mission is to realize a welfare-oriented society where the value of work is respected. The highest priorities in our activities today are to secure job security and good working conditions, reform the social security system, tackle the issue of atypical workers, and increase our membership. In the area of international activities, our basic task is to take part in worldwide activities aimed at overcoming the negative aspects of globalization. The current economic and social conjuncture in Japan is a critical one. The unemployment rate remains high at around 5 percent. Middle-aged people, in particular, have borne the brunt of continuing corporate restructuring. Each year, about thirty-two thousand people commit suicide. These problems originate in the neoliberal policies pursued by the Koizumi government. RENGO is determined to fight against those policies.

Some of the RENGO members went to attend the World Trade Organization's ministerial meeting in Cancun in 2003. Could you tell me more about it?

Today's economic globalization is problematic; it has led to poverty and increasing gaps between the haves and have-nots. However, we believe that "another world is possible." In order to realize the new world, it is important to insert social dimensions into existing international economic and trade institutions, including the World Trade Organization (WTO). We advocate changing the WTO system through participation and dialogue. It is on the basis of this stance that our members attended the WTO Cancun ministerial meeting and other meetings.

How does RENGO manage to make its voice heard within the WTO?

To ensure that the WTO contributes to the maintenance of a fair international economic order, we must introduce mechanisms to overcome the negative aspects of globalization. These mechanisms should include the institutionalized participation of trade unions and NGOs in some form within the WTO negotiations. To this end, trade unions and NGOs must take on the challenge of strengthening international cooperation, expressing their demands in a forceful way and materializing them. Another important question involves what activities trade unions and NGOs should carry out in their own countries. We believe that they should call on governments to give due consideration to their views in the WTO rounds. It is also important to work through the International Labour Organization (ILO). The ILO is a tripartite institution in which labor unions have a legitimate role. We are working to strengthen the relationship between the ILO and the WTO.

What issues within WTO negotiations concern you?

The Doha round was launched on the basis of the idea that top priority would be given to the development issues facing developing countries. However, the emphasis later shifted to coordinating the interests of the major countries. The issue of development has not been sufficiently discussed. In addition to trade and economic matters, social and environmental problems should also be taken into account in WTO negotiations. The principle of *sustainable development* must be incorporated into all areas of WTO activities. In the area of nonagricultural market access negotiations, it is vital to pay special attention to the needs and concerns of developing nations. Furthermore, we believe that public services and utilities should be excluded from the negotiations for the General Agreement on Trade in Services.

What is RENGO's position on free trade?

Let me talk a little bit about free trade agreements (FTAs). In general, RENGO is not against free trade if it brings about a fair distribution of fruits among people and decent work for workers. However, recent FTAs in East Asia have neglected social aspects both in the negotiation procedures and in the contents of the agreements. Within the process of negotiations there has been inadequate information disclosure, involvement of trade unions, and expression of the views of trade unions. The ILO core labor standards have not been incorporated into any of the agreements. We believe that FTAs should set out to complement the WTO system. Also, it is vital to incorporate fair rules into the WTO and those FTAs and EPAs, and to ensure information disclosure and the participation of trade unions and NGOs in their negotiations.

Some Japanese NGOs also involved in monitoring the WTO think that Japanese labor unions are weak. What do you think of this comment?

To confront the problems arising from globalization, we have two major issues to tackle. One is to reform the trade union movement by making our activities more attractive and promoting organizational strengthening. The other is to bolster international solidarity among trade unions for overcoming the negative aspects of globalization. Since the middle of the 1990s, the Japanese trade union movement has been losing power. There are three reasons for this: first, the neoliberal policies of our conservative government; second, the wave of globalization that has swept over Japan; and third, the failure of the Japanese trade union movement to reform itself. In 2001 RENGO adopted a new platform: "The Role and Action for the New RENGO in the Twenty-First Century." It suggests that RENGO should focus our efforts on part-time workers and other atypical workers, develop new measures for organizational strengthening, build stronger ties with NGOs, and develop new international solidarity activities. The statement "Japanese labor unions are weak" is not correct in general, but we are fully aware that we have many challenges to tackle for the future of workers in Japan and in the world.

Related Web Sites

International Confederation of Free Trade Unions: http://www.icftu.org

International Labour Organization: http://www.ilo.org

Nikkeiren (Japan Federation of Employers' Associations): http://www.nikkeiren.or.jp /english/top.htm

Nippon Keidanren: http://www.keidanren.or.jp

RENGO: http://www.jtuc-rengo.org

World Trade Organization, Trade and Labor Standards: http://www.wto.org/english/ thewto_e/whatis_e/tif_e/bey5_e.htm

Related References

Berberoglu, Berch. 2002. *Labor and Capital in the Age of Globalization: The Labor Process and the Changing Nature of Work in the Global Economy.* New York: Rowman and Littlefield.

Munck, Ronaldo. 2002. *Globalization and Labor: The New Great Transformation.* London and New York: Zed Books.

Nikkeiren. 2002. "Promoting Structural Reform to Overcome the Crisis." Tokyo: Nikkeiren.

RENGO and Nikkeiren. 1999. "Joint Declaration on Employment Stabilization." Available at http://www.jtuc-rengo.org/updates/before2003/weekly/1999/ week99oct/99oct7.html

8

CORPORATE RESTRUCTURING AND HOMELESSNESS

Kasai Kazuaki

KASAI KAZUAKI is undersecretary general of Shinjuku Homeless Support Center, an NPO corporation he cofounded in 2002. Born in Tokyo in 1962, Kazuaki has worked as a day laborer since 1991 and has also engaged in providing aid to homeless people in Sanya. He helped organize the Shinjuku Network (Shinjuku Renrakukai) in 1994 and now serves as its director. He was arrested and prosecuted in an incident of enforced eviction by the Tokyo Metropolitan Government in 1996.

When did homelessness become an issue in Japan?

Since the beginning of the 1990s, homelessness has been increasing in Japan. It depends on who counts and how one counts. According to government statistics, there are twenty-five thousand homeless people in Japan, including fifty-seven hundred in Tokyo. I think that in reality the figures are much higher. Ninety-five percent of all homeless people are single men. Within this population, 60 percent come from the day construction sector (*yoseba*) and the average age is 55.9. Others come from service sectors, including part-time workers.

Why did it become an issue? What has been the government's response?

The key reason of course is restructuring. Until the Law Concerning Temporary Measures to Support the Self-Reliance of Homeless People was passed in 2002, there was not really a system in Japan to support the homeless, and there was little recognition of homelessness as a structural rather than a personal issue. Right now we have a strange dual approach to homelessness in

Japan. On the one hand, we have this law that supposedly protects the rights of the homeless population. On the other hand, you see these blue tents here in Shinjuku Park, Ueno Park, and Shibuya Park, and many other areas in Tokyo, Osaka, and Nagoya, constantly facing the threat of eviction.

Could you tell me more about the 2002 Law Concerning Temporary Measures to Support the Self-Reliance of Homeless People?

In Japan, *giin rippō* (legislation by National Diet members) is rare. I think this new law was mostly drafted by Ministry of Labor bureaucrats when many big companies were engaged in restructuring. The age cohort of 45 to 55 was particularly hit, simply due to demographic reality. There was too much manpower in this age range, and the companies did not really have a policy to handle restructuring. Since the new law came into effect in 2002, the situation in Tokyo has improved somewhat. But the impact of restructuring in areas outside of Tokyo, like Hokkaido or Kansai remains severe. Unable to repay loans, many men would come from these areas to Tokyo in search of job opportunities. I think one problem of the law is that it focuses primarily on homelessness in big cities in Japan while neglecting the increasing spread of the phenomenon throughout the nation. In addition, there are only eight shelters with space for about two thousand people, with a maximum stay of six months, and they are not free. Most homeless people do not have access to medical service as well. Of course the most fundamental problem of all is the lack of job opportunities for this increasing population.

What is the role of nongovernmental organizations in the issue of homelessness in Japan?

There are a few nongovernmental organizations, many of them church-related groups, involved in the homeless issue. The Shinjuku Homeless Support Center was created in 2002. We have been providing meals on Sunday evenings. But most NGOs are small. There certainly is not a systematic and coordinated effort. I think NGOs face many challenges in our work. The first one is how to spread the service and advocacy to areas outside of big cities. Funding is always a big problem. Another problem concerns the division among NGOs. Migrant workers organizations, for example, do not necessarily take up the homeless issue. Yet another issue concerns the attitudes and policies of political leaders, such as Tokyo Governor Ishihara Shintarō, who consistently want to gentrify cities and remove the homeless. As you may know, in 1996, then

Tokyo governor Aoshima Yukio ordered police to evict people living in a passageway at the Shinjuku station so that the government could build a moving walkway. Finally, a big challenge is to arouse the interests of the general public. This is an enormous task, because everyone seems to be consumed by his or her own life. Even the homeless themselves tend to blame themselves. We need people to think of it as a larger societal and structural issue.

How about the role of labor unions?

This is an important question. Japanese labor unions have traditionally focused on big companies. Given that the hardest hit have been workers from medium-size and small companies as well as nonregular, part-time workers, I think the labor union response has been ineffective. The issue of homelessness should concern not just the homeless population but also all workers, because it reflects important structural changes within the labor market in Japan.

Related Web Sites

Asian Coalition for Housing Rights: http://www.achr.net/japan_2002.htm
NOJIREN (Shibuya Free Association for the Right to Housing and Well-Being of the
    Homeless): http://www.jca.apc.org/nojukusha/nojiren/declare/declare_e.html
Shinjuku Homeless Support Center: http://homepage3.nifty.com/shelter-less

Related References

Gill, Tom. 2001. *Men of Uncertainty: The Social Organization of Day Laborers in
    Contemporary Japan.* Albany: State University of New York Press.
Gucewicz, Tony. 2000. *Tokyo's Homeless: A City in Denial.* New York: Kroshka Books.
Iwata, Masami. 2003. "Commonality of Social Policy on Homelessness: Beyond the
    Different Appearances of Japanese and English Policies." *European Journal of
    Housing Policy,* 3(2), 173–192.
Kawakami, Masako, ed. 2005. *Nihon ni okeru hōmuresu no jittai* [The reality of the
    homeless in Japan]. Tokyo: Gakubunsha.
Matsushige, Itsuo, and Yasue Suzuko. 2003. *Shitte imasu ka? Hōmuresu no jinken*
    [Do you know: The human rights of the homeless]. Osaka: Kaiho shuppansha.
Ōyama, Shirō. 2005. *A Man with No Talents: Memoirs of a Tokyo Day Laborer,* translated from the Japanese by Edward Fowler. Ithaca, NY: Cornell University Press.

9

GENDER, PART-TIME LABOR, AND INDIRECT DISCRIMINATION

Sakai Kazuko

SAKAI KAZUKO is a board member of Equality Action 21. Born in Fukui in 1947, she studied at Ochanomizu University. She is a former member of the municipal assembly in the Toshima ward of Tokyo and a former joint-representative of a community union national network. Currently she is involved in research on the actual conditions of the part-time workers and in making policy proposals at Kintō Taigū Action 21. She is coauthor of *Irasuto de wakaru shiranaito sonsuru pāto & keiyaku shain no rōdōhō* [Part-time labor law: If you don't know it, you will lose].

How did you become a feminist labor activist?

I was part of the students' movement when I was in college in 1965. In the 1970s I was involved in the women's liberation movement. In the 1980s, as a member of a municipal assembly in Toshima-ku, Tokyo, I was engaged in protecting the human rights of female workers and minority women.

In the 1990s, as a full-time official of a community union, I worked on consultation with part-time workers, on organizational issues, and also in investigation. As you know, three laws were passed or revised in accordance with the Convention on the Elimination of All Forms of Discrimination Against Women (CEDAW). One of them was the Equal Employment Opportunity Law (EEOL) passed in 1985, which prohibits gender discrimination in employment. The EEOL was revised in 1997, prohibiting, among other things, sexual harassment in the workplace. Two concerns, however, remain after that revision: the issues of indirect discrimination and part-time workers (who constitute 50 percent of the women's workforce). In particular, after 1995, nonformal work increased dramatically due to globalization.

Why was Equality Action 21 established?

I think the situation of nonformal work has deteriorated since 1995 due to economic globalization. The problem is not only in Japan; we observe a similar phenomenon in every country. Women constitute the bulk of nonformal workers (*hiseiki*), contributing to the feminization of poverty (*josei no hinkonka*). Dualization is a factor—that is, half of the workforce has full-time work, dominated by men, while the other half holds part-time work. I know, for example, that it is not uncommon for full-time female workers to become dispatch workers when they get pregnant or sick. The full-time employee (*seishain*) status has become very ambiguous. In Japan it is increasingly difficult to say who is *seishain* and who is not. In 2000, thirty people, including Diet members Komiyama Yōko, Ōwaki Masako, Fukushima Mizuho, and Yoshikawa Haruko of the Democratic Party, Social Democratic Party, and Communist Party; lawyers; and women's groups, called for the formation of Kintō Taigū 21. The original name was Kintō Taigū, or Equality Action 2003, and it aimed to revise legislation to stipulate equal treatment in the Part-Time Labor Law, to prohibit indirect discrimination in the Equal Opportunity Law, and to realize equal pay for equal work by 2003. Now that 2003 has come and gone and our goal is not quite realized, we changed the name to Equality Action 21 (standing for our work in the twenty-first century). Currently we have about six hundred individual members plus labor union members. Our operation funds come from membership fees, grants, and publication sales. In 2000, Kintō Taigū 21 held symposia in Tokyo, Nagoya, Osaka, and Fukuoka, and launched a national campaign on indirect discrimination. Our objective is clear and simple: we fight for equal pay for equal work, that is, same pay per hour. In a broader sense, like any other social movement, we aim for empowerment. We aim at creating favorable conditions for women to work. For example, the EEOL is scheduled to be revised in 2006, so we are conducting surveys and studies. Of course we also lobby the deliberation councils (*shingikai*) within the Ministry of Health, Labor, and Welfare.

What is indirect discrimination?

There are various types of indirect discrimination, including discrimination by age (for example, there is an age ceiling for the bureaucrat entrance examination in many local areas), family allowance based on the assumption of a male household head, and the separation of *sōgō shoku* (management) and *ippan shoku* (general work). This separation is regarded as a form of indirect discrimination whereby men are systematically channeled into *sōgō shoku* and women into *ippan shoku*. Kanematsu, for example, recently lost a lawsuit to six women employee plaintiffs on the basis of this reason. Part-time work can also be considered indirect discrimination, because the pay and treatment are not the same and it is disproportionately occupied by women. Unlike in the European Union, these various kinds of indirect discrimination were not prohibited by the revised EEOL.

What are the obstacles you encounter in organizing against indirect discrimination in Japan?

Gender discrimination in employment received government and public attention in 1985 and 1997 when the EEOL was passed and revised. Since then, few people care about this topic, as if it is finished business. It is in part because the women's movement in Japan in the past decade has focused mainly on sexual harassment and domestic violence as human rights violations while labor issues have rarely been seen as human rights violations.

Do you advocate some sort of affirmative action for women?

In the United States, affirmative action is used to rectify racial inequality in the civil rights movement, but not so much in terms of discrimination between women and men. In Japan we use the words *positive action*. The Tokyo metropolitan government, for example, has published a report on positive action, but the report mostly contains beautiful empty words, because there is little action. As long as the government emphasizes *effort* (*doryoku*) rather than mandatory requirements, I don't think we will go very far.

What is the relationship between Kintō Taigū 21 and other labor unions and women's groups?

We are certainly connected to labor unions. They support our work and vice versa. We have labor union members and we share information and so on. In terms of connections with women's groups, we are part of the Japan NGO Network for the Convention on the Elimination of All Forms of Discrimination Against Women (CEDAW), which monitors the implementation of CEDAW by the Japanese government. We wrote the section on women's labor situation in Japan in the Japan NGO Alternative Report to CEDAW in 2003.

Related Web Sites

Equality Action 21: http://www15.ocn.ne.jp/kintou21/top.htm

International Labour Organization, Bureau for Gender Equality: http://www.ilo.org/
dyn/gender/gender.home

International Labour Organization C100 Equal Remuneration Convention, 1951:
http://www.ilo.org/ilolex/cgi-lex/convde.pl?C100

International Labour Organization C111 Discrimination (Employment and Occupation) Convention, 1958 Convention Concerning Discrimination (Employment
and Occupation): http://www.ilo.org/ilolex/cgi-lex/convde.pl?C111

International Labour Organization, Elimination of Discrimination in Respect of
Employment and Occupation (including a definition of *indirect discrimination*),
1998: http://www.ilo.org/dyn/declaris/DECLARATIONWEB.static_jump?var_
language=EN&var_pagename=ISSUESDISCRIMINATION

International Labour Organization 1996 General Survey on Equality in Employment
and Occupation (including discussions on indirect discrimination): http://www
.ilo.org/ilolex/english/surveyq.htm

Working Women's International Network: http://www.ne.jp/asahi/wwn/wwin

Related References

Brinton, Mary. 1994. *Women and the Economic Miracle: Gender and Work in Postwar
Japan*. Berkeley: University of California Press.

Broadbent, Kaye. 2003. *Women's Employment in Japan: The Experience of Part-Time
Workers*. New York: Routledge Curzon.

Hirakawa, Keiko, ed. 2005. *Onnatachi no orutanatibu: Pāto ni kintō taigū wo!* [The
alternatives for women: Equal treatment for part-time workers!]. Tokyo: Akashi
Shoten.

Kumazawa, Makoto. 2004. *Josei rōdō to kigyō shakai* [Women's labor and corporate
society]. Tokyo: Iwanami Shoten.

Nakano, Mami. 2004. "Haken, pāto no chingin to shuntō" [Wages of dispatch and
part-time workers and spring wage negotiations]. *Rōdōkumiai*, Supplement Issue,
June, 14–16.

Sakai, Kazuko. 2001. "Problems of the Equal Employment Opportunity Law."
Women's Online Media. Available at http://wom-jp.org/e/JWOMEN/kinto.html

Shimamoto, Yasuko. 2004. *Rupo Kaiko: Kono kuni de ima okite iru koto* [Layoff: It is
happening in this country]. Tokyo: Iwanami Shoten.

10

MIGRATION, TRAFFICKING, AND FREE TRADE AGREEMENTS

Ishihara Virgie

ISHIHARA VIRGIE is founder and executive director of the Filipino Migrants Center (FMC), Nagoya, Japan. Born in the Philippines in 1960 and graduated from Manuel L. Quezon University in the Philippines in 1985, Virgie served as Aichi chairperson and organizer of the Filipina Circle for Advancement and Progress in 1996. FMC serves as a source of information about the situation of Filipino migrants in Japan, particularly in Nagoya, for academics, mass media, students, government organizations, and NGOs.

Could you tell me about the Filipino migrant worker situation in the Nagoya area?

Japanese government statistics in 2003 reported 168,000 documented Filipino migrant workers in Japan, including Filipina women with entertainment visas. In addition to that, one can add at least thirty thousand undocumented entertainment workers. In Aichi Prefecture, where we are located, there are about twenty thousand documented entertainment workers. In Nagoya alone there are around five to six thousand entertainment workers, plus an unknown number who overstay their visas. These latter usually come in as tourists and stay behind. I don't know exactly the breakdown per nationality. Filipinos constitute one of the biggest groups. There are also Colombians, Uzbekistanis, and Romanians.

How old is the average Filipina who works in the entertainment industry here in Nagoya? How much do they earn?

Nowadays there are girls as young as fourteen, fifteen, sixteen, and seventeen.

The salary for a first-time-entertainer visa holder is around three hundred fifty thousand yen (about $3,500). For second-timers, it is about fifty thousand yen. Then it keeps increasing, which is why the Association for the Promotion of Businesses, of which many entertainment businesses are a member, is reluctant to hire six- or seven-timers. By the time these workers are twenty-three, no one wants them anymore.

What are some of the issues that Filipino migrant workers face here?

Not all Filipino migrant workers are in the entertainment sector. Filipino men usually work in the construction sector. The first issue concerns their labor situation. Undocumented workers in particular do not know about their rights in terms of pay and protection and so on. Then there is the issue of medical insurance. Many migrant workers, particularly those who overstay their visa, do not have access to medical insurance. Among women there is also the problem of domestic violence. In cases where they leave their Japanese husband, they might not know how to apply for their visa extension. After marriage, a Filipina will be granted a visa extension for one year, then another year on the second extension application, and then three years on the third application. The *yakuza* (crime syndicate) often extorts five hundred thousand yen from these women to act as their immigration "sponsor." The divorce rate in these mixed international marriages after five years is very high, even though of course there are also successful marriages.

In 2004 you were invited by the trafficking project team within the Liberal Democratic Party to give your views on the foreign migrant worker situation in Japan. What did you talk about in your presentation?

I emphasized two things. First, the fiscal crisis and unemployment caused by globalization is a structural problem in the Philippines. Second, the Filipino government, in my opinion, runs a labor exploitation program. Ten percent of the total population of eighty million is exported worldwide as migrant workers, the majority of whom are women. If Japan used its official development assistance (ODA) in the Philippines to create decent jobs for these women, maybe they would not leave the Philippines. The year 2006 is the fiftieth anniversary of Japanese ODA to the Philippines. It will be a good occasion for us to reflect on what ODA is about.

What are your views on the Japanese-Filipino free trade agreement that is currently under negotiation?

I am not sure it will help Filipino workers. Cheap Japanese food exports might flood the local market, causing unemployment and even possibly killing local farmers. Right now the two governments are studying the *caregiver* visa category whereby a Filipino worker can come to Japan when she is sponsored by a private company to provide care services in Japan. We don't know what will happen. I would like to see the elimination of the so-called entertainer visa category. What we want is a regular employment visa category.

Could you tell me about the activities of the Filipino Migrants Center, Nagoya?

Our center was established in 2000. We are essentially an educational and outreach organization with five goals: crisis intervention, research and information, campaigns and advocacy, networking and solidarity, and women empowerment. We run programs to support and educate young Filipina mothers. We also work with other migrant worker groups both here in Japan and in the Philippines (such as with Immigrant International, which is a Filipino umbrella NGO).

How serious is the issue of HIV / AIDS in the Filipino migrant population here?

To be honest, I don't know much about the situation. I would like to create a program on HIV / AIDS within our center.

What do you advocate in terms of migrant worker policy in Japan?

I think that, first, Filipina women with legitimate Japanese children should be given automatic permanent residency in Japan to exempt them from the regular visa extension. Second, undocumented workers should be given work permits and should have access to medical insurance. Finally, if the Japanese government is sincere about caring for the trafficked victims, it should provide skills training programs to empower them, and prosecute the traffickers rather than the victims.

Related Web Sites

Center for Japanese-Filipino Families: http://home.att.ne.jp/banana/cjff/homepage2004.htm

International Convention on the Protection of the Rights of All Migrant Workers and Members of Their Families: http://www.ohchr.org/english/law/cmw.htm

Migrants Rights International: http://www.migrantwatch.org

Solidarity Network with Migrants Japan: http://www.jca.apc.org/migrant-net

UN Special Rapporteur of the Commission on Human Rights on the Human Rights of Migrants: http://www.unhchr.ch/html/menu2/7/b/mmig.htm

Related References

Development Action for Women Network. 2003. *Pains and Gains: A Study of Overseas Performing Artists in Japan from Pre-Departure to Reintegration*. Manila, Philippines: DAWN.

Herbert, Wolfgang. 1996. *Foreign Workers and Law Enforcement in Japan*. London: Kegan Paul International.

Inaba, Nanako. 2002. "Kokusai jinken kijun to Nihon ni okeru ijūsha no kenri hoshō no genjō" [International human rights standards and the status of human rights protection of migrant workers in Japan]. In *Hanjinshushugi, sabetsu teppai sekaikaigi to Nihon* [World conference against racism, racial discrimination, xenophobia, and Japan], edited by International Movement Against All Forms of Discrimination and Racism. Tokyo: Kaiho Shuppansha.

Kalakasan Migrant Women Empowerment Center and International Movement Against All Forms of Discrimination and Racism Japan Committee, eds. 2006. *Transforming Lives: Abused Migrant Women in Japan Blaze a Trail Toward Empowerment*. Tokyo: Kaiho Shuppansha.

Migrants Rights International for the Global Campaign on Migrants Rights (MRI). 2000. *Achieving Dignity: Campaigner's Handbook for the Migrants Rights Convention*. Geneva: MRI. Available at http://www.migrantwatch.org

Roth, Joshua Hotaka. 2002. *Brokered Homeland: Japanese Brazilian Migrants in Japan*. Ithaca, NY: Cornell University Press.

Shipper, Apichai. 2002a. "Political Construction of Foreign Workers in Japan." *Critical Asian Studies* 34(1), 41–68.

Shipper, Apichai. 2002b. *Pragmatism in Activism: Organizing Support for Illegal Foreign Workers in Japan*. Cambridge, MA: Harvard University Program on U.S.-Japan Relations.

Shipper, Apichai. 2005. "Criminals or Victims? The Politics of Illegal Foreigners in Japan." *Journal of Japanese Studies*, 31(2), 299–327.

Taran, Patrick. 2000. *Human Rights of Migrants: Challenges of the New Decade*. Geneva: International Labour Organization.

United Nations High Commissioner for Human Rights (UNHCHR). 2005. *Fact Sheet No. 24: The Rights of Migrant Workers*. Geneva: UNHCHR. Available at http://www.ohchr.org/english/about/publications/docs/fs24.htm

11

NEOLIBERALISM AND LABOR ORGANIZING

Yasuda Yukihiro

YASUDA YUKIHIRO is a member of Labor Net. Born in Tokyo in 1956 and graduated from the Graduate School of Letters, Arts, and Sciences at Waseda University, Yukihiro has been providing information communication technology to social movement organizations since the 1990s. Since 1997 he has also been involved in activities at an information communication company that works with nonprofit organizations.

How did you become involved in Labor Net?

I helped Labor Net set up its Web site initially. As I learned more about Labor Net's activities, I became interested in labor issues. In 1998 I attended the International Labor Media in Seoul and was impressed by the militancy of Korean labor unions. I thought maybe we should do similar things in Japan with our labor movement. Labor Net was founded in 2001. We are connected to Labor Net in the United States and United Kingdom, as well as to Nodong in South Korea. Now we have three hundred members, most of whom are individual labor unionists and activists.

What do you do in terms of labor organizing?

Labor Net is an informal gathering of labor union activists. As you may know, labor unions in Japan are organized in such a way that cross-company or cross-sector mobilization is difficult; that is, we have company-based unions and industry-based unions under the larger umbrella national union known as RENGO. (There are also two other major labor unions: National Federation of

Trade Unions, or Zenrōren, tied to the Communist Party; and National Trade Union Council, or Zenrōkyō.) RENGO performs important functions such as raising base salaries, providing policy recommendations vis-à-vis business federations and the Japanese government, as well as carrying out campaigns on safety nets, reduction of work time, elimination of unpaid overtime work, and unequal informal work conditions. But RENGO as an institution does not critique or oppose capitalism. So we as labor activists are engaged in exploring alternatives to the existing economic structure in Japan. We meet once a month to exchange information. We organize demonstrations such as the one in front of the Ministry of Foreign Affairs in November 2004 to protest the negotiations on the Japanese-Korean free trade agreement. In addition to campaigns, we also organize the annual Laborfest, inspired by Steve Zeltser of Labor Net (USA), where we sing and dance. Labor unionists in Japan are often very serious; I think we should also rejoice and celebrate.

There are quite a few labor issues in Japan. What is the priority of Labor Net?

I think we concentrate on and build on the alterglobalization movement, that is, against unchecked neoliberalism. We have seen the results of the neoliberal economic policy of the Japanese government manifested in many ways: the dramatic increase in the informal work sector, including part-time work and contract work, through the so-called dispatch agencies; the precarization of women's work that dominates the informal sector; underemployment that is not reflected in the stable unemployment rate of 5 percent; and the end of the lifelong employment system. There is of course also the issue of migrant workers who, often because of their illegal working status, are subject to various kinds of discrimination. When the Japanese economy was booming in the past decades, many Japanese did not think about these issues. But now, because the economy is not doing well, there are a lot of antiforeigner sentiments.

Concretely, what kinds of alternatives do you advocate as a labor activist?

Korean labor unions are now planning a general strike for next week (November 1, 2004) when the Parliament passes the bill to restrict public sector workers' rights to organize and bargain collectively. In Japan we don't do general strikes anymore. We used to, in the 1960s and 1970s, but labor unions have become much weaker now. Our baseline is that we want working conditions that are secure. The lifelong employment system that existed in Japan resembled a socialist practice. I don't think we will ever return to that system, but we work toward the reduction of the wage gap, reestablishing social security, which is currently going in the American direction of privatization. If I may add, media reform is necessary. The demonstrations we organized in November 2004 in Tokyo, for example, with more than a hundred Korean labor activists and three to four hundred Japanese, were not at all reported in our press, while foreign press such as the Associated Press and Reuters were present. The Japanese press would want us to believe that neoliberalism is all good, but we want to show to the Japanese people that there are also many problems with it. There are now quite a few alternative media in Japan, such as JanJan (Japan Alternative News for Justices and New Cultures).

What do you think of the appearance of many small NGOs established by young Japanese that explore alternative work styles?

Yes, in recent years there are a few indeed, such as Body and Soul and Namake-mono Kurabu (the Sloth Club). They are interesting, but there is little horizontal connection between them, which makes it difficult for them to make any visible impact. They tend to be short-lived as well.

Related Web Sites

Anti-Restructuring Sankei Union: http://www006.upp.so-net.ne.jp/fujisankei

Asia Pacific Workers Solidarity Links Japan Committee: http://www.jca.apc.org/
    apwsljp

Bilaterals.org on bilateral trade and investment agreements: http://www.bilaterals
    .org/article.php3?id_article=865

General Union, on Japanese labor union structure, see: http://www.generalunion
    .org/affiliation.htm

Human Rights in the Work Place: http://homepage2.nifty.com/jinken

Japan Alternative News for Justices and New Cultures (JanJan): http://www.janjan.jp

Japan Computer Access Network (JCA-NET): http://www.jca.apc.org

Japan Union: http://www.jca.apc.org/j-union

Labor Net: http://www.labornetjp.org

Laborfest (International): http://www.laborfest.net/index.html

National Federation of Trade Unions (Zenrōren): http://www.zenroren.gr.jp/english/
    index.html

National Trade Union Council (Zenrōkyō): http://www.zenrokyo.org

Supporters group for the Philippines Toyota Labor Union: http://www.geocities.jp/
    protest_toyota/index.htm

Related References

Gordon, Andrew. 1998. *The Wages of Affluence: Labor and Management in Postwar Japan*. Cambridge, MA: Harvard University Press.

Kume, Ikuo. 1998. *Disparaged Success: Labor Politics in Postwar Japan*. Ithaca, NY: Cornell University Press.

Onodera, Tadaaki. 2003. *Chiiki union collaboration ron: orugu kara mita chiiki kyoutou to wa* [Theory of community union collaboration: Community joint struggle seen by an organizer]. Tokyo: Impact Shuppan Kai.

Tokyo Kanrishoku Union, ed. 2003. *Tenkanki no Nihon rōdō undō neo kaikyū shakai to kinben kakumei* [Japanese labor movement in the transitional era: Neoclass society and industrious revolution]. Tokyo: Ryokufu Shuppan.

Williamson, Hugh. 1995. *Coping with the Miracle: Japan's Unions Explore New International Relations*. London: Pluto Press.

Yanbe, Yukio. 2001. *Kōzō kaikaku to iu gensō: keizaikiki kara dō dasshutsu suru ka* [Illusion of structural reform: How to escape from economic crisis]. Tokyo: Iwanami Shoten.

12

WATER, GLOBAL COMMONS, AND PEACE

Mizukoshi Takashi

MIZUKOSHI TAKASHI is a central executive committee member of the All-Japan Water Supply Workers' Union (Zensuidō). Born in Yamanashi in 1951, Takashi entered the Waterworks Bureau in Tokyo in 1970 and became involved in the labor movement under the Zensuidō. His responsibilities in the union include water policy and organizing a panel session of the union at the People's World Water Forum held in Kyoto in 2003. He has been engaged in activities that aim at the reduction and dissolution of the public sector, and the creation of water business in which the community has autonomy over the management of water as a public good.

Could you tell me about the history and organization of Zensuidō?

The All-Japan Water Supply Workers' Union, Zensuidō, was created in 1951 by workers of prefectural and municipal utility companies and their affiliates dealing with water supply, drainage, and gas supply. We have a membership of twenty-eight thousand. We are a member of the Japan Trade Union Confederation (RENGO) as well as Public Services International, a trade union federation of more than six hundred public sector unions in more than 140 countries. Our aims are to improve the working conditions of public service employees, promote international solidarity among workers, and contribute to world peace. Currently we have nineteen paid staff members.

What has been the focus of your activities?

We have been pushing for a basic law on water, like the one in the European Union. In Japan we have eleven laws concerning water, ranging from the

Water Quality Preservation Law to the River Law, and water administration is under the jurisdiction of the Ministry of Health, Labor, and Welfare; the Ministry of Environment; the Ministry of Land, Infrastructure, and Transport; the Ministry of Agriculture, Forestry, and Fisheries; and the Ministry of Economy, Trade, and Industry. We believe water is a central part of any sustainable society and so should be a top priority of this administration. In our campaign work for the basic law on water, we want to appeal to the general public about two ideologies—one focused on public provision and the other on privatization—that are competing against each other.

Why, in your opinion, is water privatization problematic in Japan?

First, we have to place it in a larger context. Privatization of public services in Japan, like in the United Kingdom, United States, Germany, and France, has been going on for the past twenty years, beginning with telecommunications in 1985 and then railroad services in 1987. In the water sector, outsourcing has been a continuing trend for the past two decades. It began with the subcontracting of portions of operations, and now even design and management functions are subcontracted. In August 2004, the Council for the Promotion of Regulatory Reform within the Koizumi cabinet released its midterm report, outlining the introduction of market tests—in particular, privatization of public services—in fourteen sectors, including health, welfare, child care, and education. This, we see, is one of the biggest challenges faced by Japanese society today, that is, how to continue to provide public services. Unlike in Europe, where welfare states are well established, public services serve as a safety net in Japan. In addition, we see water as a public good or commons (*kōkyō zaisan*) as well as an environmental issue. We do not believe that water supply should be done on a commercial basis.

I saw your basic water law campaign poster in Cancun (at the World Trade Organization ministerial meeting) in 2003. Could you tell me what you did there?

We began our campaign for the basic water law in Japan in 2001. As you know, water privatization has become a major issue in WTO negotiations, so we are concerned. Of course the water issue in Japan is quite different from in the South where the focus has been on access, cost, and quality. In Japan our concerns are about pollution, privatization, and our working conditions. While most of our work targets the Japanese government, we think it is also important to campaign at the level of the WTO and Asian Development Bank (ADB), where the new president, Kuroda Haruhiko, is an *amakudari* (literally "descent from heaven," referring to the widespread practice of retired civil servants moving into high-profile positions in the private and public sectors from the Japanese Ministry of Finance). ADB, for example, has been pushing for privatization of public services through its conditionality loans to the Thai government. In Cancun we wanted others to know about our campaign for the basic water law in Japan, in which we lay out our basic philosophy on water as a common property of the people and part of the ecosystem.

You mentioned about improving working conditions for members of Zensuidō. Could you tell me more about your work on this?

Do you know that our wages have not increased for the past five years? There are now about four hundred thousand nonregular employees in the public sector, constituting about a third or a fourth of the public sector labor market. The total labor union membership rate in Japan is about 20 percent (10.8 million members over a total of 53.31 million employed workers in 2004). The number of nonregular workers keeps increasing each year. Now one-third of the total workforce in Japan is engaged in nonregular work, including long-term part-time workers, short-term part-timers, and contract employees. The issue of unemployment among young Japanese is also getting very serious. Public sector labor unions and other labor unions are organizing against this trend. Our president, Satō Yukio, is speaking tonight at the Hiseiki Koyō (nonregular employment) Forum's inaugural meeting. Nonregular employment is also one of the main themes in the 2004 International Confederation of Free Trade Unions (ICFTU) Congress, which was held just a few days ago in Miyazaki in Kyūshū.

Some Japanese NGOs think that labor unions in Japan are facing some sort of impasse. Could you comment on that? How do you see the relationship between labor unions and other social movements in Japan?

For sure, labor unions have been experiencing organizational decline and cuts in funding base since the 1960s. But if you look at social movements in Japan today, labor unions still play a very central role. NGOs and various kinds of citizens' movements are small. In the peace parade last night, for example, didn't you see that nearly 90 percent of the participants were from labor unions?

What is your strategy in terms of labor organizing then?

As ICFTU emphasizes, we are building toward the globalization of labor unions. We draw on the Quality Public Services Campaign of Public Services International, for example. In October 2004 we went to attend a big labor union congress in South Korea. Nonregular employment and the privatization of public services are becoming serious issues in South Korea as well. We often talk about international solidarity (*kokusai rentai*). I think we have to do it locally and regionally. For me, the water issue is just an entry point to look at labor, environment, peace, and other social issues. We have to approach it holistically.

Related Web Sites

Blue Planet Project, Council of Canadians: http://www.blueplanetproject.net/english
Center for Public Integrity: http://www.icij.org/water/default.aspx
Japan Center for a Sustainable Environment and Society (JACSES), on water privatization: http://www.jacses.org/en/sdap/water/index.html
People's World Water Forum: http://www.wateryear2003.org/es/ev.php-URL_ID=2510&URL_DO=DO_TOPIC&URL_SECTION=201.html
Public Services International: http://www.world-psi.org
UN Committee on Economic, Social, and Cultural Rights, General Comment 15, The Rights to Water: http://www.unhchr.ch/html/menu2/6/cescr.htm
Zensuidō: http://www.zensuido.net

Related References

Alexander, Nancy, and Kyōko Ishida. 2004. "Driving Forces of Water Privatization: The Multilateral Development Banks (MDBs) / IMF." Tokyo: JACSES. Available at http://www.jacses.org/en/sdap/water/report03.html
Asian Development Bank. 2001. "Water for All: The Water Policy of the Asian Development Bank." Manila, Philippines: ADB. Available at http://www.adb.org/Documents/Policies/Water/water0301.asp?p=policies
Barlow, Maude, and Tony Clarke. 2002. *Blue Gold: The Battle Against Corporate Theft of the World's Water.* Toronto: Stoddart.
Hall, David. 2001. *Water in Public Hands.* London: Public Services International Research Unit.
Holland, Ann-Christian Sjolander. 2005. *The Water Business: Corporations Versus People.* London and New York: Zed Books.
International Consortium of Investigative Journalists. 2003. *The Water Barons: How a Few Powerful Companies Are Privatizing Your Water.* Washington, D.C.: Center for Public Integrity.

Olivera, Oscar, and Tom Lewis. 2004. *Cochabamba: Water War in Bolivia.* Boston: South End Press.

Sakuma, Tomoko. 2004. "The Third World Water Forum: Concerned Citizen's Perspective on Water Privatization." Tokyo: JACSES. Available at http://www.jacses .org/en/sdap/water/report01.html

Shiva, Vandana. 2002. *Water Wars: Privatization, Pollution, and Profit.* Boston: South End Press.

PART III

FOOD SOVEREIGNTY

FIGURE 3. Japanese Farmers' Protest at the Fifth World Trade Organization Ministerial Meeting in Cancun, Mexico, September 2003

INTRODUCTION TO PART III

IF FOOD IS UNIVERSALLY CONSIDERED AN IMPORTANT PART of culture and national identity, this sentiment seems particularly strong in Japan. Public opinion surveys have consistently shown that cost-efficiency is not the only criterion
that concerns Japanese consumers. Postwar agricultural development in Japan
has resembled such progress in other developed countries, in some respects.
Agriculture has been assumed to play a supportive role in the national policy
of rapid economic development. The modernization of agriculture has meant
mechanization, specialization, intensification, and industrialization. Two
historical-political factors, however, have caused the structural vulnerability
of the agricultural sector in Japan: postwar land reform and forced agricultural liberalization under the Allied Occupation Forces. Before World War
II, only 30 percent of all agricultural land was tilled by land-owning farmers.
The land reform imposed by the United States eliminated absentee landlords
and redistributed land to farmers (four hectares per farmer in Hokkaido and
one hectare per farmer elsewhere in the country).[1] The resultant small-scale
farming pattern has often been considered a structural impediment to increasing agricultural productivity in Japan. Further, in 1954 Japan was forced
to import five billion yen worth of wheat from the United States as part of
the Mutual Security Act (MSA). Importing this so-called MSA wheat ushered
Japan into agricultural liberalization and exerted a profound negative impact
on food self-sufficiency. From that year on, for example, bread was introduced
as a staple food in schools under the School Food Law.[2]

Critics of agricultural liberalization within Japan argue that Japanese farmers are particularly vulnerable. The modernization policy espoused in the 1961 Agricultural Basic Law, coupled with land scarcity on the one hand and an aging population on the other, resulted in irreversible trends of declining self-sufficiency and increasing farm closure, health hazards, and environmental destruction.[3] Japan has the lowest calorie-based food self-sufficiency rates in the developed world—40 percent, compared to 50 percent in Korea, 71 percent in the United Kingdom, 97 percent in Germany, and 136 percent in France. Across a wide spectrum of basic foodstuffs, the self-sufficiency rate is alarmingly low: 0 percent in corn, 0.1 percent in canola, 5.2 percent in soybeans, and 36 percent in beef.[4] The amount of agricultural land has decreased from six to about four million hectares since 1961, due mostly to farm abandonment. The age bracket of the majority of Japanese farmers in 2000 was seventy to seventy-four. Under the modernization policy, pesticides and additives have been widely used, putting environmental concerns behind economic growth. The high dependence on food imports has also meant Japanese exposure to diseases such as BSE (bovine spongiform encephalopathy or mad cow disease) and the avian flu.

Agricultural trade liberalization intensified under the Nakasone administration as Japanese manufactured goods took flight in international markets. The yen appreciated by 60 percent between 1985 and 1987, after the Plaza Accord, while food imports from the United States increased by 40 percent between 1985 and 1988. Agricultural trade negotiations began under the Uruguay Round in 1986. By 1994 when the trade round was concluded, Japan had agreed to a "minimum access" of 4 percent for rice imports, 20 percent reduction of domestic support, tariffication of nontariff barriers, and a 36 percent reduction of export subsidies.[5] By 2000, total imports of all agricultural products had risen more than forty times in value since 1970, and the average dependency across the main food categories doubled from 21 percent to 42 percent. Since agricultural trade talks resumed in the Doha Round in 2001, Japan has been under pressure to further reduce tariffication, in particular for rice. Because of high price differentials, the reduction of the current tariff rate of 490 percent on imported rice will de facto mean the complete liberalization of the rice market.[6]

Centered on the Consumers Union of Japan and farmers unions, and supported by a broad spectrum of NGOs in the alternative globalization movement, a coalition called Food Action 21 Japan was formed in 1994. It has used a variety of mechanisms, from domestic legal process to issue reframing through global norms, to resist the neoliberal paradigm of agricultural liberalization. It successfully lobbied for the 1999 passage of Japan's Basic Law on Food, Agriculture, and Rural Areas, which affirms the basic principles of stable food supply, multifunctionality of agriculture, sustainability, and regional development.[7] Food Action 21 Japan participates in regional and international summit meetings, and uses global frames to lobby domestically. For example, at the Regional NGO Consultation for Asia and the Pacific on the World Food Summit in Bangkok in April 1996, Food Action 21 joined members of nearly one hundred NGOs from eighteen countries in Asia to denounce the increasing control of agribusinesses to the detriment of small local farmers and the environment.[8] Instead of the narrow trade focus of agriculture used in the WTO Agreement on Agriculture, they emphasized food sovereignty and the multifunctionality of agriculture that focuses on a variety of social goals such as food security, rural development, rural employment, cultural heritage, environmental protection, and so on.[9]

Besides liberalization, the issue of safety of genetically modified (GM) foods has also galvanized the mobilization of the food movement in Japan, especially after BSE was detected there in 2001. A nationwide No! GMO Campaign was launched as soon as GM soybeans, corn, and canola imported to Japan were approved for human consumption in 1996. Its goals are threefold: food safety, environmental sustainability, and food democracy (against control by agribusinesses).[10] Given the low food self-sufficiency in Japan, Japanese consumers have been automatically exposed to GM foods without their knowing. Take the case of corn, for example. In 2003, 40 percent of all U.S. corn was genetically modified. Given that Japan has zero self-sufficiency in corn and that Japan imported 87.6 percent of its corn from the United States in 2001, roughly 35 percent of all corn and corn-related food products consumed by Japanese in 2003 were genetically modified.[11] The immediate action of the No! GMO Campaign was to push for mandatory labeling. It successfully lobbied for the passage of the GM labeling law, the Law Concerning Standardization and Proper Quality Labeling of Agricultural and Forestry Products (under the responsibility of the Ministry of Agriculture, Forestry, and Fisheries), and the amended Food Sanitation Law (under the jurisdiction of the Ministry of Health, Labor, and Welfare) in 2001. Under the new mandatory GM labeling system, any food containing more than the threshold level of 5 percent has to be labeled "genetically modified food." The Food Sanitation Law also makes it illegal to import or sell genetically modified foods, or foods made from such foods, that have not undergone a safety assessment.[12] The third pillar of government regulations, after labeling and food safety, took the form of the Law Concerning the Conservation and Sustainable Use of Biological Diversity Through Regulations on the Use of Living Modified Organisms (Cartagena Law), subsequently passed in 2003.[13]

After the labeling battle was (partially) won, the No! GMO Campaign focused on two issues: preventing GM cultivation in Japan and stopping GM research by public research institutes through a combination of local petitions and international lobbying.[14] In July 2002, the campaign organized the Stop GM Rice National Assembly in Nagoya and handed a petition with 323,097 signatures from throughout Japan to the Aichi-Ken Agricultural Research Center, which successfully halted the center's development with Monsanto of an herbicide-resistant variety of rice called Matsuribare.[15] The following month, No! GMO Campaign joined more than two hundred NGOs from around the world in Johannesburg at the World Summit on Sustainable Development to issue the Statement of Solidarity with Southern African Nations over GM Food and Crops:

We condemn the United States' use of Food Aid as a tool of propaganda to force acceptance of GM food and crops by Southern nations on the eve of the World Summit on Sustainable Development. Peasant farmers and indigenous peoples in many Southern nations are opposing GM crops and condemning GM contamination of their land whilst the recipients of food aid are protesting the dumping of GM food that have not undergone independent safety testing. We decry the bio-imperialism of dumping food aid in Africa, the endangerment of food sovereignty and security, and the deviation from principles of self-determination.[16]

The resistance movement against GM food in Japan goes beyond national and international protests. It seeks to build a positive alternative to the dominance of agribusinesses through, for example, the nationwide Soybean Field Trust Movement, the goal of which, since 1998, is to increase the self-sufficiency of soybeans through the growth of organic crops in Japan. This food-based movement has also become part of an emergent slow food, slow life movement in Japan (itself part of a larger international movement begun in Italy in 1986). In this movement, food safety and quality become an integral component of an alternative globalization agenda.[17]

The four interviews in this section look at how Japanese consumers organize themselves against the liberalization of the agricultural market and GM foods, and at how domestic food coalitions network with farmers from around the world at international summits to reframe food as a people's sovereignty issue. Several themes emerge from these interviews. NGO mobilization against the corporatization and marketization of agriculture through the WTO and bilateral free trade agreements focuses not only on issues of safety and local farming communities but also on the nontransparent nature of the WTO's decision-making process. Several groups were born as a result of international participation, whether through organizing Asian farmers or attending a GMO symposium in Europe. These groups mobilize around the concepts of multi-functionality of agriculture and food sovereignty to create alternatives based on biodiversity, sustainable development, and community building. Even though many farmer activists see food as an issue of democracy, a stronger connection between their activity and the larger alterglobalization still needs to be made.

Notes

1. Dore 1959.
2. Ibid.
3. Ibid.
4. Food Action 2003.
5. Ohno 2004.
6. Interview with an agricultural journalist and member of the No WTO—Voices from the Grassroots in Japan Campaign, December 6, 2004.
7. Food Action 21 2004. For the entire text see http://www.maff.go.jp/soshiki/kambou/kikaku/NewBLaw/BasicLaw.html
8. These NGOs argue, "Democratic control of the food system is the ultimate test of democracy. Food security cannot be ensured by entrusting agriculture, food production and trade to global markets. Land, water, biodiversity, and traditional/intellectual practices, which are the vital resources that make food security possible, should stay under the democratic control of those who produce the food and local communities themselves, with special emphasis on establishing mechanisms to ensure the participation of women at all levels of the decision-making processes. Therefore, a new social contract needs to be established among Asian farmers, Asian peoples and Asian governments. This social contract must be people derived, people led, and people managed. It must be centred on a vision at the centre of which is the integrity of local farming communities and the food security of the national community. It must be implemented via strategies that promote social equity, ecological sustainability, people's empowerment and gender balance. Finally, this social

contract must include policies aimed at immediately countering the negative impact of forces and institutions that promote food insecurity, like the GATT Agricultural Accord and the policies of international financial institutions." "Report of the Regional NGO Consultation for Asia and the Pacific on the World Food Summit," Bangkok, Thailand, April 29–30, 1996. Accessed March 21, 2005, at http://www.fao.org/wfs/resource/english/APRCNGOE.HTM

9. Consumers Union of Japan 2005.

10. Accessed March 21, 2005, at http://www.no-gmo.org

11. Interview with executive director of No! GMO Campaign, December 8, 2004.

12. Ministry of Health, Labor, and Welfare 2006, accessed March 21, 2005, at http://www.jetro.go.jp/en/market/regulations/pdf/food-e.pdf

13. For more details, see Japan Biosafety Clearing House, accessed March 21, 2005, at http://www.bch.biodic.go.jp/english/law.html

14. The threshold level has been widely considered too high, compared to 1 percent in the European Union. Many Asian countries have since followed the lenient standards of Japan (Consumers Union of Japan 2002).

15. Consumers Union of Japan 2002.

16. Statement of Solidarity with Southern African Nations over GM Food and Crops. Wellington, NZ: Peace Movement Aotearoa. Accessed March 21, 2005, at http://www.converge.org.nz/pma/cra0815.htm

17. Tsuji 2001.

13

AGRICULTURAL LIBERALIZATION, WORLD TRADE ORGANIZATION, AND PEACE

Ohno Kazuoki

OHNO KAZUOKI is an agricultural journalist and board member of No WTO—Voices from the Grassroots in Japan. Born in Ehime in 1940 and graduated from Kenritsu Shimane Nōka University (currently the Department of Agriculture at Shimane University), he became a freelance journalist on issues of agriculture and food. Ohno has published many works on agriculture in Japan and Asia. He has also been involved in civil movements promoting exchange between farmers in Asia and acting against globalization.

How did you become involved in the alternative globalization movement?

As an agricultural journalist, I have visited villages in Japan and other Asian countries and have paid attention to people for about forty years. What I witnessed in those places is small-scale agriculture that supported people's lives collapsing, one after another. I have seen the same situation in Japan, South Korea, Thailand, and the Philippines. In particular, in the 1990s, the destruction of agriculture and farms became serious. When I thought about the causes, I came up against the liberalization of agriculture, that is, globalization. I realized that issues concerning the earth, such as poverty, the destruction of the environment, and the expansion of starvation, in addition to the destruction of agriculture, were rooted in the reality that market competition has been getting serious on a global scale. Therefore, I discussed with my colleagues; formed a network of groups dealing with workers, residents in cities, consumers, the environment, human rights, and migrant workers in addition to farmers; and established an organization called No

WTO—Voices from the Grassroots in Japan. In cooperation with farmers' and citizens' movements in the world, we are promoting a campaign against multilateral negotiations within the WTO and FTAs pushing for globalization. At the same time, I organized a small group named Asian Farmers Exchange Center with other farmers, and I am engaged in a movement aiming to help villages generate an alternative structure that respects lives, unlike the current world, where all the value judgments are given to the market, and to discuss and share experiences with farmers in Asia.

How has the farming structure changed over the past few decades in Japan?

There are some changed and unchanged things. The changes are that the absolute number of farmers and farming land has decreased while farmers are aging, and the amount of abandoned land has increased. In other words, both the quality and quantity of agricultural productivity has been deteriorating. In the 1960s there were six million and fifty thousand farmhouses, but now there are fewer than three million. Speaking of the size of farming land, in the 1960s there were 6,070,000 hectares. Now it is reduced to 4,700,000 hectares. During this time, many young people left farming. Currently, 65 percent of the farmers in Japan are over sixty-five years old. In addition, in the last few years, the area of abandoned land raising no crops is 500,000 hectares, which constitutes 10 percent of all the farming land. What hasn't changed is the Japanese agricultural structure called *small management* (*reisai keiei*), which has mostly remained despite the decrease in the farming population. Prior to the 1960s, when Japan's economy started developing rapidly, the average land size for Japanese farmhouses was one hectare. The government adopted a policy to enlarge the scale of management because it believed that small-scale farming could not be as independent an agricultural operation and could not compete with foreign countries in the market. The expansion of management scale was placed as the most important goal among the government's policies on agriculture, and a large number of grants were given. This expansion produced large-scale managers with ten or twenty hectares. This is still small compared to the United States and Europe, but they were exceptional farms. Now the average scale of operation in Japan is about 1.5 hectares per farmhouse; scale enlargement did not really proceed. Most farmers chose not to increase the scale of operation and become full-time farmers but instead maintained small-scale farming as well as working in other industries. In this way the small structure of Japanese agriculture has been preserved. Since the 1990s, real liberalization of agriculture has begun. Because of small-scale farming and high wage levels, Japanese farm products with high production costs were not competitive, and the Japanese crop market was instantly occupied by cheap imports from foreign countries. Right now, the degree of Japan's self-sufficiency in food is 40 percent in calorie-based calculations. As a result, the standard of crop price declined remarkably, and more people have given up farming and abandoned the land. I think that under globalization, Japanese agriculture overall is in danger of dismantling.

Could you tell me something about rice politics in Japan? Why is it such a touchy issue?

The most important issue in rice politics is a surplus in rice product. Before World War II, Japan actually had to import rice from Korea and Taiwan. Until 1955, Japan did not produce enough rice. Since 1970, we have been having a surplus in rice production. Since the costs are high, we could not export our rice. So the Japanese government has been encouraging rice production reduction and given farmers subsidies to convert from rice to other products, such as corn, soybeans, vegetables, and fruits, as a sort of supplementary income. Until 2004, for example, farmers had been receiving subsidies for the reduction of 30 percent of rice production. This was supposed to be a short-term policy, but it lasted for thirty-five years. There are several reasons why rice production has to be reduced. First, rice consumption has dropped from one hundred kilos per person per year before World War II to sixty kilos per person per year now. It keeps decreasing because of the increasing Japanese consumption of bread and noodles, both of which depend on imports. Over the past few decades, productivity has also increased due to technological improvement.

Until 1994, the Japanese government controlled everything from production to consumption of rice under the Food Management Law (*Shokuryō Kanrihō*), which was established soon after the war to ensure sufficient rice production. In 1994, however, this closed market policy of protection of domestic rice was seen as a violation of the Uruguay Round. Finally, Japan had to agree to a minimum access of 4 percent of rice imports (from California and China, for example) as well as a 20 percent reduction of domestic support and 36 percent reduction of export subsidies. In 1995, a new Food Law and Agricultural Policy was passed to replace the Food Management Law and introduce the market principle (*shijō seisaku*). Many farm support programs have been cut, and farmers have been encouraged to sell or merge their farmland to corporate ownership. Since 1998, the minimum access has increased to 8 percent, which amounts to about seven hundred thousand tons of imported rice that is mostly not sold in the domestic market but sent as aid to North Korea and so on. Since 2000, under the Agreement on Agriculture within the World Trade Organization (WTO), rice has been placed under tariff (490 percent on imported rice). Now the bone of contention at the WTO is the further reduction of tariff, which is considered too high by most countries (the United States, for example, imposes a 150 percent tariff on imported rice). The United States and the European Union both demand a rice tariff ceiling of 150 to 200 percent by Japan.

What would happen if the Japanese government were to comply with this demand?

Let me explain this through some calculations. The consumer price for a ten-kilo rice pack is about 4,000 yen (about $40) and the equivalent of a rice pack from China is only 500 yen. Even if you add 490 percent tariffs, the price becomes about 3,000 yen. If you reduce the tariff to 200 percent, the price will drop to 1,500 yen. While I think that most Japanese prefer Japanese rice, the economy is now bad, so people might prefer to buy cheap imported rice. Cheap imported rice is also likely to drive the overall rice price down. I am afraid that if the price continues to go down, rice farming will disappear in Japan.

What are the key issues that Japanese farmers face today?

I already mentioned aging (difficulty in finding successors) and farmland abandonment. There is also the issue of debt. Because of high machinery costs and decreasing consumer prices over a range of agricultural products, many farmers are indebted. Japan is going toward an open market approach to agriculture in which business federations now take up farming. Today we have 2.3 million farm households, but the Japanese government has said that 400,000 would be sufficient. Recent land reform policy allows companies to own land, leading to the phenomenon of the corporatization of farming. Construction companies and contractors, for example, aim to become farming corporations with one hundred hectares or more per farm, like in the United States. The government sees no future in individual farms. Another big issue is of course free trade agreements (FTAs) that the Japanese government is actively seeking with a number of countries. The current FTA negotiations with the Thai government would mean imports of many cheap Thai agricultural products, including rice, chicken, and various kinds of vegetables, and you can imagine its impact on Japanese agriculture. Because many Japanese firms have moved abroad, farmers who quit their jobs face unemployment risk.

As an activist for farmers' basic rights, how do you respond to the criticism that Japan's closed agricultural market denies access to many developing countries?

First, increased market access to Japan does not necessarily mean increased income for small farmers in Thailand, for example. It is more likely that big export farms would benefit. Second, I am not so sure that the rice export policy of the Thai government serves Thai farmers' best interests, because the price of rice has come down a lot. Third, most farmers who produce crops for export are in big farm corporations. I think the basic principle is self-sufficiency first, and farmers export only if there is a surplus. In that sense, I am against the free trade policy of the WTO.

What is problematic with the WTO?

Whether they like it or not, farmers got into globalization. Basically, I oppose the neoliberal direction of the WTO. I don't think the WTO necessarily has to be dissolved, but we need to do it differently. The WTO is a big, multilateral organization that functions in a top-down fashion. I would like to see more horizontal and equal economic relations. We must pose the question, is economic growth sufficient? What is important is not just getting materially rich; we need to take into consideration nature, for example. In a nutshell, we need to change values.

When did the No WTO—Voices from the Grassroots in Japan campaign begin? What are its main activities?

It was created in April 2003 in the context of the fifth WTO ministerial meeting in Cancun in September 2003, as well as the antiwar global march that same year. Nineteen of us from various NGOs, including ATTAC Japan; Consumers Union of Japan; No! GMO Campaign; Forum of Peace, Human Rights, and Environment (Peace Forum); labor unions, farmers' groups, and so on, decided to launch a campaign network in Japan that focuses on WTO monitoring. We did direct action at the Cancun ministerial. Now we have launched a movement toward the sixth WTO ministerial meeting in December 2005 in Hong Kong. We have also organized some educational campaigns, for example, "For Whom Is the WTO?" in Tokyo in February 2003. We want to join so many others in the world who oppose war, free trade under the WTO, and FTAs. In particular, we give high priority to making a network with Asia social movements against the WTO and FTAs. We declare that "another world is possible."

What is your alternative vision of agriculture in Japan?

I have been part of a social movement in Japan that emphasizes alternative agriculture focusing on safety, biodiversity, and community building. First, we have a strong social movement against genetically modified foods. We successfully lobbied for mandatory labeling. Second, we emphasize the relationship between agriculture and biodiversity. For us, farm work is intimately connected to nature conservation. Japan is a mountainous country; farming plays the role of flood control. Finally, we want to use regional examples of alternative, organic farming to show the importance of self-reliance. Not everything is for sale. We have two options: community-based farming alternatives and the commercialization of farming, like in the United States. For us the choice is clear.

What is your main preoccupation now?

I think that peace is the most important challenge we face as social movement activists. Farmers need to do something together. During World War II there was an emergency law whereby farmers were mobilized to support the war. In the current context of Japanese participation in the war in Iraq through the dispatch of the Self-Defense Forces, and the political movement to change the constitution to give up the use of force, I called on some farmer friends of mine to show them a 2003 farmers' declaration on the refusal to provide food, land, and water for war purposes. I got approval from thousands of farmers all over the country. Some friends sent out the declaration to consumers in their organic food delivery boxes.

Related Web Sites

Confédération Paysanne: http://www.confederationpaysanne.fr/index.php3
Institute for Agriculture and Trade Policy: http://www.iatp.org
Larzac 2003, Gathering on the Larzac Against the WTO:
    http://www.monde-solidaire.org/larzac-2003/uk/index.html

No WTO—Voices of the Grassroots in Japan: http://members.at.infoseek.co.jp/davidyt/grassroot/home.htm

Ohno Kazuoki no Nōson Tsūshin (Rural journal by Ohno Kazuoki): http://rural exblog.jp

Statement from Members of the International Civil Society Opposing a Millennium Round or a New Round of Comprehensive Trade Negotiations (1999): http://www.aidc.org.za/?q=book/view/164

World Trade Organization, Agricultural Negotiations, Backgrounder: http://www.wto.org/english/tratop_e/agric_e/negs_bkgrnd00_contents_e.htm

Related References

Kageyama, Yuri. 2004. "American Rice Growers Court Japanese." AP Online, Mar. 07. Available at http://lists.iatp.org/listarchive/archive.cfm?id=89718and http://www.highbeam.com/doc/1P1-91890799.html

Ohno, Kazuoki. 2004. *Nihon no Nōgyō wo kangaeru* [On Japanese agriculture]. Tokyo: Iwanami Shoten.

Pesticide Action Network Asia Pacific. 2000a. *Empty Promises . . . Empty Stomachs: Impacts of the Agreement on Agriculture (AoA) and Trade Liberalisation on Food Security.* Penang, Malaysia: Pesticide Action Network Asia Pacific.

Pesticide Action Network Asia Pacific. 2000b. *Past Roots, Future of Foods: Ecological Farming Experiences and Innovations in Four Asian Countries.* Penang, Malaysia: Pesticide Action Network Asia Pacific.

Yamashita, Sōichi, and Kazuoki Ohno. 2004. *Hyakushō ga jidai wo tsukuru* [The farmers create another world]. Tokyo: Nanatsumori.

14

MULTIFUNCTIONALITY OF AGRICULTURE OVER FREE TRADE

Yamaura Yasuaki

YAMAURA YASUAKI is vice chairperson of Consumers Union of Japan, lecturer at the School of Law at Meiji University, and a board member of Food Action 21. Born in Tokyo in 1949 and graduated from the Graduate School of Law at Waseda University, he has been involved in addressing issues related to agriculture, food safety, and the World Trade Organization.

Why was Food Action 21 created?

Food Action 21 was created in September 1994 when the 1961 Agricultural Basic Law was amended in response to the World Trade Organization (WTO) Agreement on Agriculture. For us, Food Action 21 is not only about food but also about the connection between food and land. Our goal was to lobby for a basic food law, which we drafted in 1994. The Basic Law on Food, Agriculture, and Rural Areas was finally passed in 1999.

Could you tell me more about the Basic Law?

We think that every country should have a basic food law. In our draft, in Articles 1, 2, and 3, we emphasized the basic right to life and the importance of food self-sufficiency and safety. Subsequent articles focus on food reserve, sustainable agriculture, revision of the Agricultural Basic Law, information disclosure, and consumer participation. Not all of these elements were incorporated into the Basic Law on Food, Agriculture, and Rural Areas, but we are happy to have a law that explicitly deals with food sufficiency, safety, multifunctionality of agriculture (the diverse roles that agriculture performs in addition to providing food), and the role of consumers.

What are the main activities of Food Action 21?

Until the Basic Law on Food, Agriculture, and Rural Areas was passed in 1999 and the corresponding Basic Action Plan on Food, Agriculture, and Rural Areas was established in 2000, we mostly focused on lobbying activities in the Diet. We had an advertising campaign for the Basic Law that cost 10 million yen (about $100,000). We also participate in international solidarity actions. For example, I attended the Regional NGO Consultation for Asia and the Pacific on the World Food Summit, in which NGOs made their position clear that food was an issue of democracy. I also went to the World Food Summit in Rome in 1996, and the NGO summits at WTO ministerial meetings, in Seattle in 1999 and in Cancun in 2003. We think that food is a big problem within globalization.

I saw the handout of Food Action 21 in Cancun. Could you tell me about your position on the WTO?

As we wrote in our position paper, we consumers in Japan favor the term *multi-functionality of agriculture* and an approach to agricultural policy based on self-sufficiency. Because liberalization of food trade has brought profit only to developed exporting countries and multinational agricultural industries, almost all importing countries' agriculture suffers a great loss due to imported foods, and developing exporting countries have not been able to win in export competition. Indeed, consumers in a few developed countries, such as Japan, have benefited from free trade in food by having access to a variety of international foods, but their traditional foods have gone out of use and their health has gotten worse with chemicals and high-calorie foods. Also, their countries' environments have been badly affected by domestic agricultural decline. Similarly, with regard to services, global industries will be able to enter into many countries, so the quality and wage levels of public service will fall down. With regard to nonagriculture market access—current negotiations to eliminate barriers to trade on all products not covered by the WTO Agreement on Agriculture—uniform tariff reduction does not bring about industrial development in developing countries, because an economic gap between developing and developed countries remains. With regard to the Trade-Related Aspects of Intellectual Property Rights, access to HIV medicines in developing countries is not fully guaranteed, in spite of the Doha Declaration in 2001. One of the biggest problems of the WTO is that the negotiations are nontransparent and noninclusive.

How about free trade agreements (FTAs) that Japan is pursuing? What is the position of Food Action 21?

We have had study and information exchange meetings, including with some Diet members, on the issue of FTAs. We are a member of the No WTO— Voices from the Grassroots in Japan campaign that has been monitoring FTA negotiations by the Japanese government. For example, in June 2004, together with some two hundred NGO members from Japan, I attended the East Asia Economic Summit in Seoul. In November 2004, Food Action 21 was part of a coalition of fifty-four Japanese NGOs and unions, together with fifty-two Korean counterparts, that protested in front of the Ministry of Foreign Affairs in Tokyo for three days against the Japanese-Korean FTA. In our appeal, we demanded (1) recognition of the basic human rights of Japanese and Korean workers, (2) information disclosure, and (3) the participation of Japanese and Korean civil society, especially in the affected sectors of labor, human rights, environment, and food.

Some proponents of genetically modified foods argue that biotechnology is the future. What do you think of that?

I think biotechnology is harmful to consumers and farmers in the world. Year 2004 is the International Year of Rice. Some proponents advertise genetically modified foods and crops. I oppose the application of biotechnology. I think that biotechnology is not the future.

How has the focus of the activities of Consumers Union of Japan changed over time?

We have traditionally focused on issues of food safety, including pesticides and pollution. More recently we have been emphasizing local production and local consumption (*chisan chishō*). We have actually worked on the issue of organic farming for thirty years. But the organic farming movement in Japan has been slow to spread because it is not really recognized. Also, not all farmers' unions are supportive.

How about public opinion on genetically modified (GM) foods? Are you satisfied with the mandatory labeling system introduced in 2001?

I think Japanese public opinion is against GM food, but the reality is that it is still being imported. The problem of the current mandatory GM labeling system is that the ceiling is a bit high at 5 percent. Under 5 percent, GM foods are not detected. There is also the risk of contamination from GM to non-GM foods. We would like to see the law revised to reduce the rate to 0.9 percent, as in the European Union.

What do you think of the emergent alternative globalization movement in Japan? Is the food movement part of this larger movement?

Despite the fact that many members of big and small Japanese farmer unions (about three hundred) went to Cancun to protest against the WTO, I don't quite see the alterglobalization NGOs as a movement yet in Japan. Certainly farmers in Japan have begun to acknowledge the need to talk to other farmers' movements worldwide, but as part of an alternative globalization movement, I think we still need to make that connection.

Related Web Sites

Basic Law on Food, Agriculture, and Rural Areas: http://www.maff.go.jp/soshiki/ kambou/kikaku/NewBLaw/BasicLaw.html

International Year of Rice 2004: http://www.fao.org/rice2004/index_en.htm

People's food sovereignty: http://www.peoplesfoodsovereignty.org/content/view/32/26/

Pesticide Action Network, Asia and the Pacific, Save Our Rice Campaign: http:// www.panap.net/ricecampaign

Report of the Regional NGO Consultation for Asia and the Pacific on the World Food Summit, April 1996: http://www.fao.org/wfs/resource/english/APRCNGOE .HTM

Related References

Food Action 21. 1995. *Inochi wo tsunagu "Shoku to nō": "Shoku no kihonhō" tōron no tame ni* [Connecting life "food and agriculture": For the discussion of the draft of the basic food law]. Tokyo: Food Action 21.

Food Action 21. 2003. "WTO Should Respect Survival Equivalent: Voice of the Grassroots in Japan." Unpublished statement at the NGO Forum of the World Trade Organization Ministerial Meeting in Cancun, Mexico, September.

Food Action 21. 2004. *Food Action 21 setsuritsu 10 shūnen kinen shūkai* [Tenth anniversary symposium: Food, agriculture, region, and environment: What our movement aims at]. Tokyo: Food Action 21, November 12.

Glipo, Arze, Laura Carlsen, Arza Talat Sayeed, Rita Schwentesius de Rindermann, and Jayson Cainglet. 2003. "Agreement on Agriculture and Food Sovereignty." Unpublished paper presented at the World Trade Organization Conference in Cancun, Mexico, September 10–14.

15

CITIZENS' MOVEMENT AGAINST GENETICALLY MODIFIED FOODS

Amagasa Keisuke

AMAGASA KEISUKE is chairperson of the No! GMO Campaign, which he established in 1996. Born in Tokyo in 1947 and graduated from the Department of Science and Engineering at Waseda University in 1970, Amagasa has written extensively on environmental and medical issues as a freelance journalist. He also started a civil group called the DNA Study Group in 1980.

How did you become involved in the anti–genetically modified organisms (GMO) movement?

I was a science journalist for a magazine back in the 1970s. In 1974, GMOs had just been developed. There was a declaration by some leading scientists arguing for some sort of GMO moratorium. I was interested in introducing the declaration to Japan. During the 1980s, many incidents related to GMOs occurred worldwide. I thought that citizens' movements really had to do something. In 1980 I was part of an association called the DNA Study Group, which opposed GMOs. We looked at issues of bioethics. Then, after 1985, many GMO incidents occurred in Europe. I attended one of the symposia organized by the citizens' movement in Europe and thought I would like to do something in Japan. So, since the early 1990s I have been involved in the anti-GMO movement in Japan.

What is the No! GMO Campaign?

In 1996, the Japanese government approved the import of GM soybeans and corn and so on. When we knew about it, members of the Consumers Union of Japan and I went throughout Japan and started the No! GMO Campaign. Our three core issues are food safety, environmental impact, and control by multinational corporations. At the beginning, the Consumers Union of Japan became the center of the campaign to demand mandatory labeling.

How significant are GM food imports to Japan?

Japan probably has the highest percentage of imported GM foods among developed countries. Given the low food self-sufficiency in Japan, Japanese consumers have been automatically exposed to GM foods without their knowing. Take the case of corn, for example. In 2003, 40 percent of all U.S. corn was genetically modified. Given that Japan has zero self-sufficiency of corn and that Japan imported 87.6 percent of its corn from the United States in 2001, roughly 35 percent of all corn and corn-related food products consumed by the Japanese in 2003 was genetically modified.

How successful has your campaign been thus far?

We did some successful lobbying first at the level of local councils. We managed to get a thousand local council resolutions demanding GM labeling. Finally, in 2001, the Ministry of Agriculture, Forestry, and Fisheries approved the mandatory labeling system. There are actually two laws that concern GM labeling in Japan: the Standardization and Proper Quality Labeling of Agricultural and Forestry Products (under the Ministry of Agriculture, Forestry, and Fisheries) and the amended Food Sanitation Law (under the Ministry of Health, Labor, and Welfare), which makes it illegal to import or sell genetically modified foods, or foods made from such foods, that have not undergone a safety assessment. A second concrete result we obtained is no GM planting in our farms. In addition, we managed to stop GM research by private Japanese corporations. What is left is GM research by national research institutes and multinational corporations, which we have been trying to stop.

Are you connected to NGOs outside of Japan that work on similar issues?

We exchange information with environmental groups. We invited the Canadian farmer Percy Schmeiser (who was sued by Monsanto for Canola seed pirating) to Japan in 2003. As a result of that, we became connected to the Council of Canadians and we wanted to do something to oppose the approval of GM wheat in the United States and Canada. Japan is the number one importer of Canadian wheat and an important importer of U.S. wheat. In 2003 we launched the campaign against GM wheat in Japan. We submitted a formal letter to Monsanto Japan, stating that 59.5 percent of Japanese consumers thought GM food was bad, only 2.9 percent thought it was good. The campaign demanded Monsanto's withdrawal of approval for its GM wheat in the United States and Canada, two major wheat exporters to Japan. At the same time, the No! GMO Campaign managed to get a consensus from the Japanese Flour Millers Association that it would not handle GM wheat. In March 2004, a delegation of Japanese consumer representatives carried a petition signed by 414 organizations in Japan representing 1.2 million Japanese people to the Canadian federal government in Ottawa and the state government of North Dakota. Two months later Monsanto announced the suspension of all development of GM wheat.

With these successes, what is the focus of the No! GMO Campaign now?

While we continue to work on the labeling issue (for example, bringing down the high threshold level of 5 percent), our ultimate goal is to increase food self-sufficiency and eliminate GM food in Japan. Since 1998, we have begun the nationwide Soybean Field Trust Movement, the goal of which is to increase the self-sufficiency of soybeans through the growth of organic crops in Japan. We have thirty-nine local production areas and five thousand consumer participants. Another movement concerns the spread of local ordinances prohibiting GM planting. The first one is likely to be in Hokkaido by the end of 2005. We hope to spread this nationwide.

It is often said that Japanese NGOs are small and have limited impact on policy change. Why do you think the No! GMO Campaign has been relatively successful?

Yes, we are not that big at all. We have two hundred individual members, two hundred organizational members, and merely six staff members. The immediate reason that contrasts with other NGOs or movements is that it is always easy to appeal to the general public about food. In Japan, the cooperative organization is very well established and strong, so we can draw on its power. Even though the Consumers Union of Japan has been the center of the campaign, we get a lot of support from other overlapping NGO members in various movements. Unlike other issues, food is also covered by the Japanese media.

What do you think of the World Trade Organization (WTO)?

I think the WTO is dominated by the United States as well as by multinational corporations such as Monsanto, which is why I oppose the WTO. I think consumers and farmers have to form grassroots movements to monitor it.

Related Web Sites

Food Sanitation Law, 2001: http://www.jetro.go.jp/en/market/regulations/pdf/
food-e.pdf
GMR (GM Rice) Watch Center Japan: http://teikeimai.net/gmr-watch
Japan Biosafety Clearing House: http://www.bch.biodic.go.jp/english/law.html
NGO Johannesburg Declaration on Biopiracy, Biodiversity and Community Rights:
http://www.biowatch.org.za/main.asp?include=docs/announcements/jhbdecl.htm
No! GMO Campaign: http://www.no-gmo.org
Statement of Solidarity with Southern African Nations over GM Food and Crops,
World Summit on Sustainable Development, Johannesburg, 2002: http://www
.converge.org.nz/pma/cra0815.htm

Related References

Amagasa, Keisuke. 2004. *Sekai Shokuryō Sensō* [World food war]. Tokyo: Ryokufu.
Bove, Jose, and Francois Dufour. 2001. *The World Is Not for Sale: Farmers Against Junk Food*. London: Verso.
Consumers Union of Japan, ed. 2005. *Shokuryō Shuken* [Food sovereignty]. Tokyo: Ryokufu.
No! GMO Campaign. 2004. "Canada-U.S. Press Conference Resume." No! GMO Campaign.
Rosset, Peter. 2002. "U.S. Opposes Right to Food at World Summit." Oakland, CA: Food First / Institute for Food and Development Policy. Available at http://www
.foodfirst.org/media/printformat.php?id=162
Shiva, Vandana. 2000. *Stolen Harvest*. Boston: South End Press.

16

SELF-SUFFICIENCY, SAFETY, AND FOOD LIBERALIZATION

Imamura Kazuhiko

IMAMURA KAZUHIKO is a veterinarian in the Research Division of the Graduate School of Medical Sciences at Kumamoto University and founding member of Watch Out for WTO! Japan. Born in Fukuoka in 1958 and graduated from the Graduate School of Nihon University, he has been engaged in the research and practice of community empowerment. Imamura is also involved in health promotion activities in Shanghai, Guilin, and Harbin.

How did you become involved in the alternative globalization movement?

I have been involved in development issues for the past eighteen years, since I was twenty-eight. I was trained as a veterinarian. Now I work on issues of poultry hygiene at a local government office in Fukuoka, and do research on food safety and risk issues from the angles of BSE (bovine spongiform encephalopathy, or mad cow disease) and bird flu.

How did Watch Out for WTO! (WOW) Japan come into being?

The Asian Development Bank (ADB) held its thirtieth annual meeting in my hometown, Fukuoka, in May 1997. I was involved in some of the local advocacy activities in terms of monitoring the lending policies of the ADB, in which the Japanese government plays a key role. I think the citizen mobilization against the WTO in Seattle in 1999 exerted a great impact on many social movements, including those in Japan. WOW Japan was created in 2001 to monitor WTO issues. In November 2002, Jose Bové gave a well-attended talk against genetically modified (GM) foods in Fukuoka. We organized a visit to an organic duck farmer in the region.

Why are GM foods problematic?

There are many risks involved. It can be a biohazard. It poses risks to our health, for example, in causing cancer. Then there is the issue of seed mono-poly. As you might be aware, food self-sufficiency in Japan is very low (in calorie-based calculations, 14 percent for wheat, 10 percent for beef, 9 percent for eggs, 7 percent for chicken, and 5 percent for pork). Foods such as tofu and soy sauce are very sensitive issues for Japanese. One of the main problems is that there really isn't that much public debate about GM foods in Japan.

What does WOW Japan do to stimulate public debate?

We are still a very young group. We try to focus on three areas: farmers' issues, foreign migrant workers, and local economic development in Kyūshū. Since 1999, many family-owned shops along the shopping streets in Fukuoka and other cities in Kyūshū have been closed. Like many other small local NGOs, such as Agri-Project Kyūshū, we do research and educational projects with students. Our objective is to encourage them to make the linkage between what they eat and what goes on at the WTO. We also exchange information and work with other local NGO networks, such as Jubilee Kyūshū, which is part of a larger international coalition on debt relief. One of our key goals is to spread alternative organic farming and consumption. One organic cooperative has four hundred thousand members in Fukuoka alone. I think this is a growing market. Japanese firms, for example, have set up operations in China to export organic foods into Japan. I would like to work on creating conditions so that large cooperatives in Fukuoka and small local farmers in China can have equal exchange relations.

How is the food movement connected to the alternative globalization movement in Japan?

The food movement is closely connected to the environmental movement for obvious reasons, but I don't think it is well connected to the alternative globalization movement.

How about the government? What is the relationship between WOW Japan and the government?

Since we are poor (we have only volunteer staff members), we cannot afford to do advocacy work at the national level. We focus on local party officials and we target especially younger members who might be more receptive to us. Otherwise, we focus more on the bureaucracy than on Diet members.

Related Web Sites

Asian Development Bank, Fukuoka NGO Forum: http://www.geocities.co.jp/
WallStreet/2253/#forum
ODA Reform Network: http://odanet.npgo.jp/archives/cat9/index.html
People's Global Action Against Free Trade and the WTO: http://www.nadir.org/
nadir/initiativ/agp/en/index.html
Trade Observatory of the Institute for Agriculture and Trade Policy: http://www
.tradeobservatory.org
Watch Out for WTO! Japan: http://wowjapan.npgo.jp

Related References

Nishimatsu, Hiroshi. 2004. "Aigamo suitō dōjisaku" [Integrated rice cultivation and
duck farming]. *Kyūshū no mura* [Kyushu Village], *15*.
Watch Out for WTO! Japan. 2001. *Dai 3 kai WTO-NGO senryaku kaigi hōkokusho*
[Report on the third WTO-NGO strategic meeting]. Fukuoka: WOW Japan.
Watkins, Kevin. 1996. *Agricultural Trade and Food Security*. London: Oxfam.

PART IV

PEACE

FIGURE 4. World Peace Now, Peace Parade in Tokyo, December 14, 2004

INTRODUCTION TO PART IV

ALTHOUGH THERE WAS a strong pacifist movement in Japan, notably against the U.S.-Japan Security Alliance, Vietnam War, and nuclear weapons in the 1960s and 1970s, and in a much more localized fashion against U.S. military bases in Okinawa, many activists feel that the peace movement in Japan had largely come to an impasse in the 1980s and 1990s due to violence within the Japanese Left and a lack of appeal to the general public.[1] Many events in the past decade, however, have re-ignited this dormant movement, giving it new forms and political colors: the 1995 rape of a twelve-year-old schoolgirl by two U.S. Marines and a sailor in Okinawa, and military base relocation; September 11, 2001, and the subsequent passage of many security-related bills; war, the dispatch of Japanese Self-Defense Forces (SDF), and hostage-taking in Iraq; political movement to revise Japan's constitution; and a whole range of international developments in which Japanese social movements have been intimately involved, including nuclear disarmament, the establishment of the International Criminal Court, and a worldwide campaign to ban landmines.

There has been a strong peace and antibase movement in postwar Okinawa, even though it has not always garnered media and public attention in mainland Japan. Between March and August 1945, the only ground battle in Japan was fought in Okinawa, causing the death of 240,000, including about 140,000 civilians (about a fourth of the Okinawan population), nearly double the number of Japanese military deaths. The end of World War II was followed by twenty-seven years of direct U.S. military rule. Land was confiscated for military base construction, with only nominal compensation to the landowners.[2] Many Okinawans mobilized for Okinawa's reversion to Japan in 1972, hoping that it would end the presence of U.S. military bases on the islands. Today, nearly forty military bases are spread throughout the Okinawan archipelago. There have been antibase protests against land seizure, impunity of the U.S. military, violence against women, and environmental destruction throughout the postwar period, but the 1995 rape mobilized eighty-five thousand people. The protests spurred the establishment of the Japan-U.S. Special Action Committee on Okinawa (SACO) to look into ways to reduce the burden of bases shouldered by the people of Okinawa. In December 1996, the SACO Final Report outlined twenty-seven recommendations concerning the return of U.S. base properties on the island. But details about the most controversial plan—relocating the major military heliport now at the U.S. Marine Corps Futenma Air Station to a fifteen-hundred-meter sea-based facility off the east coast of the main island of Okinawa, near the village of Henoko—were undecided. In December 1999, Nago City mayor Kishimoto Tateo accepted plans to move the Futenma Air Station to Henoko, thereby clearing the final political obstacle for the relocation. Some Henoko villagers have been sitting in the Henoko harbor since 1996, protesting the proposed move. They have been joined by peace activists throughout Japan since 2004, when drilling tests began off the coast of Henoko.

Military bases in Okinawa might have remained a marginalized issue, but the war in Iraq and the global antiwar movement sparked a new peace movement in Japan. The dispatch of the Japanese SDF to Iraq, albeit for humanitarian purposes, was extremely controversial, due to Japan's pacifist constitution. Peace activists in Japan vehemently opposed the successive passage of many bills—from the Special Measures Against Terrorism in 2001 to the Iraqi Reconstruction Special Measures Law in 2003 and seven war-contingency laws in 2004—strengthening the power of the SDF and allowing its dispatch to Iraq. The climax for mobilization came on April 8, 2004, when three Japanese (an NGO staff member, a freelance journalist, and another freelance writer) were taken hostage in Iraq. The Japanese NGO antiwar coalition, World Peace Now, released an urgent appeal for the release of the hostages, demanding the immediate withdrawal of Japanese troops from Iraq.[3] The hostages were finally released, although Japanese troops remain in Iraq. World Peace Now, together with many other citizens' groups, including the Article 9 Association, are now launching a nationwide mobilization against constitutional revision. In August 2005 the New Constitution Drafting Committee within the dominant Liberal Democratic Party (LDP) issued a draft of the new constitution, adding new phrases such as one about the emperor being the symbol of Japan. The national election on September 11, 2005, with the LDP winning more than two-thirds of the seats in the lower house, made it legally feasible to get a bill on a revised constitution past the lower house, although a two-thirds majority is also required in the upper house, and a majority in a popular referendum (the rules of which are yet to be hammered out).

The eight interviews collected in this section reflect a range of peace issues, from Okinawa to Iraq, from constitutional revision to the amendment of the Fundamental Law on Education, from the question of Japan's accession to the International Criminal Court to Japan's Campaign to Ban Landmines, from nuclear disarmament to the creation of a peoples-based peace movement in Asia. Many activists see distinct differences between the renewed peace movement and its predecessors in the 1960s and 1970s. Older networks tended to focus on single issues. They relied heavily on the support of the labor movement and the opposition political parties. The demise of the Social Democratic Party of Japan and the Japan Communist Party in the 1990s gave rise to opportunities for those who might not identify with the political left to participate in a broad spectrum of peace issues. Organizationally, the newer peace movements not only rely on national coalitions of youth, feminist, and environmental organizations, but also draw on regional and global networks to create a peoples-based peace movement in Asia and the world.[4] Discursively, they draw on global human rights frames. Tactically, they experiment with new ways of participation and self-expression, and expand their protest repertoire beyond peace parades and signature campaigns to include grassroots tribunals and cultural expressions. These activists face several challenges: how to change the antigovernment image of NGOs in the public's mind, funding, effective peace education, and encouraging people to make the linkages between the U.S. military bases in Japan and other peace issues.

Notes

1. Takada 2004.
2. Hein and Selden 2003.
3. http://give-peace-a-chance.jp/wpn-en/appeal_20040409.htm
4. Chan 2006.

17

"WE WANT BLUE SKY IN PEACEFUL OKINAWA"

Hirayama Motoh

HIRAYAMA MOTOH is a board member of the Grassroots Movement to Remove U.S. Bases from Okinawa and the World. Born in 1938, he majored in the history of revolution in China in the Department of Eastern History at Tokyo University and wrote *The Agricultural Theory of Lenin* and *The Ryūkyū Development Finance Corporation Theory* for his master's degree and doctoral degree credits, respectively, in the Graduate School at Tokyo University. After the assault of a girl in Okinawa in 1995, he became head of the Research Center on Okinawan Issues in the Institute of Politics and Economy.

Could you tell me a little about the U.S. military bases in Okinawa?

Year 2005 marked the sixtieth anniversary of the stationing of U.S. military troops in Okinawa and elsewhere in Japan. Between the end of World War II, with the notorious Battle of Okinawa, and Okinawa's reversion to Japan in 1972, Okinawa was under U.S. occupation. Article 3 of the 1951 San Francisco Peace Treaty specified that "the United States will have the right to exercise all and any powers of administration, legislation, and jurisdiction over the territory and inhabitants of these [*Ryūkyū*] islands, including their territorial waters." The U.S. Army forcibly took private land from local residents and farmers for military purposes. Since the reversion in 1972, the Japanese central government has been paying billions of yen per year to lease lands from Okinawan owners and then subleasing the lands to the U.S. military.

What problems do the U.S. military bases in Okinawa cause?

Okinawa represents only 1 percent of the total population (that is, roughly 1.2 million) and 0.6 percent of total land area in Japan, but 75 percent all U.S. military base lands and 40 percent of the total number of military bases in Japan are on Okinawa. U.S. forces (about twenty-eight thousand out of a total of one hundred thousand stationed in the Asia Pacific) occupy about fifty-eight thousand acres on Okinawa. When you look at the tourist map of Okinawa, the bases are not marked. Many Japanese tourists who go to Okinawa for vacation do not even know where the bases are. In addition to the land seizure issue that I just mentioned, there are also problems of crime, rape, pollution, noise, and accidents. Did you see that just three months ago, on August 13, 2004, a U.S. Marine helicopter crashed into the Okinawa International University in Ginowan City while trying to land at the base in Futenma? It was miraculous that no one was hurt. Many NGOs sent a joint statement to the university president that we wanted to keep the accident site for educational purpose. People should see this and they would realize what Okinawans experience in their daily lives. The U.S. military knows the issue of safety better than anybody else. In the report of the Special Action Committee on Okinawa in 2003, U.S. defense officials agreed to move operations from Futenma U.S. Marine Corps Air Station, located in the densely populated city of Ginowan, to a sea-based facility to be built by the Japanese. It was agreed that 21 percent of the land currently used by U.S. forces on Okinawa would be returned to Japan over the next five to seven years.

How have the people in Okinawa protested against the U.S. military bases?

The first wave of mobilization began with the Korean War in 1950, when Okinawa became the main U.S. military staging area. After the reversion in 1972 and throughout the "bubble period" (marked by skyrocketing land and stock prices in the Japanese economy) from 1986 to 1990, U.S. base-related business constituted 70 percent of the Okinawan economy. The Okinawan prefectural government was not vocal about the U.S. military bases. A turning point was the rape incident in 1995. Many new groups were created, and the women's movement came together with the peace movement. There was a prefecture-wide vote on the U.S. bases on September 8, 1996. About 60 percent of eligible voters cast ballots: 482,000 supported base reduction while 46,000 opposed it. Even taking into consideration that 40 percent did not vote, one can say that the majority were in favor of base reduction. Now of course there is a lot of mobilization against the boring tests in Henoko Bay. Have you seen pictures of those Okinawan *obā* (elderly women) demonstrating under water? Unfortunately those pictures were reported only in local Okinawan and not in national newspapers. There is now a campaign to raise one billion yen to buy a boat to continue the protests.

In what ways is the military base issue in Okinawa connected to other peace issues?

Many people in the world live under the influence of U.S. military bases. For example, we are connected to antibase grassroots movements in South Korea. For us, the military base issue in Okinawa is linked to many things. Do you know that Emperor Hirohito gave a message to the General Headquarters of the Allied Occupation in 1947 giving his benediction for the United States to use Okinawa? In that sense, the issue of military bases in Okinawa is connected to the issue of the allegedly apolitical, symbolic status of the emperor. The Okinawa issue is at the heart of debates concerning the revision or abolition of the U.S.-Japan Security Treaty. It is unfortunate that the Kōmeitō Party, which used to oppose U.S. military bases in Japan, is now silent on the issue. We believe that if Japanese citizens want the abolition of the U.S.-Japan Security Treaty, the Japanese government can end it. We have to a build citizens' movement for it. As long as U.S. military bases are present in Japan, it is not possible for Japan to have equal relationships with her Asian neighbors.

What does the Grassroots Movement to Remove U.S. Bases from Okinawa and the World advocate?

We aim at building a broad national and international citizens' movement against U.S. militarism. Concretely speaking, we want the immediate closure of the Futenma base, as well as the reduction and elimination of other military bases in Okinawa. We are also against a new offshore military base in the Henoko Bay in Nago City. We want the reduction and removal of U.S. marines, and the elimination of noise and other pollution as well as crime committed by the U.S. military. We are against the use of U.S. military bases in Okinawa for war purposes, and in particular, we are against the participation of Japanese Self-Defense Forces as part of the U.S.-controlled military operations in Iraq. Instead of the U.S.-Japan Security Treaty, we want to build a nuclear-free and U.S. military base–free Northeast Asia.

Related Web Sites

Grassroots Movement to Remove U.S. Bases from Okinawa and the World: http://
www.kusanone.org

Greenpeace Japan, Henoko Diary from the Dugong Sea: http://www.greenpeace
.or.jp/info/features/okinawa/blog_eng/categorylist_html?cat_id=2

Hitotsubo hansen jinushi kai (Hitotsubo Antiwar Landlords Association): http://
www.jca.apc.org/heiwa-sr/jp/1tubo.html

Okinawa Peace Network: http://okinawaheiwa.net

Okinawa Peace Network of Los Angeles: http://www.uchinanchu.org/uchinanchu
/020605_news_henoko.htm

Related References

Amano, Yasukazu. 2000. *Okinawa keiken: Minshū no anzenhoshō e* [The experience
of Okinawa: Toward people-based security]. Tokyo: Shakai Hyōronsha.

Arasaki, Moriteru. 1996. *Okinawa Hansen jinushi* [Okinawan antiwar landlords].
Tokyo: Kōbunken.

Field, Norma. 1993. *In the Realm of a Dying Emperor: Japan at Century's End*. New
York: Vintage Books.

Fujimoto, Yukihisa. 2005. *Marines Go Home: Henoko, Mehyang, Yausubetsu*. Video.
Mori no Eigasha. Available at http://www.ourplanet-tv.org/main/contents/
review.html

Hahei Chekku Henshūiinkai, ed. 1996. *Nichibei Ampo "saiteigi" wo yomu* [Read-
ing the "redefinition" of the U.S.-Japan security alliance]. Tokyo: Hahei Chekku
Henshūiinkai.

Hein, Laura, and Mark Selden, eds. 2003. *Islands of Discontent: Okinawan Responses
to Japanese and American Power* (Asian Voices). New York: Rowman & Littlefield.

Iha, Yōichi, and Nagai Hiroshi. 2005. *Okinawa kichi to Iraku sensō: beigun heli
tsuiraku jiko no shinso* [Military bases in Okinawa and the Iraq war: Deep inside
the U.S. military helicopter crash accident]. Tokyo: Iwanami Shoten.

Johnson, Chalmers, ed. 1999. *Okinawa: Cold War Island*. Tokyo: Japan Policy
Research Institute.

Kerr, George. 2000. *Okinawa: The History of an Island People*. Boston: Tuttle.

Kumamoto, Hiroyuki. 2005. "'Henoko' kara Henoko e" [From 'Henoko' to Heno-
ko]. In *Gunshuku Chikyūshimin* [Global citizens for disarmament], Special Issue:
"Okinawa kara / Okinawa e" [From Okinawa / to Okinawa], *2*, 65–71.

Makishi, Yoshikazu. 2000. *Okinawa wa mō damasarenai: Kichi shinsetsu-SACO gōi
no karakuri wo utsu* [Okinawa won't be cheated anymore: Taking a shot at the
SACO Agreement]. Tokyo: Kobunken.

Medoruma, Syun. 2005. *Okinawa "sengo" zero nen* [Okinawa "postwar" year zero]. Tokyo: NHK Shuppan.

Nomura, Kōya. 2005. *Muishiki no shokuminchi: Nihonjin no beigun kichi to Okinawa-jin* [Unconscious colonialism: Japanese U.S. military bases and the Okinawans]. Tokyo: Ochanomizu Shobo.

Ota, Masahide. 1996. *Kyozetsu suru Okinawa: Nihon hukki to Okinawa no kokoro* [Resisting Okinawa: Return to Japan and Okinawan heart]. Tokyo: Kindaibun-geisha.

Ota, Masahide. 2000a. *Minikui nihonjin: Nihon no Okinawa ishiki* [Ugly Japanese: Japan's awareness of Okinawa]. Tokyo: Iwanami Shoten.

Ota, Masahide. 2000b. *Okinawa, kichi naki shima eno dōhyō* [Okinawa, a guidepost toward the islands without military bases]. Tokyo: Shueisha.

Ota, Masahide. 2000c. *Okinawa no ketsudan* [Okinawa's decision]. Tokyo: Asahi Shimbun Sha.

Teruya, Kantoku. 2002. *Okinawa kara yūjihō–sensōhō wo kangaeru* [Thinking about the emergency law–war law from Okinawa]. Uruma, Japan: Yui Shuppan.

Yui, Akiko. 2005. "The Okinawan Anti-Base Movement Regains Momentum: New U.S. Base Project Off Henoko Beach Met with Effective Non-Violent Resistance on the Sea." Available at http://www.europe-solidaire.org/spip.php?article5147

18

WORLD PEACE NOW

Hanawa Machiko, Tsukushi Takehiko, and Cazman

HANAWA MACHIKO is an organizing member of World Peace Now (WPN). Born in Tokyo in 1977, she started working at a company in Tokyo after college graduation. When WPN was established, she appealed, along with others, to NGOs working on the environment, emergency aid, peace, and human rights to join the activity of WPN. She has been engaged in creating a new, broad-based coalition.

TSUKUSHI TAKEHIKO is a member of World Peace Now and the secretary-general of the Foundation for Human Rights in Asia. Born in Fukuoka in 1943, Tsukushi was involved in movements such as the anti–Vietnam War movement as the chairperson of a student union at Kyūshū University. After graduation, he became a secretariat member of the Workers Union and secretary-general of the Kitakyūshū Anti-War Youth Committee. He also worked as an editor of *Civil Movement* magazine in Tokyo and as a policy secretary for a member of the House of Councilors. Currently he is involved in the activities of the Association for the Best Use of Japan's Constitution, WPN, and the World Conference on Article 9.

CAZMAN is an innovator using visual communication as a medium. Living in Tokyo, he has been involved in activities promoting the participation of diverse peoples and equal relationships, including organizing for World Peace Now (WPN), Earth Day Tokyo 2004, and the NGO Village at the Fuji Rock Festival. He has also been involved in designing the logo of WPN and the Web site of Don't Let It Be: World Poverty.

How did you become a peace activist?

HANAWA: I was very shocked by the incident on September 11, but I think there was a big problem in the response of George W. Bush, that is, the war on terrorism, both in terms of its violence and in the suppression of individual freedoms. Therefore, I wanted to do something to actualize peace in the nonviolent way. Since September 23, 2001, I have participated in weekly peace demonstrations. In October 2001, the attack on Afghanistan began, and then the attack on Iraq was approaching. In Japan at the time, the movement against the war was still small. Practically, in demonstrations that we members of CHANCE! pono2 held, there were only about fifty participants. Accordingly, we thought that it would be necessary to join hands widely with civic groups in each field as well as with individuals seeking peace. That led to the formation of World Peace Now (WPN) in Tokyo.

How did WPN come into being?

HANAWA: WPN came into being as an amorphous network when youth-centered groups centered around CHANCE! pono2 and many civic groups (dominated by relatively older people) taking action against the attack on Iraq got together and organized the first demonstration on October 26, 2002. In this first attempt, eight hundred people joined. WPN started as a broad coalition of individuals in citizens' groups, religious groups, and international NGOs who have agreed on four principles: no more war, opposition to the attack on Iraq, opposition to the Japanese government's support and cooperation for the attack on Iraq, and nonviolent action. There were some thirty organizations at the beginning, but currently the number has increased to fifty. Until this kind of coalition came into being, many NGOs in Japan focused on a single theme and acted separately. In order to overcome this, we requested the participation and self-expression of NGOs in different fields, including Peace Boat and Green Peace Japan. In this way, on January 18, 2003, before the start of the attack on Iraq, seven thousand people participated in the demonstration in Tokyo, and fifty thousand people joined on March 21, 2003, right after the attack was started. After December 2003, when the Japanese Self-Defense Forces (SDF) joined the occupation of Iraq, opposition to the occupation of Iraq and immediate withdrawal of SDF became WPN's demands. In March 2004, the first anniversary of the U.S. invasion of Iraq, WPN also joined the international antiwar action again. This time, 130,000 people in 120 places across Japan marched on the streets.

Why is the Japanese government's cooperation with the occupation of Iraq problematic? Could you tell me more of the role of the Japanese SDF in Iraq?

TSUKUSHI: During the Persian Gulf War in 1991, Japan contributed $13 billion to the U.S. military operations but did not send the SDF. It is because Article 9 of the constitution forbids the use of force as the way to solve international disputes and the right to wage war. Therefore, in 1992, the Japanese government overbearingly enacted the so-called Peace Keeping Operations Cooperation Law, approving the SDF to join the UN Peacekeeping Operations and thereby beginning to crack open Article 9 gradually. This attracted big criticism inside Japan, and as a result of an internal discussion, the opposition Social Democratic Party submitted to the Diet a counter bill arguing for international cooperation by civilians without relying on SDF, and took a strong stand against the law. In 1992, when the Peacekeeping Operations (PKOs) Law was passed, SDF were dispatched to Cambodia to engage in road construction in safe areas, while election monitoring, which was dangerous, was done by the Japanese civil police. Since then, whenever SDF are sent to PKOs around the world, armament has been reinforced, and a permissible range of the use of weapons has been legally extended. Upon such a fait accompli, the Japanese government enacted the Anti-Terrorism Special Measures Law in October 2001, right after 9/11, and this made it possible for SDF to support the attack on Afghanistan by the United States. It amended the SDF Law and extended the range of operations of SDF within the country. In addition, the government enacted three wartime emergency laws in the event that Japan becomes the country involved in war situations. Under these laws, when the government declares war, not only the freedoms and rights of all the administrative organs, private enterprises, workers, and residents are restricted, but everyone will have to cooperate with the operations of U.S. troops and SDF. This is equivalent to the revival of the 1938 National Mobilization Act during World War II, and according to a plan that was developed by a secret research group in the SDF in 1963. The Japanese government, which promptly supported the attack on Iraq by the Bush administration, enacted the Law Concerning the Special Measures on Humanitarian and Reconstruction Assistance in Iraq in 2003 and dispatched SDF to the war front for the first time. Since then, about five hundred members of the SDF have been stationed in Iraq. Even though this defense army holds up "humanitarian" purposes, it actually complements the occupation of Iraq by U.S. troops, and it fits the idea of "the right of belligerency" prohibited by the Constitution of Japan (because occupation is part of the right of belligerency).

In addition, the Air SDF dispatched to Kuwait keeps transporting armed U.S. soldiers and military resources to Iraq, and it undertakes a part of the actual use of force (this is also violating Article 9 of the constitution). The government claims that "places to which SDF are sent are not battle areas." But the reality is that more than two thousand American soldiers and several tens of thousands of Iraqi people have lost their lives up to now. Before and after the war began, we have asserted that peace cannot be achieved by military power. We do not want to see Japanese troops in Iraq. In April 2004, when the Japanese hostage crisis happened, WPN protested in front of the prime minister's office day after day, and the release of hostages came true.

Could you tell me a little about the peace movement in Japan? What is new about WPN?

TSUKUSHI: The postwar peace movement in Japan (after World War II) centered on the Social Democratic Party, its supporting labor unions, the Communist Party, religious people with no party affiliation, and civic groups that were loosely connected. Although the movement for the prohibition against atomic and hydrogen bombs spread widely, the confrontation between the Social Democratic Party and the Communist Party left a scar that never quite disappeared. Since the 1960s, independent social movements such as Beheiren (Anti–Vietnam War Alliance) have developed, and "women power" also emerged, but the confrontational structure of left parties was not overcome. Due to violence and murder within movements of extreme left students, student movements broke up and disappeared, and the youth could rarely be seen in social movement scenes. Moreover, at the end of the 1980s, Sōhyō (General Council of Trade Unions of Japan, the largest national center of labor unions), which was linked to the Social Democratic Party, was dissolved, and RENGO (Japan Trade Union Confederation), which emphasizes capital-labor cooperation, was created. In practice, the labor movement no longer represents the key actors of the peace movement. In the past "lost decade" (or two decades), the peace movement in Japan has not recovered. That is why the appearance of WPN, through which many young people and citizens with no party affiliation gather, is a hope to recover from this negative history. At the same time, it shoulders a big challenge: the movement in Japan is not large compared with social movements around the world that stood up against the war in Iraq. WPN refuses to work under any particular political party, and in so doing we want to go beyond the traditional split in the movement due to confrontation among political parties. However, that is not our main purpose. What is important is to develop a peace movement in which many young people and citizens can express their opinions freely. The slogan "No War!" had become popular in Japan until 2003. We work toward cooperation among groups, the respect of autonomous actions, and the creation of new styles of activism. For instance, in WPN's demonstrations, we can see the participation and expression of many cultural groups, including those using Samba dance, South Korean drum, and traditional Okinawan drum and dance (eisā). The group called Momoiro Gerira (Pink Guerrilla), with both women and men activists all dressed in pink, attracted a lot of attention. Some people who were behind the times did not approve of them, but we want to respect diverse and delightful expressions.

Why do you think so many people responded to the call?

CAZMAN: When we started our actions, before the war in Iraq began, many people thought they could stop the war. For many Japanese it was their first demonstration. I think we attracted many people because it was easy for them to join. Many Japanese are hesitant to join protests organized by the labor unions, for example. But in our case, we encourage individuals to express themselves and we respect the diversity of their expressions for peace. Many designed their own antiwar buttons and carried all kinds of banners at the parades. Green Peace Japan published a peace march advertisement in a Japanese daily whereby people could color the ad the way they wanted. Many, young and old, carried their colorful ads on placards to the marches.

How do you raise your activity funds?

CAZMAN: Since the spirit and practice of citizens' donations to social movements and NGOs have not yet developed in Japan, it is hard to raise funds. WPN has covered necessary expenses by donations from many participants in meetings and by selling several tens of thousands of antiwar badges and T-shirts.

Are you connected to other peace issues in Japan?

TSUKUSHI: For example, many of us network with movements on the withdrawal of U.S. military bases from Okinawa and the construction of new bases. In addition, we focus on the recent global reorganization and transformation of the U.S. army and the Japanese SDF becoming a part of it. We also cooperate with social movements against U.S. military bases throughout Japan and South Korea. We emphasize our position against revising the constitution (Article 9 referring to the renunciation of war and demilitarization being the focus) as advocated by the dominant party as well as the biggest opposition party.

What issues do you face in your peace movement?

TSUKUSHI: As the trend of sending SDF overseas and revising the constitution has become serious, there have been frequent serious incidents in which people distributing antiwar leaflets have been arrested and prosecuted. In addition, there is a big problem that the major media in Japan hardly report the issues concerning U.S. military bases in Okinawa, the revision of the constitution, and the peace movements, or report our movement negatively. In terms of the SDF in Iraq, the actual conditions are not reported in detail. In particular, since Prime Minister Koizumi and the Liberal Democratic Party won an overwhelming victory in the general election in September 2005, the shrink in the critical spirit of the press has been striking.

Related Web Sites

Anti-Terrorism Special Measures Law: http://www.kantei.go.jp/foreign/policy/2001/anti-terrorism/1029terohougaiyou_e.html

CHANCE! pono2: http://www.pono2.jp

Don't Let It Be: World Poverty: http://hottokenai.jp/english/index.html

Introduction to Japan Defense Agency and Self-Defense Forces by Globalsecurity.org: http://www.globalsecurity.org/military/world/japan/jda.htm

Momoiro Gerira (Pink Guerrilla): http://www.gameni.org/momoirogerira

World Peace Now: http://www.worldpeacenow.jp

Related References

Goodman, Amy. 2004. "Mass Antiwar Protests in Japan, Fate of Iraq Hostages Remains Unclear," Democracy Now! April 12. Available at http://www.democracynow.org/article.pl?sid=04/04/12/1423256

Lummis, Douglas. 2005. "Why Are the Japanese Self-Defense Forces in Iraq?" Available at http://www.ppjaponesia.org/modules/tinycontent1/index.php?id=8#cont

Mutō, Ichiyō. 2003. *Empire Versus People's Alliance.* Tokyo: Shakai Hyoronsha.

Yamamoto, Mari. 2004a. *Grassroots Pacifism in Post-War Japan: The Rebirth of a Nation.* London and New York: Routledge Curzon.

Yamamoto, Mari. 2004b. "Japan's Grassroots Pacifism." Available at http://japanfocus.org/products/details/2102

19

ARTICLE 9 AND THE PEACE MOVEMENT

Takada Ken

TAKADA KEN is under-secretary-general of No to Constitutional Revision! Citizens' Network, and a secretariat member of the Article 9 Association. Born in Fukushima in 1944, he established and became representative of the Institute of International Economy in 1986. In 1993 he formed the No to Constitutional Revision! Citizens' Network and started the movement against the revision of the Diet Act for the establishment of the Research Commission on the Constitution in 1997. In 2000 he established the Citizens' Surveillance Center of the Research Commission on the Constitution (currently the Constitution Citizens' Forum), and in 2002 he proposed the creation of World Peace Now.

Could you tell me the background to the current debates on constitutional revision in Japan?

In Japan, the political move to revise the constitution has been around since the 1950s. Though the revision movement was defeated by the end of the 1950s due to strong popular opposition, the idea has lingered on in the minds of some politicians within the Liberal Democratic Party. Former Prime Minister Nakasone Yasuhiro (1982–1987) just recently reiterated his ideas on the topic. In his draft, the first article of the amended constitution stipulates that the emperor is to be the "head of state of Japan." He wants to rename the Self-Defense Forces as Defense Forces and wants the forces to be dispatched overseas. The constitutional revision movement is linked to U.S.-led globalization. Article 9 has become the target so that the United States and Japan can develop joint military defense capability on a global scale.

How did the No to Constitutional Revision! Citizens' Network come into being?

There has been a strong citizens' movement against constitutional revision since the 1980s. In 1999, one hundred of these groups came together to form the No to Constitutional Revision! Citizens' Network (Renrakukai in Japanese) to oppose the current political trends to amend the constitution. We have been alarmed by the fact that the Research Commission on the Constitution in the Diet has moved from researching the constitution to revising the constitution. In 2002, the chairman of the Research Commission on the Constitution, Nakayama Tarō, made the remark that by 2005 there should be a standing committee on constitutional revision in the Diet. We oppose the stance of the constitutional revision camp that Japan should become a "normal country" with military power.

Concretely, what do you do to stop the constitutional revision movement?

To change the constitution, you need two-thirds of votes in the Diet and then 50 percent of votes in a popular referendum. It used to be that the opposition parties always constituted more than a third of the votes in the Diet, so it was hard to amend the constitution. But now, since the pro-revision camp controls almost 90 percent of the seats, constitutional revision becomes a possibility. We thought if we could not change the political processes within the Diet, we could at least mobilize public opinion. All we need is more than half of the voters who say no to revision on the referendum. So we have launched a nationwide campaign on Article 9. We organize public talks on the constitution, participate in demonstrations, and hold an annual gathering on Constitution Day (May 3). In particular, we monitor the Research Commission on the Constitution in the Diet very closely. The Renrakukai now has more than two hundred groups and five hundred individual members. We draw on their individual networks to spread our movement.

You are also a Secretariat member of the Article 9 Association. Could you tell me a little about it?

The Article 9 Association (9-jō no kai) was founded in June 2004 when nine Japanese intellectuals decided to come together to support Article 9. These are well-known individuals—Inoue Hisashi (novelist), Katō Shūichi (commentator and doctor), Miki Mutsuko (UN Women's Society), Oda Makoto (writer), Ōe Kenzaburō (novelist and Nobel Laureate), Okudaira Yasuhiro (constitution scholar), Sawachi Hisae (writer), Tsurumi Shunsuke (philosopher), and Ume-hara Takeshi (philosopher). If you look at their political leanings, you have Miki Mutsuko on the Liberal Democratic Party side and Inoue Hisashi on the left side. Of course there are differences between these individuals, but the common base among them is that they want to keep Article 9. This is also the opinion of more than half of the population in polls. This group has been giving talks in nine major cities in Japan, with around thirty thousand participants so far. There are now local 9-jō no kai in eighteen hundred places throughout Japan. We want to spread the movement further, creating an unprecedented citizens' movement.

Are you connected to other peace groups, in Japan or internationally?

I was one of the founding members of World Peace Now in 2002. We are certainly connected to the international peace movement. We participated in the peace march in January 2003 against the impending war in Iraq. I think the goal of 9-jō no kai is to reach out to the average Japanese.

Is your movement supported by the Japanese public?

If you look at recent polls (both by Yomiuri and Asahi Shimbun), more than 50 percent of Japanese are against the revision of Article 9 of the constitution. In that sense, I think there is a gap between the Japanese government and the people. I think our movement will succeed.

Related Web Sites

Article 9 Association: http://www.9-jo.jp/en/index_en.html
Constitution of Japan: http://www.solon.org/Constitutions/Japan/English/english
-Constitution.html
No to Constitutional Revision! Citizens' Network: http://www.annie.ne.jp/kenpou/
index.html
Short speeches by Mr. Nakayama Taro, Chairman, Research Commission on the
Constitution, House of Representatives: http://www.shugiin.go.jp/itdb_english
.nsf/html/kenpou/english/speech.htm

Related References

Beer, Lawrence W., and John M. Maki. 2002. *From Imperial Myth to Democracy: Japan's Two Constitutions, 1889–2002*. Boulder: University Press of Colorado.
Hook, Glenn D., and Gavin McCormack. 2001. *Japan's Contested Constitution: Documents and Analysis*. London and New York: Routledge.

Kato, Yoshiteru. 2000. *Kenpō kaikaku no ronten: 21 seiki no kenpō kōsō* [Points of constitutional revision: A conception of the Constitution in the twenty-first century]. Tokyo: Shinzansha.

Mutō, Ichiyō. 2004b. "Upper House Elections Mark the Beginning of the End of the Koizumi Era: A Major Confrontation Is Impending over the Peace Constitution." Available at http://www.europe-solidaire.org/spip.php?article1853

Samuels, Richard. 2004. "Constitutional Revision in Japan: The Future of Article 9." Roundtable luncheon of the Brookings Institution Center for Northeast Asian Policy Studies, available at http://www.brookings.edu/fp/cnaps/events/20041215 .pdf

Takada, Ken. 2004. *Goken wa kaiken ni katsu* [Constitutional protection will win over constitutional revision]. Tokyo: Gijutsu to ningen.

20

FUNDAMENTAL LAW OF EDUCATION, PEACE, AND THE MARKETIZATION OF EDUCATION

Nishihara Nobuaki

NISHIHARA NOBUAKI has been a teacher at Shin'ei High School in Kanagawa since 1992 and is an executive committee member of the union of high school teachers in Kanagawa. Born in Kanagawa in 1964, he earned a degree in Japanese history from the Department of History at Aoyama Gakuin University in 1989. Since 2002, as under-secretary-general of the Organization Bureau of the Japan Teachers Union (Nikkyōso), he has been in charge of movements on peace, human rights, and the environment. He was also director of the Education and Culture Bureau of the Japan Teachers Union from 2004 to 2006.

Could you give me some background to the current debates on the amendment of Japan's Fundamental Law of Education?

Article 26 of Japan's constitution talks about the right to education and about free compulsory education for both boys and girls. This is the only provision on education within the constitution. The 1947 Fundamental Law of Education lays out the general principles in education. To elaborate on those principles, we have thirty-three laws concerning education in Japan. The movement to amend the Fundamental Law of Education dated back to the early 1950s. From 1947 to 1951, when the San Francisco Peace Treaty was signed, the right-wing current in Japan could not do much because Japan was still under occupation. With the onset of the Korean War in 1951, right-wing groups became active in seeking the amendment of the Fundamental Law of Education, together with the movement to revise the constitution. They never succeeded, but the idea remained. On March 20, 2003, the Central Council of Education submitted a report entitled "The Modality of a New Fundamental Law of Education Befitting to the New Times and a Basic Plan for Education" to the Ministry of Education, Culture, Sports, Science, and Technology (MEXT). Several changes were proposed, including the "restoration of the ability of the home to educate children" and fostering "respect for tradition and culture, and a sense of love and respect of the country and home and internationalism." The report was submitted when the war in Iraq began. In addition, few people knew much about the Fundamental Law of Education, so the report attracted little public attention. Now the ruling party is looking into a bill to revise the Fundamental Law of Education.

Who is pushing for the amendment?

It is mainly pushed by conservative politicians within the ruling Liberal Democratic Party. The opposition Democratic Party is split on the issue. The amendment of the Fundamental Law of Education is not an isolated phenomenon. You have the same right-wing support groups that are also pushing for constitutional revision, the reinstatement of the emperor as the head of state, revisionist history textbooks, backlash against gender-free education, and so on. So this is part of a wider conservative movement in Japan.

What, in your opinion, is problematic about the amendment of the Fundamental Law of Education?

We believe in children-centered education, as advocated by the UN Convention on the Rights of the Child. We don't want to see education controlled by the nation-state. The Fundamental Law of Education concerns one's individual right to education and the freedom of thought and conscience. In our opinion, to legally mandate *aikokushin* (a sense of love and respect for the country) or patriotism as a purpose of education contravenes the freedom of thought and conscience stipulated in the constitution as well as the same principle in modern law. The Fundamental Law of Education is a conceptual document. Article 11 specifically states that, if necessary, appropriate laws shall be enacted to carry the foregoing stipulations into effect. Hence, we should use Article 11 and create appropriate laws to realize specific policies. If we were to amend the Fundamental Law, it would become cumbersome. We do think something within the existing set of education laws needs to be changed, but we think the current conservative political context does not provide the perfect timing for it.

What is the position of Nikkyōso on this issue?

Nikkyōso is clearly against the amendment. But RENGO (the Japan Trade Union Confederation), of which we are a member, is split on the issue. Because RENGO has many member organizations, there are times, depending on the issues, when there is no consensus. The overall stance of RENGO right now is to follow Japanese public opinion. Nikkyōso believes that we need more debates, both within the Diet and among the public. Only then should we decide whether the Fundamental Law should be changed or not.

Could you tell me about the situation concerning the compulsory observance of the Hinomaru and Kimigayo during school ceremonies?

The Hinomaru and Kimigayo were adopted as the national flag and national anthem in 1999. In the Diet, the government maintains that the law does not mandate that people must observe the national flag and the national anthem. However, boards of education have made it compulsory for teachers and students to observe them during school ceremonies. In 2004 there were more than two hundred cases in which teachers who did not sing Kimigayo or stand up while it was being sung were punished by the Board of Education. Nikkyōso's position is that we oppose the compulsory observance of Hinomaru and Kimigayo. The power to organize educational programs resides in schools. We need to clearly protect that. It is similar to the textbook issue. We advocate the reexamination of the screening and authorization (*kentei*) process whereby MEXT approves the textbooks that have to be adopted by school boards. We believe that both primary and middle schools should be able to decide.

You mentioned the current backlash against gender-free education earlier. Could you tell me more about it?

The Japanese government passed the Basic Law on Gender-Equal Society and the Basic Plan for Gender Equality in 1999. Within that framework, there were many initiatives on gender-free education in local areas. But now there is a backlash against the gains we have made since the late 1990s. A particularly sensitive issue is sex education. I am afraid, when compared to the United States and Europe, we are very behind in sex education in Japan. Some people still tend to emphasize *kinyoku kyōiku* (abstinence education) and *yobō kyōiku* (prevention education).

How about futōkō *(school refusal)? It has attracted quite a bit of public and political debate. What is the position of Nikkyōso on this?*

I think, first of all, that there are all kinds of cases and viewpoints and it is really difficult to generalize. Though the debates have often focused on the children themselves, schools can be the source of problems as well, such as bullying and teachers' treatment of students. But basically the phenomenon of *futōkō* reflects the fact that schools are not the only place to learn. There are many different ways of learning, and what is best depends on the individual child. There is an increasing image that schools are not a liberating space for children. As long as we are still a *gakureki shakai* (credentialing society), the pressure is on.

I saw that Nikkyōso is a member of Education International (an international teachers' union association), which has been active in mobilizing against the General Agreement in Trade in Services (GATS) within the World Trade Organization (WTO). What is Nikkyōso's take on GATS?

We think the education sector should be excluded from GATS. Japan has a high percentage of private provision in education (40 percent in high schools and 80 percent in higher education in terms of student enrollment). Since the early 1980s, many private U.S. universities have set up offshore campuses in Japan as *senmon gakkō* (technical-vocational schools). Since Koizumi came into power in 2001, the situation has gotten worse. He has made special exceptions for private corporations to set up schools. In Arakawa district in Tokyo, Benesse Corporation provides part-time English teachers for primary schools. In Ishikawa Prefecture, an Internet company has just set up a school. In Japan, besides schools, we have a lot of private educational institutions, such as *juku* ("cram schools," which are special private schools that conduct lessons after regular school hours and on the weekends). It is a reality that public education and *juku* function like two wheels of a car. There are now cases where cram schools own other schools. Recently, Toyota, Japan Railway Tōkai, and Chūbu Electric set up a school jointly in Aichi Prefecture. Prime Minister Koizumi's motto is "structural reforms without exceptions." Nikkyōso opposes the introduction of a market ideology and competition that destroys public education.

[*Postscript*: The Fundamental Law of Education was revised in November 2006.]

Related Web Sites

Basic Law for a Gender-Equal Society, 1999: http://www.gender.go.jp/english/basic_
law

Central Council for Education, "Amendment of the Fundamental Law of Education,"
2003: http://www.mext.go.jp/english/org/reform/09.htm

Fundamental Law of Education, Japan: http://pegasus.phys.saga-u.ac.jp/Education/
law-of-educationE.html

Japan Teachers Union: http://www.jtu-net.or.jp/nikkyoso/nikkyoso.htm

Related References

Kyōiku kihonhō kaiaku sutoppu! Zenkoku shūkai [National forum to stop the revision of the Fundamental Law of Education]. 2004. *Kyōiku kihonhō kaisei mondai
no ronten* [Debates surrounding the revision of the Fundamental Law of Educa-
tion]. Tokyo: Advantage Server.

Okamura, Tetsuo. 2004. *Kyōiku kihonhō "kaisei" to wa nani ka* [What is the revision
of the Fundamental Law of Education?]. Tokyo: Impact.

Takahashi, Tetsuya. 2004. "'Kokumin' kyōiku to gisei poritikusu" [National education and the politics of sacrifice]. *Gendai Shisō* / Revue de la pensée d'audourd'hui
[Contemporary thought]. Tokushū: Kyōiku no kiki [Special issue: Educational
crisis], *32*(4), 70–75.

Ukai, Satoshi. 2000. "Hata no kanata no kaisō: naze hinomaru wa 'omedetai'" no
ka [Reminiscence across the flag: Why is Hinomaru auspicious?]. *Impaction*,
Tokushū: Hinomaru, Kimigayo no kobami kata [Special issue: Ways to refuse the
Hinomaru and Kimigayo], *118*, 28–38.

21

JAPAN AND INTERNATIONAL WAR CRIMES

Higashizawa Yasushi

HIGASHIZAWA YASUSHI is a lawyer admitted to the bar in Japan and in New York and California. He is also professor in the Graduate Law School at the Meijigakuin University. He attended the Rome Conference for the International Criminal Court in 1998 as one of a few members from Japanese civil society. He is a council member of the Japan Federation of Bar Associations, a member organization of the International Criminal Bar; and director of the Japan Civil Liberties Union.

How did you become involved in the International Criminal Court (ICC) issue?

In 1997, several international NGOs, including Human Rights Watch, sent a letter to the Japan Federation of Bar Associations (Nichibenren) outlining the priority focus of the international human rights society to conclude an agreement on the ICC and urging Nichibenren to take up its role in domestic mobilization on the issue. It was reported that the Japanese government had been reluctant to discuss the treaty, particularly with regard to reparations for war victims. The Japanese government objected to connecting civil litigation to criminal litigation. In order to observe the Japanese government's position, Nichibenren decided to send me as an observer to the Rome Conference in 1998. I have been involved in representing "comfort women" in Japan, as well as participating in the Women's International War Crimes Tribunal on Japan's Military Sexual Slavery in Tokyo in 2000. I believe that criminal justice is necessary to redress the damage done by Japan during World War II.

What happened at the Rome Conference?

Nichibenren did not take any position on the issue. I became involved, however, in the NGO Coalition for the ICC and discussed strategy. I tried to keep myself from getting involved with the Japanese government delegation, and I contributed only to setting up briefings with the Japanese delegation at the request of many Asian NGOs. At the conference, the Japanese government changed their position on reparations and expressed support for the ICC. Ambassador Owada Hisashi played an active role in obtaining a compromise, but Japan did not sign the Rome Statute.

What did you do upon your return to Japan?

I belong to the Committee on International Human Rights within Nichibenren. I set up a working group on international human rights and law and started to discuss the ICC. My first priority upon returning from the conference was to have Nichibenren's support on the issue. A second activity was related to the establishment of the International Criminal Bar (ICB) in 2002, just before the Rome Statute came into effect. The Rome Statute contains provisions for establishing the court and recruiting judges and prosecutors, but little on the legal representation of both sides. Nichibenren along with legal society in the world felt that we should have a voice in the development of this third important pillar. Nichibenren joined the ICB and, with its recommendation, I was elected as an ICB board member. Negotiations on the recognition of the ICB by state parties continue today. Rule 21 of the Rome Statute, on evidence and procedures, focuses on legal conduct, legal assistance, and legal education. The ICB, for example, was working on a draft of the code of conduct for the ICC based on the experiences of the International Criminal Tribunal on Yugoslavia and the International Criminal Tribunal on Rwanda. The ICB has also been providing guidance on issues such as freedom of choice and training of lawyers in the ongoing investigation in the Congo. So this is what Nichibenren has been involved in at the international level.

My third activity was to try to raise awareness of the ICC in Japan, first within legal circles and then in the media, through writing articles. I am also involved in the Japan Network for the ICC, which was set up by the Japan Chapter of the World Federalist Movement. The International Human Rights NGO Network, a homegrown coalition within Japan, also began distributing information on the ICC among network member groups and to the public.

What kinds of issues have you encountered in your outreach work?

There are several problems in educating the legal society. Japanese lawyers tend to be cautious about introducing new criminal laws, especially in accordance with international conventions. The establishment of the ICC in 2002 coincided with discussions on the controversial June 2003 passage of Emergency Measures in Japan, which allowed the Self-Defense Forces (SDF) to be deployed in case of invasion by foreign powers as well as for humanitarian purposes in international conflicts, such as in Iraq. Discussing the Rome Statute and talking about war crimes responsibility became a very sensitive thing to do, because there was a possibility that this might slide into supporting the Emergency Measures and the revision of Article 9 of the constitution. Many legal scholars believe that we should not talk about war crimes or the introduction of humanitarian laws in Japan because we have not been involved in military conflicts since World War II. I have tried to distinguish the Emergency Measures from the ICC statute, but it has become a fine line for us to walk, between our desire to respect international human rights and the risk that our cause will be hijacked by the current conservative government's agenda to expand the powers of the SDF.

What is the Japanese government's position on accession to the Rome Statute?

The main opposition party, the Democratic Party, supports Japan's accession to the Rome Statute. Kōmeitō, part of the leading coalition group, has decided to support it as well. The ruling Liberal Democratic Party has been discussing reforms of the Japanese legal system, including internationalizing it. But most Diet members do not know what the ICC is; this is because they are so busy with other changes surrounding the Emergency Measures that they do not feel that the ICC is necessary. I have been invited to give a lecture to members of the leading party, but more consciousness-raising needs to take place. The Rome Statute itself does not oblige states to introduce domestic legislation, but the Japanese government believes that it needs to introduce comprehensive legislation so as to give maximum protection to Japanese soldiers against prosecution for war crimes in order to accede to the Rome Statute. I advocate for the ICC to connect to the war crimes responsibility of Japan during World War II as well as to focus on the many unpunished atrocities in Africa, Latin America, and Asia. Japan should have a leading role in this.

Related Web Sites

Coalition for the International Criminal Court: http://www.iccnow.org

International Criminal Bar: http://www.bpi-icb.org/en

Rome Statute of the International Criminal Court: http://www.un.org/law/icc

Statement by Ambassador Owada Hisashi at the United Nations Diplomatic Conference of Plenipotentiaries on the Establishment of an International Criminal Court, Rome, June 15, 1998: http://www.un.org/icc/speeches/615jpn.htm

Related References

Amnesty International Japan. 2002b. *Nyūmon Kokusai keiji saibansho* [Introduction to the International Criminal Court]. Tokyo: Gendaijinbunsha.

Broomhall, Bruce. 2004. *International Justice and the International Criminal Court: Between Sovereignty and the Rule of Law.* Oxford, UK: Oxford University Press.

Cassese, Antonio, Paola Gaeta, and John R.W.D. Jones, eds. 2002. *The Rome Statute of the International Criminal Court: A Commentary.* Oxford, UK: Oxford University Press.

Jackson, Judy. 2006. *The Ungrateful Dead: In Search of International Justice.* Video. Saltspring Island, BC: Judy Films.

Sands, Phillipe. 2003. *From Nuremberg to The Hague: The Future of International Criminal Justice.* Cambridge, UK: Cambridge University Press.

Schabas, William. 2001. *An Introduction to the International Criminal Court.* Cambridge, UK: Cambridge University Press.

22

LANDMINE BAN AND PEACE EDUCATION

Kitagawa Yasuhiro

KITAGAWA YASUHIRO is a founding member and coordinator of the Japan Campaign to Ban Landmines (JCBL). Born in Tokyo in 1927 and graduated from Waseda University, he joined Nippon Telegraph and Telephone Public Corporation in 1952. From 1963 to 1965, he worked in the Cambodian Ministry of Post and Telecommunications as a Japanese government technical cooperation expert. He established JCBL in July 1997. In collaboration with the International Campaign to Ban Landmines (which won half of the 1997 Nobel Peace Prize), he has been working energetically with the Japanese government, media, NGOs, and individuals on activities to ban landmines.

How did the Japan Campaign to Ban Landmines come into being?

In 1979, a Japanese NGO called Association for Aid and Relief (AAR) was founded and began offering assistance services to refugees in Indochinese countries. Other NGOs, such as the Japanese International Volunteer Centre (JVC) and the Japan Sōtōshū Relief Committee (now Shanti Volunteer Association) were formed in 1980. In 1989, AAR began distributing wheelchairs to Cambodian mine victims in the refugee camps near the Thai-Cambodia border. Then they opened a vocational training center for Cambodian mine victims in 1992. But AAR's activities were limited in victim assistance. In 1992, the International Campaign to Ban Landmines (ICBL) was started and the mine ban campaign became worldwide. In Japan, in 1995, several Japanese NGOs, including the Japanese Red Cross Society, the JVC, the National Christian Council in Japan, the Tokyo YMCA, and the People's Forum on

Cambodia, Japan (PEFOC, J), organized independent publicity campaigns about mine issues. The campaign activities included a landmine symposium and a photo exhibition of mine victims. I created Phnom-Penh-no-Kai (PPNK, or Association of Phnom Penh) in 1992 and began to dispatch orthoprosthetists to the Limb Center of a U.K.-based NGO, the Cambodia Trust, in Phnom Penh. In the course of my activity I learned a lot about landmine issues, and participated in the Landmine Working Group of the PEFOC, J. At that time AAR had not yet begun the mine-ban campaign. It was in 1996 that AAR changed its policy. In January 1996, AAR organized the first landmine NGO international conference in Japan. AAR published a children's book, *Not Landmines, but Flowers*, which sold more than four hundred thousand copies in the first year. From Cambodia I learned about the ICBL activities and that the Cambodia Campaign to Ban Landmines had already been created in Cambodia. I thought someone should create the same campaign NGO in Japan. I consulted with JVC, the Tokyo YMCA, and AAR, and created the JCBL in July 1997. Forty NGOs, except AAR, and about three hundred individuals joined us. In August, the JCBL submitted a letter to then Prime Minister Hashimoto Ryūtarō to request that Japan join the Oslo Conference to prepare the final draft of the Mine Ban Treaty with no exceptions, reservations, and loophole conditions. In November, JCBL submitted another petition with thirty-five thousand signatures requesting Japan to join the treaty to then Foreign Minister Obuchi Keizō. AAR joined the JCBL later, in 1998.

What was the Japanese government's position on the landmine ban?

When JCBL started in July 1997, the Japanese government had not yet decided to sign the treaty. At the treaty draft meeting in Oslo in September, the Japanese government supported the U.S. position of *exceptionalism*; that is, the United States wanted to use landmines, for example, in South Korea. On September 11, Obuchi Keizō was appointed as the new foreign minister. Obuchi had been sympathetic to the landmine issue. At a press conference on September 17, Foreign Minister Obuchi Keizō made an unexpected remark that it would not make sense for Japan to oppose the treaty while cooperating in demining activities in Cambodia. Indeed, between 1993 and 1997 the Japanese government had spent $300 thousand in demining activities in mine-affected countries. The biggest opposition to the treaty came from the Japan Defense Agency (JDA), whose position was that landmines were important for the defense of the shores of the Japanese islands. Obuchi did his best to persuade the government and the Diet; he seemed to have convinced the secretary of defense, who came from the same faction of the Liberal Democratic Party as Obuchi. By the end of November 1997, the Japanese government decided to participate in the Ottawa Process, and on December 3, 1997, in Ottawa, Obuchi himself signed the Convention on the Prohibition of the Use, Stockpiling, Production and Transfer of Anti-Personnel Mines and on Their Destruction, or in short, the Mine Ban Treaty.

What was the role of JCBL in the process? What are the activities of JCBL?

Until Japan signed the treaty, JCBL collected about thirty-five thousand signatures and submitted them to Foreign Minister Obuchi. Citizens' power encouraged Obuchi's resolution to persuade the opposition members in the government and the Diet. JDA finally agreed to sign the treaty. The following year, in 1998, it had become clear that the government was still reluctant to ratify the treaty. So JCBL collected another two hundred thousand signatures to urge Japan, as one of the first forty members, to ratify the treaty so that it could enter into force, which Japan did on September 30, 1998, becoming the forty-third member state to do so. At the same time, the Law Concerning the Prohibition of the Production of Antipersonnel Landmines was passed in the Diet. I think one Asahi journalist, Momose Kazumoto, played an important role in drawing public attention to the landmine issue. He was a journalist posted to Iran during the early 1980s and was himself a mine victim. He has been writing articles on landmine issues since 1992. Since Japan ratified the treaty, our activities have focused on public education, treaty monitoring, and newsletter publication. For example, Japan had about one million landmines in 1999. The treaty required member states to get rid of their stock, except for a small provision for training and research purposes. So we monitored that the stock in Japan was reduced by about 250,000 per year. As of December 2003 there were 8,359 left for training and research. The bigger issue, however, is the removal of existing landmines that are in the ground of mine-affected countries worldwide. At the current rate of two to three hundred thousand removals per year, the current stock of sixty to seventy million landmines will take a few hundred years to remove. There are 250,000 mine amputees today worldwide, with 22,000 new victims each year, which is why public education by our campaign successors is so crucial. Every year we organize lectures and symposia, including at high schools and colleges.

We have been training speakers and landmine educators as well. In March of this year (2004) we organized the Second Tokyo Seminar on Landmines, called Storytellers Bring up a Course.

What are some of the issues that ICBL and JCBL face now that the treaty is in force?

The Nairobi Summit on a Mine-Free World, the first review conference on the treaty, was just held in December 2004. Many issues were raised there. The most controversial concerned the interpretation of Articles 1, 2, and 3 of the treaty, about obligations, definitions, and exceptions. Questions like whether antivehicle mines with sensitive fuses should be under treaty coverage, and how many mines could a member state keep for training purposes, and so on, were debated. The overall atmosphere was one in which most member states were unwilling to reopen the package or add new things. For ICBL, one of the questions was to rethink its relationship with governments. ICBL, for example, receives money from the Canadian and Swedish governments. Since 1997, Canada has disbursed $150 million through the Canadian Landmine Fund. For JCBL, we also ask ourselves similar strategic questions. In terms of priority, should we work on Articles 1 to 3, or ask for more money and support to affected countries? The Japanese government has spent $141 million in the past ten years. But the Japanese government has not pledged its funding for the next five years. Also, we think the government should spend more money on victim assistance than on development of demining technology.

How do you see this international movement going in the near future?

The key word of our movement is the *universalization* of the treaty. Since 1997, I think, regional and local initiatives have become the focus of both ICBL and JCBL. ICBL today has fourteen hundred member organizations in ninety countries. It aims at local and sustainable solutions to landmines. The movement as a whole has also been emphasizing mine-risk education. Being an NGO network, the financial capacity of JCBL is very small. Still, we are providing small-scale aid under $5,000 per project to our fellow campaign NGOs in Afghanistan, Bangladesh, South Korea, Nepal, and the Philippines. As I said earlier, educating the next generation of campaigners is an imperative.

Related Web Sites

Association for Aid and Relief, Japan: http://www.aarjapan.gr.jp

Convention on the Prohibition of the Use, Stockpiling, Production and Transfer of Anti-Personnel Mines and on Their Destruction: http://www.icbl.org/treaty/text/english

E-Mine Database of Mine Action Investment: http://www.mineaction.org/overview.asp?o=27

Geneva International Center for Humanitarian Demining: http://www.gichd.ch

International Campaign to Ban Landmines (ICBL): http://www.icbl.org

Japan Campaign to Ban Landmines: http://www.jcbl-ngo.org/

Japan's Action on Anti-Personnel Mines, Zero Victims Initiative: http://www.mofa.go.jp/policy/landmine/pamph0411.pdf

Landmine Action (UK): http://www.landmineaction.org

Landmine Monitor: http://www.icbl.org/lm

Landmine Survivors Network: http://www.landminesurvivors.org

Mine Action Information Center at James Madison University: http://maic.jmu.edu

Mines Action Canada: http://www.minesactioncanada.org

Young Professionals International Mine Action Program: http://www.minesactioncanada.org/home/index.cfm?fuse=Youth.Ypimap

Related References

Adachi, Kenki. 2004. *Otawa purosesu: taijin jirai kinshi rejīmu no keisei* [The Ottawa process: Formation of antipersonnel landmine ban regime]. Tokyo: Yūshindo.

Cameron, Max, Robert Lawson, and Brian Tomlin, eds. 1998. *To Walk Without Fear: The Global Movement to Ban Landmines*. New York: Oxford University Press.

Mekata, Motoko. 2000. "Building Partnerships Toward a Common Goal: Experiences of the International Campaign to Ban Landmines." In *The Third Force: The Rise of Transnational Civil Society*, edited by Ann Florini. Washington, DC: Carnegie Endowment for International Peace.

Mekata, Motoko. 2002. *Jirai naki chikyū e: yume wo genjitsu ni shita hitobito* [Toward an Earth without mines: People who made it a reality]. Tokyo: Iwanami shoten.

23

NUCLEAR DISARMAMENT, ADVOCACY, AND PEACE EDUCATION

Nakamura Keiko

NAKAMURA KEIKO is secretary-general of Peace Depot. Born in Kanagawa in 1972, she completed a degree in gender and development at the Graduate School of the Monterey Institute of International Studies in the United States in 2001. Her research and publications include *Kakuheiki, kakujikken monitā* [Nuclear arms/nuclear tests monitor], a bimonthly information magazine; and *Kakugunshuku, heiwa* [Nuclear disarmament/peace], a yearbook published every summer.

How did you become a peace researcher?

I completed my master's degree at the Monterey Institute of International Studies in August 2001. It was just before the September 11 attacks happened. It was not easy for me to find a job in the United States in the field of nuclear disarmament, so I returned to Japan. I became one of the few paid peace researchers working in NGOs in Japan. It was my first job and I experienced several culture shocks: returning to Japan after having lived in the United States for nine and a half years, entering the field of nuclear disarmament research, and finding myself being half researcher and half activist. I am taking advantage of it though. I enjoy being both a researcher and an activist.

What is the history of Peace Depot?

The founder of Peace Depot, Umebayashi Hiromichi, was a professor in nuclear physics. In 1980 he resigned from teaching to be a full-time peace campaigner and researcher. In Japan, a country with firsthand experience of the atomic bombs, there is a long history of antinuclear movement. When the United States began to send Tomahawk missiles into the Pacific region in 1984, an international antinuclear movement emerged and Japanese nongovernmental groups were part of it. When Greenpeace launched the Nuclear Free Seas Campaign in 1987, its young researchers used the U.S. Freedom of Information Act to research nuclear armament trends. Under this influence, Umebayashi began to think about creating a peace movement in Japan that, first, would be based on systematic research and that, second, would employ a paid professional staff funded by public donations and motivated by the public's desire for peace. In 1995, the international movement against nuclear testing by the French government became a mobilizing opportunity for us in Japan. We then began our fortnightly bulletin, *Nuclear Weapon and Nuclear Test Monitor*. In 1997, Peace Depot was formally established and we obtained nonprofit organization (NPO) status under the Japanese NPO Act in 2000.

What does Peace Depot do?

Peace Depot is a nonprofit, independent peace research, education, and information institution that aims to build a security system that does not rely on military power. We have seven specific goals: (1) being a think tank on peace issues to serve citizens and grassroots organizations and to support peace education; (2) collaborating with NGOs around the world to change the prevailing view that peace is assured by military power; (3) promoting activities consistent with an understanding of the unique part that Japanese people may play in advancing world peace, based on Japan's pacifist constitution, its experience of atomic bombings, and reflection with regret on its aggressive wartime role; (4) emphasizing accurate information based on primary sources and easy-to-understand analysis; (5) public information disclosure; (6) encouraging new cooperative relations between grassroots movements and specialist communities; and (7) increasing the social value of peace NGOs in Japan by fully utilizing the status of Peace Depot as an NPO. In terms of our activities, we focus on four areas: nuclear disarmament; regional security in the Asia Pacific, especially U.S. troops in Japan; training NGO activists and researchers for peace; and finally, emergency projects such as the India-Pakistan Special Update in 1998. We publish two bulletins per month and our annual yearbook. We also participate in Nuclear Non-Proliferation Treaty (NPT) preparatory committees and review conferences. Last year we did workshops during the preparatory committee meeting for the NPT review conference and gave a presentation on our proposal to the Northeast Asia Nuclear Weapon-Free Zone. But in terms of my daily schedule, I spend 80 percent of my time on administration, trying to help run our NPO, because we have only three paid staff members. I even have to sell our yearbook myself. We published thirteen hundred copies of the 2004 yearbook, but even that amount was hard to sell!

What is the Japanese government policy on nuclear disarmament?

Despite the fact that Japan is a country that was affected by atomic bombs, the Japanese government's policy on disarmament is not a peaceful one. Japan relies on the U.S. nuclear umbrella. The current administration is very subservient to the United States, which is now very aggressive in its nuclear policy. Since 2002 we have published an annual Japan's Report Card on Nuclear Disarmament, in which we evaluate the Japanese government's commitment on the issue. You can see, for instance, in the 2004 report that while the Japanese government did make some efforts to encourage countries like China to ratify the Comprehensive Test Ban Treaty through bilateral negotiation, it is far more reluctant to speak up to the United States concerning the moratorium on nuclear weapons testing, for example (the United States introduced a bill calling for a reduction in the test readiness time to resume nuclear tests). Missile defense is another good example. Many Japanese NGOs believe that missile defense is not useful (it is scientifically proven), yet the Japanese government continues to purchase missiles. In 1998 the government said that they just wanted to do research, but now they are saying that they want to develop missiles. Many diplomats think that the Japanese government is keen on disarmament issues, but I think the Japanese government practices double standards, that is, that there is a gap between what Japan portrays internationally and what it actually does.

What is the alternative model advocated by Peace Depot?

The current Japanese government policy is based on military power. For us, we want to build peace through confidence building, dialogue, and mutual trust among countries. We think the situation has changed since the end of the Cold War, but governments' mentality has not changed that much. They still use the word *deterrent* and they don't trust each other. In this region, we have a tragic history of war. We have to stop the predominant way of thinking. One of our concrete proposals is a Northeast Asia nuclear-weapon-free zone (NWFZ). There are already four NWFZs in the world, and the Southern hemisphere is almost nuclear free. The Japanese government may not think it is realistic because of North Korea. We have a model treaty that is based on the Three plus Three Nations Arrangement. This involves the three key non-nuclear states of the region, namely, the Republic of Korea, the Democratic Peoples Republic of Korea (DPRK), and Japan, as the central players, and three neighboring nuclear weapons states, namely the United States, China, and Russia, as supportive players in the arrangement.

What are some of the issues that you face in your research and educational work?

One of the biggest problems is that the Japanese people are not interested. I think about it every day: how to create an opportunity for young people to be interested in this issue. Almost everyone knows about Hiroshima and Nagasaki, but few make the links between them and current nuclear issues. It is an educational issue. I have heard that sometimes parents are reluctant to bring kids to see the peace museums in Hiroshima and Nagasaki because it is too ugly to see. Another problem is the role of the Japanese media. The reports (on DPRK, for example) are often sensationalized. When it comes to important issues of nuclear policy, they are often not reported or are reported without evidence. Another issue is the image of NGOs. I think the antigovernment image of NGOs is still strong. Japanese civil society for a long time was objecting to government policy without being capable of providing an alternative policy. That image has to be changed before dialogue with the government is possible.

What are your strategies, then, in making the work of Peace Depot more effective?

We are connected to and draw upon the resources of many international movements, such as Abolition 2000, a network of more than two thousand organizations in more than ninety countries working for a global treaty to eliminate nuclear weapons; and Mayors for Peace, another international NGO of mayors in 1,002 cities in 110 countries who are working to transcend national borders and work together to press for nuclear abolition. Now we are forging the link between these mayors for peace and NGOs, because with each mayor we hope to get ten thousand citizens to support our movement. We expect more than one hundred mayors and one thousand NGOs, a total of more than one million people, to go to New York Central Park in May 2005 for the

2005 NPT Review Conference. Year 2005 marks the sixtieth anniversary of Hiroshima and Nagasaki; it is an important year for Japan and the world to commit to nonproliferation.

On a more personal note, how has your experience been working as a paid staff member of an NGO in the past three years?

To be honest, I never thought I would be interested in nonproliferation issues, because my major was actually in gender and development. But I wanted to do something where I could put my hands on. I was interested in Japanese NGO activities and I wanted to be a researcher. I never thought I would become an activist. In the United States I saw NGO people wearing different hats. Sometimes they were researchers; at other times, they raised funds. Being an activist in Japan is a very different thing, not only because of the antigovernment image that I mentioned already, but also because very few are actually paid activists. Perhaps the best part of my job is the strong motivation that I have concerning this issue. I see that there is a big problem that is a matter of life and death. Maybe I can change the way the Japanese government works. I began to feel connected in many ways. But there are also many issues involved in working in an NGO. Some of my "real researcher" friends working in bigger research institutes seem to be able to spend more time on research. Working in a small NGO is almost like being self-employed. The pay is not good and I have to do everything. The work is endless. That is the culture. I belong to the first generation of paid NGO professionals, if you will. Some of my friends would remark, "You are such a lucky girl!" I am not sure it is a really fair remark. For my friends who have full-time regular jobs, they do NGO activities as an after-six hobby. I think a lot of people who work in NGOs share this frustration. We are not recognized as professional researchers. The pay is also an important issue. I got married last year. My husband is a regular businessman with a decent enough salary, so I can keep my current job. A friend of mine, for example, quit his job at an NGO two years ago after his child was born. The reality is that an NGO salary cannot support a family! If I were a thirty-year-old or so, thinking of starting a family, I simply could not afford to work at an NGO. The fact is that, overwhelmingly, women in my age bracket, or young men in their twenties, or people over fifty and sixty work as full-time staff members in NGOs. There is a huge gap in the middle. I would like to see, within the next decade, that NGOs, government, and the private sector become equally attractive options for graduates. I would also want to see the professionalization of Japanese NGOs, in terms of organization, funding, management, and so on.

You gave a workshop last Saturday at one of the community centers in Yokohama. Could you tell me more about it?

I bought thirty thousand toy blood capsules, which represent the total number of nuclear warheads on earth today. I asked the thirty-five participants to close their eyes. After I dropped the first one into a bowl, I said, "This is Hiroshima on August 6, 1945." Then I said, "This is Nagasaki on August 9, 1945," after dropping the second one. I dropped all thirty thousand of them one by one. As I was doing that, even I felt the chills down my spine. I was doing the workshop for university students, which was not a natural crowd for nuclear disarmament issues. I had to be very careful about not giving a lecture, to make it as participatory, interactive, and attractive as possible. I have to think constantly about how to reach a wider public.

Related Web Sites

Abolition 2000: http://www.abolition2000.org
Agency for the Prohibition of Nuclear Weapons in Latin America and the Caribbean
    (OPANAL), Nuclear-Weapon-Free Zones Around the World: http://www.opanal
    .org/NWFZ/NWFZ's.htm
Disarmament and Security Centre: http://www.disarmsecure.org
Global Security Institute: http://www.gsinstitute.org/index.html
Japan's Report Card on Nuclear Disarmament, 2005, Peace Depot: http://www
    .peacedepot.org/e-news/nd/toplist.html
Mayors for Peace: http://www.mayorsforpeace.org
Model Treaty on the Northeast Asia Nuclear Weapon–Free Zone, by Peace Depot:
    http://www.peacedepot.org/e-news/workingpaper1.pdf
Parliamentary Network for Nuclear Disarmament: http://www.gsinstitute.org/pnnd
Peace Depot: http://www.peacedepot.org

Related References

Green, Robert. 1999. *Fast Track to Zero Nuclear Weapons: The Middle Powers Initiative*. Christchurch, NZ: Disarmament and Security Center.
Green, Robert. 2000. *The Naked Nuclear Emperor: Debunking Nuclear Deterrence*. Christchurch, NZ: Disarmament and Security Center.
Peace Depot. 2005. *Year Book: Nuclear Disarmament and Nuclear Weapon–Free Local Authorities*. Tokyo: Peace Depot.

24

BUILDING A CITIZENS' PEACE MOVEMENT IN JAPAN AND ASIA

Ōtsuka Teruyo

ŌTSUKA TERUYO is coordinator of the Asia Pacific Peace Forum and secretary in the office of Tsujimoto Kiyomi of the Japan House of Representatives. Born in Tochigi in 1966, she graduated with a bachelor's degree in sociology from Tsuda College in 1989, and completed her master's degree in social policy at the University of Manchester. She worked for ten years at the Pacific Asia Resource Center, one of the Japanese NGOs working on international solidarity.

How did you become a peace activist?

I had worked at the Pacific Asia Resource Center (PARC) for ten years before becoming a parliamentary assistant for Inami Tetsuo, a Lower House Member of Parliament and member of the Democratic Party. I learned a tremendous amount while I was at PARC. The most important thing for me during those years was meeting individuals and building a human network. I had the opportunity to meet with a lot of Asian people and grassroots groups, so working for peace in Asia is a natural idea for me. PARC was involved in the antiwar movements in Japan and in Asia from the beginning. But now, with the issue of funding, it has become very difficult to do antiwar activities. PARC became one of the fifty group members of World Peace Now, which was founded in 2002 as a coalition. So I have been active within World Peace Now and also as a parliamentary assistant within the Diet.

Why was the Asia Pacific Peace Forum (APPF) created?

After September 11 and before the United States attacked Afghanistan, differ-

ent peace groups in Japan saw the need to create a broad-based peace movement within Asia. With veteran and young peace activists, we established a
citizens' coalition to oppose the war in Afghanistan in the winter of 2001.
One of the things we did was invite Congresswoman Barbara Lee (a Democrat
from Oakland, California, the only member of Congress who opposed a resolution authorizing President Bush to use military force after the September 11
terrorist attacks) to come to Japan in August 2002. Then we invited Richard
Becker from International A.N.S.W.E.R. (Act Now to Stop War and End Racism), a U.S.-based nongovernmental coalition formed in response to the rush
to war following the September 11 attacks.

What does the Asia Pacific Peace Forum do?

Our aim is to create a citizens' peace movement in Asia. We work at three
levels: parliamentary, local government, and grassroots. Our four areas of activities are peace NGO networking in Japan, Asia, and internationally; peace
education; research; and information sharing. Right now, concretely, we want
the Japanese Self-Defense Forces (SDF) to come home from Iraq. Because we
cannot do this by ourselves as Japanese, we try to connect internationally in
addition to our national lobbying activities. APPF is still very small. We have
only voluntary, nonpaid staff members and ten active members from various NGOs and labor unions—including the Japan Forum for Peace, Human
Rights, and the Environment; White Ribbon of Peace Campaign Fujisawa;
and the Japan Center for a Sustainable Environment and Society—and another parliamentary assistant like myself. Because we have a limited budget
(we pay for our own activity), currently we mostly work through the coalition
group, World Peace Now.

Since September 11 and especially after the war in Iraq began in 2003,
there have been a lot of antiwar activities in Japan. How do you see this
movement going?

If you look at World Peace Now and APPF, you will see the connections between the various groups and issues represented in both coalitions. But then
the question is about our breadth and depth. We have been working very hard
on bringing together various peace movements in Japan, but if you compare
our movement with other antiwar movements worldwide, we could only mobilize a hundreth or even a thousandth of the numbers elsewhere. The two
to three decades after the end of the Vietnam War saw a decline of citizens'

movements in Japan because of infighting and bad public image. I think the peace movement in Japan right now is still weak, which is why we emphasize the need to connect regionally and internationally.

How about at the level of national politics? Why has mobilization by World Peace Now, APPF, and other groups failed to make a substantial impact on Japanese government policy concerning war and terrorism?

First, the opposition Democratic Party of Japan (DPJ) was in principle against the dispatch of Japanese SDF and their extension in Iraq. But the party spent a lot of time and energy solving its internal frictions on the issue. Some members of DPJ were concerned about being seen as leftist if they opposed the dispatch of SDF. Some other members of DPJ opposed their fellow members who opposed. Although DPJ did try to push for more parliamentary debate, it was not strong enough and it was too late. Another problem reflects a structural issue of power and domination within the Diet. Traditionally, the ruling Liberal Democratic Party has been able to decide policies by themselves. Take the issue of the extension of Japanese SDF in Iraq, for instance. Prime Minister Koizumi basically decided all by himself; there was no parliamentary process involved. Until we change this, we will not be able to exert our influence. If you look at public opinion polls, there are more Japanese who oppose rather than support the dispatch of SDF in Iraq. But there is a gap between this public antiwar sentiment and the actual mobilization by the peace movement. Then there is yet another gap between the social movement and the political process within the Diet. I think we need to level up our movement, that is, create a better connection between Diet members, citizen groups, and international NGOs.

Other than this problem of gap or disconnection (zure), what other issues have you faced in your peace organizing activities in Japan?

In addition to the issue of funding, there is the problem of representation. Because we emphasize international connection, the question of who goes and represents APPF or World Peace Now at these international gatherings has to be addressed. When we commit to an action at an international conference, who is actually responsible for following up or carrying it out once we get back home? Another problem concerns understanding and reflecting on who we are as a peace coalition. We don't know how long we will last. If we want to continue, we have to think strategically about what works and what doesn't.

A last issue is about the peace education of young Japanese people. How do we attract young people? I think coalitions like World Peace Now give many grassroots movements in Japan an opportunity to come together, but we have to work on a lot of these difficult issues.

Related Web Sites

Asia Pacific Peace Forum: http://www.bbnowar.org/newpage1.htm
Asia People and Social Movements' Call to Action (Seoul June 2004): http://www
.europe-solidaire.org/spip.php?article713
International A.N.S.W.E.R.: http://www.internationalanswer.org
World Peace Now: http://www.worldpeacenow.jp

Related References

Asian Regional Exchange for New Alternatives: http://www.arenaonline.org/
details/103816730831637.shtml
Focus on the Global South. 2002. "The Struggle for Peace in Asia." Available at http://
www.focusweb.org/publications/declarations/APA-declaration-2002.html

PART V

HIV / AIDS

FIGURE 5. Information Booth of the Japanese Network of People Living with HIV/AIDS at the Seventh International Congress on AIDS in Asia and the Pacific, Kobe, Japan, July 2005

INTRODUCTION TO PART V

ASIA IS EMERGING as a crucial new battleground in the fight against HIV / AIDS.[1] In 2004, an estimated 8.2 million adults and children in the region were living with HIV / AIDS. Although most attention has been paid to countries with high prevalence rates, including India, China, Cambodia, and Thailand, Japan faces its own set of challenges in terms of confronting HIV / AIDS. In the mind of the average Japanese, AIDS affected hemophiliacs through contaminated blood products in the 1980s. Since the Ministry of Health and Welfare apologized in 1996, most people believe erroneously that there is no AIDS problem in Japan. Despite a small per-capita population of people living with HIV / AIDS—twenty thousand as of 2003—studies show that if measures are not taken, the figure could more than double, increasing to fifty thousand by 2010.[2] Japan is the only developed country in the world that registers increasing rates of HIV infection. The vulnerable populations are men who have sex with men (MSM), migrant workers, sex workers, and drug users. Prevalence among males accounts for 70 percent of HIV-positive cases and 85.9 percent of AIDS cases. In terms of mode of transmission, out of all Japanese males infected with HIV, the largest percentage (53.9 percent) are MSM. Of all new infections among Japanese nationals, the largest share (35 percent) are young people, especially males, in their twenties. Non-Japanese nationals account for 33 percent of HIV cases. Among females with HIV, nonnationals occupy 71.9 percent.[3]

There are many reasons to be concerned about the situation of HIV / AIDS in Japan. There is a striking difference between Japan's financial commitment to global efforts on AIDS and the lack of a coherent national AIDS policy. Under the leadership of former prime minister Mori Yoshirō, Japan pledged $3 billion in aid through the Okinawa Infectious Diseases Initiative (IDI) in 2000 during the G8 Summit in Okinawa, even though the IDI failed to give priority to HIV/AIDS (only 8 percent of total expenditure went to HIV/AIDS-related projects).[4] Japan further pledged $265 billion and, in July 2005, another $500 billion to the Global Fund to Fight AIDS, Tuberculosis, and Malaria at the Seventh International Congress on AIDS in Asia and the Pacific held in Kobe. But HIV/AIDS remains marginalized as a policy issue area in Japan. The semigovernmental Japan Foundation for AIDS Prevention was created in 1987. Then the Law Concerning the Prevention of Infectious Diseases and Patients with Infectious Diseases, and the corresponding National Guidelines for HIV/AIDS Prevention and Care were established in 1999. HIV/AIDS treatment is available at medical centers called AIDS Care Core Hospitals. But migrant workers face many challenges in obtaining access due to language and information barriers, lack of national health care coverage, and lack of a community support system. Often these foreign nationals visit hospitals only after they have reached advanced stages of AIDS, and some die literally on the doorstep.[5]

In the case of sex workers and drug users, issues of illegality can make testing, reporting, and treatment difficult. Both prostitution and drug use are illegal in Japan. Although transmission via drug injection remains at under 1 percent of all seropositive cases reported and thus is not considered a major channel for spreading the epidemic in Japan, there may be a problem of underreporting. MSM, although they have a legal existence in Japan, face stigma and discrimination.[6] Consciousness of AIDS among the general populace is overall very low. The NGO community in Japan—more than one hundred groups—has engaged in various outreach activities.[7] For example, Friends of the Global Fund Japan, a nongovernmental network created under the initiative of the former Prime Minister Mori Yoshirō in March 2004 to promote understanding of the Global Fund within Japan, organized a symposium entitled Promoting Global Cross-Sectoral Partnership for An Effective Response to Major Communicable Diseases: Accomplishments and Challenges of the Global Fund to Fight AIDS, Tuberculosis and Malaria. OCCUR (the Japan Association for the Lesbian and Gay Movement), a pioneer gay rights NGO in Japan, created the Life Guard workshop program in bars and nonbar settings, as well as informational booklets, including "HIV Next Door" for MSM.[8] Sex

Work and Sexual Health, a sex workers' rights group, created Open Space in Shibuya through a grant from the Levi-Strauss Foundation. Some other outreach projects are funded by the Ministry of Health, Labor, and Welfare, but most of these resources go to the bigger NGOs.

The three interviews in this section explore issues confronting the AIDS NGO community in Japan, from sex education to the lack of affordable treatment for undocumented migrant workers. Several themes emerge. The AIDS issue irrupted into the Japanese political scene in 1987 through the blood contamination scandal and largely disappeared from the public radar screen after an apology and settlement in 1996. AIDS activists in Japan point to a curious gap between Japan's leadership in the global fight against HIV / AIDS (through calling for the establishment of the Global Fund and significant financial contribution) and the lack of a coherent domestic policy on HIV / AIDS. International summits such as the International Conference on AIDS in Yokohama in 1994 became a galvanizing opportunity for many local support and advocacy groups to be formed. While some activists approach the access issue from a human rights perspective, especially in the case of undocumented migrant workers, others are conscious of the limits of a rights-based approach. Many NGOs in the field of HIV / AIDS remain small. In the absence of major governmental support and AIDS foundations in Japan, fundraising remains a bottleneck issue for many NGOs. AIDS education remains a difficult challenge. A conservative political current has made sex education and condom distribution in schools a delicate task.

Notes

1. Asia Society 2004.
2. Japan Center for International Exchange 2004.
3. Ibid.
4. Ibid.
5. Sawada Takashi, founder and director of SHARE, "Situation of HIV Positive Migrants in Japan," presentation at the International Symposium on Immigrants and HIV / AIDS in Japan, December 2004.
6. Naito 2005.
7. See Japan Center for International Exchange 2004.
8. Naito 2005.

25

HIV / AIDS FROM A HUMAN RIGHTS PERSPECTIVE

Tarui Masayoshi

TARUI MASAYOSHI is professor of philosophy and ethics at Keio University and vice president of the Japan AIDS and Society Association, an organization dedicated to dispersing information on HIV / AIDS to strengthen prevention and educational efforts among researchers, journalists, the business sector, and the general public. A graduate of Keio University and the University of Muenster in Germany, he has authored numerous publications on the subject of HIV / AIDS and other global issues. He also served on the organizing committee for the Seventh International Congress on AIDS in Asia and the Pacific held in Kobe in July 2005.

How did you become involved in the AIDS issue in Japan?

I teach social philosophy at Keio University and focus on bioethics, which includes human rights issues. When the AIDS scandal broke out in Japan in 1987, I saw it as a human rights concern. Between 1982 and 1985, about fourteen hundred hemophiliac patients were infected with contaminated blood products, and until the mid-1990s they constituted more than half of the Japanese living with HIV / AIDS. Lawsuits against the Ministry of Health and Welfare as well as five pharmaceutical companies began in 1989, but it was not until 1996 that the ministry made a formal apology and accepted responsibility. In 1991 I joined an NGO called the Japan AIDS and Society Association as part of efforts to fight for the rights of the infected population.

How has the AIDS issue evolved in Japan?

One can broadly categorize the development of the HIV / AIDS issue in Japan in five phases. From the identification of the virus in 1982 until 1994, it was understandably dominated by the blood scandal. Little known, however, was that since the first half of the 1980s, AIDS had several faces beyond the hemophiliacs: for example, gay men and migrant female workers, especially from Southeast Asia. The two major issues concerning the migrant workers were the denial of treatment and compulsory testing. Phase two was marked by the World Health Organization-sponsored International Conference on AIDS in Yokohama in 1994. The Japanese Ministry of Health and Welfare had to support it, but domestically the AIDS issue was primarily concerned with the hemophiliacs, and the Japanese government really did not pay attention to the issue internationally. At the conference there was a parallel NGO meeting. The conference became a catalyst for both the Japanese government and NGOs. For example, the Yokohama city government helped organize a civil coalition among the Chamber of Commerce, YMCA, Catholic groups, and a network called AIDS Culture Forum for Citizens; this coalition still meets today at the beginning of every August. Phase three began with most media and public attention focused on the blood scandal after the 1994 conference. In 1996, after the Ministry of Health and Welfare apologized, most Japanese considered the issue closed. The media did not talk about AIDS anymore, with the exception of reporting by Miyata Kazuo of *Sankei Shimbun*. After 2000, in phase four, the AIDS issue picked up again in Japan. At the Okinawa G8 Summit in July 2000, Prime Minister Mori Yoshirō wanted to show leadership and chose infectious diseases as his issue. The Infectious Diseases Initiative (IDI) was proposed and the Ministry of Foreign Affairs organized an international conference on infectious diseases in December 2000. The conference became an important networking opportunity for Japanese NGOs, which had to strategize to give a fifteen-minute presentation at the plenary session. Subsequently, an NGO coalition (of which the Japan AIDS and Society Association is a member) was formed to sit on the Global Issues Initiative–Infectious Disease Initiative Advisory Council. The Japanese government called for the establishment of a global fund, a proposal announced by Kofi Annan at the UN Millennium Summit. After U.S. President George W. Bush agreed to the proposal in 2001, a decision to implement it was made at the G8 Summit in Genoa in 2001 and announced at the UN General Assembly on HIV / AIDS. The fund was established in 2002. Japan is the fourth contributor, after the

United States, United Kingdom, and Italy. The Ministry of Foreign Affairs wanted to contribute more, but it was blocked by the Ministry of Economy, Trade, and Industry.

How about Japanese NGO mobilization on this issue? How has it changed over time?

Domestically, after public interest peaked in 1996, a few NGOs worked independently of one another. By 2000, AIDS had become an international issue for globally oriented Japanese NGOs such as the Africa Japan Forum and Place Tokyo. Since highly active antiretroviral therapy (HAART) was presented at the 1996 International Conference on AIDS, the discrepancy in access to treatment between the North and the South became a central rallying cry for NGOs and developing countries. NGO mobilization at the 2001 Durban conference was very strong. The public health clause in the Trade-Related Aspects of Intellectual Property Rights (TRIPS) Agreement (that it "can and should be interpreted and implemented in a manner supportive of World Trade Organization [WTO] members' right to protect public health, and in particular, to promote access to medicines to all") at the 2001 WTO Doha Round was a hard-won victory for the global AIDS movement. In preparation for the International Conference on AIDS in Durban, the Japanese NGO Coalition on HIV/AIDS was formed, with some seventy to eighty individual members working on an infected population of about ten thousand. The conference became a renewed opportunity to mobilize for awareness within Japan, with the objective of increased networking among the NGOs in Japan and GIPA—Greater Involvement with People Living with HIV/AIDS, a principle that was set forth at the Paris Summit in December 1994. For example, one of the main activities of the Japan Network of People Living with HIV/AIDS is to train speakers to undertake AIDS education and outreach work in schools and communities.

What does the Japan AIDS and Society Association do and what is its relationship with the Japanese government?

We are essentially an advocacy and educational group. Unlike other groups, we do not provide direct support to the HIV/AIDS population. We are not entirely clear in terms of lobbying priorities for policy change, because the Japanese government has no clear policy. MOFA itself has no policy on HIV/AIDS, because no one specializes in it. Before the Infectious Disease Law was passed in 1999, several laws were in place: one related to leprosy, one on infectious disease in general, and one on HIV prevention. The main intention of these laws was social defense (that is, to separate the general public from the affected population), which has been strongly criticized from a human rights perspective. The new Infectious Disease Law remains very abstract. In 1999, the AIDS Prevention Guidelines were issued, but because these are guidelines, they are like announcements; that is, they are very weak.

What do you think are the issues faced by Japanese NGOs working on HIV/AIDS?

Such NGOs are weak, have no money or manpower, and have too many tasks, including supporting HIV-infected populations, and advocacy. Advocacy is not easy on this issue. Despite its financial commitment, the Japanese government's international policy on AIDS is unclear. Internationally speaking, two of the main issues are access to treatment and development of a vaccine. Denial of treatment due to costs constitutes a basic human rights violation. Our task is to reconstruct the structure of social rights, especially in the field of health. The relationship between property rights and the right to health should be reconsidered. As the report "Macroeconomics and Health: Investing in Health for Economic Development," by the Commission on Macroeconomics and Health to the director general of the World Health Organization in 2001, demonstrates, from the point of view of developing countries, investing in health is not charity but both a cost-effective investment and a basic human right. As a philosopher, I know that in the short term such investment is unlikely to gain returns, but in the long term it benefits everybody.

Related Web Sites

AIDS Culture Forum in Yokohama: http://www.yokohamaymca.org/AIDS/index .htm
Campaign for Access to Essential Medicines: http://www.accessmed-msf.org/ campaign/campaign.shtm
Campus AIDS Interface: http://www.cai.presen.to
Japan AIDS and Society Association: http://asajp.at.webry.info
Japan Foundation for AIDS Prevention: http://www.jfap.or.jp/english
Japan HIV Center: http://www.npo-jhc.com
Japanese Network of People Living with HIV/AIDS: http://www.janpplus.jp
Japanese Society for AIDS Research: http://jaids.umin.ac.jp
Seventh International Conference on AIDS in Asia and the Pacific, Kobe, 2005: http://www.icaap7.jp

Related References

Feldman, A. Eric. 1999. "HIV and Blood in Japan: Transforming Private Conflict into Public Scandal." In *Blood Feuds: AIDS, Blood, and the Politics of Medical Disaster*, edited by A. Eric Feldman and Ronald Bayer. New York: Oxford University Press.

Japan AIDS and Society Association. 2001. *Eizu wo siru* [Learning about HIV / AIDS]. Tokyo: Kadokawa Shoten.

Japan Association for the Lesbian and Gay Movement (OCCUR). 1999. *Eizu Yobōshishin: Sono kaisetsu to kadai* [AIDS prevention: Commentary and guidelines]. Tokyo: OCCUR.

Japan Center for International Exchange. 2004. *Japan's Response to the Spread of HIV / AIDS*. Tokyo: JCIE.

Japan Center for International Exchange. 2005. *East Asian Regional Response to HIV / AIDS, Tuberculosis, and Malaria*. Tokyo: JCIE.

World Health Organization. 2001. "Macroeconomics and Health: Investing in Health for Economic Development." Available at http://www.un.org/docs/ecosoc/meetings/hl2002/RT.K.MacroeconomicsHealth.pdf

Yamamoto, Tadashi, and Satoko Itoh, eds. 2006. *Fighting a Rising Tide: The Response to AIDS in East Asia*. Tokyo: Japan Center for International Exchange.

26

HIV / AIDS, GENDER, AND BACKLASH

Hyōdō Chika

HYŌDŌ CHIKA is a researcher at Place Tokyo. She completed the Ph.D. program requirements in the Faculty of Education at Tokyo University and has since been engaged in activities dealing with HIV / AIDS. She also teaches in the Hirayama Ikuo Volunteer Center at Waseda University.

How did you become involved in the HIV / AIDS issue?

When I began my research on sexuality education during graduate school, I was thinking of using a personal approach to look at sexuality. After I went to the International Conference on Population and Development in Cairo in 1994 and then to the Fourth World Conference on Women in Beijing in 1995, I wanted to do lobbying and look at sexuality from a social structural approach. I became involved in networking within Asia and lobbying internationally. In 1994, Japan hosted the Tenth International Conference on AIDS in Yokohama. The director of Place Tokyo served as an NGO member on the Japanese government delegation. The coming together of the concepts of reproductive rights and sexual rights at the conferences represented a milestone. I conducted my research as a visiting scholar in population studies at the University of Michigan in 1999 and worked in the UN Population Fund office in Thailand. I felt that I was an activist while being in a UN bureaucracy. Now I am a researcher at Waseda University on reproductive rights issues from an international relations perspective; I also work at Place Tokyo. For me, HIV / AIDS from a sexuality point of view and health from a women's rights point of view are issues concerning justice.

How was Place Tokyo created? What are its main activities?

Ikegami Chizuko created Place Tokyo in 1992. She went to the United States and worked as a freelance writer on sexuality issues. She translated the book *Women's Bodies*. After she came back to Japan she was committed to the HIV/AIDS issue and sexuality education. Place Tokyo has one paid staff member and many volunteer members. We are a direct service group that provides medical, mental, and social welfare services. We do not focus on antidiscrimination. In terms of our main activities, we run Nest Group, which is a buddy service for people living with HIV/AIDS. We do research funded by the Ministry of Health, Labor, and Welfare. My current project looks at youth contraceptive usage, at issues such as why Japanese youth don't use condoms and how to promote sexual health among young people. We have created some educational videos and pamphlets. Projects by other researchers look at lifestyle issues of HIV-positive people. We also run a telephone hotline and a self-help group.

What is the relationship of Place Tokyo with the Japanese government?

In terms of strategy, we focus on health policy. We are more concerned with medical access and health services in general than with gay rights. For instance, if an HIV-positive person applies for social welfare as "disabled," the costs of HIV drugs per year drop to around $4,000 to $5,000 per year, which makes a big difference. Instead of being antigovernment, we want to enter the government. I think our basic stance is not radical or antigovernment. We do lobbying, but we focus on dialogue. For me personally, I think research and empirical data are important.

Could you tell me some of the challenges that you face in working on the HIV/AIDS issue in Japan?

I think the current political environment in Japan is one of backlash. After the Tenth International Conference on AIDS in Yokohama in 1994, the International Conference on Population and Development that same year, and the Fourth World Conference on Women in Beijing in 1995, there was a very powerful women's movement in Japan, which led to the passage of the Basic Law on Gender Equality and the Domestic Violence Prevention Law. Since 2000, there has been backlash at different levels. There is a lot of feminist bashing at the political level (for example, comments made by Tokyo Governor Ishihara Shintarō) and in the media, for example, the use of the term *feminist Nazism*.

Gender-free education is very much under attack. It has become very difficult to do sex education. With the emphasis on abstinence only, teaching about intercourse or condoms is prohibited. Despite the stipulation by the Basic Law on Gender Equality and local ordinances requiring measures to promote gender equality, little has been done concretely in schools. This backlash is organized. I know that some Japanese groups went to the United States to study about abstinence-only sex education. In that sense, you can see the links between George W. Bush and Ishihara Shintarō.

What are some of the issues you are concerned about in AIDS organizing?

The key slogan at the XV International AIDS Conference in Bangkok in 2003 was "Access for all" because of huge gaps among countries in access to HIV / AIDS drugs. Many Asian AIDS activist groups were there, including the Seven Sisters (a coalition of seven Asia Pacific regional networks on HIV / AIDS; lesbian, gay, bisexual, and transsexual groups; migrant workers' organizations; sex workers' groups; and drug-user groups). I worked as an Asian activist. One of the issues was the clash between the political stance of Japanese sex workers in organizations like SWASH (Sex Work and Sexual Health) on sex workers' rights and mainstream feminists' stance on sex work. There were also tensions between Japanese sex workers and Asian sex workers within Japan, an issue that was never explicitly addressed. Then there was the problem related to talking about the HIV-positive drug users in Japan. It is difficult to talk about this population because drug use is illegal in Japan. In our work, we try not to define things too much. For example, concerning sex work, we build solidarity without too much debate on the definition of *sex work*. If we discussed too much, there would be no more solidarity because we would talk for many hours. One last issue: I think it is very difficult to use the concept of "right to self-determination" (*jiko ketteiken*). In the Japanese context, for instance, how would you advise about the right to self-determination to single mothers who have no social welfare? When their options are so constrained, what does the right to self-determination mean? In Japan there are two camps on this issue: for and against *jiko ketteiken*. Personally, I am in neither camp. I use a pragmatic approach. I don't use a moral approach vis-à-vis the girls who practice *enjo kōsai* (assisted dating, a form of prostitution). I work on how to protect their health.

You mentioned feminist backlash earlier. Could you tell me about some of the current debates within Japanese feminism?

One of the current feminist debates in Japan concerns the introduction of foreign maids in domestic service. Because of our low fertility rate (1.2 percent), immigration seems to be one of the solutions. Feminists in Japan are concerned about the impact of foreign maids on gender relations. Will Japanese women employ foreign maids? How might class affect gender relations? What would be the role of men in middle-income families? Another big issue is part-time work of women, especially as *haken* (short-term dispatch workers). This is a broader issue of the increase of nonregular work under economic globalization.

You are one of the few activists who have a university-based research position. How do you juggle both?

I think the two are connected. The Ministry of Education, for example, has launched this major global research initiative. One of the components is on globalization, women and labor, violence and globalization, and so on. However, few within Japanese academia are interested in activism. This, I think, could be challenged. I see myself as both a researcher and an activist.

What would be your priority from now on?

I think it is important to emphasize the voice of the people living with HIV / AIDS—that is, their own perspectives as gays, positive women, and sex workers—instead of having an academic domination. I think the upcoming Seventh International Conference on AIDS in the Asia Pacific in Kobe in July 2005 will be more issue-focused regarding gays, gender, youth, foreigners, and so on. Place Tokyo wants to work more on providing information to people living with HIV / AIDS, including e-mail counseling. I also think we are not doing enough outreach to the general population.

Related Web Sites

Act Against AIDS: http://www.actagainstaids.com
Place Tokyo and Place Tokyo jōhō: http://gf.ptokyo.com
Seven Sisters (Coalition of Asia Pacific Regional Network on HIV / AIDS): http://www.7sisters.org
United Nations Development Programme HIV / AIDS Portal for Asia Pacific: http://www.youandaids.org
Web Nest: http://web-nest.ptokyo.com/about

Related References

Hunter, Susan. 2005. *AIDS in Asia: A Continent in Peril*. New York: Palgrave Macmillan.

Irwin, Alexander, Joyce Millen, and Dorothy Fallows. 2003. *Global AIDS: Myths and Facts*. Cambridge, MA: South End Press.

Kimoto, Kinuko. 2001. "Barriers to Safer Sex Practices Among Commercial Sex Workers in Osaka, Japan: Scope for Prevention of Future HIV Epidemic." Boston: Harvard School of Public Health. Available at http://www.hsph.harvard.edu/takemi/RP181.PDF#search='antiprostitution%20law%20in%20Japan'

Law, Lisa. 2000. *Sex Work in Southeast Asia: The Place of Desire in a Time of AIDS*. London and New York: Routledge.

Micollier, Evelyne. 2004. *Sexual Cultures in East Asia: The Social Construction of Sexuality and Sexual Risk in a Time of AIDS*. London and New York: Routledge Curzon.

Narain, Jai P., ed. 2004. *AIDS in Asia: The Challenge Ahead*. Thousand Oaks, CA: Sage.

Sherr, Lorraine, Catherine Hankins, and Lydia Bennett. 1996. *AIDS as a Gender Issue: Psychosocial Perspectives*. London and Bristol, PA: Taylor & Francis.

Tlou, Sheila. 2002. "Gender and HIV / AIDS." In *AIDS in Africa*, edited by Max Essex, Souleymane Mboup, Phyllis Kanki, Richard Marlink, and Sheila Tlou. New York: Kluwer Academic / Plenum.

World Bank. 1993. *Social and Gender Dimensions of the AIDS Epidemic in Asia*. Washington, DC: World Bank.

27

MIGRANT WORKERS AND
HIV / AIDS IN JAPAN

Inaba Masaki

INABA MASAKI is a board member of Africa Japan Forum. Born in Kyoto in 1969 and graduated from the Faculty of Letters at Tokyo University in 1995, Inaba started his work in Japanese civil society in the early 1990s. Since 2002 his work has focused on HIV / AIDS both in Japanese civil society and in the global community, especially in Africa.

How did you become an HIV / AIDS activist?

I was program director on advocacy in OCCUR, the Japan Association for the Lesbian and Gay Movement, a gay and lesbian organization in Japan that was founded in 1986. I think the Tenth International Conference on AIDS in Yokohama in 1994 had an important impact on the HIV / AIDS issue in Japan. Around that time there were not many NGOs in Japan that worked on this issue area internationally (there were OCCUR, the Japan AIDS and Society Association, and some other organizations). Within OCCUR there were only a few people who consistently worked on the HIV / AIDS issue. I began attending international conferences on AIDS in the Asia Pacific as a member of OCCUR. By the 1990s, AIDS had become a mainstream global issue. I became committed to the international movement on HIV / AIDS mainly in the Asia and Pacific context. OCCUR was one of the leading organizations for lesbian and gay rights. From the mid-1990s, my concern about the lack of internal democratic structure in the organization had increased, and I finally decided to leave OCCUR in 2001. At that time, Africa Japan Forum (AJF), an NGO working on African issues, wanted to start its program on advocacy for global AIDS issues. I had a desire to do more work globally on HIV / AIDS, so I joined the organization as the program coordinator on HIV / AIDS and infectious diseases.

How and why was AJF created?

In 1993, the first Tokyo International Conference on African Development (TICAD I), a multilateral intergovernmental conference held once every five years, took place. Despite the significance of African NGO activities, neither African nor Japanese NGOs were invited to the conference. Japanese NGOs called on their African counterparts and organized a counter forum. After TICAD I, the organizing committee of the counter forum developed itself to organize AJF in 1994. It set its mission to support the regional independence of African nations through partnerships with the African people. AJF experienced an organizational reform from 1998 to 2001, and since 2002 we have two paid staff members responsible for two working groups, one on food security and one on HIV / AIDS; about thirty volunteer (mostly student) staff members, including both students and workers; and 250 members, including researchers and NGOs that work on African issues in Japan. There has been increasing interest among students in development and NGOs.

What issues do you face in mobilizing on the HIV / AIDS issue?

The biggest issue is funding, not only locally, but also globally. I just returned from the board meeting of the Global Fund to Fight AIDS, Tuberculosis, and Malaria (the Global Fund). The Global Fund didn't have enough money to launch Round 5, which is the new round for developing countries to apply for new grants from the fund under its current financial management regulations. There were serious debates between donors and recipients on issuing Round 5, but the Global Fund failed to launch it at the board meeting. As you know, in his 2003 State of the Union address George W. Bush launched his own initiative, the President's Emergency Plan for AIDS Relief, pledging $15 billion over five years. To date, more than forty-five countries as well as other donors have pledged $5.9 billion to support Global Fund programs in 127 countries till 2008, but this falls short of the original budget of $7 billion a year. At its sixth meeting, in October 2003, the board of the Global Fund agreed to establish a funding model, the voluntary replenishment mechanism, based on periodic replenishment, in place of the current system, and the replenishment process is chaired by UN Secretary General Kofi Annan.

How about domestically? What are some of the challenges?

You may have heard about the hemophiliac blood contamination scandal. After the infected patients got an apology and some kind of settlement from the Ministry of Health and Welfare, public attention quickly diminished. Despite the fact that the gay community accounted for 60 percent of all infections in Japan, the Ministry of Health and Welfare of Japan didn't recognize the urgent need of taking measures for HIV infection prevention and raising awareness on HIV/AIDS among Japanese gay communities. After much lobbying by OCCUR, the population of gays and other MSMs (men who have sex with men) were finally included as one of the focus populations within the Japanese National HIV/AIDS Prevention and Care Guidelines in 1999. We also managed to insert a clause to prevent discrimination based on sexual orientation, under Definitions in Article 2 in the draft Human Rights Protection Bill.

You recently organized an international symposium on HIV/AIDS and foreigners living in Japan? Could you tell me more about it?

There are about thirty thousand Africans living in Japan. The biggest group is from Nigeria (about six to eight thousand), then Ghana (five to seven thousand), Uganda (three thousand), and about a thousand each from Senegal, South Africa, Tanzania, Guinea, and Ethiopia. They include students, professionals, laborers, and embassy staff. More than half are unregistered migrants, who don't have valid visas to stay in Japan. One of the problems concerning HIV-positive Africans living in Japan is the lack of affordable access to HIV drugs for unregistered migrants. The Japanese government has been refusing unregistered migrants access to its social security programs for health care, including the national health insurance program, so unregistered migrants have to pay all the medical fees by themselves. All the antiretroviral drugs in Japan are branded, so antiretroviral therapy usually costs more than $10,000 a year. It is impossible for almost all of the unregistered migrants living with HIV/AIDS to pay such a huge amount of money to get treatment. If they can access Japanese public health care programs, they can get antiretroviral therapy for $50 to $100 a year. Another issue is the lack of access to HIV drugs for unregistered migrants in detention centers, which are operated by the Ministry of Justice. There are three detention centers in Japan and more than one thousand unregistered foreigners. Most of them have court cases against the ministry on their visa or refugee status. These detention centers are notorious for their inappropriate or lack of medical services for detainees. In terms of

NGO work, Japanese NGOs don't have enough formal relationships with African communities. There are quite a few Japan-Africa cultural exchange groups in which the Japanese members know a lot of Africans, but they are not necessarily connected to NGOs working on African issues. As of now, we don't have enough capacity to provide services to the African populations. For example, there are HIV / AIDS counseling services in Thai, Spanish, English, Chinese, and Portuguese in Japan, but not in French, one of the major languages among people from Francophone African countries. A more general issue concerns the invisibility of African migrants in Japan. Together with stigmatization against HIV / AIDS itself and against people living with the disease, it makes consciousness-raising about this population very difficult.

What kinds of changes do you advocate?

I think migrants in Japan should have access to HIV treatment and care regardless of their visa status, as with tuberculosis. HIV treatment should also be available during detention. Finally, we would like to focus on building civil society response. Adding to our efforts to lobby the government, we have to find ways to increase our staff members and funding, to augment our capacity for direct action, and to work on our relationships with policy makers and parliamentary members.

Related Web Sites

Africa Japan Forum: http://www.ajf.gr.jp
Friends of the Global Fund Japan: http://www.jcie.or.jp/fgfj/e/diet.html
Fund the Fund: International Campaign to Increase Funding for the Global Fund: http://www.fundthefund.org
Global Fund links to civil society, governmental, and intergovernmental organizations working on HIV / AIDS: http://www.theglobalfund.org/en/links_resources/our_partners/#civil_society
Global Fund, Sixth Board Meeting: http://www.theglobalfund.org/en/about/board/sixth
Global Fund, Voluntary Replenishment Mechanism: http://www.theglobalfund.org/en/about/replenishment
Human Rights Protection Bill of Japan: http://imadr.org/old/tokyo/Human%20Rights%20Protection%20Bill%20of%20Japan.html
U.S. President's Emergency Plan for AIDS Relief Fact Sheet: http://www.whitehouse.gov/news/releases/2003/01/20030129-1.html

Related References

D'Adesky, Anne-Christine. 2004. *Moving Mountains: The Race to Treat Global AIDS.* London and New York: Verso.

D'Adesky, Anne-Christine. 2005. *Pills, Profits and Protest.* Video. New York: Outcast Films.

Iwamuro, Shin'ya. 1996. *AIDS ima nani wo dō tsutaeru ka* [AIDS: What and how we should convey now]. Tokyo: Taishūkan Shoten.

Munakata, Tsunetsugu, Mako Morita, and Kazumi Fujisawa. 1994. *Nihon no AIDS* [AIDS in Japan]. Tokyo: Akashi Shoten.

Nemoto, Tōru. 2004. "HIV/AIDS Surveillance and Prevention Studies in Japan: Summary and Recommendations." *AIDS Education and Prevention, 16* (Supplement A), 27–42.

UNAIDS, UNICEF, and WHO. 2006. *Epidemiological Fact Sheets on HIV/AIDS and Sexually Transmitted Infections (Japan).* Available at http://www.who.int/hiv/pub/epidemiology/pubfacts/en

PART VI

GENDER

FIGURE 6. Women's Association Against the Path to War, Relay Talk
in Yūrakuchō, Tokyo, December 4, 2004

INTRODUCTION TO PART VI

THE 1990s REPRESENTED A WATERSHED DECADE in Japan in terms of discursive and legal changes related to women's rights. A national machinery on the status of women and local women's centers has been gradually institutionalized since the International Year for Women in 1975, and Japan's ratification of the Convention on the Elimination of All Forms of Discrimination Against Women (CEDAW) in 1985 resulted in the amendment of the Nationality Law and school curricula, and the passage of the Equal Employment Opportunity Law. But it was the Fourth World Conference on Women in Beijing in 1995 that galvanized the women's movement in Japan on the issue of gender-based violence. Between 1997 and 2001, a series of legal changes were introduced to mandate prevention of sexual harassment in the workplace, prohibit child pornography and prostitution, outlaw domestic violence, and promote gender equality at all levels of government. Central to these pivotal developments is mobilization on global human rights norms—reproductive health, commercial sexual exploitation, and violence against women—by women's groups in Japan.[1]

Several issues, however, have caused much soul-searching within the women's movement in Japan since the late 1990s. First, transnational and local debates on the politics of location have opened up the whole issue of power and representation.[2] Although there has been relative success on the mobilization of more "mainstream" feminist issues such as sexual violence, "minority" feminisms remain largely marginalized. Half a century after the end of World War II, despite much international mobilization against contemporary and historical military sexual slavery, the women's movement in Japan is still divided over the redress of the estimated two hundred thousand former "comfort women" who have been drafted to serve the sexual needs of the Japanese military largely because of their race (80 percent of the comfort women were Korean). Similarly, the serious issue of the trafficking of young women from Asia, Latin America, and Central Europe was not picked up by mainstream feminist groups until 2003, when the Japan Network Against Trafficking in Persons was formed. Further, movements addressing sexual rights and sex workers' rights have remained largely outside the women's movement in Japan.

Just as their foreign counterparts have attempted to inject a feminist agenda into the global justice movement,[3] feminists in Japan have also been trying to articulate their resistance and formulate alternatives to neoliberal globalization, nationalism, and militarism within Japan from a gender perspective. Whether the issue is labor, food, peace, ecology, sexuality, or racism, women in Japan are not only affected but also have consistently fought for their rights. Conceptually, CEDAW prohibits *all forms* of discrimination. The Beijing Platform for Action, in particular, lays out comprehensive areas for action by governments and NGOs, from poverty to education, health, violence, peace, economy, and politics. Empirically, feminists in Japan have been involved in the emergent alterglobalization, antiwar, and antidiscrimination movements. For nongovernmental networks such as Equality Action 21 (*Kintō Taigū*), labor restructuring, for example, is clearly a feminist issue. Employment deregulation affects all workers but has an arguably disproportionate impact on women, who constitute the bulk of nonformal workers and face gender-specific indirect discrimination.[4] On the antiwar front, not only have women traditionally been heavily involved in the peace movement, but they have, in particular, focused on the gender aspects of militarism. Recent feminist historical research has looked at the role that women played in the military expansions of Japan. Many women's groups in Japan—Women in Black Tokyo, Feminist Art Action Brigade, Women's Association Against the Path to War, and Group on Women and the Emperor, to name just a few— have been involved in recent antiwar demonstrations. Women's groups such as Femin Women's Democratic Club, No! Rape No! Base Women's Group, Violence Against Women in War—Network Japan, and Women's Network Against U.S. Bases in Japan are also members of large peace networks such as World Peace Now (see Appendix 1A).

The eight interviews grouped in this section look at how women in Japan engage in resistance, in particular through the use of UN human rights mechanisms, on issues ranging from human trafficking to reproductive rights, lesbianism, sex work, violence against women in war, and feminist art resistance. Several key themes emerge from this set of interviews. Although coalitions such as the Japan NGO Network for CEDAW have become increasingly savvy in international lobbying, they are confronted with issues of coordination, weak domestic lobbying power, and practical constraints in doing follow-up monitoring work. Several feminist activists have also cautioned about diversity and the need for the direct participation of ethnic and sexual minorities in the women's movement in Japan. As illustrated with trafficking, one of the best political opportunity structures for NGO network mobilization remains *gaiatsu* (foreign pressure). When the U.S. State Department put Japan on the Tier II Watch List of the Victims of Trafficking and Violence Protection Act of 2000, the Japanese government was spurred into action by the revision of the Immigration Control Act to allow special residence permits for trafficking victims and by making trafficking a criminal offense under the Penal Code. Finally, backlash against the movement for gender equality has consumed much of the feminist energy in Japan since the late 1990s. While the government pays lip service to the discourse on women's empowerment through labor participation and child care support, the conservative political reality on the ground threatens to take away the gains that feminists have made in the past few decades. In the era of "small government," national and local women's centers have become targets of administrative reforms. Sexual education that emphasizes a rights perspective has been under attack. Larger developments in nationalism, including the amendment of the Fundamental Law of Education, have called for a return to traditional family values. In this context, feminist activists aim beyond legal and political reforms; they work to change people's consciousness and behavior, and they continue to focus on empowerment and community building.

Notes

1. Chan-Tiberghien 2004a.

2. Kaplan 1994; Mackie 2002; International Movement Against All Forms of Discrimination and Racism 2002.

3. International Gender and Trade Network 2003; International March of Women 2004; and Shiva 2000. For a feminist critique of the World Trade Organization, see Chan-Tiberghien 2004b.

4. Hirakawa 2005.

28

INTERNATIONAL LOBBYING AND JAPANESE WOMEN'S NETWORKS

Watanabe Miho

WATANABE MIHO works as a researcher at the National Women's Education Center, an institution promoting gender equality. She is in charge of research on trafficking, and organizing international seminars on leadership and empowerment. Born in Tokyo in 1967, she spent several teenage years on the West Coast of the United States. After earning her bachelor of arts degree in law from Waseda University, Watanabe began her career in international financing at a securities company. In 2002 she graduated from the School of Industrial and Labor Relations at Cornell University with a master's degree in professional studies. She is a member of the Japan NGO Network for CEDAW.

Could you tell me how the Japan NGO Network for CEDAW (JNNC) was formed?

After I finished my master's in industrial and labor relations at Cornell University in 2001, I wanted to work at an NGO. Because I was an active member of the Japanese Association of International Women's Rights, an NGO focusing on promoting the Convention on the Elimination of All Forms of Discrimination Against Women (CEDAW) in Japan, I participated in a CEDAW lobbying training workshop organized by the International Women's Rights Action Watch Asia Pacific (IWRAW) in 2002. I learned that the CEDAW committee would review Japan's Fourth and Fifth Periodic Reports in its twenty-ninth session in summer 2003. (Japan ratified CEDAW in 1985.) So in December of that year a handful of Japanese feminists, including Yamashita Yasuko, Hara Yuriko, Saito Fumie, and Omi Miho, called for the establishment of JNNC.

Concretely, what did JNNC do until the review meeting?

First of all, we called on the major NGOs working on various issues to join together to lobby for the review of Japan's reports. To facilitate the discussion and the coordination of various groups, we created a homepage and mailing list. Because the Japanese government had to respond to the questions posed by the CEDAW committee before the review meeting, the idea was that we had to intervene before that meeting in July 2003; so we began lobbying CEDAW at a presession working group meeting in January 2003. Ten of us went to New York to participate in the working group, providing the CEDAW experts with the NGOs' view of the persisting women's issues. Our input into the presession working group had been reflected in the list of issues posed by the committee members to the Japanese government. We met with members of the Japanese Association of Parliamentary Women (Josei Giin Kondankai) and organized a small study session with them. The involvement of parliamentary members has been crucial to carrying out the aim of JNNC. We held consultation meetings twice with the Japanese government ministry staff to let them know the views of Japanese women's NGOs on the issues. We compiled alternative reports to the Fourth and Fifth Periodic Reports of Japan on CEDAW by issue area and submitted them to the CEDAW committee. JNNC grew to become a network of forty-six women's and human rights NGOs in Japan.

And in New York? What happened at the review meeting in July 2003?

In New York the director general of the General Equality Bureau from Japan, who led a fifteen-member governmental delegation, summarized the Fourth and Fifth Periodic Reports in her presentation to CEDAW committee members and experts, focusing on four key areas: strengthened machinery, legal measures, targets set, and international cooperation. In addition to a summary on the general situation of Japanese women, which covered aggregated statistics on the participation of Japanese women in education, employment, agriculture, and NGO activities, the second part of the two reports detailed changes in Japan article by article: violence against women (article 2), national machinery (article 3), women in decision making (article 4), sex-role stereotypes (article 5), prostitution (article 6), public fields (article 7), women in international decision making (article 8), discrimination in foreign service (article 9), education (article 10), employment (article 11), health (article 12), rural areas (article 13), and finally amendment to the Civil Code (article 16). We lobbied the CEDAW experts during recess time. We set up an informal input meeting with CEDAW experts during lunchtime in which we presented our issues. JNNC member groups coordinated sixteen NGOs, which came to New York to present their views in limited time slots. In addition to issues in health, education, employment, and public office, other issues related to trafficking and minority women groups—the Buraku, Koreans, Ainu, Okinawans, migrant workers, women trafficked into the sex industry, and non-Japanese women married to Japanese men—drew the attention of the experts.

What came out of that mobilization?

Some of the issues that we raised are reflected in CEDAW's concluding comments to the Japanese government after its twenty-sixth session. It was the first time that CEDAW mentioned minority women in Japan in its report. I think we played a crucial role. The challenge is domestic follow-up work. One problem was for us to try to identify the government bureaucracy that would be responsible for following up on the recommendations of CEDAW. Under the National Plan of Action on Gender Equality, a special commission was set up to evaluate progress. We have been lobbying for this commission to follow up on the government's implementation of CEDAW recommendations—for example, by setting up a gender focal point within each ministry. For the NGO groups, it was important that we learned the importance of organizing and of solidarity on different issues, which were critical for the successful lobbying of the government and CEDAW committee. It also helped the members from different groups to understand each other better and to work on other issues, because it all leads to gender equality and human rights.

You are now a researcher at the public National Women's Education Center (NWEC). Could you tell me about NWEC and your work there?

NWEC (created after the International Women's Year in 1975) focuses on research, training, and information exchange. Local government employees of gender equality divisions and staff members of regional women's centers and women's NGO groups participate in the training seminars and forums conducted by NWEC. I work as a full-time researcher. Major research areas of NWEC this year are gender statistics, gender equality programs (for men), and women's career building. Also, the current national concern is to increase the number of children in Japan (to offset an aging population), and the government has been putting in place policies on women's participation in the workforce and women's career development, especially in decision-making positions and in fields such as science and technology, child care support, job segregation, and part-time work. For example, there was a symposium in summer 2004 on careers of women in science. To prepare for that, we did research on how many women publish in academic journals in Japan. We also have programs for men. For example, to address the so-called 2007 crisis—the gender social structure related to the retirement of postwar baby boomers, who were the driving force in shaping today's Japanese economic success—we are conducting research on programs to be carried out at local women's centers to help these men adapt to the home environment and society while they gradually change their gender discriminatory views.

What issues do you face in your gender research?

First of all, there has been a strong backlash against initiatives to promote gender equality. Because NWEC was established as a national institution to promote gender equality and women's education, there has been a strong pullback in its initiatives. We still have a long way to go before there is a general understanding that the gender-equal society is not just for women but for both men and women. As in many other public and private institutions, most of the staff members are men, and the value of gender equity is not recognized by all. This is one of my dilemmas working at NWEC—the difference between the government and my own feminist stance—but I hope to change it little by little from within. Year 2004 was also a difficult time for NWEC because the issue of whether NWEC was necessary was raised in the Committee for Deregulation (Kisei kaikaku iinkai). Now may not be the *best* time for gender research in Japan, but it is a very *important* time.

Related Web Sites

Alternative Reports to the Fourth and Fifth Periodic Reports of Japan on CEDAW: Voices of Minority: http://www.jaiwr.org/jnnc/20030701jnncsummaryreport(en).pdf

CEDAW's Concluding Comments on the Japanese Government's Fourth and Fifth Periodic Reports: http://daccessdds.un.org/doc/UNDOC/GEN/N98/355/16/IMG/N9835516.pdf?OpenElement and http://daccessdds.un.org/doc/UNDOC/GEN/N02/600/19/IMG/N0260019.pdf?OpenElement

International Women's Rights Action Watch Asia Pacific: http://www.iwraw-ap.org/index.htm

Japan NGO Network for CEDAW: http://www.jaiwr.org/jnnc/english

Japan's Fourth and Fifth Periodic Reports to CEDAW: http://www.mofa.go.jp/policy/
    human
Japanese Association of International Women's Rights: http://www.jaiwr.org/
    jaiwrpre29.html
Lunchtime presentation to CEDAW members by JNNC, July 7, 2003: http://www
    .jaiwr.org/jnnc/030707lunchpresen.html

Related References

Japan NGO Network for CEDAW. 2004. *Josei sabetsu teppai jōyaku to NGO* [The UN
    Convention on the Elimination of All Forms of Discrimination Against Women
    and NGO]. Tokyo: Akashi Shoten.
JoJo. 2004. *Onnatachi no benrichō* [Directory of women's groups in Japan]. Tokyo:
    JoJo.
New Japan Women's Association. 2004. *NGO Alternative Report: Comments on
    the Response of the Government of Japan to the Questionnaire on Implementa-
    tion of the Beijing Platform for Action (1995) and the Outcome of the Twenty-
    Third Special Session of the General Assembly (2000)*. Tokyo: New Japan Women's
    Association. Available at http://www.shinfujin.gr.jp/c_4_english/4_resource/
    files/b+10njwareport.pdf

29

GENDER, HUMAN RIGHTS, AND TRAFFICKING IN PERSONS

Hara Yuriko

HARA YURIKO is under-secretary-general and program manager at International Movement Against All Forms of Discrimination and Racism; an organizing member of Japan NGO Network for CEDAW; and a steering committee member of Japan Network Against Trafficking in Persons. She received a master's degree in human rights from the Graduate School of Essex University, United Kingdom. She served as a coordinator for foreign media at the 2000 Women's International War Crimes Tribunal on Japanese Military Sexual Slavery. She teaches part-time at Meiji University and Sōka Women's College.

How did you become involved in human rights issues in Japan?

I worked in the United States (New Jersey) for a big Japanese construction company for two and a half years. In 1996, when I returned to Japan, I first got involved in the issue of women in development through lobbying activities against the Asian Development Bank (ADB), which was going to hold its annual meeting in my hometown, Fukuoka, in May 1997. Together with my friend Imamura Kazuhiko, who subsequently formed the Watch Out for WTO Japan group, we established ADB Fukuoka NGO Network. Through various activities of this NGO I got into the issue of women's rights. Then I went to the University of Essex between 1999 and 2000 for my master's studies in human rights. I wrote my dissertation on trafficking in Japan. I was interested in looking at the issue through multiple perspectives: gender, race, ethnicity, nationalism, and the emperor system. I interviewed a staff member in the Geneva office of the International Movement Against All Forms of Discrimination and Racism (IMADR) for my dissertation. There I became sympathetic to IMADR's perspective on and approach to discrimination and trafficking. In June 2000, during my volunteering work at the Beijing-Plus-Five Conference in New York, I was asked by the late Matsui Yayori to help prepare for the Women's International War Crimes Tribunal on Japanese Military Sexual Slavery scheduled for December 2000 in Tokyo. I worked for the tribunal as a media coordinator. The following year I joined IMADR as a staff member, focusing my work on issues of minorities, especially minority women.

You were one of the coordinating member-facilitators of the Japan NGO Network for CEDAW (JNNC), which had an impact on CEDAW's concluding comments on the Japanese Government's Fourth and Fifth Periodic Reports. Could you tell me about that lobbying and networking experience?

In terms of lobbying and networking, what is in question is the power to coordinate. Because I recognized the importance of forming a coalition and taking common action when the report of the Committee on the Elimination of Racial Discrimination (CERD) was examined, I thought it would be great if I could coordinate by making good use of the experience and ability of each member at CEDAW. One of the issues that the women's movement in Japan faces is weak lobbying power vis-à-vis the central government. Another issue is lack of consciousness of minority voices within the movement. So when JNNC was formed, the target for us was not only the government but also the women's groups themselves. As a result, we were able to make the best use of a coalition in various ways, such as negotiating with the government and politicians, providing information through lobbying, having briefing sessions with the CEDAW committee, and engaging in media tactics. I think that in this regard the younger members within the coalition have made a significant contribution. How we do follow-up work back in Japan remains a challenge. Structurally there was no place to monitor the CEDAW conclusions and recommendations. We had been lobbying the government to set up some kind of monitoring system under the Council for Gender Equality so that the council would be responsible for doing the follow-up work. For instance, we want to see the issues addressed in the concluding comments of CEDAW reflected in the next National Plan of Action. In terms of the women's movement, I think the overall lobbying capability is still low. The movement is not connected to young people. I think the movement should be open to many perspectives as well.

Could you describe the trafficking situation in Japan?

Japan has been criticized as a big trafficking recipient country. Most trafficking victims come from the Philippines, Thailand, Colombia, Eastern Europe, and the former Soviet Union. A common pattern is that women from developing countries are approached by recruiters and deceived about finding "good work" in Japan. They are issued false passports and do not know that they would have to engage in prostitution. Once in Japan, they are moved around by *yakuza* (crime syndicates). These women often incur a fictitious debt of about 5,500,000 yen (about S50,000), because the *yakuza* tells them that they are sold for that amount, plus rent and food, and that they have to work to repay that debt. Japan signed the Protocol to Prevent, Suppress, and Punish Trafficking in Persons, Especially Women and Children (one of the Palermo Protocols), which supplemented the UN Convention Against Transnational Organized Crime, in 2002, but has not yet ratified it.

How was the Japan Network Against Trafficking in Persons (JNATIP) formed?

Various NGOs and women's groups, including shelters, have been concerned about trafficking in Japan, but there was not one single, focused network on the issue. In 2000, the United States passed the Victims of Trafficking and Violence Protection Act of 2000, and the State Department has been monitoring the efforts of other countries in combating trafficking. Japan has been placed on the act's Tier II Watch List, which means that Japan has not fulfilled the minimum standards, such as increased investigations, prosecutions, and convictions of trafficking crimes, and better assistance to victims. We used this fact as a tailwind for setting up a coalition to combat trafficking. JNATIP was formed in October 2003 through a coalition of twenty-five NGOs and one hundred individual members. Our aim is to formulate effective and comprehensive laws to prevent trafficking in persons, to provide relief to victims, and to ensure the punishment of traffickers. In order to materialize this goal, we lobbied the government, and each political party, and started a project to compile data on the situation of human trafficking in Japan.

What is the prospect of having a new law on trafficking in Japan anytime soon?

This is a difficult question. In order to ratify the Protocol to Prevent, Suppress, and Punish Trafficking in Persons, the government has set up an interministerial task force to look into necessary legal reform. As a result, the government plans to revise the Immigration Control Act to permit the issuance of a "special residence permit" to trafficking victims. The Penal Code would also be revised to include the act of trafficking as a criminal offense, at last. In other words, the government would take several steps to combat trafficking, as long as it would be in line with national policy, that is, strengthening crime control. That is the limit. As for the protection of victims, the government has no political will for legislation; it will stop at a national plan of action. The current approach of the Japanese government treats trafficked victims as illegal overstayers, while being extremely lenient with the traffickers. We would like to see a new law that criminalizes trafficking as an organized crime and, at the same time and more important, gives protection to trafficked victims. It remains unclear whether such a law will be passed in the Diet, particularly now, when the ruling coalition is preoccupied with various kinds of emergency legislation and with the move to revise the constitution. The government might very well go for a softer version, some sort of a national plan of action, which we think is not sufficient.

What do you think are the biggest obstacles in combating trafficking in Japan?

It is about whether we can change people's fundamental consciousness and behavioral patterns. Legal reforms represent only the tip of an iceberg in which people's consciousness and behavior, and the social and economic structures, are anchored. It involves discrimination against foreigners. Many people do not understand the root of the issue and feel that trafficked people have to shoulder self-responsibility, because they come here to make money, and that is what they want. In addition, there is the consciousness that it is acceptable to buy women. The goal is to change such consciousness. The entertainment sector, in which most trafficked victims work, is huge and plays a big role in the Japanese economy. The Association for the Promotion of Businesses, of which many entertainment businesses are members, is an important lobbying group. Further, from an immigration perspective, the Ministry of Justice fears that a new law providing victim protection might increase long-term residency of illegal immigrants. I think that until now neither the government nor the media looks at this issue from a gender or racial perspective, that trafficking is a violation of women's basic human rights. In the United States, trafficking issues are talked about on the Oprah Winfrey show. In Sweden, teachers use videos to talk about it.

Related Web Sites

Choike Portal on Southern Civil Societies: http://www.choike.org/nuevo_eng/
informes/1763.html

Global Alliance Against Traffic in Women: http://gaatw.net

Japan Network Against Trafficking in Persons: http://www.jnatip.org/aboutthejnatip
.html

Protocol to Prevent, Suppress, and Punish Trafficking in Persons, supplementing
the United Nations Convention Against Transnational Organized Crime (2000):
http://www.ohchr.org/english/law/protocoltraffic.htm

Trafficking in Persons Report, 2004: http://www.state.gov/g/tip/rls/tiprpt/2004

U.S. State Department Office to Monitor and Combat Trafficking and Victims of
Trafficking, and Violence Protection Act of 2000: http://www.legislationline.org/
legislation.php?tid=178&lid=4107&x=1&y=7

Related References

Coomaraswamy, Radhika. 2000. *Integration of the Human Rights of Women and
the Gender Perspective: Report of the Special Rapporteur on Violence Against
Women.* Available at http://www.unhchr.ch/Huridocda/Huridoca.nsf/0/
e29d45a105cd8143802568be0051fcfb/$FILE/G0011334.pdf

Japan Network Against Trafficking in Persons, and Yoko Yoshida, ed. 2004. *Jinshin
baibai wo nakusu tame ni: ukeire taikoku Nihon no kadai* [Toward the elimination of human trafficking: Issues in the big receiving country of Japan]. Tokyo:
Akashi Shoten.

Kyoto YMCA, Asian People Together. 2001. *Jinshin baibai to ukeiretaikoku Nippon: sono jittai to hōteki kadai* [Trafficking and the big recipient country, Japan:
Reality and legal issues]. Tokyo: Akashi Shoten.

Malarek, Victor. 2003. *The New Global Sex Trade.* Toronto: Viking Canada.

National Network in Solidarity with Migrant Workers. 2002. *Protecting Foreigners
in Japan: Some Proposals.* Tokyo: National Network in Solidarity with Migrant
Workers. Available from http://www.hurights.or.jp/asia-pacific/no_29/03mnet
japan.htm

30

GENDER, REPRODUCTIVE RIGHTS, AND TECHNOLOGY

Ōhashi Yukako

ŌHASHI YUKAKO is a freelance editor and writer, and a member of Soshiren (Starting from a Female Body), a women's group advocating reproductive freedom. Born in Tokyo in 1959 and graduated in sociology from Sophia University in Tokyo in 1982, she worked in the editorial departments of *Nihon dokusho shinbun* [*Weekly Book Review*] and *Honyaku no sekai* [monthly magazine about translation]. Her publications include *Karada no kimochi wo kīte miyō: Joshi kōsei no tameno sei to karada no hon* [Let's listen to our bodily feelings: Book on sexuality and body for high school girls].

How did you become involved in reproductive rights issues in Japan?

In 1982, I read a newspaper article by a women's group concerning its opposition to the prohibition of abortion. I had just graduated from college. I was dating at the time and worried about getting pregnant, so I went to the women's group meeting. Several women's grassroots organizations that sprang up as a result of the International Year on Women and the Asia Women's Association headed by the late Matsui Yayori had just that year formed the Network to Stop the Revision of the Eugenic Protection Law. The network did stop the movement to prohibit abortion. In 1984, the International Meeting on Women and Health was organized by the Women's Global Network for Reproductive Rights in Amsterdam. In 1987 we organized a similar conference in Japan entitled Starting from a Female Body (*Watashi/onna no karada kara*). Although at the time we did not use the term *reproductive rights*, the conference was about reproductive freedom. Already at that time we debated about the language of *rights*, and women were split on the issue. Many felt that *rights* might not be the appropriate language, because many women who aborted did not really have a choice.

How was Soshiren formed?

Abortion has been technically illegal in Japan under Article 26 of the Criminal Code since 1880. The 1948 Eugenic Protection Law provided conditions whereby abortion could be obtained without criminal charges. Essentially, under eugenics thinking, "undesirable" people should not have children; maternal protection also became part of that law. The first conservative movement to remove one of the conditions—the economic reasons clause—for abortion while adding a new condition allowing the abortion of fetuses with disabilities within the Eugenic Protection Law occurred in 1972. Of course the economic reasons clause accounted for 98 percent of all abortions by Japanese women; removing it de facto made abortion illegal. It was the height of the women's liberation movement in Japan then, and the opposition from both women's groups and disability groups was strong. The revision never took place. In 1982, when there was another conservative move to once again remove the economic reasons clause, Soshiren (which was the Japanese abbreviation for the Network to Stop the Revision of the Eugenic Protection Law) was formed to halt the revision, and we were once again successful.

Who pushed for the revision of the Eugenic Protection Law?

In 1982, there was a *mizuko* (literally "children of the waters," or aborted fetuses) boom in Japan. The general population was declining, so pro-life religious groups like Seichō No Ie (Truth of Life) were vocal against abortion, citing that women who aborted were "selfish," and so on. The conservative movement was largely pushed by these groups who had strong influence on the dominant Liberal Democratic Party.

How about now? What issues does Soshiren focus on?

In the late 1980s a member of our group attended an international meeting on in-vitro fertilization (IVF) technology organized by the Feminist International Network Against Reproductive and Genetic Engineering. After that, in 1990, Soshiren organized a symposium on IVF. Although those of us at Soshiren clearly saw IVF as continuous medicalization of the woman's body and were hence against IVF and reproductive technology in general, our critiques were somewhat softened as we realized that there were women who wanted

IVF. In December 2004 we organized a symposium on the commodification of women's eggs. The Japanese government is very enthusiastic about stem cell research, and researchers need eggs and stem cells from aborted fetuses for that purpose. Unlike in the United States, where the antiabortion groups are also anticloning, in Japan we are pro-choice but anticloning. The debates around the ethics of cloning have become very complicated. Many medical researchers have been pushing for stem cell research. Some scholars who oppose this have argued for restrictions on abortion so that aborted fetuses would be less readily available. Although we are also anticloning, we want to draw a line between ourselves, who fight for women's reproductive freedoms, and those academics.

So is Soshiren against all reproductive technology?

Fundamentally, we are against reproductive technology, but we don't want to oppose women who want to use it. There are a few infertility self-help groups in Japan, including Finrrage no kai (FINRRAGE: Feminist International Network of Resistance to Reproductive and Genetic Engineering), where debates about reproductive technology take place. Some Japanese couples go overseas for solutions, because surrogate mothers are still prohibited in Japan. We know that most obstetricians and gynecologists in Japan are in favor of reproductive technology. Other groups are split. Some patient groups are close to the position of doctors, while some self-help groups are more skeptical about medical opinion. What we are against is the lack of public debate and discussion on issues of reproductive technology within the Ministry of Health, Labor, and Welfare's committee on cloning. We are also worried that the power hierarchy between doctors and users in Japan is so big that it might be difficult for uninformed users to say no to doctors.

What is new about the 1996 Mother's Body Protection Law, which replaced the Eugenic Protection Law?

In this new law, the word *eugenics* (the purpose of which is to prevent the birth of unhealthy fetuses) and the list of conditions for abortion were removed. Since then, only physical or economic reasons and rape became the conditions under which abortion is allowed. However, abortion remains criminalized, and we can't say that women's reproductive rights are guaranteed. On the other hand, because of developments in prenatal diagnosis, it is a reality that people obtain abortion on the basis of "economic reasons" when they identify fetal disorder. This can be considered discrimination against fetuses with disability, and disability groups have launched a movement to prohibit abortion due to fetal disorder in the Disability Anti-Discrimination Bill. There is certainly the fact and history that women with disability have not been allowed to give birth. It is natural that those women claim their right to give birth, but I think the problem is that perspectives on freedom not to give birth are not taken into consideration. What if they would like to abort? In addition, while I personally do not agree with abortion based on fetal disorder (selective abortion), I think the idea that it should be prohibited in the law is dangerous. So I have been participating in a group discussion on the Disability Anti-Discrimination Bill.

What are your preoccupations now concerning the reproductive health and rights movement in Japan?

Our ultimate goal is complete decriminalization of abortion in Japan. Right now the conservative movement is very strong in Japan. One of the most vocal Diet members against abortion is Yamatani Eriko. She preaches abstinence-only sex education. In May 2002, the thirty-two-page *Love and Body Book*—a textbook using a reproductive rights and health perspective that we really welcomed—was designed by the Mothers' and Children's Health and Welfare Association, a privately funded organization supervised by the Health, Labor, and Welfare Ministry. Although more than one million copies were freely distributed to middle school students in Japan, Yamatani Eriko was one of those who vehemently critiqued "radical sex education" in the Diet. In August 2002 the association had to put inserts into the booklet, clarifying that "the best way to avoid these troubles (disease infection and unwanted pregnancy) is to refrain from having sex." The distribution of the *Love and Body Book* was stopped, and unwanted copies were destroyed. In Japan now, the backlash on the movement to legalize abortion and promote sex education and gender-equal education is strong. I think this is synchronized with both a wider backlash in the world and a conservative movement within Japan to revise the constitution and restore the state and the "standard family" as the basic unit at the expense of individual freedoms. We strongly oppose this and work to stop this movement.

Related Web Sites

Article 29 of the Criminal Code, prohibiting abortion, www.soshiren.org/shiryou/
   dataizai.html

Eugenic Protection Law of 1948: http://www.soshiren.org/shiryou/yuseihogohou
    .html; replaced by Mother's Body Protection Law in 1996: http://www.soshiren
    .org/shiryou/botaihogohou.html
FINRRAGE: Feminist International Network of Resistance to Reproductive and
    Genetic Engineering: http://www5c.biglobe.ne.jp/%7Efinrrage
Professional Women's Coalition for Sexuality and Health: http://square.umin.ac.jp/
    pwcsh/englishhome.htm
Seichō No Ie Japan: http://www.snitruth.org
Soshiren: http://www.soshiren.org
Yamatani Eriko: http://www.yamatani-eriko.com/message/index.html

Related References

Ashino, Yuriko. 2001. "Reproductive Health / Rights: The Present Situation of Japan
    and Its Problems." Tokyo: Women's Online Media. Available at http://wom-jp
    .org/e/JWOMEN/repro.html
Katō, Masae. 2005. *Women's Right? Social Movements, Abortion, and Eugenics in
    Modern Japan.* Leiden, the Netherlands: Leiden University.
Norgren, Tiana. 2001. *Abortion Before Birth Control: The Politics of Reproduction in
    Postwar Japan.* Princeton: Princeton University Press.
Ōhashi, Yukako. 1997. "Umu umanai wa watashi ga kimeru" [I decide whether to give
    birth]. In *Nihon no feminism 5 bosei* [Japanese feminism 5 motherhood], edited
    by Teruko Inoue, Chizuko Ueno, and Ehara Yumiko. Tokyo: Iwanami Shoten.
Ōhashi, Yukako. 1998. "Ekkyōsuru" [Transgressing the Border]. In *Gender de
    manabu shakaigaku* [Learning sociology through gender], edited by Kimio Ito
    and Kazue Muta. Kyoto: Sekai Shisō Sha.
Ōhashi, Yukako. 2001. *Karada no kimochi wo kīte miyō* [Let's listen to our bodily
    feelings]. Tokyo: Yukkusha.
Ōhashi, Yukako. 2003. "Umu umanai wa watashi ga kimeru soshite undemo umana-
    kutemo watashi wa watashi" [I decide whether to give birth and I am me whether
    I give birth or not]. In *Yūseihogohō ga okashita tsumi* [Crimes committed by the
    Eugenic Protection Law], edited by Yūsei shujutsu ni taisuru shazai wo motomeru
    kai [Committee asking for apology for eugenic surgery]. Tokyo: Gendai Shokan.
Saito, Yukiko. 2002. *Botai hogohō to watashitachi* [The Mother's Body Protection
    Law and us]. Tokyo: Akashi Shoten.
Takenobu, Mieko. 2004. "Bashing Gender Equality: Establishing a System That
    Skews the Population on All Sides." Available at http://www.ppjaponesia.org/
    modules/tinycontent/index.php?id=9

31

AS A LESBIAN FEMINIST IN JAPAN

Wakabayashi Naeko

WAKABAYASHI NAEKO is a member of Regumi Studio Tokyo, Japan's first lesbian group aimed at broadening the lesbian network in Japan. Born in 1947 in Tokyo, Wakabayashi began to get involved in the women's liberation movement in 1970. From 1975 to 1976 she worked at the Feminist Women's Health Center in Oakland, California, as a health counselor. She also organized a self-help clinic in Japan from 1976 to 1982.

How did you become involved in the women's movement in Japan?

In 1970, I read an article in the newspaper about a women's liberation demonstration in Ginza, Tokyo, by members of Group Tatakau Onna (Fighting Women). They put up a sign that said, "Mother, are you happy in your marriage?" I felt a strong sympathy because my mother had a hard time in her marriage and I did not want to live like her. That was my first occasion to think about sexual discrimination. I did participate in some anti–Vietnam War activities while I was in college. At the time there were ideas but not yet a movement about women's liberation. After I finished college, the women's liberation movement in Japan was in full bloom. I was very much attracted to the idea of questioning the system of marriage and family. But back thirty-some years ago, the norm for women was to get married, and it seemed like a radical idea for women not to marry and to live independently. In addition, I had polio when I was one year old and I received a lot of care from my parents. It was extremely difficult for me to leave home. But at the age of twenty-four I ran away from home with my younger sister. That was the beginning of independent living for me.

When did you begin your lesbian activities in Japan?

When I was part of the women's liberation movement, I was not aware of the fact that I was a lesbian. I was conscious about sex discrimination, but I had prejudice against lesbians, both because I had no lesbian friends around me and because the media portrayed a negative image of lesbians. When I was twenty-seven, I went to the United States. I became a member of the Feminist Women's Health Center and worked at a women's choice clinic as a health counselor who provided gynecological services, including abortion. There were many lesbian staff members and I shared a house with two lesbian women by chance. I think this work and living experience changed my consciousness about lesbianism. I fell in love with a woman for the first time there and I felt so happy. Toward the end of my stay I traveled for two months in the United States, including giving a talk at the University of Michigan on the Japanese women's liberation movement. I was twenty-eight when I first had a sexual relationship with an American woman and felt that I was a lesbian. When I returned to Japan, the lesbian movement had just begun to take shape. Several lesbians got together and published the book *Subarashii onnatachi* [Wonderful women]. I organized the women's self-help clinic and helped to spread the women's health movement in Japan. I learned how to use the speculum in the United States, and in turn shared my experiences in Japan. In 1982, six other women and I published a book called *Onnatachi no [Women's] Rhythms/Menstruation: Messages from Our Bodies.* I wanted to work on women's health and lesbian issues, but it was difficult. In order to have some economic stability, I opened my own natural foods store while continuing my lesbian activities.

Could you tell me some of your activities at Regumi?

In 1985 we did a workshop on lesbian issues at the International Feminist Conference held at the National Women's Education Center in Saitama, Japan. After that workshop, the lesbians decided to hold a lesbian-only conference in November 1985. We used the name The International Women's Conference (*Kokusai Josei Kaigi*) to reserve the place, but it was a lesbian conference, with half Japanese and half international participants. This gathering has continued for twenty years and contributes to creating a lesbian network in Japan. In 1986 I was invited to the eighth International Lesbian Conference in Geneva. Asian lesbians from Thailand, Bangladesh, India, Japan, and the United States created an Asian lesbian network. Until then, the International Lesbian Conference was mostly dominated by white Anglo-European lesbians. Regumi

Studio Tokyo (the first lesbian office in Japan) was started in 1987 to broaden the lesbian network in Japan. In 1990, the first Asian Lesbian Network (ALN) conference was held in Bangkok, and it was a memorable meeting for me. Two years later, in 1992, we organized the second ALN conference in Japan. There were more than 140 participants.

What were some of the issues encountered in the second ALN conference?

After the first ALN conference, we had a serious discussion on who the members of ALN are. Asian lesbians who live in the West and face racism insisted on an Asian-only space. However, many Asian lesbians from Asia who live in very isolated situations wanted to keep the connection with and get support from Western lesbians who live in Asia. We managed to hold Asian-only plenary sessions and workshops while parties were mixed at the second ALN conference. It worked out fine. Many attendants from other Asian countries spoke English because they had studied in Western countries (many were more than middle class), but many Japanese did not speak English. Many Japanese have an inferiority complex vis-à-vis the North Americans and Europeans, but a superiority complex vis-à-vis the Asians. At that time, many of us did not know about lesbian issues in Asia. There was an embarrassing incident, when the emcee introduced only "Japanese lesbians." A *Zainichi* (Korean resident) lesbian was ignored.

And now, what are the preoccupations of Regumi as a lesbian group?

I think our first priority is to create a lesbian network in Japan. Still, the prejudice and the discrimination against lesbians are strong, and many are living in the closet. For the past eighteen years we have been publishing a monthly newsletter in which lesbians can express our feelings freely. Otherwise, we want some basic legal rights as lesbians. For example, because a lesbian couple is not recognized legally as a family, we can't live together in public housing and don't have hospital visitation and inheritance rights and so on. We do not see a big demand for the recognition of lesbian marriage in Japan because of the difficulties of coming out. I personally doubt the marriage system, but I think we need the legal recognition of same-sex partnership. In Japan there are few feminist lesbians, so it is not always easy to merge the two perspectives—sexual and homophobic discrimination.

Related Web Sites

Groups for Asian / Pacific Lesbian / Bisexual Women: http://www.geocities.com/
    WestHollywood/Heights/5010/wgroups.html#japan
Lesbians of Undeniable Drive: http://www.space-loud.org/loud/modules/english1
Regumi Studio Tokyo: http://regumi.sakura.ne.jp/index.html
Tokyo Lesbian and Gay Parade: http://parade.tokyo-pride.org/6th/english

Related References

Chalmers, Sharon. 2002. *Emerging Lesbian Voices from Japan*. London and New
    York: Routledge Curzon.
Izumo, Marou, and Claire Maree. 2001. *Love Upon the Chopping Board*. Melbourne,
    Australia: Spinifex Press.

32

SEX WORKERS' MOVEMENT IN JAPAN

Kaname Yukiko

KANAME YUKIKO is founder and board member of Sex Workers and Sexual Health, which supports sex workers in Japan. Born in Osaka in 1976, her published works include *Fūzokujō ishiki chōsa hōkokusho* [Report of attitude survey on women working in the sex industry] and two coauthored books, *Uru uranai wa watashi ga kimeru* [I decide whether to sell or not] and *Sei wo saikō suru* [Rethinking sex].

How did you become involved in the sex workers' movement in Japan?

In 1999, a sex worker was arrested by the police at a bar in Ikebukuro. The policeman was very condescending and kept saying to her, "Is this the only thing you can do?" After the incident, I thought that the only way to improve the working conditions of sex workers was for them to speak out as sex workers, just like sex workers have done elsewhere in the world.

Why was Sex Work and Sexual Health (SWASH) created?

SWASH was created in Kyoto in 1999, and then the Tokyo branch was established by both sex workers and supporters. We have three main goals: creating a safe working environment in terms of health, eliminating discrimination against sex workers, and international networking. For example, we participated in the Asian Sex Workers Conference as well as in the international AIDS conference. In terms of activities, we conduct study meetings, for example, on sexually transmitted diseases (STDs) and HIV / AIDS. We exchange information and create pamphlets on STDs and HIV, which we put in sex workers' magazines and on the Internet. We co-organize events with gay sex workers. We also have a consultation desk, where we handle one to two cases per week. We meet in cafés, go to movies and drinking parties, and offer massage to one other as a way of support. When the members bring their children to our meetings, we take turns babysitting. The key for us is empowerment and community building.

What are some of the issues that sex workers confront in Japan?

Because prostitution is illegal in Japan, we work under the constant fear of being caught. If we could register in a legal way, this would not happen. In Japan, labor unions are weak, and the issue of sex work has not received any attention from them, so our working conditions are not safeguarded. For example, when we do not receive proper payment from our clients, we have little recourse. Another issue is sex education. Recent conservative political trends have made it very difficult to teach about sex in schools. The Minato Ward Office in Tokyo, for example, prepared a pamphlet on condom use, but it could not be distributed to middle and high schools, because the board of education considered it "too radical" and "expressive." I think there is not enough information in schools, in particular for girls in middle school. They often begin sex work too early.

What is the relationship between the sex workers' movement and the women's movement in Japan?

In the history of the women's movement in Japan, the emphasis was on women's liberation. Sex workers were not considered part of it. One might say that the women's movement has been antisex. There is a generation gap as well. Some older feminists are against sex work. They show no understanding of our movement, and they believe that society would be better without the sex industry. For these feminists, the sex industry equals sexual discrimination. Their moral position ignores the practical reality of the needs and rights of the sex workers themselves. Younger activists are more supportive of our movement. Our goal is not to get rid of the sex industry but to improve its working conditions. I think empowerment of sex workers in Japan is important, and I think change needs to come from the perspective of the marginalized.

Do you work with foreign sex workers in Japan?

We actually do not. SWASH has only Japanese members. The main issue is language. We don't have the capacity to provide assistance to them. In Japan, shelters like HELP (Housing in Emergency of Love and Peace) take care of foreign sex workers. But shelters do not have a positive opinion of sex workers. For example, in the current campaign to ban human trafficking to Japan, sex workers are considered victims who need to be protected.

What kind of policy change does SWASH advocate?

We want to overturn the Prostitution Prohibition Law (1956) because it discriminates against the intercourse-service industry. Sex workers are not bad women, and we do not need protection from the government. What we want is recognition as workers, and our basic rights.

What do you think of the recent peace rallies against the war in Iraq?

I think the actions of the recent peace coalitions are too soft. I mean they are not very strategic. It is we who chose Koizumi, after all, and we bear that responsibility. I am not sure how many protesters think about this. I think our actions need to be strategically based on public opinion. I am against constitutional revision, but I am afraid that the Japanese leftist movement is powerless. The issue is what we need to do to make change happen. Ideology alone is not sufficient. Our actions need to be more professional, if you will, and focus on specific results.

Related Web Sites

Asia Pacific Network of Sex Workers: http://apnsw.org/apnsw.htm
Network of Sex Work Projects: http://www.nswp.org
Sex Work and Sexual Health (SWASH): http://www.geocities.jp/swashhp/index.html

Related References

Kaname, Yukiko. 2003. "Sekkusu wāku to iu mondai teiki: sekkusu wāku to jinken" [From the viewpoint of sex work: Sex work and human rights]. In *Sei wo saikō suru: sei no tayōsei gairon* [Rethinking sex: A conceptual analysis of sexual diversity], edited by Hideo Hashimoto, Hanatate Tsuyoshi, and Shimazu Takeo. Tokyo: Sekyusha.

Kempadoo, Kamala, and Jo Doezema, eds. 1998. *Global Sex Workers: Rights, Resistance, and Redefinition*. New York: Routledge.

Nohno, Chieko. 2004. *Sei dōitsu sei shōgaisha seibetsu toriatsukai tokureihō* [On the special law on sexual difference treatment for gender identity disorder]. Tokyo: Kajo.

33

WOMEN'S ACTIVE MUSEUM ON WAR AND PEACE

Watanabe Mina

WATANABE MINA is secretary-general of Women's Active Museum on War and Peace. Born in 1970 and graduated from International Christian University in Tokyo, she has been involved in various women's movements since the 1990s. She is currently involved in preserving the documents and testimonies of "comfort women," and in organizing actions to end violence against women in conflict situations.

Could you tell me about the Women's Active Museum on War and Peace (WAM) project?

The museum was the idea of the late Matsui Yayori, a feminist journalist who had consistently fought against violence against women in Japan and Asia until her death in 2002. Yayori used to say that she had given her life for the Women's International War Crimes Tribunal on Japan's Military Sexual Slavery, which had been held in Tokyo in 2000 to end the cycle of impunity for wartime sexual violence. To prepare for this people's court, massive amounts of material were collected, including relevant documents of the Japanese military, and testimonies of the victimized women and perpetrating soldiers. After the tribunal, a space was needed in which to keep these records and open them to the public, especially because the reference to "comfort women" had been taken out of Japanese junior high history textbooks. An effort to remember and pass on to others the experience of the victimized women itself is a struggle now. We launched the project in December 2002, and we opened the museum in the summer of 2005, the year marking the sixtieth year after the end of World War II. Just before the opening, we decided to add the word *active* to the name of the museum so that the finalized official name now is the Women's Active Museum on War and Peace. Because we wanted to make clear that WAM is not a static museum, only for exhibitions, but an action center as well, in order to realize justice for the survivors of Japan's military sexual slavery (also known as the "comfort women" system), and at last to eliminate violence against women in armed conflicts and around where armed forces are throughout the world today.

Why is it important to document history from the perspectives of women who have suffered sexual violence?

If you look at the real history of Japan during World War II, you will find that between 1932 and 1945, tens of thousands of women were sent throughout Asia to serve Japanese soldiers; young women and girls were taken from their homes and sent to "comfort stations," where they were raped every day. Upon its defeat, the Japanese military gave order to burn in secret most of their documents related to possible war crimes prosecution, including the sexual slavery system. Now, these facts are not recorded in the official male history. A history without gender perspective, without women's voices, is not whole but covers only half of the population. We need to pass on to the future generations the whole story, so that they will be able to learn from them and not repeat the same mistakes. In terms of Japan's military sexual slavery, the research to find and keep a full picture of the system has to be done urgently, because those who experienced it firsthand are now dying one by one. Much has to be done to hear and record the experience of the victimized, the perpetrator, and the eye witness wherever the Japanese military were, and to do full research into what is left of the official documents of the time. History has long remained silent about wartime sexual slavery, because the women who suffered it have been forced to stay silent. The survivors of Japan's military sexual slavery broke this historical silence. They have been struggling so that no other women will have to suffer what they have suffered. The record of their struggle is also part of history, which we want to pass on.

I see that you wear many hats. Could you tell me some of your other activities?

Besides being a staff member for WAM, I continue to be an active member of three other women's groups: the Violence Against Women in War–Network

Japan, the Asian Women's Resource Center, and Video Juku (a feminist group that produces video documentary for gender justice). Please have a look at their Web sites for detailed information. These three groups actively support the WAM too. I am also involved in two campaigns right now: one concerning a lawsuit against Tokyo governor Ishihara Shintarō, the other with a women's group on nonpartisan electoral campaigns.

In fall 2001, Ishihara said in an interview with *Shūkan Josei*, a weekly magazine for women, "Old women who live after they have lost their reproductive function are useless and sinful. (Men have reproductive functions even in their eighties and their nineties; however, women cannot bear children after they reach their menopause. It is said that it is evil and malicious for the world that these people live until the age of Kinsan and Ginsan [famous twin sisters who lived over one hundred years of age]. . . . I agree with the idea but cannot say it as a politician.)" One hundred and thirty-one women in Japan stood up and filed a lawsuit against Mr. Ishihara because this is an extreme form of verbal violence against women, made by an influential politician. We lost the lawsuit on technical grounds, but he has again made the same kind of remark, against which we'll file another lawsuit. We won't give up until he apologizes and retracts discriminatory remarks.

The other campaign, called *Josei ga kaeru: senkyo kyanpēn* (Women to Bring Change: Electoral Campaign), started originally to say no to the male members of Parliament (MPs) who made sexist remarks. But negative campaigns are prohibited in Japan by public office election law. So we ran a survey instead and researched how the MPs had been working in the Diet, and we provided our findings through the Internet. You know, in Japan lawmakers do not draft laws, administrators do it for them! Through these actions we learned more about our electoral system and found that the law was for politicians, not for people. We published a booklet, "Take Back the Election into People's Hands!" I think people in the United States should also question the presidential election system in order to make change.

As a young feminist, what are some of the issues that you face in feminist organizing in Japan?

I have been involved in women's movements in Japan for a decade now. For me personally, I don't find much of a generation gap now, and I enjoy working with some of the older feminists. It is hard to generalize, because the experience and wisdom of each feminist differs. When I was younger, one of the problems I faced was that there were only young women and old women, no age in between. A major reason why there is an age vacuum in the middle is that only young people can afford to have a lower salary or volunteer for tremendous amounts of work. The problem for the women's movement in Japan is the lack of money to keep experienced persons as paid staff. The money should be paid according to the quality of work, but it is not realistic yet. Women's NGOs that focus on changing Japanese society rarely receive support from the government, and receive no tax reduction and no foreign funds, because Japan is regarded as a rich country.

Do you see a kind of renewal of the Japanese Left through the recent social activism on peace and other issues?

I think there is a wide spectrum of NGOs and NPOs, from the ideological Left to those who are concerned but don't think very much about ideology. I think these groups need to network and become a political mass in order to change the increasingly militarized government. But right now I don't think there is a common platform among them yet. Another challenge for the Left is to reach out to the general public in Japan. Yes, there are demonstrations, but as long as the average Japanese does not have access to alternative media and information, I wonder how effective the renewed social movements can be. The Japanese media as a whole is in a miserable state now. It is not functioning as a watchdog against power and authority as it should, but is rather acting like their pet. This was symbolically shown in the case of the television program about the Women's Tribunal 2000. NHK (Nippon Hōsō Kyōkai, or the Japan Broadcasting Corporation) distorted their program severely because of the pressure put on them by top politicians. Even the other media corporations did not question the intimate relationship between the public media and politics. I have a feeling that how the civil society in this country might actually manage alternative media for people may be a key to the social movement in Japan from now on.

Related Web Sites

Asia-Japan Women's Resource Center: http://www.ajwrc.org/english/index.html
Center for Research and Documentation on Japan's War Responsibility: http://space
.geocities.jp/japanwarres/center/english/index-english.htm
Korean Council for the Women Drafted for Military Sexual Slavery by Japan: http://
www.womenandwar.net/english/menu_01.php

Video Juku: http://www.jca.apc.org/video-juku/index-eng.html

Violence Against Women in War—Network Japan: http://www1.jca.apc.org/
vaww-net-japan/english

Women's Active Museum on War and Peace: http://www.wam-peace.org/eng

Women's Caucus for Gender Justice: http://www.iccwomen.org/wigjdraft1/Archives/
oldWCGJ/index.html

Related References

Asian Centre for Women's Human Rights. 2000. *From the Depths of Silence: Voices of
Women Survivors of War.* Quezon City, the Philippines: Asian Centre for Wom-
en's Human Rights.

Berndt, Caroline M. 1997. "Popular Culture as Political Power: Writing the Reality of
Sexual Slavery." *Journal of Popular Culture, 31*(2), 177–187.

Boling, David. 1995. "Mass Rape, Enforced Prostitution, and the Japanese Imperial
Army: Japan Eschews Legal Responsibility?" *Columbia Journal of International
Law, 32,* 533–590.

Chinkin, Christine. 1994. "Rape and Sexual Abuse of Women in International Law."
European Journal of International Law, 15(3). Available at http://www.ejil.org/
journal/Vol5/No3/art2.html#TopOfPage

Cho, Sangmie, ed. 2000. *Comfort Women Speak: Testimony by Sex Slaves of the
Japanese Military.* New York: Schellstede Hornes and Meir.

Coomaraswamy, Radhika. 1997. "Reinventing International Law: Women's Rights
as Human Rights in the International Community." Edward A. Smith Visiting
Lecturer Human Rights Program, Harvard Law School, September.

Dolgopol, Ustina. 1995. "Women's Voices, Women's Pain." *Human Rights Quarterly, 17*(1), 127–154. Available at http://muse.jhu.edu/journals/human_rights_
quarterly/toc/human_rights_quarterlyv017.html

Dudden, Alexis. 2001. "'We Came to Tell the Truth': Reflections on the Tokyo
Women's Tribunal." *Critical Asian Studies, 33*(4), 591–602.

34

ART, FEMINISM, AND ACTIVISM

Shimada Yoshiko

SHIMADA YOSHIKO is an artist and founder of Feminist Art Action Brigade. Born in Tokyo in 1959, she graduated in humanities and studio art from Scripps College in Claremont, California, in 1982. She has produced a series of etchings concerning war and women based on historical photographs. Since then she has expanded her media into installation, video, and performance. She lectures and exhibits worldwide, including in Europe, North America, and Asia.

How would you describe your work as an artist?

I think I am most influenced by conceptual art from the 1970s, and I consider my work to be conceptual art. That is, my work is not just for art's sake. It is not about making a beautiful object, although I do not totally discard the notion of beauty. For me, art is a means to explore the relationship between the surrounding world and myself.

Why did you create the Feminist Art Action Brigade (FAAB) in Japan?

There was or still is a feminist art organization in Japan called the Women's Art Network, of which I am not a member, although I am on their mailing list. I was somewhat frustrated about the relative inactivity of the group. It was around the time of the war in Afghanistan, and then later the war in Iraq, that I proposed to a group of artists, scholars, and curators to set up the FAAB to engage seriously in social issues and actually do something together. Some members of the Women's Art Network joined us. Since 2002 we have done some war protest group art shows, collaborations with Women in Black Tokyo (part of an international women's peace activist group), and a group exhibition with women artists from South Korea. But several problems arose. First, many of my artist friends declined to join us because they did not want to associate themselves with some kind of old-fashioned, dogmatic, and out-dated feminists. Most of the members are academics and museum staff people rather than artists. Second, some artists who joined thought that FAAB would be some sort of a self-help fraternity. They did not always understand the professional requirements of exhibition work. Third, a big issue was fundraising. It strikes me as odd that many Japanese women would be willing to spend one hundred thousand yen (or about $1,000) for a brand-name bag while they are hesitant to donate a thousand yen to our group. Finally, many women remain observers rather than participants.

How do you see the relationship between art, feminism, and resistance?

Recently I have been thinking that art is not for resistance. I don't think feminism is for resistance either. When we talk about resistance, we have to ask the question, *Resistance against what?* In Japan in 2005 we do not have a clear enemy. I think having a clear enemy itself is a false notion. We are not in the 1960s anymore. Our lives and world politics have become much more complicated. In my opinion, we cannot simply blame men, authority, and the capitalists. In some sense, the enemy is within us. Art makes people think of this complicated situation. Art can show people where they are in relation to this world and make them see it from a completely new viewpoint. Feminism gives hope to this impossible situation. I don't think feminism is anti-something. The aim of feminism is to make some difference in this rigid system of hierarchy, but not in a violent, destructive way. I make art with this feminist conviction.

You recently organized an international symposium on diaspora and art, focusing on the Korean diaspora, in Tokyo, November 2004. What were your motivations? Do you see a connection between art and minority rights, in particular in Japan?

I was one of the organizers of the art exhibition and artist talk section. I thought art can provide a new way of viewing the diaspora issue instead of sticking to the old binary of Japanese versus Korean residents in Japan. I also wanted to show some of the young Korean residents' artworks to a wider audience. I have worked with Korean minority women in making a family-photograph art project. It was worthwhile bringing out the experiences of the Korean minority to a majority audience. But somehow I felt that it remained within the cliché of "minority women sad stories." I tried to provoke the majority audience by including my own family's relationship to Koreans, but most of the majority audience remains silent, or they just consume the sad but not unsettling old stories. Perhaps my visual language was not strong enough to provoke thoughts. I was unsure of what I could have done better with the stories by the minority women. As an artist and as a Japanese, I did not want to make their narrative just material for my work. It would be too arrogant. But on the other hand, I was too afraid to change anything they provided in order to make the whole work more convincing. I thought it would be better if it was done by the minority women artists themselves. But there are very few minority women artists in Japan. There may be some, but most do not get to be shown in major venues. I wanted to encourage a younger generation of artists who have fresher artistic language to tell their stories. There is, for example, a third-generation Korean woman artist whose work I really like. I want her to be better known, more successful. But I found out recently that some older generation Korean women criticized this young artist because she used both her Korean and Japanese names. While it might be natural for a third-generation Korean woman to feel both Korean and Japanese, the older generation thinks that it is a sell-out. She was even accused of exploiting her ethnicity to become famous. I think there is a lot of power play between generations when it comes to minority and diasporic relations. The older generations might think they are the ones who possess the "right" identity. Another issue that emerged in the aftermath of the symposium on diaspora and art was the difficulty in maintaining dialogue with some older Korean residents in Japan. Considering the past and present discrimination inflicted by Japanese, I can perfectly understand their reluctance to have dialogue with me concerning their identity. I was simply hoping that art could become a means to bridge a minority and majority audience.

What, according to you, is the relationship between art and activism?

When I talk about art and activism, I do not make art from the viewpoint of the oppressed or the victimized. I make art to make the oppressors think of what they do from where they are. But there is no clear borderline between the oppressors and the oppressed anymore. When the line was clear, it might have had meaning to make art of resistance, but I don't think it works anymore.

You have worked on the "comfort women" issue through your art production. Could you tell me more about that and about your feelings about war issues in Japan today?

I did not intend to make artwork about the comfort women. It was about us, the Japanese women who turned a blind eye to the issue for a half a century after the war. What have we been seeing all this time? What can we say to these women? These were questions I tried to ask my audience. Of course a part of it was to make people aware of the issue itself, because it was not widely publicized in the world as it is now, but it was not my main point. Previous to this work I made a series of prints depicting Japanese women's participation in the war. I wanted to make them rethink the existing image of women and war, women as victims, women as peace-loving mothers, and so on. Now the situation has gotten a lot worse. People in Japan are even less informed about the war issues, and they do not seem to care to think.

Do you see art as a means of educating the public about a variety of global, regional, and local issues? Could you give me some concrete examples?

I think art can be an educational tool, but it is only a small part. The problem with activists is that they think art is just a tool to illustrate the existing problems. As illustration, they want it to be simple, black and white. They also value the issues and problems depicted there more than the artwork itself. Sometimes they value the works only because they are made by the victimized themselves. This may sound awfully arrogant but art made by a person who has suffered does not automatically make it good art. Good art needs to have the power to unsettle people, to make them rethink and question the existing world order. In order to do so, it must reach a certain level of beauty (or ugliness) to attract attention. If one has to know the background of the artist beforehand in order to appreciate a piece of artwork, the artwork at hand is speaking only to the converted.

Japanese popular art has attracted a large following in the West. What is your reading of that?

Japanese popular culture and visual art, including design, *manga*, *anime*, and pop art, have been very popular overseas in the past decade. In recent years, governmental cultural institutions are increasingly supportive of them. Like the "Cool Britannia" campaign in the United Kingdom, Japan is promoting "Japanese cool." Because this "J-pop" is a product of the highly developed capitalist and consumerist society, it is very easy for them to get corporate as well as government support. After a decade of recession, public funding has been cut from cultural institutions. Now many of the museums have no money to put together exhibitions without corporate support. Therefore, most of the public and private support goes to J-pop, leaving other artistic expressions, especially minority cultural expression, almost totally without support.

Related Web Sites

Feminist Art Action Brigade: http://home.interlink.or.jp/reflect/FAAB/index.html
Frontiers of Gender Studies, Ochanomizu Women's University: http://www.igs.ocha.ac.jp/f-gens/index_e.html
n.paradoxa (international feminist art journal): http://web.ukonline.co.uk/n.paradoxa
Ota Fine Arts gallery: http://www.otafinearts.com
Women in Black Tokyo: http://home.interlink.or.jp/reflect/WIBTokyo/home.html

Related References

Kitahara, Megumi. 1999. *Art Activism*. Tokyo: Impact.
Kō, Fua-Jon. 2004. "Bunka to teikō" [Art and resistance]. *Zenya*, 1 (Founding Issue), 2–3.
Lloyd, Fran, ed. 2002. *Consuming Bodies: Sex and Contemporary Japanese Art*. London: Reaction Press.
Pollock, Griselda, ed. 1996. *Generation and Geographies*. New York: Routledge.
Shimada, Yoshiko. 2000. "Defining Experiences: Feminist Exhibitions in the 1990s. A Response from Yoshiko Shimada." *n.paradoxa*, 13. Available at http://web.ukonline.co.uk/n.paradoxa/define.htm

PART VII

MINORITY AND HUMAN RIGHTS

FIGURE 7. Diversity in Japan T-shirt by Issho Kikaku at the World Conference Against Racism, Racial Discrimination, Xenophobia, and Related Intolerance NGO Forum, Durban, South Africa, August 2001

INTRODUCTION TO PART VII

THE HOMOGENEOUS-NATION MYTH remains strong in Japan. As late as October 2005, Japanese Minister of Foreign Affairs Aso Taro remarked that Japan is a monoethnic nation-state. What makes it difficult for social movement groups to mobilize are not only the enormous domestic political challenges and low public consciousness, but also the lack of institutionalization of minority rights norms at the international level. Whether it pertains to indigenous peoples' rights (Ainu and Okinawan), caste (Buraku), or reparations for colonialization (Koreans, Taiwanese, and Chinese), the absence of a specific human rights convention means that it is difficult for social movement groups to rally around a global human rights frame to push for domestic political change. In other areas of minority rights—refugees, torture, the death penalty, and migrant workers—existing international human rights instruments are either weak or mostly ignored by the Japanese state.

Since the 1990s, various minority rights NGO coalitions have been formed within Japan, often around a specific world conference or human rights convention. The first minority rights network—NGO Liaison Group for the World Conference on Human Rights—emerged in 1992 to prepare for the Vienna conference in 1993. The Japan Citizens' Coalition for the UN International Decade of the World's Indigenous People was also formed the same year to monitor the decade's activities. In 1997, a network of eighty-seven NGOs formed the Solidarity Network with Migrant Workers Japan to lobby for Japan's ratification of the UN Convention on the Rights of Migrants. A minority rights coalition, Durban 2001 Japan, was organized to lobby at the World Conference

Against Racism in Durban. In particular, minority women in Japan, who have been invisible within both the women's and minority movements in Japan, mobilized around the concept of *intersectionality*—"a conceptualization of the problem that attempts to capture both the structural and dynamic consequences of the interaction between two or more axes of subordination . . . [and] specifically addresses the manner in which racism, patriarchy, class oppression and other discriminatory systems create background inequalities that structure the relative positions of women, races, ethnicities, classes, and the like."[1] In the 2003 NGO Alternative Report on the Fourth and Fifth Periodic Reports of Japan to CEDAW, Buraku, Ainu, Okinawan, and Korean as well as migrant women from Japan criticized the inattention of the Japanese government to the specific discriminatory situations of minority women in Japan:

Minority women do exist in Japan, being discriminated against not only on the basis of gender but also of nationality, ethnicity, indigenity, descent, lack of citizenship or documentation, status of migrant worker, asylum-seeker or refugee. Generally speaking, they suffer multiple discrimination with different factors compounded, being socially and economically marginalized, and are faced with more difficulties in almost every aspect of life than both male members of the same group and Japanese women belonging to the majority. Consequently, they are vulnerable to abuse, violence, and exploitation. However, Japan's periodic reports contain hardly any information, neither on the actual situation of minority women who suffer multiple discrimination, nor on measures to protect them from acts contradictory to the treaty provisions, to remedy violations, and to promote their rights and status in the society.[2]

Further, neoliberal globalization, nationalism, and militarism exert a disproportionate impact on minorities in Japanese society. This section groups twelve interviews, beginning with the exploration of an antidiscrimination law in Japan. It moves on to cover international networking on indigenous peoples' rights from Ainu and Okinawan perspectives; Buraku, Korean, and migrant workers' rights; and lobbying for the UN Convention on the Rights of Persons with Disabilities by the Japan Disability Forum. It ends with three largely unknown issues: prisoners' rights, refugees' rights, and the abolition of the death penalty in Japan. Several themes emerge from the discussion. Just like the renewed antiwar movement, the antidiscrimination movement in Japan is a loose coalition of many minority groups that differ in objectives and strategies. Even though the goal may be the same, to create a society for everyone to live in without discrimination, patterns of mobilization vary across groups and networks. Many minority rights NGOs use the UN human rights system strategically by attending the Permanent Forum on Indigenous Issues and the UN Working Group on Indigenous Peoples or by inviting the UN High Commissioner for Human Rights or members of various human rights committees. But they are also keenly aware of the limits of the state-based UN system. Since the World Conference Against Racism in Durban in 2001, NGOs in Japan have become more conscious of multiple discriminations, from the perspectives of race, gender, class, disability, nationality, and so on. As seen in the case of the city of Kawasaki (discussed in Chapter Thirty-Eight), local governments can play a leadership role in the advancement of minority rights. Activists work toward a law on the elimination of racial discrimination, the establishment of a human rights institution independent of the Ministry of Justice, and broad public human rights education. As is true for those involved in the alterglobalization and antiwar movements, antidiscrimination activists recognize the need to create a movement that appeals to the Japanese society.

Notes

1. Crenshaw 2000, 7.
2. http://www.jaiwr.org/jnnc/20030701jnncsummaryreport(en).pdf

35

PROPOSAL FOR A LAW ON THE ELIMINATION OF RACIAL DISCRIMINATION

Fujimoto Mie

FUJIMOTO MIE is a lawyer admitted to the Japanese Bar in 1993 and a board member of the Japan Civil Liberties Union (JCLU). Born in Tokyo in 1967 and a graduate of the University of Tokyo (LL.B., 1991) and University of California, Berkeley (LL.M., 2000), she practices as a corporate law lawyer and participates in research and policy advocacy activities as a member of the JCLU's Subcommittee for the Rights of Foreigners.

How did you become involved in foreigners' rights issues in Japan?

I have been involved in foreigners' rights issues in Japan for the past ten years. When I became a lawyer in 1993, there were a lot of newcomers to Japan from South Asia and Brazil, and we were already seeing some problems emerging. Some of the issues for these newcomers were similar to those for earlier foreign residents from Korea and China, but others, such as bad working conditions, were new. Because many of these foreigners were overstaying their visas, it was hard for them to receive help when they encountered trouble. I used to live in the United States as a young student. I could sympathize with the insecurity that foreigners felt in Japan and I thought I might be able to help. Because I spoke English, I felt I could use my legal skills in a field other than business law. So I joined the Subcommittee for the Rights of Foreigners within the JCLU when I was a legal trainee. As soon as I registered as a lawyer, I joined a group and a hotline, one on criminal cases and the other on civil cases.

Could you tell me about your work in the Subcommittee for the Rights of Foreigners?

The JCLU, formed in 1947, is composed of mainly lawyers and scholars, but with an increasing number of students and other nonlawyers. We are not a lobbying group, but we make legal proposals. When I joined, the subcommittee was working on a proposal on amnesty for foreigners who overstayed their visas. But just around that time the Japanese economy began to stall and the situation got worse. Public opinion about foreigners was not favorable, so we thought it was not a good time to introduce our proposal on amnesty. In 1997 we published a book on the rights of foreign children and, on the occasion of the fiftieth anniversary of JCLU, a white paper on foreigners' rights. Afterward, we started drafting a foreigners' rights ordinance for local governments. We thought we would start with local governments, but the project was suspended. When I left for a year to work on my master of laws degree at Berkeley, only three other members were active in the subcommittee.

Why did the subcommittee begin drafting a proposal for a law on the elimination of racial discrimination?

Japan ratified (with reservations) the International Convention on the Elimination of Racial Discrimination (CERD) in 1996, but the government maintains that there is no need for the passage of new laws on racial discrimination. The Japanese government has been working on setting up a national human rights institution in Japan. We felt that even if the government sets up such an institution, we would still need a substantive law to be applied by that body. Many thought that we drafted this bill because of CERD, but in reality this came as an afterthought. The way we proceeded in drafting our proposal was the following. First, we looked at existing laws overseas and we asked Japanese scholars to talk about their research in this area. For example, we invited a lawyer who worked on an antidiscrimination law on disability (a proposal by Nichibenren, the Japan Federation of Bar Associations, that was not passed as a law). We drafted a first version in March 2003. We published it as a subcommittee proposal and solicited public comments. JCLU is well known for its protection of the freedom of expression, so we knew there would be opposition. Then we drafted the second version, to which we added the actual sections, and published it in August 2004. That's when we really began to get opposition.

What were the main oppositions?

In addition to concerns about the freedom of expression, one objection was concerned with broad criminal sanctions. The opponents feared that such sanctions might be abused, especially if they were imposed on acts such as harassment. Others objected to compulsory measures about discriminatory acts in general. They did not think the national human rights institution should be able to take such measures in areas related to the freedom of expression.

Why do you think a law on the elimination of racial discrimination is necessary in Japan?

Until our proposal, the only legal recourse in Japan for someone who suffers racial discrimination is tort. If it is tort, you can ask for damages, and if the problem continues, you can ask for legal protection so that the other person refrains from his or her acts. But under tort the victim has the burden to bring the case, and the compensation is small. The Japanese government says that the existing law covers racial discrimination. In reality, first, there is no definition on racial discrimination in tort law. Second, the standards applied by our courts are too lenient. Third, racial discrimination in public services, such as employment in public offices, falls outside of existing legal coverage. If we had a law specifically prohibiting racial discrimination, the situation would be quite different.

What are the special features within the JCLU subcommittee proposal for a law on the elimination of racial discrimination?

One very important feature to note is that we have added nationality to the definition of race. In the European Union's Racial Equality Directive, for instance, different treatment based on nationality is excluded. We have seen in court precedents in Japan, confirmed by the Japanese Supreme Court, that judges invoke the reasonable-distinction-based-on-nationality argument under Article 14 of the Japanese constitution. We think that this standard is too relaxed. We want a sentence in a new law that says that racial discrimination due to nationality is not OK. Another important feature in Article 6 of the second version of our proposal is punitive provisions that impose criminal sanctions on racial harassment by public officials, in addition to all direct and indirect discriminations. In Japan there has been a campaign by the police on their claim of rising crime by foreigners. It has been going on for some time, but it is getting worse. They manipulate crime figures and create the impression that Japan is under attack by foreigners. With the harassment clause of

Article 6, we hope to catch this kind of behavior. Finally, we have also added remedial measures for victims in our second version.

Does the JCLU subcommittee proposal touch on the issues of multiple discrimination and affirmative action?

There is no specific provision on multiple discrimination on gender and race in our proposal. The issue was pointed out but it never got discussed in detail, for example, concerning what kinds of provisions would be necessary. Similarly, there is no specific mention of positive action except that the proposal does include the phrase, "special measures will not constitute racial discrimination."

How has the Japanese government responded so far?

We are yet to receive any response from the government, but if our proposal is discussed, we expect to have a lot of opposition. Why our proposal is so controversial is that, if passed, it has drastic implications in many areas. For example, there will be many professions in which foreigners can apply. There will also be many social rights, such as social security, to which foreigners will be entitled. This is completely opposite to the current government position, and opposite to the court position or interpretation. There will also be changes concerning freedom of association and foreigner participation in groups. For example, some golf clubs have a nationality—that is, Japanese only—clause.

You mentioned about the government proposal to set up a human rights commission in Japan. Could you tell me more about it?

The government set up a group to examine the issue almost seven years ago, around 1997. This working group recommended the establishment of a human rights commission. The Ministry of Justice (MOJ) then came up with a proposal. One of the reasons for this could be that, since the adoption in 1993 of the UN Paris Principles on national human rights institutions, many Asian countries have set up national human rights commissions and the Japanese government felt some sort of pressure to set up one in Japan. There are several issues in the current MOJ proposal. It does not cover any human rights issue in employment, which is under the jurisdiction of the Ministry of Health, Labor, and Welfare. Also, as a substantive law, it does not sufficiently provide for specific rules regarding human rights violations, including discrimination. That is why we feel that the antidiscrimination law we are proposing is necessary.

In addition, there is a lot of opposition from the media about the freedom of expression, because the bill specifically targets privacy issues in media reporting. Finally, there is the whole question of independence. Under the current proposal, the commission will be established under the authority of MOJ.

What is your agenda from now on?

Our first goal is to make our proposal an official JCLU proposal. For that we are organizing a symposium on December 4, 2004. We want to publish a booklet on this proposal. In October 2004, Nichibenren organized a symposium on foreigners' rights in Miyazaki. Nichibenren has been working on a declaration on a basic law on foreigners' rights. Some members of Nichibenren have invited NGOs to form a network as a new movement that brings together newcomers and "oldcomers." We had an informal meeting of the NGOs and I believe a network will be formed by early 2005, with NGOs working on and with migrant workers, Korean, Chinese, Nikkeijin (foreigners of Japanese descent), and so on. I think it might be difficult to push for a basic law on foreigners' rights, but we can use it as a tool for changing the government's attitude.

Related Web Sites

Japan Civil Liberties Union: http://www.jclu.org/index_e.shtml

Japan Federation of Bar Associations (Nichibenren): http://www.nichibenren.or.jp/en

Proposed Outline for a Law on the Elimination of Racial Discrimination (Draft Proposal Ver. 1 of JCLU Subcommittee for the Rights of Foreigners): http://www.jclu.org/katsudou/bills/racial_discrimination/outline_e.html

Universal Principles (JCLU newsletter): http://www.jclu.org/katsudou/universal_principle/main.shtml

Related References

Goodman, Roger, and Ian Neary, eds. 1996. *Case Studies on Human Rights in Japan.* Surrey, UK: Japan Library.

Human Rights Forum 21. 1998. *Nihon no Jinken Hakusho* [White paper on human rights in Japan]. Tokyo: Kaihō Shuppansha.

Japan Civil Liberties Union. 1997. *Nihon de kurasu gaikokujin no kodomotachi: Teijūka jidai to kodomo no kenri* [Foreign children living in Japan: The era of long-term residency and children's rights]. Tokyo: Akashi Shoten.

Yamazaki, Koshi. 2005. "Proposed Human Rights Commission in Japan: A Critique." *Asia Pacific News, 39.* Available at http://www.hurights.or.jp/asia-pacific /039/04 .htm

36

ANTIDISCRIMINATION, GRASSROOTS EMPOWERMENT, AND HORIZONTAL NETWORKING

Morihara Hideki

MORIHARA HIDEKI is secretary-general of the International Secretariat and Japan Committee of the International Movement Against All Forms of Discrimination and Racism. Born in Japan's Ishikawa Prefecture in 1972 and graduated from the Department of Economics at Keio Gijuku University in Tokyo, he served as secretary-general of the Japanese NGO Forum for Habitat at the second UN Conference on Human Settlement in 1996. In 1997 he worked at Amnesty International Japan as a campaign coordinator. He has also been a lecturer at Seigakuin University since 2005.

Could you tell me about your personal background?

I grew up in an upper-middle-class family. My mother is a full-time housewife and my father is a regular salaryman. We lived in Setagaya district in Tokyo— the area often described as an upscale residential neighborhood. I think I can say very clearly that I grew up in a privileged majority society. I didn't live in downtown, where there were a lot of foreign migrant laborers. I entered college in 1991 and majored in economics, not because I chose to but because I got good grades on my university entrance examinations. It was right after the end of the Cold War and the bubble economy had collapsed in Japan. In college I saw how difficult it was for women to find jobs. At that time it was cool to do things related to *kokusaika* (internationalization), so I joined AIESEC, an international group of mostly economics and business students. As the president of the local committee at my college, I was responsible for overall management and fundraising. I met a lot of personnel managers in foreign companies in

Japan and got quite a bit of money for our club. At that time I was thinking only of personnel skill development and international exchange. I didn't think there was any problem with that. I became the national president of all chapters of AIESEC in Japan. I felt my English was poor and I wanted some challenge. I became the vice president for external relations at AIESEC International head-quarters and spent a year and a half in Brussels between 1994 and 1995. There I wanted to change AIESEC. I saw a gap between students from the North and the South. Many ambitious students from rich countries were preoccupied only with climbing up their career ladder and becoming global business lead-ers. They thought that poverty and human rights had nothing to do with them. Despite the fact that AIESEC had consultative status with the UN Economic and Social Council (ECOSOC), it did not concern itself with corporate social responsibility or peace. So I created a few programs, such as internships in NGOs, encouraging youth participation in processes for international policy formulations. Just around that time, in 1995, the World Summit on Sustainable Development (WSSD) was held in Copenhagen and the Fourth World Confer-ence on Women took place in Beijing. I began to realize that business growth did not equal peace. The ideas laid out in the Human Development Reports of the UN Development Programme better matched my beliefs. I wanted to do something in that direction.

What did you do upon your return to Japan?

I experienced this sort of epiphany outside of Japan. Until then, I did not real-ize what was problematic with gross domestic product growth as the main goal of Japan's development. When I returned to Japan, I worked in the secretariat of a new NGO network that was created to monitor the domestic follow-up of the WSSD and prepare for the Second UN Conference on Human Settlements (Habitat II) in Istanbul in June 1996. Just around that time, the homeless peo-ple in Shinjuku were forcibly evicted by the Tokyo Metropolitan Government. I had never met any homeless people until then and I had to think about what I could really offer to them. Through this new NGO network, I also met Buraku people for the first time. I remembered that my father's company used to keep a Buraku list (so that the company could avoid hiring them). I went to Istanbul and participated in my first demonstration. I saw some Kurds being arrested. It was the first time I had firsthand experience of state power and oppres-sion. That was probably the first big opportunity for me to become involved in human rights issues.

What did you do after Istanbul?

I was still a bachelor at the time and was looking for a job. Amnesty International (AI) Japan was hiring and I joined them for five years. I continued international campaign work and government lobbying as well as press relations on various human rights issues. I met a lot of people, interviewed refugee applicants, and learned a tremendous amount about various human rights issues. Two of my preoccupations were how to connect Habitat II to the kind of civil and political rights work that I was doing at AI, and how to spread our human rights activities in Japan. I became the secretary-general of the International Human Rights NGO Network, a coalition of Japanese NGOs in various areas of human rights.

How did you shift from AI Japan to the International Movement Against All Forms of Discrimination and Racism (IMADR)?

While I had a great experience at AI, there were several issues. One was the fact that AI did not work on structural issues. For example, AI intervened after a person was detained or tortured. It did not look at why the person was detained in the first place. Another issue was that AI was primarily a group that appealed on behalf of someone who had no voice. That really was the core of the AI mission. It was a support group. In that sense, there was a question on the relationship between the victims themselves and their supportive NGO. I wanted to do more work with people who were fighting for their own rights. So I joined IMADR.

What is the focus of the activities of IMADR?

IMADR was formed in 1988 by the Buraku liberation movement. It is an international NGO with ECOSOC consultative status that focuses on minority rights worldwide. In Japan, *sabetsu* (discrimination) has become government terminology. The governmental approach is, if we all become kinder persons, *sabetsu* will disappear. I think IMADR wants to reflect on what an antidiscrimination movement really means in Japan. We emphasize historical and structural conditions, including colonization and postcolonialism, that have an impact on minority communities. I think three characteristics of IMADR are that (1) it is run by the minority members themselves, (2) it is an international human rights NGO based in Japan (that is, outside Europe and North America), and (3) it prioritizes minority empowerment. We try to approach discrimination in a broad and intersectional way. We have activities on minority rights, migrants' rights, multiple discrimination, trafficking, and so on.

IMADR is one of the NGOs in Japan that are most active in UN lobbying. Could you tell me more about your work in this area?

Yes, the work of IMADR has been very UN-focused. We try to use the UN human rights mechanisms for our purpose of eliminating racial and other discrimination. But I am cautious about the limits of the UN human rights system. The UN is still a state-based system. For instance, indigenous peoples' rights are not recognized. I don't think the UN system can deal with structural issues such as colonization or postcolonialism. We were active in the process of the World Conference Against Racism in Durban in 2001, but now there is little follow-up on that process at the UN level. If you looked at the current war in Iraq, to take another example, you would see that the UN is limited in many ways. But on the caste issue, for instance, we are using the UN system, and we lobbied for the appointment of two special rapporteurs on discrimination based on work and descent—a proposal by the Subcommission on the Promotion and Protection of Human Rights. But we are conscious of our role of reforming the UN and not being just a UN agent. That is why our work is not only about lobbying at the UN. It is also about grassroots empowerment, horizontal networking between various minority communities, and then facilitating their voices in the UN.

What do you think are the connections between the antidiscrimination, antiwar, and alterglobalization movements in Japan?

I think the old kind of leftist activism is sometimes ineffective. We have to approach globalization and militarism from an antidiscrimination perspective, which is why we organized one of the plenary panels on trafficking at the 2004 World Social Forum (WSF) in Mumbai. To the extent that a lot of minority members themselves participated at WSF, it could be considered a success. But at times the discussions were dominated by leftist intellectuals.

Do you have any reflections on Japanese NGOs as a whole?

The number of NGOs has increased. Many now have legal status. But I want to focus on the civil and political rights of NGOs. There is a growing trend in Japan in which NGOs become just service providers to the government. They are supposed to constitute the third sector, but some are co-opted. That can have an impact on the social-movement role of NGOs. I would like to see Japanese NGOs construct more relationships with other NGOs in Asia.

Related Web Sites

Amnesty International Japan: http://www.amnesty.or.jp

International Movement Against All Forms of Discrimination and Racism: http://www.imadr.org

United Nations Development Programme Human Development Reports: http://hdr.undp.org/reports/global/2003

World Social Forum 2004: http://www.wsfindia.org

Related References

Bayefsky, Anne. 2002. *How to Complain to the UN Human Rights Treaty System*. New York: Transnational. International Human Rights NGO Network. 1999. *Wocchi! Kiyaku Jinken Iinkai: Doko ga Zureteru? Jinken no Kokusai Kijun to Nihon no Genjō* [Watch! Human Rights Committee: Where is the gap? International human rights standards and the situation in Japan]. Tokyo: Nihon Hyōronsha.

International Human Rights NGO Network. 1999. *Wocchi! Kiyaku Jinken Iinkai: Doko ga Zureteru? Jinken no Kokusai Kijun to Nihon no Genjō* [Watch! Human Rights Committee: Where is the gap? International human rights standards and the situation in Japan]. Tokyo: Nihon Hyōronsha.

International Movement Against All Forms of Discrimination and Racism. 2001. *Kokuren Kara Mita Nihon no Jinshu Sabetsu* [Racial discrimination in Japan from UN perspectives]. Tokyo: IMADR.

International Movement Against All Forms of Discrimination and Racism, ed. 2002a. *Mainoriti Josei ga Sekai wo Kaeru!* [Minority women change the world!]. Tokyo: Kaihō Shuppansha.

International Movement Against All Forms of Discrimination and Racism, ed. 2002b. *Hanjinshushugi, Sabetsu Teppai Sekaikaigi to Nihon* [World conference against racism, racial discrimination, xenophobia, and related intolerance and Japan]. Tokyo: Kaihō Shuppansha.

37

MULTIPLE IDENTITIES
AND BURAKU LIBERATION

Mori Maya

MORI MAYA is a member of the Buraku Liberation League and director of the Tengawa Youth meeting group, and assistant to Matsuoka Toru, Member of the House of Councillors. Born in the Tengawa Buraku community, Kyoto, in 1981, she was a leader of the Students' Association for Buraku Liberation, which provided students with high school and university scholarships. She is currently enrolled in a master's program in sociology, and her study focuses on the marginalized situations of Buraku women.

How did you become involved in Buraku issues in Japan?

I was born in a Buraku community called Tengawa in Kyoto in 1981. My paternal grandfather is a first-generation resident in Japan, with Taiwanese and Chinese roots. My mother is Buraku. I have multiple identities. My older brother, who died at the age of six, was dumb. I remember that I had to be imaginative to communicate with him because I could not use words. In terms of the current situation of my father, he chose *mukokuseki* (statelessness) in 1981 for the sake of his daughter. He gave up his own Chinese nationality so that his own child could live in Japan, instead of pursuing justice in keeping his own nationality. In 1991, at the time of the Persian Gulf War, I went on Peace Boat. I saw American planes from our boat. Until then I had only heard about the war from my grandmother. My mother was involved in after-school programs for Buraku children, which were established through the movements to win the special educational measure for Buraku children. I myself went to these kinds of after-school tutorials, and also began to organize other after-school meetings. My grandparents created the Tengawa chapter of the Buraku Liberation League (BLL). They had to sell their house and property, including rice fields and other crops, in order to raise money for their activities. There were tensions between my grandparents, and I saw that my grandmother suffered from domestic violence. My parents were active in BLL. I thought I would like to do similar things.

What have been your activities so far?

At first I was active in the Children's Club in BLL. I received a scholarship from BLL to attend high school and then college. In high school I helped organize meetings on themes like dropouts and *freeta* (nonregular employment). Our activities were not about theories of liberation. Instead, we focused on concrete discrimination issues within the community, as well as on the connections between various kinds of discrimination, due to gender, ethnicity, and other statuses. In college I became more empowered. I kept thinking about the issue of connections between Buraku liberation and antidiscrimination.

You attended the World Conference Against Racism in Durban in 2001. Could you tell me about your experience?

BLL was a member of the NGO coalition Durban 2001 Japan. Many BLL members went to Durban. Until then, I was not aware of the caste issue, even though I had been to Nepal when I was small. In Durban I felt very strongly about the advocacy by *tōjisha* (minority members themselves), as well as about NGO activism. After Durban, I got to thinking more about my own complex identity. Also, I wanted to learn more English. I felt there were many things I needed to learn. I spent six months in San Francisco and was exposed to many different social movements. I met a friend who was a third-generation Korean resident in Japan who was living in the United States. I met people in the gay and lesbian movement and the peace movement. The time I spent in the United States made me think about my identity as a Buraku with Japanese nationality and about my brother who was a Buraku with disability. In addition, my partner is also Buraku.

How would you like to continue your work from now on?

I've just begun work as an assistant to Matsuoka Toru, a member of the House of Councillors. I took up this position because I wanted to learn more about our political system. When I reflect on what I want to do from now on, I feel that our political power is very weak. We do not have much organizing capacity. A lot remains to be done in terms of connecting the various antidiscrimination movements together.

Related Web Sites

Buraku Liberation League: http://blhrri.org/index_e.htm

Human Rights Watch, End Caste Discrimination Campaign: http://hrw.org/campaigns/caste/index.htm

Suiheisha Declaration of Human Rights in Japan (1922): http://www.hurights.or.jp/asia-pacific/no_27/07suiheisha.htm

Related References

Buraku Liberation League. 2005. "What Is Buraku Discrimination?" Available at http://blhrri.org/blhrri_e/blhrri/buraku.htm

Human Rights Watch. 2001. *Caste Discrimination: A Global Concern. A Report for the UN World Conference Against Racism, Racial Discrimination, Xenophobia and Related Intolerance*, Durban, South Africa, September. Available at http://www.hrw.org/reports/2001/globalcaste/index.htm#TopOfPage

International Movement Against All Forms of Discrimination and Racism. 2002. "Summary of Caste Discrimination: A Global Concern Symposium": http://www.imadr.org/old/project/dalit/smita.html

Ishikawa, Yuka. 2001. "Rights Activists and Rights Violations: The Burakumin Case in Japan." Available at http://imadr.org/old/tokyo/ishikawareport.html

Neary, Ian. 1989. *Political Protest and Social Control in Pre-War Japan: The Origins of Buraku Liberation*. Manchester, UK: Manchester University Press.

Neary, Ian. 1997. "Burakumin in Contemporary Japan." In *Japan's Minorities: The Illusion of Homogeneity*, edited by Michel Weiner. London: Routledge.

Miyazaki, Shigeki, ed. 1999. *Kokusaika jidai no jinken to dōwa mondai* [Human rights in an era of internationalization and the Buraku issue]. Tokyo: Akashi Shoten.

Takeuchi, Junko. 2002. "Hisabetsu Buraku Shusshin no Josei no Tachiba Kara" [From the standpoint of women of Buraku origins who have experienced discrimination]. In *Mainoriti Josei ga Sekai wo Kaeru!* [Minority women change the world!], edited by International Movement Against All Forms of Discrimination and Racism. Tokyo: Kaihō Shuppansha.

Tomonaga, Kenzō. 1999. "Buraku Mondai" [Buraku issue]. In *Wocchi! Kiyaku Jinken Iinkai: Doko ga Zureteru? Jinken no Kokusai Kijun to Nihon no Genjō* [Watch! Human Rights Committee: Where is the gap? International human rights standards and the situation in Japan], edited by International Human Rights NGO Network. Tokyo: Nihon Hyōronsha.

38

INDIGENOUS PEOPLES' RIGHTS AND MULTICULTURAL COEXISTENCE

Uemura Hideaki

UEMURA HIDEAKI is professor at Keisen University in Tokyo and has been founding president of Shimin Gaikō Centre, Diplomatic Centre for the Rights of Indigenous Peoples, since 1982. Born in Kumamoto in 1956, he graduated with a bachelor's degree in political science from Keio University in 1979 and obtained his master's degree in economics from the Graduate School at Waseda University in 1981. He has long been involved in the human rights movement for indigenous peoples, in particular for the Ainu, the Okinawans, and the South Pacific islanders, and founded the International Human Rights NGO Network in 1990 and the Japan NGO Network on UN Reform in 2005.

How did you become involved in minority rights issues in Japan?

I have family members who were born and lived in Taiwan under Japanese colonial rule. My grandmother, who acted as my foster mother, was born there and was forced to return to Kyūshū, Japan, with her children in the aftermath of World War II. The community in Kumamoto, the city in which I was born, was made up of a lot of Japanese returnees or refugees from Harbin, Seoul, Singapore, and Taipei. I heard a lot of stories from my grandmother about military rule and discriminatory structures. When I was in my last year of college in 1979, I wrote a thesis about the British formal and informal empires. That was how I got into the subject of Japanese imperialism and its victims. At that time, and even now, at schools we were taught that the start of Japanese imperialism was the annexation of Taiwan in 1895, but I became rather interested in both Hokkaido and Okinawa, because that was where Japanese imperialism began.

So I took up the issue of Ainu rights in my master's studies and began to visit Ainu leaders in Hokkaido in 1979. Around that time they were reflecting on what strategy they should use to protect their rights. In 1984, the Ainu Association of Hokkaido adopted a draft of a new Ainu law and began to campaign for the enactment. When I met with the Ainu leaders, I deeply understood that many of them disliked and distrusted Japanese in a very real sense, and I was often asked, seriously, the question about Japanese responsibility. I challenged myself over my obligation, in particular about what I could do for the Ainu on an equal basis. Subsequently, in 1981, I wrote my master's thesis on Ainu rights in their colonial history, especially because the average Ainu does not have the opportunity to know about his basic history and being deprived of his rights in the Japanese education system. Then I decided to become an activist rather than a researcher.

How was the Shimin Gaikō Centre established? Could you tell me some of its activities so far?

The Shimin Gaikō Centre was established in 1982 by me and my friends who supported the second UN Special Session for Disarmament held in New York. The center focuses on peace, human rights, environment, and development issues internationally. From the beginning we supported indigenous peoples and their human rights, which had long been ignored in Japanese society. We felt that the Japanese political system presented a high wall on minority and indigenous rights under the myth that Japan was a monoethnic nation-state. Whether it was the ruling party or the opposition parties, no one ever talked about minority or indigenous rights at that time. So, since 1987 we have been sending delegations to the UN Working Group on Indigenous Populations (WGIP) in Geneva along with the Ainu delegations, and we have been doing research at the UN level on international standards to protect minority and indigenous rights. In 1990, Shimin Gaikō Centre was a founding member of the International Human Rights NGO Network in Japan, because my friends and I strongly felt the need for a network to share common concerns. Many from this network participated in the World Conference on Human Rights held in Vienna in 1993. In 1996 we dared to begin supporting the participation of the Okinawa Ryūkyū peoples in the WGIP. In addition, since 1988 we have been making an annual contribution to the UN Voluntary Fund for Indigenous Populations for encouraging the wider participation of the indigenous peoples in the UN system. In 1995 we established a special fund and began financially supporting the translation and publication of international human rights instruments into indigenous languages. Through this program, indigenous peoples' organizations in Asia, Latin America, and Africa succeeded in disseminating their rights in the international context in their own languages. As a result of these activities, in 1999 we became the first Japanese grassroots NGO to be given special consultative status at the UN Economic and Social Council. In 2001, as you know, Shimin Gaikō Centre was a core NGO in the Japanese NGO coalition Durban 2001 Japan at the UN World Conference Against Racism.

There are quite a few minority issues in Japan. What is your priority?

The point is to introduce international human rights standards, including indigenous rights, into Japanese society and to correctly inform international society of the real situations and aspirations of the indigenous peoples in Japan. Simply speaking, this is globalization. Although we also approach Okinawa from an indigenous rights point of view, the structure of oppression is quite different for the Ainu compared to the Okinawans. The Okinawans have their own prefecture; therefore the Japanese government is able to deny their rights easily by using a central-local administrative structure. We are surely interested in indigenous issues in Asia, where indigenous rights have been increasingly ignored in the process of economic globalization, and where supporting NGOs like ours are too weak and fragile to inform the public of the real situation. In general, when there is no language and concept to describe a phenomenon, people cannot understand what has happened. For instance, if there is an international instrument that refers to land rights for indigenous peoples, we can introduce that concept or article to improve human rights abuses in Japan. Most Japanese came to know about the Ainu Culture Promotion Act of 1997, but no one knows about indigenous rights in its entirety—namely, the meanings and limits of the act. Educating people about the human rights language is absolutely crucial.

What are your criticisms of the Japanese government concerning minority rights in Japan?

First, there is lack of a rights-based approach. Through the Ainu Culture Promotion Act, Japan legally moved to a multicultural society, but we call it cosmetic multiculturalism. Even in this society, the Japanese government doesn't recognize any rights of minorities or indigenous peoples. For example, Japan ratified the UN Convention on the Rights of the Child (CRC), which includes the rights of minority and indigenous children, but it has not revised any old laws on education to translate CRC into a domestic reality. I think human rights are very much under threat right now in Japan and in the world. Therefore, we have to build our solidarity, for example, by creating civil society solidarity in at least Japan and East Asia. In this regard, I have great expectations that civil society solidarity will be built between South Korea and Japan.

Shimin Gaikō Centre is one of the oldest advocacy NGOs in Japan. What changes do you see in the NGO and NPO scene since the passage of the NPO Law in 1998?

Indeed, we called ourselves a Jurassic Park (that is, as old as a dinosaur) NGO before the term *NGO* appeared in Japan. It is obvious that I don't know all NGOs in Japan, but my great concern about NGOs since the passage of the NPO law in 1998 is the partnership between NGOs and the central and local governments. As a result of the NPO law, a lot of money has been invested in NGOs by the governments in the guise of partnership. So, NGOs like the ones in Japan Platform have big budgets, beautiful offices, and full-time paid staff members. They are like a business, and we have new words, such as *NGO business* or *business-oriented NGOs*. We have to remind ourselves of the raison d'être of NGOs: critical independence from authority, namely the governments, and activities in support of citizens. Fortunately (or unfortunately), human rights NGOs, including ours, remain critical about the governments, and our budgets are severely limited. But I am proud that our projects are funded solely by membership donations through what we call a peace tax. Our problem, one that is shared with other human rights NGOs, is how to gain new members to support our activities.

You are also president of the Commission on the Promotion of Human Rights in Kawasaki. Could you tell me about the work of this commission?

In order to protect and promote human rights, in my opinion, the role of local governments is so crucial. In this regard, the city of Kawasaki has a prominent history and is one of the leading local governments in Japan. In 1996 the city government established a foreigner advisory committee on issues that directly concern foreigners, and in 2001 appointed an ombudsperson on human rights. Even now there are a few councils and no ombudsperson system like the one in Kawasaki elsewhere in Japan. Besides the foreigner advisory committee, the city has two specific committees on women's rights and children's rights. To comprehensively promote human rights, including in these areas, the Commission on the Promotion of Human Rights in Kawasaki was formed in 2000. As its president in 2003–2004 and 2005–2006, I recognize that my mission is to protect victims of human rights abuses under the impact of globalization. They are foreigners, including foreign workers and victims of human trafficking; homeless people; and women and child victims of domestic violence. We emphasize not only remedies in cases of human rights violations, but also recommend positive action for foreigners and other minorities, such as that the city committees concerned should have at least one foreigner member or observer. As we laid out in the 2003 midterm and 2004 annual reports, the key is human rights education for the construction of multicultural and multiethnic coexistence so that various social concerns can be shared with all residents in Kawasaki.

Related Web Sites

Ainu Culture Promotion Act of 1997: http://homepage2.nifty.com/paper/lawcollection.htm

Japan Platform: http://www.japanplatform.org

Shimin Gaikō Centre: http://www005.upp.so-net.ne.jp/peacetax/#English

UN Permanent Forum on Indigenous Issues: http://www.un.org/esa/socdev/unpfii

UN Voluntary Fund for Indigenous Populations: http://www.ohchr.org/english/about/funds/indigenous/Contributions.htm

Working Group on Indigenous Populations, UN High Commissioner for Human Rights: http://www.unhchr.ch/indigenous/groups-01.htm

World Conference Against Racism: http://www.un.org/WCAR

Related References

Citizens' Diplomatic Centre for the Rights of Indigenous Peoples. 2001. "Written Statement on the World Conference Against Racism," submitted to UN Commission on Human Rights, January. Available at http://www005.upp.so-net.ne.jp/peacetax/#English

Human Rights Forum 21. 2002. "Japanese National Human Rights Commission." Available at http://www.hurights.or.jp/asia-pacific/no_28/05japanesehrc.htm

Kawasaki jinken keihatsu suishin kyōgikai [Commission on the Promotion of Human Rights in Kawasaki]. 2005. *Iken-gusin: Kawasaki-shi no jinken seisaku ni tsuite* [Report: Opinions on the human rights policy of Kawasaki City]. Kanagawa, Japan: Kawasaki City Government.

Uemura, Hideaki. 2002. "Dāban e no nagai michinori, soshite, sabetsu teppai no mirai e no shiza" [The long road to Durban and the vision toward elimination of discrimination]. In *Hanjinshushugi, sabetsu teppai sekaikaigi to Nihon* [World conference against racism, racial discrimination, xenophobia, and related intolerance and Japan], edited by International Movement Against All Forms of Discrimination and Racism. Tokyo: Kaihō Shuppansha.

Uemura, Hideaki. 2003. "The Colonial Annexation of Okinawa and the Logic of International Law: The Formation of an 'Indigenous People' in East Asia." *Japanese Studies*, 23(2), 213–222.

Uemura, Hideaki. 2004. "Escape from Freedom in the Information Age: Insecure Society Generated by Globalization and the Sacrificed Human Rights of Minorities." *Asia Rights Journal*, 1. Available at http://rspas.anu.edu.au/asiarightsjournal /Uemura.html

39

ON THE RECOGNITION OF THE INDIGENOUS PEOPLES' RIGHTS OF THE AINU

Sakai Mina

SAKAI MINA is a member of the Association of Rera. Born in Obihiro, Hokkaido, as Ainu in 1983 and graduated from the Department of International Studies at Obirin University, she has been active in conferences of indigenous peoples held by the UN and NGOs, and in conveying the message as an Ainu to the world. Since her childhood, she has studied traditional Ainu dance and currently performs and lectures on Ainu dance and songs across Japan and abroad.

How did you become aware of your own Ainu culture?

I was born in Hokkaido and lived there until I finished high school. Then I moved to Tokyo for college. My father is Ainu and my mother is non-Ainu. From kindergarten to high school I went to a study group called the Tokachi Eteke Kanpa Group for two hours per week. Because many Ainu children were behind in their school performance due to bullying, discrimination, and unfavorable family situations, many would go to the extracurricular study group. I started to go to the Eteke Study Group when I was seven years old. I also started to learn Ainu traditional dance, which I enjoyed very much.

Did you suffer from any bullying yourself when you grew up?

Compared to others, not so much. Other people faced taunts like "Look, there is an Ainu" or "Ainu are stupid [*baka*]." In schools we were laughed at because of our "thicker eyebrows" or "hairy appearance." In society the Ainu people were sometimes suspected of theft or other petty crimes. We always stood out (*medatsu*) because we look different.

Do you speak Ainu?

No. I can neither speak nor use Ainu. Maybe my father could (he passed away when I was five). My grandparents passed away before I was born. I can speak only Japanese, but I would like to learn Ainu. With the new Ainu Culture Promotion Act (1997), now there are Ainu language radio programs. But there are few opportunities to use it in our daily lives. In Hokkaido, people in their eighties and nineties may be able to speak Ainu, but others mostly can't. The government does not collect reliable census data on the Ainu, so we don't know how many Ainu there really are in Japan today. Many Ainu don't know that they are Ainu or would not admit that they are Ainu. A common figure puts our population at about twenty-five thousand.

What do you think of the Ainu Culture Promotion Act?

I think it is better to have a law than none. But that being said, I think there should be more emphasis on human rights. A common critique of the new law is that it focuses only on cultural aspects while we also need human rights protection. It is good to create an environment where people can now enjoy the Ainu language, dance, and other cultural activities, but most people who struggle to make a living might not be able to take full advantage of the changes. There are areas, such as employment, that fall outside the law.

What rights issues are the Ainu people most concerned about today?

I think the first issue is land rights. The Ainu did receive some compensation for land that was forcibly taken away from them by the Japanese government after 1872, but the compensation was small and unfair. Some have filed lawsuits, but the process is very slow. Another problem is hunting and fishing rights. Traditionally, Ainu people depended on hunting and fishing for food, but this was prohibited by the Japanese government from the Meiji Era. My father did fish despite the prohibition. Of course he was caught and fined. A related issue is the right to gather wild plants and vegetables. Besides the fact that these rights were taken away from us, a more fundamental problem is the lack of consciousness among the Ainu people that we are actually entitled to those rights that we once owned. So how to change the educational system so that the Ainu people will feel empowered to demand their rights is a big challenge. Besides these specific rights, the Ainu people also face key issues, including employment and education.

Could you tell me more about the educational issues that the Ainu people face?

The Japanese government does not recognize ethnic education in Japan. As I mentioned earlier, the Ainu language is not taught in formal schools. The formal education system does not teach anything about the Ainu. I believe that there needs to be more support for education and empowerment of the Ainu. Ainu language, culture, and history should be included in the formal education system. The Ainu Culture Promotion Act is not enough. The Japanese government needs to address the more serious problems that Ainu face today.

Related Web Sites

Ainu Association of Hokkaido: http://www.ainu-assn.or.jp
Foundation for Research and Promotion of Ainu Culture (FRPAC): http://www
.frpac.or.jp/eng/index.html
Sakai Mina's personal homepage: http://www.ainupride.com
Senjūminzoku no Jūnen Shimin Renraku Kai (Japan Citizens' Coalition for the UN
International Decade of the World's Indigenous People): http://indy10.at.infoseek
.co.jp/e-introduction.htm

Related References

Ainu Association of Hokkaido. 1999. "A Statement of Opinion Regarding the Partial Revision of ILO Convention No. 107." Olympia, WA: Center for World Indigenous Studies. Available at ftp://ftp.halcyon.com/pub/FWDP/Eurasia/ainu.txt

Ifunke no kai, ed. 1991. *Ifunke: aru Ainu no shi* [Ifunke: The death of an Ainu]. Tokyo: Sairyusha.

Japan Times. 1997. "Japan and Multiculturalism." Editorial on the Law to Promote Ainu Culture and Disseminate Knowledge of Ainu Traditions. May 13. Available at http://www.hurights.or.jp/asia-pacific/no_9/no9_multi.htm

Kayano, Shigeru. 1994. *Our Land Was a Forest: An Ainu Memoir*. Boulder, CO: Westview Press.

Loos, Noel, and Osanai Takeshi, eds. 1993. *Indigenous Minorities and Education: Australian and Japanese Perspectives on Their Indigenous Peoples, the Ainu, Aborigines, and Torres Strait Islanders*. Tokyo: Sanyusha.

Siddle, Richard. 1996. *Race, Resistance, and the Ainu of Japan*. London: Routledge.

Sonohara, Toshiaki. 1997. "Toward a Genuine Redress for an Unjust Past: The Nibutani Dam Case." *Murdoch University Electronic Journal of Law*, 4(2). Available at http://www.murdoch.edu.au/elaw/issues/v4n2/sonoha42.html

Stevens, Georgina. 2001. "The Ainu and Human Rights: Domestic and International Legal Protections." *Japanese Studies*, 21(2), 181–199.

Stevens, Georgina. 2003. "UN Expert, R. Stavenhagen, Meets with Ainu Indigenous People." Available at http://www.imadr.org/old/pub/web/r.stavenhagen-ainu .html

Uemura, Hideaki. 1999. "Ainu minzoku no kenri to Okinawa no jinken jōkyō" [Ainu people's rights and the human rights situation of Okinawa]. In *Wocchi! Kiyaku jinken iinkai: Doko ga zureteru? Jinken no kokusai kijun to Nihon no genjō* [Watch! Human Rights Committee: Where is the gap? International human rights standards and the situation in Japan], edited by International Human Rights NGO Network. Tokyo: Nihon Hyōronsha.

40

"I WOULD LIKE TO BE ABLE TO SPEAK UCHINĀGUCHI WHEN I GROW UP!"

Taira Satoko

TAIRA SATOKO has been a member of the Association of Indigenous Peoples in the Ryūkyūs since college. Born in Okinawa in 1979, she graduated with a degree in international social studies from the Graduate School at Keisen University in 2005. Since 2005, Taira has been a member of the Okinawa Social Mass Party, and as a member of the Naha Municipal Assembly has been involved in action aiming for political self-determination for Okinawans.

Could you tell me how you became aware of the Okinawa issue?

I first became conscious of my Okinawan identity in 1995, when there was widespread mobilization in Okinawa after the rape incident in 1995 (in which a school girl was victimized by three U.S. soldiers). At that time I was twelve years old. My friends were saying, "I would like to be able to speak *Uchināguchi* when I grow up!" In the first year of high school, I started to notice that our textbooks never talked about Okinawans. There was actually a supplementary text (*fukudokuhon*) that included information on Okinawans. But because of the typhoons, classes were often suspended and the teachers almost never got to use the supplementary text. Also, questions on Okinawa never came out in examinations, so teachers did not teach about Okinawa. In college I took a course on international peace studies at the Okinawa International University, where a U.S. Marines helicopter recently fell. In one of the classes, a member of the Association of Indigenous Peoples' Rights in the Ryūkyūs (AIPR) reported on the progress of negotiations on indigenous peoples' rights within the United Nations. I realized two things for the first time: first, Okinawans, as indigenous peoples, have the right to self-determination (*Okinawajin ga okinawa no koto wo jibun de kimeru*); and second, the problems confronting indigenous peoples worldwide are common. That was a catalytic moment for me, and I was very happy to learn about my own identity. In addition, my father is a high school teacher and a peace activist. He was involved in the postwar land struggles (when the U.S. military forcibly took private land for military purpose) and the antimilitary base movement in the 1980s. We live in South Okinawa, where many Okinawans died during the last battles of World War II.

Do you speak Uchināguchi?

Our languages, the languages of the Ryūkyū Archipelago, were forbidden in 1879. My grandparents did not teach my parents to speak it. My parents can understand but not speak it. In turn, my parents never spoke to me in Uchināguchi. I can neither speak nor understand it; so, for example, I cannot speak to my great grandparents.

What are the goals and activities of the AIPR?

AIPR was established in 1996 in the context of Okinawan citizens' movements. AIPR declares that Okinawan people are indigenous peoples as defined by international law. The aim of our movement is the recovery of the self-determination of Okinawan people, and to achieve the solution of Okinawan problems by Okinawan people themselves through the human rights regime of the United Nations. We organized a study group called International Human Rights and Okinawa, which meets once every month. Every year our members attend the Permanent Forum on Indigenous Issues in May, and the UN Working Group on Indigenous Populations in July. We also monitor and make position statements on various UN human rights conventions, including the UN Convention on the Rights of the Child, the Convention on the Elimination of All Forms of Discrimination Against Women, and the International Convention on the Elimination of Racial Discrimination, from Okinawan perspectives. For example, we talked about the impact of military bases on children in schools around the Futenma base in our statement to the Committee on the Rights of the Child.

Okinawans have been going to the UN Working Group on Indigenous Populations since 1996. Could you tell me more about it?

Okinawans have been attending the meetings of the UN Working Group on Indigenous Populations since 1996, the year following the rape incident, in part because it has been very difficult to access the domestic justice system. At the UN we have been fighting for our right of self-determination. For example, despite the fact that Okinawa represents only one percent of the total population, 75 percent of all U.S. military bases are concentrated in Okinawa. Domestically, there seems to be nothing we can do about this confiscated land.

What are your views on indigenous peoples' rights at the UN level?

I think that the protection of indigenous peoples' rights within the UN system is still weak. Especially after September 11, there has not been much attention to the issue. But we still try to use the UN human rights system. For example, the Human Rights Committee, in one of its deliberations on Japan, urged the government to recognize Okinawans as a minority within Japan.

Do Okinawans want to be independent from Japan?

The issue of independence is very tricky. Only about 30 percent of Okinawans are pro-independence. But if you ask them, "Are you Japanese?" most would reply, "I am Okinawan." Until now, most Okinawan activists don't use the term *indigenous peoples*, because it has a rather pejorative image. For example, people would think of the Aboriginals in Australia, or the Native Americans, or the Ainu within Japan. I think some Okinawans make the distinction between self-rule (*jichi*) and independence (*dokuritsu*).

As a young Okinawan woman, what do you think are the gender dimensions of the various social movements on and in Okinawa?

In the 1950s and 1960s, men were the actors in the land movement and women were the supporters. Seventy-five Okinawan women attended the Fourth World Conference on Women in Beijing in September 1995. The rape incident occurred right after the Beijing conference, which helped catalyze the women's movement within Okinawa. Rape has always been around, but the Beijing Platform for Action provided an international definition and standard that rape constituted a violation of women's rights, something that Okinawan women's groups have emphasized.

What is it like for you to live near the military bases?

There are twenty-seven bases in Okinawa. It is very noisy. The planes flying overhead make us think of bombs. The noise and air pollution have a bad impact on our health. For example, in Okinawa the average birth weight for babies is 2.5 kg, which is much lower than the national average. In addition to accidents, as a woman you are worried about rapes. There is also the issue of *Amerajians* (Amerasians, or children of U.S. soldiers stationed in Okinawa and local women). They have Japanese nationality. Sometimes they can't find their dads in the United States and the women don't have alimony fees. I think that military bases lead to all kinds of human rights violations. Because bases are used to launch wars, such as the war in Vietnam and the current war in Iraq, it's like we are killing people. It gives us that burden, in effect.

What is the relationship between the women's movement in Okinawa and the peace movement in general?

It is hard to say in general, but let me give you an example. Members of the Okinawan women's group Kichi/guntai wo yurusanai kōdō suru joseitachi no kai (Association of Women in Action Against the Bases and the Military) go to the United States to participate in symposia and demonstrations for peace.

What would you like to do from now on?

AIPR has only about ten active members, so one of our main issues is how to spread our movement within Okinawa. I have been to the UN Working Group on Indigenous Populations. That experience makes me search for or reconfirm my own Okinawan identity. I don't speak the Okinawan language, I don't know how to do Okinawan dance. I want to find my own Okinawan-ness, and I think that search is related to the ethnic memory of my people. From now on I want to look into the concept of self-determination. Also, if my friends are serious about learning Uchināguchi, we need to claim our educational rights, including the right to curriculum in our language. Some cultural centers offer Uchināguchi courses, but we need them in schools. This is part of our claiming indigenous peoples' rights. I think the media is a big problem in Japan. There is almost no reporting in the mainland about Okinawa. Within Okinawa, not all Okinawans think of themselves as indigenous peoples. The challenge is how to problematize our situation. Okinawa is a small island and the communities are small. People got used to living with military bases and became dependent on the military-base economy. There is a saying that Okinawa relies on three Ks: *kankō* (tourism), *kichi* (military base), and *kōkyō jigyō* (public enterprise)! For example, the city government of Nago does not object to the current proposal to build a new offshore military base in Henoko Bay as long as it receives money from the central government.

Because of this structural political-economic dimension, I think this will be a long and difficult fight for us.

Related Web Sites

Citizen's Network: A Call for Withdrawal of Bases for World Peace: http://www.jca.apc.org/heiwa-sr/jp

Indigenous Peoples' Rights Network (Japan): http://jns.ixla.jp/users/indigenousnet566/index.html

Okinawa Environmental Network: http://homepage1.nifty.com/okikan/en/index.htm

Okinawa Women Act Against Military Violence: http://www.space-yui.com/koudou.htm

Related References

Angst, Linda Isako. 2003. "The Rape of a Schoolgirl: Discourses of Power and Women's Lives in Okinawa." In *Islands of Discontent: Okinawan Responses to Japanese and American Power*, edited by Laura Hein and Mark Selden. New York: Rowman & Littlefield.

Association of Indigenous Peoples in the Ryūkyūs. 2004. *Kokusai jinken hō to Ryūkyū, Okinawa* [International human rights law and Ryūkyū, Okinawa]. Tokyo: AIPR.

Chinen, Hidenori, and Izena Kasumi. 1998. "Education in Okinawa and the Okinawan Languages: A Position Paper on the Rights of the Okinawans to Education and Languages." Tokyo: Shimin Gaikō Centre. Available at http://www005.upp.so-net.ne.jp/peacetax/e5.html

Shimin Gaikō Centre. 2004. "Use of Depleted Uranium Munitions and Related Contamination in and Around Military Training Areas in Okinawa, Japan." Tokyo: Shimin Gaikō Centre. Available at http://www005.upp.so-net.ne.jp/peacetax/e6.html

Takazato, Suzuyo. 1996. *Okinawa no onnatachi: jose no jinken to kichi, guntai* [Women in Okinawa: Women's human rights and military bases, army]. Tokyo: Akaishi Shoten.

Thornberry, Patrick. 2002. *Indigenous Peoples and Human Rights*. Manchester, UK: Juris and Manchester University Press.

Uemura, Hideaki, Fujioka Mieko, and Nakano Kenji. 2004. *Gurōbaru jidai no senjūminzoku: "Senjūminzoku no jūnen" to wa nan datta no ka?* [Indigenous peoples in the era of globalization: What was the International Decade of the World's Indigenous People?] Kyoto: Hōritsu Bunkasha.

41

ART ACTIVISM AND
KOREAN MINORITY RIGHTS

Hwangbo Kangja

HWANGBO KANGJA is a representative of Mirine (Chōsenjin jūgun'ianfu mondai wo kangaeru kai, or Association of Korean Comfort Women). She was born in Osaka of Korean parents in 1957. She produced *Guraedo Salawatta* [And yet we survived: Women forced into the Japanese military sexual slavery system], an educational documentary on "comfort women," as well as *Ijebuteo* [From now on: Korean women in Japan of three generations], which portrays the histories of succeeding generations of Zainichi Korean women. She continues to research the life histories of minority women living in Japan.

How did you become involved in Korean issues in Japan?

I was born in Osaka in 1957, a 2.5–generation Korean in Japan. In 1991, after Korean "comfort woman" Kim Hak Sun visited Japan, I established Mirine (Chōsenjin jūgun'ianfu mondai wo kangaeru kai, or Association of Korean Comfort Women), a group working in Kansai on the issues of Korean victims of the Japanese system of military comfort women.

What are the main activities of Mirine?

We do public lectures and produce documentaries. For example, I produced *Guraedo Salawatta* [And Yet We Survived: Women Forced into the Japanese Military Sexual Slavery System] in 1994, and *Ijebuteo* [From Now On: Korean Women in Japan of Three Generations]. In 1996 I met Shimada Yoshiko through her exhibition "Gender: Beyond Memories" at the Tokyo Metropolitan Museum of Photography, in which she explored issues related to Japanese war responsibility and the military comfort women system. Together with

Shimada Yoshiko we began our donation to the House of Sharing for the surviving comfort women in Korea.

You had an exhibition of family pictures of Koreans in Japan in Vancouver,
Canada, in 2001. Why did you choose to focus on family pictures?

It was in part through the inspiration of Shimada Yoshiko's own artworks that
I began to think of new ways to express ourselves concerning Korean issues in
Japan. Until then, we had always lectured and talked about the "coming out" of
the comfort women. Though it had certainly become easier for us to talk about
it, we thought our message might be even more accessible through photos. In
my family we had many photos, including marriage photos, photos of our up-
bringing, relatives' photos, and so on. I remember that when my mother died,
some photos surprised me. There was a picture of my mother in 1939; I was
shocked to see how beautiful she was. In sieving through my family photos, I
learned about the Zainichi history and saw my family photos in a new light.
There was another photo of me in kimono on the day of high school graduation. I wanted badly to wear a kimono and not a traditional Korean *hanbok*. I
remember that I didn't want to show the marriage photos of my parents and of
my aunt and uncle in traditional Korean clothes. I thought it was very strange
for them to wear such traditional Korean wedding costumes even though they
only spoke Japanese. Those photos changed my consciousness as a Korean and
I saw my own family in a different way. I think what we wanted to do in Vancouver was to use our own expression, together with the expression of many
other minorities in the world, to rethink our own identity and work against
the common stereotypes of Koreans (for example, as dirty and smelly).

What issues do you face in your daily life as a Korean resident in Japan?

First of all, we don't have citizenship rights. We have to carry our alien cards
that show our legal status as *tokubetsu eijūsha* (special permanent residents).
I think it is unacceptable that we have no voting rights and other basic rights
because we are non-Japanese nationals. For instance, I am a teacher. Koreans
are barred from working in more than half of all public school districts in
Japan. There are few public schools where Koreans can be employed as teachers, and they are recent.

Did you consider becoming a Japanese national through immigration
procedures?

The Japanese government tries to ask us to adopt Japanese nationality. We don't do it, not only because there is a cumbersome review process, but also because we feel discriminated against. We want to fight for recognition as Koreans, not as Japanese.

What do you do to bring about change in the current situation?

We used to go the Ministry of Justice and protest, but now we focus much more on our practical social rights such as employment, education, and welfare. For example, we have asked for a government grant to do a survey on bullying against Korean children in schools. We spend most of our energies on educating our own children in our own region. There are Korean schools, but they are not formally recognized and they are few and far between. Our goal is to create an environment within the mainstream educational system where Korean children feel fine and happy, where they can use their Korean names and are free from bullying, where they can enjoy Korean songs and culture.

Related Web Sites

Half-Moon Tsuushin (newsletter): http://www.han.org/a/half-moon
Nihongun ianfu rekishikan kouenkai (Association to Support the Japanese Military Comfort Women Museum): http://www.nanum.org/eng/menu05/index.html

Related References

Ebara, Mamoru. 2003. *Minzoku gakkō mondai wo kangaeru* [On the issue of ethnic schools]. Kyoto: Agenda Project.

Fukuoka, Yasunori. 2000. *Lives of Young Koreans in Japan*. Melbourne: Trans Pacific Press.

Kim, Puja. 1996. "'Jūgun Ianfu' Mondai: Undō to sono Imi" [The question of comfort women: The movement and its meaning]. In *Jendā* [Gender], edited by Hiroko Hara, Mari Osawa, Makoto Maruyama, and Yasushi Yamamoto. Tokyo: Shinseisha.

Okamoto, Masataka. 1999. "Zainichi Korean Mainoriti" [Korean resident minority]. In *Wocchi! Kiyaku Jinken Iinkai: Doko ga Zureteru? Jinken no Kokusai Kijun to Nihon no Genjō* [Watch! Human Rights Committee: Where is the gap? International human rights standards and the situation in Japan], edited by International Human Rights NGO Network. Tokyo: Nihon Hyōronsha.

Ryang, Sonia, ed. 2001. *Koreans in Japan: Critical Voices from the Margin*. London: Routledge.

Schellstede, Sangmie Choi, ed. 2000. *Comfort Women Speak: Testimony of Sex Slaves of the Japanese Military*. New York: Holmes and Meier.

42

ETHNIC DIVERSITY, FOREIGNERS' RIGHTS, AND DISCRIMINATION IN FAMILY REGISTRATION

Tony László

TONY LÁSZLÓ is a writer and founding director of Issho Kikaku, an organization that has been researching multicultural issues of Japan since 1991. A U.S.-born Hungarian-Italian, he has been living in Japan since 1985. He served as a representative in the Japanese NGO delegation to the UN World Conference Against Racism in Durban, South Africa, in 2001.

How did you become involved in foreigners' rights issues in Japan?

I first arrived in Japan in 1985. Around that time, many newcomers began to arrive in Japan to study and work. The key concern was not so much discrimination as that the newcomers were simply looking for deeper interactions with people around them. In some sense it was a quest for some level of normalization. The first activities were essentially self-help. This then became more holistic. Over time I began to experience various kinds of discrimination and problems, and I became increasingly aware of people facing similar issues, some more dire than others. My associates and I wanted to take on tasks that would be less hectic and thus easier to sustain over time. We wanted to do something more, on a weekly, monthly, and quarterly basis.

How did Issho Kikaku come into being?

In 1987 I created an NGO called SPEAK! This was an organization designed for nonnative speakers of Japanese, so that they might debate and make speeches in Japanese together, thus empowering themselves. In addition, SPEAK! also invited Japanese native speakers to take part in open sessions. While SPEAK!

did draw a line between native and nonnative speakers of Japanese, it succeeded in its goal of breaking down the barriers between national and foreigner. SPEAK! flourished for several years, making a meager contribution
in the areas of empowerment and normalization. However, Japan's economy
started to slow down, and the number of people who were willing to travel
down the path that SPEAK! had opened decreased. In 1992, as SPEAK! entered its period of decline, I formed Issho Kikaku, to pursue related activities
that were beyond the limitations of SPEAK! The group's initial mandate was
to produce a theatrical piece that I had begun writing around that time. The
project aimed to underscore the diversity among foreigners, and was a reaction to the national versus nonnational dichotomy by which foreigners were
simply lumped together as "the Other." I decided it would be best to make the
project a collaborative one. The name of the play (*Issho*) and the group (Issho
Kikaku) reflects the collaboration aspect, on the one hand (*Issho* means "together," *Kikaku* means "project"). On the other hand, it reflects the notion that
all people share commonalities due to their membership in the human race
(*Issho* also means "the same" in another usage). After the staging of the *Issho* in
1994, I received other requests from various bodies and agencies and did more
projects. Then, in 1998, I was invited to sail from Africa to South America on
board Peace Boat, an NGO that periodically sails around the world for peace
education. I staged *Hone, Hone, Hone* on the ship, with a cast and crew made
up of passengers. In 1996, Issho Kikaku entered a transformation, essentially
leaving behind the costly and time-consuming theater projects and becoming
more research and advocacy oriented. The transformation was spurred on by
the group's use of the Internet for communications between members and
publishing of materials. In conjunction with this technology and methodol-
ogy shift, and because of the resulting adjustment in the group's mandate,
Issho Kikaku expanded its interests to include diversity and multiculturalism around the world while maintaining its basic focus on matters related to
Japanese society.

What are the main activities of Issho Kikaku?

At Issho Kikaku we have chosen to engage in research issues first because research is easier to do than rescue. We also limit our focus on human diversity
to ethnicity and similar matters; we do not cover issues such as gender. We have
broadened our organization to include international issues so that people can
compare and link, for instance, global issues and local issues in Asia. Around

the time of the World Conference Against Racism in Durban in 2001, our Web site became multilingual, with material available in ten languages or so. Our big hope is that individual communities in Japan and broader Asia can better find each other and communicate through our network—particularly our Web site—by exchanging information on their shared issues and concerns. We want to assist people globally to find information and connect across the language barriers. In terms of organization, we keep it simple. SPEAK! had a formal structure. Issho Kikaku is administrated primarily by two people: myself and Ana Bortz, a video-journalist by trade. Bortz is well known for her victory in an important antidiscrimination court case after, in 1998, a jewelry shop owner in Hamamatsu attempted to force her from the premises on the basis of her being a Brazilian national. It was the first time the International Convention on the Elimination of Racial Discrimination (ICERD) was invoked in a Japanese court—in this case to prove that the store manager's actions were illegal. Issho Kikaku maintains very low operating costs and does not have membership fees at this time. We consider anyone who is demonstrably active in the organization's various projects to be a member.

How did you begin your international lobbying work?

Japan ratified the ICERD in 1995. When the ICERD committee reviewed Japan's First and Second Periodic Reports in 1999, I went to Geneva as part of an NGO coalition. Issho Kikaku submitted two counterreports on discrimination and multiple discrimination. The first of these was entitled "Report on Racial Discrimination Within the Residents Registration Law." In the case of foreigners who are married to Japanese, their names can appear neither in the *koseki* (family registration) nor in the *jūminhyō* (resident registration). Both registration systems are based on the Japanese family unit rather than on individuals; while the Japanese nationals in the household appear on the documents, the spouse of a Japanese (and any other nonnational in the household) does not. In the case of the *jūminhyō*, this has been an issue of multiple discrimination in Japan because it has disproportionately affected women. In 99 percent of the cases, the men become the household head. Concerning the *jūminhyō*, there was an *administrative guidance* (formal regulation issued by a government agency) in 1962 that if a foreigner is the actual head of household, then the person's name should be written in the "remarks" column. But for most female foreigners, even if they were the head of household, they would never be recorded. Because foreigners cannot accomplish *nyūseki* (entry into the family register), many issues arise. It has implications for inheritance issues when the Japanese spouse passes away. It is also a resident issue, because the *koseki* is also a basic document to prove residency. The problem can also be as mundane as cellular phone companies not offering subscription discounts to such families. We at Issho Kikaku considered it an issue of considerable concern, affecting about one million people, so we launched the *Jūminhyō* for Everyone Issho Project (JEIP). The project was launched by a number of female foreign spouses to Japanese, many of whom had lived in Japan for decades while struggling with these issues. A report they created on this issue was included in the NGO ICERD report from Japan.

What came out of your mobilization on this issue?

After Issho Kikaku's JEIP project team researched the issue and formed a consensus on the matter, it began lobbying through petition and appeals. On March 1, 2002, the then vice-minister of the Ministry of Internal Affairs and Communications took up the issue in a Diet committee meeting. In particular, his reading of a statement prepared by one of the JEIP members apparently moved the members of the Diet. As a result of his presentation, the ministry issued a March 15 advisory to Japan's local municipalities that stipulated that Japanese spouses (even those who were not heads of household) should be able to have their names written in the remarks column in their resident registration if they requested it. Now almost all cities and towns comply with that guidance. However, due to a trend of increased decentralization of authority, local governments have become more independent and more prone to treat guidance from the ministry as an advisory (in the past it had been considered more of an order from above). In a later development, the Democratic Party, Japan's largest opposition party, has been noting the issue in its party manifesto since 2003. Specifically, the party has been pledging to resolve the problem via legislative revision.

What other issues do non-Japanese residents in Japan face?

There have been some political debates on the right to vote, particularly at the local level, for non-Japanese residents. However, there is also a significant backlash to the scheme, especially from the Liberal Democratic Party (LDP), one of the parties in the ruling coalition. Some members within the opposition Democratic Party also oppose the plan. Those who oppose generally take the position that only Japanese nationals have or should have the right to vote in elections held in Japan. As an alternative mechanism for giving foreign residents a voice, some municipalities and prefectures have put into place a foreigners' advisory council system whereby members of that council (all or partly foreigners, depending on the model) can debate and discuss issues and submit proposals directly to the mayor (or governor, as the case may be).

I remember that before you went to the World Conference Against Racism in Durban in September 2001, Issho Kikaku drafted a proposal on a Japanese law against racial discrimination. Could you tell me more about it?

In October 2000, Issho Kikaku presented the proposal to Fukushima Mizuho (Social Democratic Party), Kaneda Seiichi (Democratic Party) and Ishige Eiko (the human rights minister of the Democratic Party's shadow cabinet) at a special conference on racial discrimination held at the Diet. Subsequently, Fukushima created a bill, inspired in part by our contribution. Her bill did not pass through the legal committee review stage and was never tabled for Diet discussions. A few years later, the Japan Civil Liberties Union also created its own proposal. There are two ways of approaching such a bill. One way is to look at which international treaties Japan has ratified and what Japan has done (or not done) to fulfill its obligations under those treaties. Another way is to simply consider what Japan can do, realistically. I think ours was more the former approach, because we proposed a law that would provide penalties against discrimination offenses. Such penalties are common in antidiscrimination laws around the world.

Issho Kikaku was very active at the World Conference Against Racism. Could you tell me about your experience?

Issho Kikaku was active in the Durban 2001 Japan NGO coalition. I myself was one of the coalition leaders. In that capacity I helped to organize a press conference in which the Japanese government delegation fielded questions from the audience and the press. At the NGO Forum, Issho Kikaku co-organized and participated in a workshop on colonialism, nationalism, and racism in Japan. When we sign onto a given network, I want to make sure that our members agree on the issues. In Japan, NGOs that back the LDP or the Communist Party or the New Kōmeitō Party often have rigid platforms on multiple issues, which doesn't make it easy for them to mix with each other. But there might well be points of agreement among such groups, which appear so different at first glance. The challenge is to find those points of agreement so that NGOs can work together more effectively. In the end our work should be about serving the public better.

Your wife wrote a best-selling manga *(comic book),* Dārin wa gaikokujin *[My Darling Is a Foreigner]. Could you tell me about it?*

She wrote two volumes of *Dārin wa gaikokujin*, to which I contributed a few essays. Together we wrote a related book entitled *Dārin no atama no naka* [Inside Darling's Mind]. All of these books are *manga* and have been unexpectedly popular. The books are humorous works that portray our life together but, particularly in the case of the first two, also manage to take up a few of the issues faced by foreigner residents in Japan, including family registration and housing discrimination. Thanks to the popularity of the series, some of the issues taken up by Issho Kikaku have reached a considerably wide audience.

What is your priority from now on?

I think it is important to be open and to understand that we don't know everything. It is important for NGOs like ours to have a logical, clear, fair, and broad mandate, and a set of criteria. We should avoid illogical favoritism. I hope that we may continue to research multiethnic and multicultural issues in Japan, East Asia, and globally.

Related Web Sites

Exclusion of Foreign Residents' Names from the Resident Certificate: http://www
.issho.org/juminhyocerdreport.html
Issho Kikaku: http://www.issho.org/index.php
Issho Report on the World Conference Against Racism and Racial Discrimination:
http://www.hri.ca/racism/analyses/issho.shtml
Proposal for an Antidiscrimination Bill: http://www.issho.org/kinshiho-modelbill
.html
Race and Nationality-Based Exclusions Occurring at Private and Quasi-Public
Establishments in Japan: http://www.issho.org/exclusion-cerdreport.html
Tony László: http://talking.to/tony

Related References

Arudou, Debito. 2004. *Japanese Only: The Otaru Onsen Refusals and Racial Discrimination in Japan*. Tokyo: Akashi Shoten.

Kondō, Atsushi. 2001. *Gaikokujin sanseiken to kokuseki* [The right to vote and nationality of foreigners]. Tokyo: Akashi Shoten.

László, Tony. 1998. "Gaikokuseki jūmin wo fukumu atarashii shakai ketsugō" [A new social cohesion inclusive of foreign residents]. In *Gendai Nihon no paburikku firosofi* [Public Philosophy of Modern Japan], edited by Naoshi Yamawaki, Mari Ōsawa, Wataru Ōmori, and Ryūichirō Matsubara. Tokyo: Shinseisha.

László, Tony. 2002. "Jūminhyō ga kazoku to chiiki wo bundan suru: kisai sarenai gaikokujin haigūsha" [Resident certificate as divider of families and communities: Non-Japanese spouses go unrecorded]. *Sekai*, 7, 182–189.

Oguri, Saori. 2002. *Dārin wa gaikokujin* [My darling is a foreigner]. Tokyo: Mediafactory.

43

DISABILITY AND GENDER

Hirukawa Ryōko

HIRUKAWA RYŌKO worked for the Japan National Assembly of Disabled Peoples' International as a secretariat member for five years. A person with disability, she had the opportunity to be in touch with the activities of people with disabilities in the United Kingdom and New Zealand when she was a student and became interested in those activities. Currently she has suspended group activities except as part of a research group on domestic violence.

Could you tell me about the work of the Japan National Assembly of Disabled Peoples' International?

Japan National Assembly of Disabled Peoples' International (DPI Japan) was established in 1986 as a grassroots disability movement in Japan. We have ten staff members and some volunteers. Our funding comes mainly from membership fees and donations. Money from foundations or the government does not cover personnel; it covers only specific projects. For example, we recently received money from the Japan International Cooperation Agency to launch a new training course, targeting ten leaders with disabilities from Southern African countries—Mozambique, Zimbabwe, Botswana, Swaziland, Lesotho, Namibia, Zambia, the Republic of South Africa, and Malawi. DPI Japan focuses its activities in the following areas: deinstitutionalization and independent living in communities, amendment of the Fundamental Law for Disabled Persons, the enactment of an antidiscrimination law for persons with disabilities, and disclosure of the names of companies not meeting the employment quota. Personally, I focus on issues of domestic violence. DPI Japan also set up the DPI Advocacy center ten years ago, and an individual telephone and fax counseling hotline. DPI Japan is currently lobbying for a UN convention on the rights of persons with disabilities.

How did you become interested in disability issues from a gender perspective?

In 2002, the sixth DPI World Assembly was held in Sapporo, Hokkaido. DPI Japan wanted many Japanese participants, especially women, to attend the assembly, because few women were involved in the disability movement in Japan. Some women were active in peer counseling, but within DPI Japan there were few women. At the time of the assembly, as a woman with disability, I was already conscious of gender issues, but I wanted to revisit disability issues from a gender perspective. Before the fifth World Assembly in December 2001, I joined the Project Team on Multiple Discrimination Against Minority Women organized by Hara Yuriko and Kumamoto Risa at the International Movement Against All Forms of Discrimination and Racism (IMADR). They gave me a gender perspective. The next year I set up our study group, made up of both disabled and able-bodied women and men, and discussed issues of sexuality, violence, education, and independent living for people with disability—the themes of the World Assembly. I wanted to look further at issues of access to employment and other concerns, but I had to stop because of my own physical and financial condition.

What issues do women with disabilities face in Japan?

Some issues are commonly faced by both men and women with disabilities. For example, in employment, big companies in Japan are required by law to hire people with disabilities as 1.8 percent of their total employees or otherwise face a fine. In a survey in 2000, we found that 9,040 companies in Tokyo did not abide by the law. Also, women don't always get the same kind of work as men, especially those who are physically challenged like I am. Some quit after a few years because of their health.

In September 2003, you gave a statement to the Japanese government before the Domestic Violence Prevention Law was revised. What was your message?

The Domestic Violence Prevention Law was passed in 2001, and the first revision was due in 2004. A subcommittee was set up within the Research Committee on Coexistence in the House of Councillors to look into the matter. Until the revision, the disabled and foreigners were not included in the scope of the Domestic Violence Prevention Law. People didn't find that women with disabilities also suffer from domestic violence, so there were issues related to service provision for such women. The government does not have any data on the situation. In shelters, hand signing services are not available. Many women with disabilities may not be able to access regular domestic violence hotlines, which are mostly run by telephone. So, as disabled women, we submitted the statement to the subcommittee. We mentioned the fact that Recommendation 26 by the CEDAW committee at its twenty-ninth session in 2003 urged Japan to strengthen measures to protect victims of domestic violence. We called for expanding the definition of *domestic* to include institutions where people with disabilities reside, better service provision to cater to the needs of women with disabilities, and so on. In addition to giving our petition, we lobbied the Diet members. Now disabled women are included in the revised version of the law.

You mentioned that DPI Japan is lobbying for a UN convention on the rights of persons with disabilities. Could you tell me more about it?

DPI Japan was an active member in creating the Japan Disability Forum (JDF), a coalition of nine disability-related NGOs and networks in Japan established in 2004, right after the World Assembly. Members of JDF have served on Japanese governmental delegations in the preparatory meetings for the UN convention on the rights of persons with disabilities. You can see our position in our paper "Regarding a New International Human Rights Convention for Persons with Disabilities."

In your work, do you see connections among the various antidiscrimination movements in Japan?

I think the various movements are not entirely separate. When I joined the Project Team on Multiple Discrimination Against Minority Women organized by IMADR, I discovered some commonalities among the Buraku, Ainu, and disability movements. Until then I was not fully aware of the similarities. However, each movement has a different reach. I think our final aims are the same, that is, lives without discrimination in the society.

What would you like to focus on from now on?

In the process of lobbying for the inclusion of disabled women in the revised Domestic Violence Prevention Law, I wanted to research disabled women who were abused. One disabled woman college professor did a survey in Nagoya.

We would like to do a survey in Tokyo. Until we have more data, we would not know our needs and cannot lobby effectively. In addition, I would like to focus on how disabled women who suffer from domestic violence actually experience the services provided, and how we can provide information as best we can.

Related Web Sites

Convention on the Rights of Persons with Disabilities: http://www.un.org/esa/socdev /enable/rights/ahcfinalrepe.htm
Disabled Peoples' International (DPI) Sapporo Declaration at the Sixth DPI World Assembly: http://www.dpi-japan.org/8wa/declaration2002e.htm
International Day of Disabled Persons 2004: http://www.un.org/Pubs/chronicle/2004 /e_alert/120304_DisabledPersons.asp
Japan National Assembly of Disabled Peoples' International: http://www.dpi-japan .org/english/english.htm
Japan Position Paper Regarding a New International Human Rights Convention for Disabled People: http://www.worldenable.net/bangkok2003/paperjapan2.htm
Resources on women and disability: http://v1.dpi.org/lang-en/resources/topics_ list?topic=12
United Nations Enable: http://www.un.org/esa/socdev/enable

Related References

Asia-Pacific Human Rights Information Center. 2003. *Shōgaisha no Kenri* [Rights of persons with disabilities]. Tokyo: Gendaijinbunsha.
Disabled Peoples' International Japan. 2003. *Sekai no shōgaisha: warerajishin no koe* [Disabled people of the world: Our own voices]. Tokyo: Gendai Shokan.
International Movement Against All Forms of Discrimination and Racism Project Team on Multiple Discrimination Against Minority Women, ed. 2003. *Mainoritijosei no shiten wo seisaku ni! Shakai ni!* [Policy and society from the perspectives of minority women]. Tokyo: IMADR JC.
Kusunoki Toshio, 2005. "Rights of Disabled Persons and Japan: Regarding a New International Human Rights Convention for Persons with Disabilities." Available at http://www.hurights.or.jp/asia-pacific/no_29/04rightsdp.htm
Nakamura, Karen. 2002. "Resistance and Co-optation: The Japanese Federation of the Deaf and Its Relations with State Power." *Social Science Japan Journal*, 5, 17–35.

44

THE UN CONVENTION ON REFUGEE AND ASYLUM PROTECTION IN JAPAN

Ishikawa Eri

ISHIKAWA ERI is senior researcher in charge of public relations as well as foreign communications at the Japan Association for Refugees (JAR), an NGO supporting refugees established in 1999. Born in Tokyo in 1976, she graduated from the Department of Law at Sophia University in 1999. In 2001 she became a staff member of JAR, which is under contract to implement business with the office of the UN High Commissioner for Refugees (UNHCR) Japan and has already provided support for more than a thousand asylum seekers and refugees.

How did you become involved in refugee issues in Japan?

I was in high school when the genocide in Rwanda happened in 1994. I joined a study group on peace-building issues within Peace Brigade International. Then I volunteered at Amnesty International Japan, where I learned a lot about the UN human rights system and different human rights issues in Japan. In 1998, an NGO called Immigrant Review Task Force (Nyūkan mondai chōsa kai) published a report on the deportation process in Japan. Its findings subsequently appeared in the recommendations of the Human Rights Committee. In 1998, Amnesty International, lawyers' groups, individual case support groups, and social welfare organizations were all involved in refugee support in Japan, but there was no specialized NGO. In 1999, the Japan Association for Refugees (JAR) was formed to cater better to the needs of refugees and asylum seekers in Japan.

What are the main activities of JAR?

We have three areas of activities: support for refugees and asylum seekers (for example, free medical consultation), research and advocacy, and public information and education. In terms of public education, for example, three times a year we organize a two-day long seminar to train refugee assistants. Those who complete the seminar can then go on to an advanced course. Usually college students and journalists attend these courses.

What issues do asylum seekers face in Japan?

First of all, we don't know much about how Japanese immigration officials receive asylum seekers at Narita Airport. Some people have called the procedure a "black box." We know that the number of applications at Narita used to be very small. In 2000, a case of ill treatment of two Tunisian visitors to Japan was reported by Amnesty International. It says that they were beaten, detained at the Landing Prevention Facility for five days, and denied access to medical facilities and their embassy. Detention is a big issue in Japan. Visa overstayers who apply for refugee status, including children, pregnant women, and the sick, could be detained while their applications are being processed. There are two types of detention centers in Japan: short-term (up to twenty months) *shūyōjo* (detention facility) and *shūyō sentā* (detention center). It is said that there are about one hundred asylum seekers now in detention centers in Japan. They can apply for limited social assistance when their applications are being processed. But in the event that their asylum applications are turned down and they decide to appeal to the court, they will no longer be eligible for social assistance during the appeal process, which usually lasts for two years. In case of denial of refugee status, no explanation is given. No time frame is set for the administrative procedures of refugee recognition. There was a case that took nine years to reach a final decision. During the application and appeal process, an applicant has no right to work in Japan.

Could you tell me about the appeal process in Japan?

The Ministry of Justice processes the applications and the appeals. An asylum seeker who loses the appeal can take her or his case to the district court. Some of the cases that go to the district court win. If the applicant wants to appeal the district court's decision, the case goes to high courts. But many cases that go to high courts lose. There are many challenges in this process. There is no state-funded legal aid system in Japan, and there are not enough lawyers to help asylum seekers. Members of NGOs, including JAR, are not entitled to attend first hearings at the Ministry of Justice, but many applicants do not have legal representation and have to file their own case for appeals at the level of the district and high courts. In 2004 there are about 430 asylum applications in Japan, one of the biggest number in the past twenty years. The number of successful applicants per year is very low: two in 1995, one in 1996, one in 1997, sixteen in 1998, another sixteen in 1999, and twenty-two in 2000. In 2003 the figure dropped back to eight.

Hasn't Japan ratified the 1951 UN Convention Relating to the Status of Refugees as well as the 1967 Optional Protocol?

Yes, Japan joined both in 1981, soon after it made an exception to accept refugees from Indochina on a quota basis due to pressure from the United States. For other groups, including Kurds, Burmese, and Chinese, Japan has accepted some of them (excluding Kurds) on an individual case basis.

What does JAR advocate?

We want a transparent immigration procedure for asylum application. We advocate an appeal system that is independent from the Ministry of Justice. We also believe that asylum seekers should have access to social assistance while their applications are being processed. In March of this year (2004), the Refugee Council Japan, a coalition of ten NGOs, including JAR, was formed in order to coordinate our activities vis-à-vis the Japanese government (specifically, the Refugee Policy Coordination Council, an interagency council in the Cabinet Office).

Related Web Sites

Immigration Review Task Force: http://hw001.gate01.com/sasara/nyukan/englis/report.htm

International Council of Voluntary Agencies: http://www.icva.ch

Japan Association for Refugees: http://www.refugee.or.jp/index_e.html

Office of the UN High Commissioner for Refugees: http://www.unhcr.org/admin.html

Protocol Relating to the Status of Refugees, 1967: http://www.unhchr.ch/html/menu3/b/o_p_ref.htm

Refugee Council Japan: http://www.issj.org/english/Intercountry/ic27-2e.htm

UN Convention Relating to the Status of Refugees, 1951: http://www.unhchr.ch/html/menu3/b/o_c_ref.htm

Related References

Amnesty International. 2002a. "Welcome to Japan?" AI Index: ASA 22/002/2002, May. Available at http://web.amnesty.org/library/index/engasa220022002

Foster, Karen. 2006. "Japan Can't Stop the Tide of People: UNHCR Chief."
    Japan Times December 7. Available at http://search.japantimes.co.jp/print/
    nn20061207f1.html

Ishikawa, Eri. 2003. "Nihon ni okeru nanmin hogo no kakuritsu e mukete: Nanmin
    shinseisha, nanmin no seikatsu jittai chōsa hōkoku yori" [Toward a system of
    refugee protection in Japan: A survey report on asylum seekers and refugee living
    conditions]. *Rīgaru eido kenkyū* [Legal aid research], 8, 37–54.

Ogata, Sadako. 2005. *The Turbulent Decade: Confronting the Refugee Crises of the
    1990s*. New York: Norton.

Sano, Hideo, and Makoto Sano. 2005. *Yoku wakaru nyūkan tetsuzuki* [Understand-
    ing immigration procedures]. Tokyo: Nihon Kajō Shuppansha.

45

TORTURE, PENAL REFORM, AND PRISONERS' RIGHTS

Akiyama Emi

AKIYAMA EMI has been a paid staff member at the Center for Prisoners' Rights Japan since 2002. Born in Tokyo in 1976 and a graduate of Meiji University in Law in 2000, she produced the documentary *Keimusho wa kawarunoka: Nagoya keimusho jiken kara 3 nen* [Will a prison change? Three years since the Nagoya jail incident], which won Our Planet TV's planning prize. She is currently a student specializing in criminal procedure law in the Graduate School of Law at Meiji University.

How did you become involved in prisoners' issues in Japan?

I took a course on criminal justice with Professor Kikuta Kōichi at Meiji University when I was in college, and I volunteered at the Center for Prisoners' Rights Japan in 1999 (at that time the center did not yet have a paid staff member). It was the first time I learned about prisoners' issues in Japan.

How was the Center for Prisoners' Rights Japan created?

One of the founding members, attorney Kaido Yūichi, did consultation for prisoners. As the number of cases continued to increase, he thought that a group should be created in Japan. In 1993, he and some other lawyers went to the United Kingdom and visited Penal Reform International (PRI). Upon their return, they wanted to create PRI Japan. Just around that time, members of Human Rights Watch came to Japan and did research on prisoners' conditions. They wanted support from Japanese NGOs. The Center for Prisoners' Rights (CPR) Japan was created in 1995. Until the center came into being, there were several lawyer groups and individual case support groups. In 2005 we are going to celebrate our tenth anniversary.

What are the main activities of the CPR Japan?

Our basic work is to give advice to prisoners. Prisoners can mail letters only to registered family members and lawyers, so they send letters to our lawyers. Depending on their specific situations, we try our best to give them information and advice. So I spend most of my time answering letters. I receive about 800 letters, 150 phone calls, and 50 e-mails per year. One-third of the letters are about penalty and solitary confinement, another third relate to medical issues, and the remaining third are general complaints. In addition, we do advocacy work for policy change and lobby in the Diet. In Japan the prison law is almost one hundred years old. A penal reform committee was set up inside the Ministry of Justice in 2003. We also maintain external relations with embassies in Japan, such as the U.K. Consulate and the European Union offices.

Could you tell me some of the issues that prisoners in Japan face?

To begin with, there are a lot of limits on letter writing and *menkai* (meetings). In addition to being restricted to writing only to registered family members and lawyers, the letters of prisoners can be censored. Prison staff members are present during visits. A more serious issue is penalty, including *chōbatsu* (punishment such as sitting straight for eight hours without moving). Again, the decision-making process for *chōbatsu* is not clear. Some prisoners get up to sixty days of *chōbatsu* penalty. There is supposedly a petition system, but it is not functioning. Even more serious is the length of solitary confinement in Japanese prisons. It is supposed to be three months, which can be extended. But when we researched the issue, we found a case of thirty-seven years of solitary confinement. Today there are about two thousand people in solitary confinement in Japanese prisons. Then there is the issue of access to medical services. All prisoners are entitled to medical services, but in reality they are often first seen by a nurse, who may ask them to *gaman* (bear with it). Often it is not until a prisoner is in threatening health condition that he or she receives care. Many medical treatment cases are related to diabetes. The living conditions in Japanese prisons are not optimal. For instance, heating is available only in Hokkaido. Another issue is overcrowding. There were 73,734 prisoners as of December 2003. Currently, the capacity of Japanese prisons is over 100 percent. For instance, eight inmates may share a cell built for six.

The trend of lengthier sentences leads to an increased prison population. Of course one solution may be to build new prisons. But for us, building more prisons would not solve the fundamental problem of an increasing criminal population. Japan is moving in the same direction as the United States in privatizing prisons. There is a plan to open the first private prison in Yamaguchi Prefecture in 2007. Finally, it has become increasingly difficult, if not impossible, for those with life sentences with parole to actually get parole, because of the increased prison population. The current figure is that only six out of a thousand get parole.

How about torture? Is torture an issue in Japanese prisons?

In 2002 there was a torture incident in a prison in Nagoya in which a prison guard used a leather handcuff for restraint. The intestines of the prisoner got hurt. So far, we know of three deaths and a few injuries due to torture in Japanese prisons. The founding members of CPR Japan knew about the torture situation and had publicly spoken about it before the center was established. Even the UN Human Rights Committee knew about the situation in Japan and mentioned "the harsh rules of conduct in prisons that restrict the fundamental rights of prisoners . . . use of harsh punitive measures including resort to solitary confinement . . . and frequent use of protective measures, such as leather handcuffs, that may constitute cruel and inhuman treatment" in Article 27 of the concluding observations in Japan's Fourth Periodic Report in 1998. In 2003 we did a campaign and invited a member of the UN Committee Against Torture and medical expert Ole Vedel Rasmussen to come to Japan. After our campaign, leather handcuffs became forbidden in Japanese prisons. Now we are hoping that it would be incorporated into the penal reform through the revision of the prison law. Kikuta Koïchi, one of the founders of CPR, served as an academic commission member for penal reform between April and September 2003 (the commission itself is not made up only of academics; he is one of the members and he is an academic). After ratifying the Convention Against Torture and Other Cruel, Inhuman, or Degrading Treatment or Punishment (CAT) in 1999, the Japanese government was supposed to have submitted its First Periodic Report to the CAT committee in 2000, but the government still has not done so.

Are there any other concerns that you think need to be addressed?

A big problem with the penal system in Japan is the lack of transparency. When there is a case of discrimination, it goes to the Ministry of Justice because we don't have any independent human rights commission in Japan. I think we need a third independent body, an ombudsperson system. Right now, prisoners have no recourse. When they write to us, they might be bullied by prison staff. Another issue I have not mentioned is the situation of women prisoners. There are four women's prisons in Japan. There was a case in the women's prison in Tochigi in which a child was taken away from the prisoner after birth. Some rape incidents were also discovered and reported, even though we have no data on inmate rape.

How about the death penalty?

Of course we oppose the death penalty, but it is not the focus of our work. Forum 90, a coalition of NGOs in Japan that advocates the abolition of the death penalty, is the main actor.

What problems do you confront in your work on prisoners' rights in Japan?

We are the only advocacy NGO in Japan that deals with prisoners' rights. There is a group called the Prisoners Union Japan, made up of both inmates and external supporters and focused on information sharing. Most Japanese have no knowledge of this issue in Japan. The majority think that these are criminals and so have nothing to do with them. The negative reporting by Japanese media does not help.

Are you connected with other antidiscrimination movements in Japan?

We are connected in the sense that what the prisoners suffer is discrimination. In the case of foreigner prisoners, we collaborate with other NGOs. When the UN High Commissioner for Human Rights, Louise Arbour, came to Japan in November 2004, four human rights NGOs in Japan—Amnesty International Japan, Citizens' Diplomatic Centre for the Rights of Indigenous Peoples, the International Movement Against All Forms of Discrimination and Racism, and the Japan Civil Liberties Union—organized a dialogue between the High Commissioner and twenty-eight human rights NGOs, one of which is CPR. Collectively, we compiled an NGO report to the High Commissioner on the human rights situation in Japan.

[*Postscript*: On May 18, 2005, the House of Councillors unanimously enacted a new law to update a nearly one-hundred-year-old prison law. The new law is aimed at clarifying the rights and obligations of prisoners, which were ambiguously defined in the old law, while making correctional education in prison mandatory and establishing a panel to monitor prisoner treatment.]

Related Web Sites

Center for Prisoners' Rights Japan: http://www.jca.apc.org/cpr

Convention Against Torture and Other Cruel, Inhuman or Degrading Treatment or Punishment (adopted in 1984, entered into force in 1987, and ratified by Japan in 1996): http://www.unhchr.ch/html/menu3/b/h_cat39.htm

Optional Protocol to Convention Against Torture and Other Cruel, Inhuman or Degrading Treatment or Punishment (adopted in 2002, not yet ratified by Japan): http://www.unhchr.ch/html/menu2/6/cat/treaties/opcat.htm

Penal Reform International: http://www.penalreform.org/index.php

Prisoners Union of Japan: http://www.kangoku.org

UN Committee Against Torture: http://www.unhchr.ch/tbs/doc.nsf

Related References

Akiyama, Emi. *Keimusho wa kawarunoka: Nagoya keimusho jiken kara 3 nen* [Will a prison change? Three years since the Nagoya jail incident]. Video. OurPlanet TV. Available at http://www.ourplanet-tv.org

Center for Prisoners' Rights. 2004. "The Latest Situation of Japanese Prisons." Tokyo: CPR.

Japan Federation of Bar Associations. 1992. *Prisons in Japan: The Human Rights Situation in Japanese Prisons.* Tokyo: JFBA.

Keiji Rippō Kenkyūkai. 2005. *Keimusho kaikaku no yukue: Kangokuhou kaisei wo megutte* [On prison reform: Regarding the revision of the Prison Law]. Tokyo: Gendaijinbunsha.

UN Human Rights Committee, Sixty-Fourth Session. 1998. "Concluding Observations to Japan's Fourth Periodic Report." Available at http://www.unhchr.ch/tbs/doc.nsf/(Symbol)/5a2baa28d433b6ea802566d40041ebbe?Opendocument

46

DEATH PENALTY AND HUMAN RIGHTS

Takada Akiko

TAKADA AKIKO is Secretary General of Forum 90 for the Ratification of the Second Optional Protocol to the International Covenant on Civil and Political Rights. She works in the office of Yasuda Yoshihiro, a lawyer in charge of most of the capital punishment cases in Japan. Born in Sapporo in 1963, since 1990 Takada has been a member of the civil group Forum 90 for the Ratification of the Second Optional Protocol to the International Covenant on Civil and Political Rights.

How did you become involved in the issue of the death penalty in Japan?

In a social studies class in junior high school, I learned about the *Taigyaku Jiken* (high-treason incident), in which people such as Koutoku Shūsui were executed. I felt vaguely that there was something wrong with the death penalty. Since then, the feeling has remained in my mind. Later, when I was in university, I learned about the activities of Amnesty International. I thought there might be something I could do to abolish the death penalty, so I joined them. That is how I began my work against the death penalty. That was already twenty-four years ago.

How was Forum 90 created?

In December 1989, the UN passed the Second Optional Protocol to the International Covenant on Civil and Political Rights (ICCPR), which aimed at the abolition of the death penalty. With this as a start, a lawyer named Yasuda Yoshihiro, who was my boss and handled many cases of the death penalty in

Japan, thought that the "death penalty will not be gone only by fighting in the court. What is necessary is a movement that appeals to society." He appealed to civic groups throughout Japan to unite and form a loose movement body aiming at only the abolition of the death penalty. That was the start of Forum 90.

How many people have been executed in Japan recently? How many are now on death row?

Fourteen were executed between 1981 and 1990, and thirty-nine between 1991 and 2000. Now there are about seventy-eight prisoners on death row in Japan (as of December 22, 2005).

What is problematic with the death penalty in Japan?

In terms of legal procedures, the current situation is that there is no factual inquiry in criminal trials in the Supreme Court of Japan. It offers no more than a constitutional decision, and a three-tiered judicial system for the accused person does not really exist in Japan. In addition, retrials are rare in Japan. In practice, it has not been functioning. Moreover, in December 1999, a death-row convict was executed while appealing for retrial. Death-row convicts can make requests for amnesty, but there has not been a single case of penalty reduction through amnesty since 1975. The result is announced only to the death-row convict, and execution is carried out at the time the result is given. The decision is not communicated even to lawyers, so protests cannot be made. This situation is against the UN resolution regarding "the safeguards guaranteeing protection of the rights of those facing the death penalty," which targets countries that have not abolished the death penalty. Executions are usually carried out six or seven years after confirmation of the death sentence. They often occur when the Diet is not sitting, so that questions cannot be asked in the Diet. In addition, neither the prisoner nor his or her family is given advanced notice of the execution. On the morning of the execution, the prisoner will be called suddenly and be informed of the execution. The Japanese execution method is hanging. A prisoner is handcuffed and blindfolded, and the hanging rope is placed around the prisoner's neck. It is said that at a signal the floor splits in two and the prisoner falls down below the floor with great force and goes into hard convulsions. Once a doctor who stands by below the floor confirms the death, the body is washed and cleansed. The person who does this sequence of things after the execution is a guard at the scene who has taken prior care of the prisoner.

*What are the main activities of Forum 90's requesting the ratification of the
Second Optional Protocol to the ICCPR?*

Forum 90 is a civic movement of about four thousand individuals, including ordinary people throughout Japan, lawyers, scholars, and Diet members.
It consists of three core groups in addition to Amnesty International Japan,
and prominent individuals including the former Chief Justice of the Supreme
Court Dandō Shigemitsu and writer Kaga Otohiko. It is a loose movement
that is connected at only one point—we aim at the abolition of the death penalty—without trying to form an organization or adopt a membership system.
In terms of our activities, we aim to play a role in activating the debate on the
death penalty by holding events, lobbying, and publishing books. Our first
event in 1990 attracted twelve hundred participants. Between December 1989
and March 1993 there was a de facto moratorium, when no death penalty was
carried out in Japan. The Minister of Justice at the time, Satō Megumu, entered Buddhist priesthood and did not sign off on any paper ordering execution. During this period there was hope among our fellow members that the
death penalty would be abolished as it was, and our movement got into swing.
However, the society in general believes that the death penalty is a crime deterrent. It is important to remember that during this period without execution, vicious crimes conversely decreased.

*I heard that there is a coalition of Diet members against the death penalty.
Could you tell me more about it?*

The ultrapartisan Parliamentary Association for the Abolishment of the Death
Penalty was formed in 1995. Tamura Hajime, former Speaker of the House of
Representatives, was the first chairman of the association. Many Diet members were enthusiastic and active about the abolition of the death penalty, and
more than a hundred Diet members have participated since the start of the association. The activities of the Parliamentary Association for the Abolishment
of the Death Penalty include holding various study meetings on the death
penalty, receiving groups of inspectors from foreign countries and the UN,
holding seminars, meeting the Minister of Justice in person, and appealing
to the minister to abolish the death penalty. Kamei Shizuka, the current and
fourth chairman of the Parliamentary Association, tried to submit a bill for
abolishing the death penalty. However, a consensus within the dominant Liberal Democratic Party could not be obtained, and unfortunately the bill was
never submitted. However, I think it was significant that the Parliamentary

Association started to take a concrete step toward the abolition of the death penalty. Kamei used to be in the police, but he is a politician who is prompt in action as well as a firm death-penalty abolitionist claiming that a false charge can inevitably occur. We want to put our hopes on his future leadership of the Parliamentary Association for the Abolishment of the Death Penalty.

Is Forum 90 connected to the international movement against the death penalty?

The closest international group is Amnesty International. Other than that, we invite leading figures from countries that have abolished the death penalty, learn the process leading up to the abolition, and request that countries around the world put pressure on the Japanese government to pursue the abolition of the death penalty. In concrete terms, in 1993 we invited Robert Badinter—the ex-Minister of Justice when the death penalty was abolished in France—to Japan, and we organized study meetings, including with Diet members. In addition, in 2002, when members of the Council of Europe came to Japan, we held seminars inside the Diet, and the Minister of Justice at the time and other concerned people participated in them. After that, the Council of Europe passed a resolution that considered removing Japan's observer status unless the government of Japan made efforts toward the abolition of the death penalty. However, unfortunately, the Japanese government has not yet tried to make such efforts. We cooperate not only with Europe. In 1993 we invited to Japan people engaged in the movements for the abolition of the death penalty in South Korea, Singapore, Taiwan, and the Philippines and held the Asia Forum on the Abolishment of the Death Penalty. In terms of countries that have not reached the abolition of the death penalty, we cooperated with them and built up the foundation so we could fight together toward the abolition of the death penalty. Above all, the movement for the abolition of the death penalty has grown in South Korea. Ex-president Kim Dae-Jung was a death-row convict and he never signed off on any death penalty when he was the president. In October 2001, after approval signatures by more than half of the parliamentary members (155 out of 273), a bill on the abolition of the death penalty was put on the agenda. It is an epoch-making situation. Taiwanese president Chen Shui Ben is also for the abolition of the death penalty, and a change has been occurring in other Asian countries. In addition, Forum 90 is currently a member of the nongovernmental World Coalition Against the Death Penalty, created in 2002.

What issues does Forum 90 face in mobilizing against the death penalty in Japan?

First, there is an issue of activity expenses. We cover our activity expenses with a donation of 814 yen (because 814 is *haishi*, which also means "abolition"). We sometimes go into the black, but in general we face deficit finances. In addition, the number of supporters dropped from fifty-five hundred at a peak period to four thousand. This is because the number of supporters decreases each time vicious crimes are committed, including the sarin gas attack in a Tokyo subway in 1995. In terms of networking with other nations, the second Asia Forum was held in South Korea in 2003, after which no country has taken up the lead. It seems that the movement faces difficulty in all countries. Also, we would like to request that European countries that have abolished the death penalty put more *gaiatsu* (foreign pressure) on the Japanese government. But there is also a trivial matter: the inability to use English freely has been an obstacle.

Why do you think it is so difficult to mobilize public support for the abolition of the death penalty in Japan?

I think that there are many reasons. The primary reason is that there is practically no information on the death penalty in Japan. The Ministry of Justice operates in secret. It does not release information even to Diet members. The Ministry of Justice claims that the death penalty in Japan is maintained on the basis of public support. However, because there is no information about the death penalty, people do not have doubts about it, and accordingly there is no controversy. In 2003, opinion polls showed that 88 percent of Japanese were in favor of keeping the death penalty. I think it is all because of the result brought by this secretism. In the first place, the abolition of the death penalty should not follow the trend of public opinion; rather, the government should take the initiative in discussing the death penalty and abolish it. Considering the current situation in Japan, public opinion needs to be shaped and to back up the politics. We think it is important to build up movement power (*undō tairyoku*) and develop engaging movements that would attract people more.

Related Web Sites

Amnesty International campaign against the death penalty: http://web.amnesty.org/
    pages/deathpenalty-index-eng
Amnesty International Japan, campaign against the death penalty: http://www
    .amnesty.or.jp

Forum 90: http://www.jca.apc.org/stop-shikei/index.html

National Coalition to Abolish the Death Penalty: http://www.ncadp.org

Second Optional Protocol to the International Covenant on Civil and Political
 Rights: http://www.unhchr.ch/html/menu3/b/a_opt2.htm

World Coalition Against the Death Penalty: http://www.worldcoalition.org/modules/
 accueil/index.php?sel_lang=english

Related References

Forum 90. 2001. *The Hidden Death Penalty in Japan: The Legal Process and the Legal
 Challenge in Japan.* Report presented at the First World Congress Against the
 Death Penalty, Strasbourg, France. Tokyo: Forum 90. Available at http://www
 .ncadp.org/html/intlreport1.html

Hood, Roger. 2002. *The Death Penalty: A Worldwide Perspective.* Oxford, UK:
 Clarendon Press.

International Federation of Human Rights. 2002. "Death Penalty in Japan." Paris:
 FIDH. Available at http://www.fidh.org/article.php3?id_article=1499

Johnson, David. 2002. The Japanese Way of Justice: Prosecuting Crime in Japan. New
 York: Oxford University Press.

Lane, Charles. 2004. "Why Japan Still Has the Death Penalty." *Washington Post,*
 January 16, B01. Available at http://www.washingtonpost.com/wp-dyn/articles/
 A11306-2005 Jan15.html

Nenpō Shikeihaishi Henshū Iinkai, ed. 1996. *"Aum ni shikei wo" ni dō kotaeruka* [How to respond to the voice, "Sentence Aum to death"]. Tokyo: Impakuto
 Shuppankai.

Nenpō Shikeihaishi Henshū Iinkai, ed. 1997. *Shikei: sonchi to haishi no deai* [The
 death penalty: Encounter of maintenance and abolition]. Tokyo: Impakuto
 Shuppankai.

Nenpō Shikeihaishi Henshū Iinkai, ed. 1998. *Hanzai higaisha to shikei seido* [Victims
 of crime and the death penalty]. Tokyo: Impakuto Shuppankai.

Nenpō Shikeihaishi Henshū Iinkai, ed. 1999. *Shikei to jōhō kōkai* [The death penalty
 and information disclosure]. Tokyo: Impakuto Shuppankai.

Nenpō Shikeihaishi Henshū Iinkai, ed. 2000–2001. *Shūshinkei wo kangaeru*
 [Examining the life sentence]. Tokyo: Impakuto Shuppankai.

Nenpō Shikeihaishi Henshū Iinkai, ed. 2002. *Sekai no naka no Nihon no shikei* [The
 death penalty of Japan in the world]. Tokyo: Impakuto Shuppankai.

Nenpō Shikeihaishi Henshū Iinkai, ed. 2003. *Shikeihaishi hōan* [A bill to abolish the
 death penalty]. Tokyo: Impakuto Shuppankai.

Nenpō Shikeihaishi Henshū Iinkai, ed. 2004. *Mujitsu no shikeishūtachi* [Innocent
 death-row convicts]. Tokyo: Impakuto Shuppankai.

Nenpō Shikeihaishi Henshū Iinkai, ed. 2005. *Aum jiken jyūnen* [Ten years since the Aum incident]. Tokyo: Impakuto Shuppankai.

Schmidt, Petra. 2002. *Capital Punishment in Japan*. Leiden, the Netherlands: Brill.

PART VIII

YOUTH GROUPS

FIGURE 8. Peace Boat

INTRODUCTION TO PART VIII

ALTHOUGH JAPANESE social movement activists often lament the generation gap (that is, young Japanese seem to be unresponsive), the national crisis triggered by the prolonged economic recession since the early 1990s seems to have opened up space for youth participation and networking. Labor re-structuring has created a "nagging sense of job insecurity" not only among middle-aged white-collar workers but also among the young in the so-called lost decade (the 1990s).[1] Since 1999 the unemployment rate for males aged fifteen to twenty-four has persistently exceeded 10 percent, more than double the national average.[2] The number of *freeta*—freelance part-time workers, or in a stereotypical image, "those who will not (or cannot) hold a steady job or those who soon quit"[3]—has continued to rise to more than two million while that of NEET (fifteen- to thirty-four-year-olds *not* in *e*mployment, *e*ducation, or *t*raining) reached 890,000 in 2002.[4]

The corporate warrior model and lifelong employment system are being questioned, and many young people in Japan have become involved in the mini NPO and NGO revolution since the Kobe earthquake in 1995, when there was an outpouring of nonprofit efforts. Statistics by the Japan NGO Center for International Cooperation show that youth between ages twenty and thirty currently constitute more than 60 percent of paid NGO staff despite a signifi-cant salary gap compared with the private sector (three-fourths to one-half).[5] At the Japan Global Expo in Aichi in 2005, young activists dominated the planning and operation of the NGO Global Village.[6] Thirty NPOs and NGOs shared their approaches to environmental problems, international collaboration, peace, and development through participatory experiences.[7] Increasingly, many young Japanese have also taken up the challenge of creating their own NGOs, in the fields of international development, peace, ecology, children's rights, sex work, HIV / AIDS, and alternative media (for example, CHANCE! pono2, Body and Soul, Action Against Child Exploitation, Sex Workers and Sexual Health, Services in Health in Asia and Africa Regions, and JanJan).

Not only are more young people involved in nongovernmental activities, but they are also transforming social movement styles and tactics. Rather than being bound by the old and rigid ideologies of the Left, young activists are searching for new means of participation and self-expression. The colors, sounds, and liveliness in recent antiwar parades in Japan may not always be shared by veteran activists, but the unprecedented participation of the general public and youth has given new life to some dormant mass movements.[8] Youth activists also challenge the very makeup of the postwar economic and social model that they have inherited from their baby boomer parents, a model based on economic growth, efficiency, competition, mass production and consumption, technology development, waste, and genetic engineering that is unsustainable. The alternatives they seek are globally inspired but locally focused. As part of a worldwide trend, the slow food–slow life movement, for example, has taken root in Japan since the late 1990s. Centered on ecological thinking and tied to peace and education, the "sloth" movement promotes "the concept of 'doing' less, living simply, minimizing our destructive impact, and finding joy in our life without consuming an endless chain of meaning-less things . . . [a] shift from the culture of the 'more, faster and tougher' to that of 'less, slower and non-violent.'"[9] Organizations like the Sloth Club, BeGood Cafe, and Body and Soul all emphasize the journey of self-realization that is changing the world by changing our thinking and living.

This last section explores some of the newest trends in youth organiz-ing in Japan. I present the profiles of four youth groups involved in peace education, environment, food, and slow life. Topics explored include par-ticipation, international advocacy, the meaning of going slow in Japan, alter-native work, regional exchange, and connections between youth and other new social movements. Several themes come out of this discussion. Youth groups tend to encourage hands-on organization—whether through travel, exchange programs, agricultural projects, or open talk events—and direct action. Many go beyond national boundaries to network with youth activists in Asia and other areas. A constant preoccupation is the need to keep their activities and activism on peace, ecology, and human rights fresh, cool, and natural in order to attract the young population that might hesitate to join the more established labor, women's, and antiwar movements. Besides having funding issues, youth activists also struggle with the predominant negative image of the alterglobalization movement in Japan, on the one hand, and question the efficacy of their networking in producing action and change, on the other.

Notes

1. Genda 2005a.
2. Ibid.
3. Ibid, 53.
4. Genda 2005b.
5. Suzuki 2002.
6. Participant's observation at the Aichi Expo, July 2005.
7. For a list of all thirty participating NGOs, see http://www.global-village.expo2005.or.jp/en/participate/participate.html
8. Takada 2004.
9. http://www.slothclub.org/pages/who/why.htm

47

EXPERIENCE, ACTION, AND THE FLOATING PEACE VILLAGE

Yoshioka Tatsuya

YOSHIOKA TATSUYA is founder and director of Peace Boat. Born near Osaka in 1960, he cofounded Peace Boat in 1983 after encountering the South Korean Democracy solidarity movement. As its director he has engaged internationally in such projects as peace education for Israeli and Palestinian youth, Eritrea-Ethiopia peoples' peace talks, and North Korea-Japan peoples' dialogues. Yoshioka is author of two books, one on the former Yugoslavia and the other on the Russia-Japan Northern Territories dispute. He also serves as a member of the International Steering Group for the Global Partnership for the Prevention of Armed Conflict (GPPAC), and is head of the Secretariat for Northeast Asia GPPAC. He is currently working on the launch of the Global Article 9 Campaign to Abolish War.

Could you tell me a little bit about your personal background?

In my experience, discrimination in Japanese society, especially against Koreans, is very serious. I grew up in Osaka. I came to Tokyo when I was only twenty years old. Discrimination against Koreans in Osaka was very severe and very overt. For example, people would say that Koreans were dangerous. I remember that when I was young, one of the teachers described discrimination as inhuman and that we had the responsibility to learn the history of why we discriminated against others. So when I was a teenager I joined a grassroots study group and had Korean friends. I think I was particularly marked by one incident. My high school was famous for good entrance rates into top national universities. In our class there was a small group that always had trouble with teachers and also criticized Koreans. They bullied the Koreans using very bad words. I always argued against them. Then one of the members of that group got kidney problems and had to give up his entrance examination. Out of sympathy I visited him in the hospital and we reminisced about school. All of a sudden he told me, "I would like to confess. My name is Japanese, but I am Korean." He apologized and then continued, "I don't know Korean and I have no friends in Korea. For Koreans in Japan, only three kinds of jobs are available: lawyers, doctors, and yakuza. Maybe it is difficult for you to imagine but I won't be able to have a regular job in big companies." I felt shame. My knowledge about Koreans was only from books. I did not know about their reality. I felt at the time that I must have inflicted on him a lot of pain.

What shaped you as a peace educator?

I had strong interests in the student movement. In 1981, after the regime of Park Chun-hee had ended, after the Kwangju massacre, there was a campaign in Japan to save Kim Dae-jung. I joined the movement and started to learn something about international solidarity and the importance of peace issues in Asia. Just around that time the history textbook problem emerged in Japan. The Ministry of Education approved textbooks that replaced the word *invaded* with *sent troops*. All governments in China, Korea, and the Philippines were upset and criticized the new textbooks. From 1979 a new kind of university center examination system was put in place in Japan. Everybody had to pass two exams: the national exam that was common to all, and then a university-specific exam. I was the first generation of that new system. Because of this new exam structure, teachers stuck tightly to the curriculum and forced us to remember the textbooks. I was twenty-three years old and I failed my university entrance exams twice before finally getting in. Maybe that is why I hated the system! [Laughter.] It was a big shock for me to see how history textbooks were completely manipulated by the government. A couple of us in college thought, "Let's go abroad, meet the Asian people, see the reality of their lives, and learn what they think about history. If we can cooperate with other Asians, we should do something." At that time, the dollar was very expensive, about 260 yen. It was too expensive to go to Asia by air. We heard that boats were cheap during the typhoon season. In 1983, one hundred and fifty of us decided to charter a boat. We incurred a big debt, and because of the debt we were fed up with our initiative and decided that there would be no more Peace Boat. But we had a democratic system; the debt was completely equally divided among us.

Why did you decide to go outside of Japan and to Asia in particular?

We couldn't trust the textbooks and we couldn't trust the media either. We thought that to make real friendship with Asians, we had to know what the Japanese had done in Asia. We had to know history well. The people who did it, the aggressors, could forget, the but victims would not, especially concerning rape and genocide. That is completely understandable, so we should know what the victims think. This remains a strong core philosophy of Peace Boat; that is, we have to know the truth. If we watch CNN twenty-four hours a day, we cannot know the truth. We have to begin our study through experience.

Besides the cost factor, why did you choose to go on a boat?

A boat was a countermovement to the peace movement of the 1970s. In 1972 there was the *Asama-sansō* scandal, in which some members of the students' movement were killed by their colleagues. The students' movement became perceived by the Japanese government and public as dangerous. I was at Waseda University at the time. The university was locked after 9 or 10 p.m. The students' activities were controlled. By the early 1980s it had become difficult for students to gather anywhere after 9 p.m. and we didn't have space for our activity. Ships have a lot of space. We could play radical movies and invite speakers who might otherwise hesitate to join. It was like a school festival. We were thirsty for such a space. We felt that ships were an interesting space, like a mobile university. We started our second boat in 1984 and we sailed to Nanjing in China.

How are the activities of Peace Boat structured?

When we launched our first Peace Boat in 1983, we were not very conscious about program planning. For our second boat, we have become a little bit more organized; for example, volunteers can join with a discount. As an NPO we try to keep a simple structure. We have a horizontal organizational structure, with an executive committee and a large board with more than one hundred members. We practice direct democracy. All board members meet once every month, and they have a high level of responsibility. For instance, if we incur a debt because our voyages are not successful, we divide the debt between all of us. We have one hundred full-time paid staff members. We have about a thousand passengers per voyage, and 3.5 voyages per year. There are many programs, group activities, and free projects. Five years ago we started the global university program on board. Each time, fifty out of a thousand passengers (mostly people who would like to work for NGOs) participate in this program. There is also the global English training program. We think that communication is crucial for peace. It is unfortunate that English is the lingua franca of the world. Our program is designed not to teach English according to the Anglo-Saxons, but to teach English for global people. We are fine with Singlish (Singaporean English), pidgin, and vernacular. We also organize an international student program once a year. We invite young students and NGO activists from conflict areas such as Israel, Palestine, India, and Pakistan. Our idea is that when they share and contextualize their own experiences, they will realize the commonality among conflicts and begin to come together to build mutual understanding.

How do you fund your activities?

We are completely independent and receive no financial support except the participants' fees (around $13,000 per voyage that lasts about three months). I think it is very important for NGOs to maintain their independence. Some NGOs receive money from the government and cannot say, for instance, antiwar comments to the Japanese government. Some people say that Peace Boat does good work but charges too much. We prefer to do it this way rather than selling our souls. Some NGOs receive government money to work in Iraq and they don't join antiwar demonstrations. In such a sensitive political situation, when there is a superpower, I think what these NGOs do in Iraq is questionable.

What is the philosophy of Peace Boat?

Peace Boat is like a small Earth. It is a floating university, a floating peace village, and a floating people's media. Our key is civil society building. Each year we lead around 3,500 people to visit countries in the North and South. What we recognize on board is that the global civil society is very unfair. For instance, in Japan everybody can buy a mobile phone. But in Sudan, how many die as a result of poverty, displacement, and war? We see huge slums in Brazil. We see AIDS in Mozambique, where close to 30 percent of the adult population is HIV-positive. It is difficult to recognize that we live in the same world. I really think we have to reconsider the so-called globalization that destroys and creates unfairness. We have to create alternatives. Networking is increasing all over the world.

What peace issues concern you most right now?

Peace Boat is the Northeast Asia regional secretariat of the Global Partnership for the Prevention of Armed Conflict (GPPAC), an initiative of UN Secretary General Kofi Annan and a project started by the European Center for Conflict Prevention, which aims at strengthening the conflict-prevention and peace-building partnership among civil society, the UN, and governments world-wide. Right now we are working on the Korean peninsular issue. It is not easy to make it successful, but I think it is very important to create civil society in Northeast Asia. Because of the North Korea nuclear issue, the cross-Straits issue, Sino-Russia relations, and Japan's growing militarism, we face the danger of war. George W. Bush has already shown us how war can be launched without a UN mandate. But the United States is only one superpower. If the United States is still democratic, civil society can change the situation.

Do you see any connection between your work and the work of antidiscrimination NGOs in Japan?

I think the links between antidiscrimination and peace are crucial. Why do people kill each other? How can the Israeli government be so cruel to Palestinians? I think the hatred is based on discrimination. An interview of Bosnian Serbs who committed mass rapes of Muslims found that their acts were completely due to discrimination. We have seen the same in Japanese history in World War II when Japanese soldiers killed Chinese because of discrimination. A Japanese solider, when asked why he killed twenty-five Chinese during the war, said, "At that time we didn't think Chinese were human beings." For me, the work of various antidiscrimination movements is very important. I think the big challenge for us is how to cohabit this small world. Passengers on the boat have to find ways to cohabit. After a while they begin to find compromise.

Are you connected to the larger alternative globalization movement in Japan or worldwide?

We have been sending our staff members to the World Social Forum (WSF) since 2002. From an educational point of view, experience is crucial. Anyone who studies alternative globalization has to go to WSF. We thought that maybe Peace Boat could provide such a vessel. In 2004 our boat actually stopped in Mumbai. Six hundred passengers from Peace Boat went to the WSF.

As a peace educator, what do you think of the WSF?

I am always thinking about this question! Peace Boat also functions as an alternative medium; that is, people themselves observe, experience, and distribute information in our society. Such an activity is very important for our society, and I think that WSF has that function. However, I think a key challenge for this global movement, not only WSF, at this point is to reflect seriously on how much energy, time, and money it should spend on activities like the WSF. It is not easy to create horizontal linkages. There is a lot of discussion on the Internet and lots of ideas are circulating, but the important question is whether such networks can produce action. Only action can change things. Without it there is no democracy.

How do you evaluate the peace education done by Peace Boat?

We don't have any formal evaluation, but we know that Peace Boat graduates have gone on to do many wonderful things. Some of them are working in schools in Cambodia. Some have become active members of Friends of the Earth Japan. Some have taken up leadership after the recent Niigata earthquake. Another has joined the Japan Campaign to Ban Landmines. For many, Peace Boat has changed their lives. Experience is important. Action is important.

Related Web Sites

10.7 Peace Renaissance (Japan): http://www.peace-renaissance-japan.org/
European Centre for Conflict Prevention: http://www.conflict-prevention.net
Global Partnership for the Prevention of Armed Conflict: http://www.gppac.net
Peace Boat: http://www.peaceboat.org
Peace Links (U.S.): http://www.peacelinks.us
World Social Forum: http://www.wsfindia.org

Related References

Peaceboat, ed. 2003. *Sensō wo okosanai tame no 20 no hōsoku* [Twenty rules for preventing war]. Tokyo: Poplar Sha.
Peaceboat, ed. 2005. *Peaceboat daikōkai jidai: 84 ka kan chikyū isshū cruise 94 ōgon no utatane* [Age of great voyages by Peaceboat: Cruise around the globe for eighty-four days in 1994: The golden siesta]. Tokyo: Dai san shokan.
Salomon, Gavriel, and Baruch Nevo Baruch, eds. 2002. *Peace Education: The Concept, Principles, and Practices Around the World*. Mahwah, NJ: Erlbaum.
Tongeren, Paul van. 2005. *People Building Peace II: Sixty-Five Inspiring Stories*. Boulder, CO: Lynne Rienner.

48

ECOLOGY, YOUTH ACTION, AND INTERNATIONAL ADVOCACY

Mitsumoto Yuko

MITSUMOTO YUKO is a secretariat staff member of A SEED Japan, an international youth environmental NGO. Born in 1983 and graduated from the Faculty of Environmental Information in the Shōnan Fujisawa Campus of Keio University, Mitsumoto attended the World Summit on Sustainable Development in Johannesburg in 2002. She was in charge of preparing a policy proposal for the People's World Water Forum held in Kyoto in 2003. She also participated in the ministerial meetings of the World Trade Organization in 2003 and 2005, and prepared advocacy policy proposals on investment and agriculture to submit to the Japanese government.

Could you tell me a little about A SEED Japan?

A SEED (Action for Solidarity, Equality, Environment, and Development) International Campaign was started in 1990 by the European Youth Forest Action, an umbrella organization of about three hundred European youth environmental groups. The objective of the campaign was to encourage strong alliances among young people committed to a socially just and ecological world through a decentralized network that supports local, national, and regional youth movements. In response to that call, A SEED Japan was established in 1991 as part of an international youth mobilization on the environment and social justice, particularly at the 1992 United Nations Conference on Environment and Development (also known as the Rio Earth Summit). Our aim was to insert the youth voice into the process. Principle 21 in the Rio Declaration, Chapter 25 in the Agenda 21, the Rio Declaration on Environment and Development, and the nongovernmental Youth Treaty talk specifically about youth

participation. A SEED Japan is part of this global youth movement on environment and development. We have two paid staff members, between thirty
and fifty volunteers, and twelve hundred members.

How did you become involved in the youth movement?

As part of our campaign on the World Summit on Sustainable Development
(WSSD) in Johannesburg in 2002, members of A SEED Japan held a demonstration on corporate responsibility in environmental issues for public educational purposes in Shibuya in downtown Tokyo. Members of three Japanese
NGOs, on African issues, women, and development, served as NGO representatives in the Japanese governmental delegation to WSSD. We tried to give our
opinion to the Japanese government through these NGO members, but unfortunately they had little impact on the government. I went to WSSD in August
2002 as a member of A SEED Japan. Every morning we did direct action inside
the conference venue. We wore "CORP RULE" on tags on our backs, held big
banners, and sang.

How did you feel about your experience at the WSSD in Johannesburg?

It was my first international experience. It made a big impression on me. I
saw huge demonstrations by various movements in South Africa, including
the powerful landless movement. I joined a "reality tour" and we visited some
townships near Johannesburg where there was no potable water. I saw five
people living in a tent no higher than a table. I had never before seen that kind
of poverty. Until then I had heard a lot of critiques of globalization, but it was
in South Africa that I finally saw why people were so angry.

For you, what is problematic with the current model of economic globalization?

I think the global alterglobalization movement raises important questions
about economic globalization. We are concerned about increasing poverty
and the wealth gap, our environment, violations of human rights, insecurity,
and the transparency of organizations such as the International Monetary
Fund and the World Bank. Take the case of water, for instance. I think water
development should be community based and more aid should be channeled
that way. Right now, the negotiations under the General Agreement on Trade
in Services for the liberalization and privatization of the water sector are
having an impact on access to water, which is a basic human right. I think

the multinational corporations will limit the actions of local communities. In Japan, parts of our water services, for example, quality control and water treatment, have already been privatized and we have seen a price increase. Or look at what Japanese corporations do in financing development projects, for example, in Russia; often what they do is sanctioned through Japanese aid (see an analysis by Friends of the Earth Japan at http://www.foejapan.org/aid/jbic02/sakhalin/index.html).

What does A SEED Japan do to raise consciousness about these issues within Japan?

In addition to our bimonthly newsletter *Tanemaki*, we have several project teams on ecosaving, youth NPO bank, ecoculture, Millennium Development Goals (MDG) watch, and eco-employment. We also run specific campaigns and participate in international conferences. For example, we organized a Freeze WTO Campaign in preparation for the ministerial meeting of the World Trade Organization (WTO) in Cancun in September 2003. We organized study groups on WTO-related issues and events in different universities. We put together a report on our actions and the results of this campaign in *The Guide to Globalization* in 2004. We emphasize looking at environmental issues from a structural and long-term perspective. We think the participation of youth and NGOs is important. We want to change the stereotypical bad image of the alterglobalization movement. For us, NGOs equal peace. When we do a march, we sing.

What are some of the issues you face in organizing the youth environmental movement in Japan?

There are many youth groups, especially within universities, but they are small and informal. For example, there is a youth network called Eco League, which is a national network of university students. They organize a big gathering every year, but they remain local and don't do advocacy work. Part of the mission of A SEED Japan is to nurture and train future activist leaders. It is a bottom-up process rather than one that is driven by the government. Many young people are expressing a lot of criticism about old movement styles and tactics. Many are hesitant to join the labor or women's movement because they do not appeal to them. We want to create a new image of NGOs that is fresh, cool, and natural. We want to emphasize that we are not a service NGO; we focus on structural inequalities.

Because a lot of the activities happen within universities, are academics involved in this movement?

Some academics are involved but only in specific campaigns. For example, a professor from Keio University is involved in our ecosaving project. Other than that, we are really focused on youth.

What are your priorities from now on?

Now we are focusing on the MDG campaign in Japan. We want the Japanese people to think about why poverty is still around and how that is related to globalization. In September 2005 we plan to attend the UN summit to review the implementation of the Millennium Declaration. Between now and then we will be organizing study groups on trade, debt, official development assistance issues, and a review of development strategy. We also do advocacy work vis-à-vis the Japanese government's commitment to the MDG goals. Personally, after graduation I would like to join an international NGO such as Friends of the Earth to learn more about NGO organizing. I am interested in the Education for All movement, fair trade, and child-soldier issues.

[*Postscript:* The MDG Watch Campaign and the youth NPO bank project by A SEED Japan were completed in 2006.]

Related Web Sites

A SEED Japan: http://www.aseed.org/english/index.html
Agenda 21: http://habitat.igc.org/agenda21/index.htm
Millennium Development Goals: http://www.un-ngls.org/MDG/Basics.htm
Rio Declaration on Environment and Development: http://www.unep.org/Documents
    /Default.asp?DocumentID=78&ArticleID=1163
UN Conference on Environment and Development: http://www.un.org/geninfo/bp/
    enviro.html
World Summit on Sustainable Development: http://www.un.org/events/wssd
Youth Treaty: http://habitat.igc.org/treaties/at-41.htm

Related References

A SEED Japan. 2004. *Guide to Globalization*. Tokyo: A SEED Japan.
Hughes, Christopher W. 2004. *Japan's Security Agenda: Military, Economic, and Environmental Dimensions*. Boulder, CO: Lynne Rienner.
International Institute on Sustainable Development. 1995. *Youth Sourcebook on Sustainable Development*. Winnipeg, Canada: IISD. Available at http://iisd.ca/youth/ysbk000.htm

Kimura, Takashi, ed. 2002. "Kore ga NGO to iu ikikata da!" [This is the lifestyle of NGOs!]. *Stage, 9.*

Wong, Amy. 2001. *The Roots of Japan: International Environmental Policies.* New York: Garland.

49

ORGANIC FOOD, EDUCATION, AND PEACE

Shikita Kiyoshi

SHIKITA KIYOSHI is the founder and a representative of BeGood Cafe. Born in Tokyo in 1951 and graduated from the Department of Science and Engineering at Waseda University in 1973, he has worked in the field of foreign trade, including representing European artists and manufacturing music fashion. Since 1999, using BeGood Cafe as a nonprofit social hub, he has been focusing on the theme of sustainable society and peace.

Could you tell me how BeGood Cafe came into being?

I was involved in the student and antiwar movements when I was in college in the late 1960s and early 1970s. During the 1980s, Japan grew into an economic power and had the second largest gross national product. But when you look at the environment, there is a huge gap in our economy. There are a lot of issues that cannot be measured or solved by material wealth. BeGood Cafe began in January 1999 with a talk in Harajuku. There were about twenty to thirty participants.

What are the main activities of BeGood Cafe?

We organize the once-a-month Open Talk in which invited speakers as well as the audience share freely their ideas on a particular theme. For example, for our last talk, in November 2004, we invited Okinawan activist Taira Natsume, who talked about the antiwar movement in Okinawa, the local culture, and art activism. Some of the themes in the past two years have included slow food, peace in East Asia, the power of poetry, peace, and media, organic food, and NGOs. So far we have held Open Talks in thirteen cities throughout Japan. Although our core focus is ecology, we approach it from many related angles, including peace, education, and art. We attract a lot of young people: 43 percent of our participants are in their twenties and 29 percent are in their thirties. BeGood Cafe also acts as an interface between NPOs and the public. Over the past five years we have profiled more than two hundred NPOs in the areas of environment, peace, education, and human rights through our activities. In addition, we run an organic catering service. In 2001 we also started a workshop on permaculture in Nagano Prefecture so that the participants could not only talk about but actually experience nature. Finally, we have a program called Kids' Space in which we run field camps for children.

Could you tell me more about your permaculture workshop?

The permaculture movement began in 1973 with the objective of building sustainable human communities. Since 2001 we have had access to a field of about seven hundred square meters in Nagano Prefecture where students and young people can experiment with sustainable agriculture and development. The issue for us is not so much that we cannot build sustainable development projects, but how widespread can those projects and communities eventually be? To mainstream the idea of permaculture, we need far more education and financial resources.

According to you, what are the elements of a sustainable lifestyle?

The key concept for the twenty-first century, I think, is community, whether it relates to agriculture, economy, education, energy, or ecology as a whole. A sustainable lifestyle focuses on community-based solutions, including alternative currency, ecovillages, kids' camp, renewable types of energy, and so on. There are already fifteen thousand ecovillages in the world. We have to connect with these existing resources.

BeGood Cafe organized a big project at the Aichi Expo 2005. Could you tell me more about it?

We featured an organic garden and our organic café within the NGO Global Village. The permaculture organic garden was about twelve hundred square meters big. We held workshops on organic farming, recycling, and sustainable energy. There was also a "trace and smile" program in which people could connect through their mobile phones or the Internet to the farmers who produced the food they had just eaten. Through the organic garden and café, we want to encourage visitors to think about where and how our food has been grown, and get closer to nature through what we eat. We want to bring the message that organic growing and eating bring us closer to nature.

Organic farming is not only the non-use of agricultural chemicals, but also a practice that ensures a fair and appropriate income for laborers in developing countries.

What issues do you face in your work on environment and youth education?

Money! We have been in a deficit since we began in 1999. Our funding comes from event fees and some grant money, but it is not sufficient. As long as we don't compromise our own agenda, I think cooperation with the private sector and the government is fine. We have seen such kinds of partnerships for Earth Day already. Nowadays, companies such as Toshiba and Panasonic are active in corporate social responsibility. BeGood Cafe might consider partnership with the private sector and the government.

Related Web Sites

Aichi Expo 2005, NGO Global Village: http://www.expo2005.or.jp/en/venue/village
    .html
BeGood Cafe: http://www.begoodcafe.com
Global Ecovillage Network: http://gen.ecovillage.org

Related References

Kawamura, Ken'ichi, and Hiroyuki Kokado. 1995. *Sustainable community jizoku kanō na toshi no arikata wo motomete* [Sustainable community: Searching for ways to sustain cities]. Kyoto: Gakugei Shuppansha.
Kaya, Yōichi, and Keiichi Yokobori, eds. 1997. *Environment, Energy, and Economy: Strategies for Sustainable Development*. Tokyo and New York: United Nations University Press.
Sawa, Takamitsu. 2000. *21 seiki no mondaigun jizoku kanō na hatten e no michi* [Issues in the twenty-first century: A path to sustainable development]. Tokyo: Shinyō sha.

50

"ANOTHER WORK IS POSSIBLE": SLOW LIFE, ECOLOGY, AND PEACE

Takahashi Kenkichi

TAKAHASHI KENKICHI is founder and president of Body and Soul. He is a student in the Graduate School of International Studies at Meiji Gakuin University. Born in Aichi in 1979, he has been involved in educational assistance in Cambodia and in exchange projects between Japan and South Korea. At Meiji Gakuin University he has helped to establish several NGOs, including Body and Soul. He continues to focus on peace, the environment, poverty, and the development in Japan of civil media aimed at youth participation.

Why did you create Body and Soul?

In my senior high school I belonged to the student council. I expected that the high school would be different from the compulsory junior high school. However, there was no change in the rather uniform education, and I felt suffocated. I lost the balance between my mind and my body. After I graduated from high school, I was a *freeta* (a person between the age of fifteen and thirty-four who is either unemployed or not employed full-time). I did volunteer work at various NGOs and was a staff member at the Cambodia Education Assistance Fund. I decided to go to college when I was twenty-two. My major is international relations and my interest is in citizens' movements in Korea. I was not very enthusiastic about my studies; I wanted to do something more closely related to society. I started Body and Soul here in Meiji Gakuin University in December 2002. Body and Soul is an NGO that aims at developing, as its name suggests, a balance between the body and the soul, and a better understanding of relationships among people and between people and nature. Body and Soul emphasizes a return to one's self and to one's humanness. There are many groups involved in volunteer activities in Japan. However, many of these groups are run by people who are not students, so it can often be difficult for young people to participate. I wanted to create a group that caters to young people and connects to Korean students.

Why do you focus on the body and soul balance?

It was in Cambodia, a land far away from Japan, that I recovered myself. When I went to a cram school to prepare for my college entrance qualification examination, I met a teacher who was involved in educational aid in Cambodia. I participated in a study tour to Cambodia. Instead of convenience and advanced technology, it was the warmhearted people and beautiful nature that welcomed me. In Cambodia, to fill one's stomach one did not buy prepackaged chicken at a supermarket but had to slaughter the chicken first. I learned the importance of feeling through my body and that humans live as part of nature. In Japan we now live in an information society and everything is too fast. Now more than thirty thousand people commit suicide every year. People living in Japan are separated from their bodies and far away from human nature and the innate abilities humans have. I think that such a distortion might be linked to current societal problems such as *futōkō* (refusal to attend school), which I personally experienced; youth withdrawal from society (*hikikomori*); and increasing suicides.

Could you tell me about the activities of Body and Soul?

We have about fifty members now. Our main activity is Korean-Japanese exchange. We hold an event every two weeks in which we see movies or invite guest speakers on a specific topic related to peace, ecology, or slow life. We just published a booklet called *Peace Kitchen*. We also have an agricultural project. We managed to borrow a field in Yokohama. Our student members have been growing rice, vegetables, yams, and peppers without the use of pesticide. In Japan, as elsewhere in the world, we have the problem of overuse of pesticides, and the mad cow disease. We want to give people the chance to experience agriculture.

What is the connection between agriculture and peace?

When you plant seeds, you have to think about the environment. I think it was Gandhi who said that peace in the world began with peace in our hearts. One of the ways of obtaining peace in our daily life is through agriculture.

Could you tell me more about your activities relating to Korea? Why do you focus on Korea?

The exchange between Japan and Korea was launched because I felt a contradiction between the historically negative legacy, such as comfort women, and the relationship between Japan and Korea, which seems to be getting closer now. Once every two weeks we hold a regular meeting with international students. We discuss the issues of history and watch films together. I believe it is important to face each other directly and sustain that relationship. In August 2004 we led a two-week summer study tour to Korea. We met with students and NGO activists, and visited the house where some comfort women are currently living. The objective of the tour was to create our own relations with Korea. On September 17, 2004, two years after the Japan–Democratic People's Republic of Korea Pyongyang Declaration was signed, Japanese and Korean NGOs came together. I helped organize an event entitled Human Letter Okkedonmu to create a peaceful future in East Asia. Tonight you saw the hip-hop group KP in our event Eco and Peace Work. Jewong and Liyoon are Korean residents in Japan. We invited them because they use music creatively to express their Korean cultural identity and issues of multiethnicity in Japan.

How are you connected to other youth and peace groups?

There was a strong peace movement in the 1960s and 1970s, and some citizens' movements in the 1980s and 1990s in Japan. But most of these activists are in their fifties. Now we see some young people involved in the recent peace marches against the wars in Afghanistan and Iraq. We are a member of World Peace Now and participate in peace marches. But I think there is a gap between the older generation and our generation. We have to think about how to appeal to the young people, to emphasize our own expressions, and to make the peace movement accessible.

What are your plans for the future?

One of my concerns is how to make our work sustainable over the long term. We are still striving for recognition. Another issue is funding. Right now, we have eight staff members, all volunteers. Our funding comes only from membership dues and event fees. I also want to create our own media, for example, documentaries. In Japan, alternative media like JanJan have begun to appear. I think it is an important part of this new youth movement. My dream is to lead a comfortable life, in an environment where I feel comfortable, in a place that is also comfortable for people around me.

Related Web Sites

Body and Soul: http://www.body-and-soul.org

Cambodia Education Assistance Fund: http://www.boreas.dti.ne.jp/%7Eakiyukio/ceaf/index.html

"I want to be a friend." Phrase written on the ground with candles by participants from Japan and Korea at a youth gathering: http://www.janjan.jp/living/0409/0409188996/1.php

Japan Alternative News for Justices and New Cultures (JanJan): http://www.ojr.org/japan/internet/1051767575.php

Namakemono kurabu (The Sloth Club): http://www.slothclub.org

Slow Food: http://www.slowfood.com

Related References

Body and Soul. 2004. *Peace Kitchen*. Tokyo: Body and Soul.

Shiva, Vandana. 2001. "Caring in Agriculture: We Need to Move Away from the Violence of Science." *Resurgence*, 208. Available at http://www.resurgence.org/resurgence/issues/shiva 208.htm

Tsuji, Shin'ichi. 2001. *Sulo izu byutifuru* [Slow is beautiful]. Tokyo: Heibonsha.

Sensō ni chikara kasanai [I will not give assistance to war]

Sensō no tame ni wa
Nani hitotsu chikara kasanai
Sensō no tame ni wa
Watashi no chikara kasanai

For the sake of war
I will not give a helping hand at all
For the sake of war
I will not give my assistance

Words by Sugi Goro
Music by Ichino Munehiko
Translated by Hara Hiroko

CONCLUSION

Social Movements and Global Citizenship Education

Resistance lies in self-conscious engagement with dominant, normative discourses and representations and in the active creation of oppositional analytic and cultural spaces. Resistance that is random and isolated is clearly not as effective as that which is mobilized through *systemic politicized practices of teaching and learning*. Uncovering and reclaiming subjugated knowledge is one way to lay claim to alternative histories.

Chandra Mohanty, quoted in hooks 1994, 32 (italics added)

THE PAST TWO DECADES have seen the rise of various resistance movements—on labor, the environment, women's rights, sexual rights, HIV / AIDS, migrants' rights, food sovereignty, indigenous peoples' rights, water, and so on. These movements have been against the existing global governance structures—primarily the United Nations, Bretton Woods institutions (the World Bank and the International Monetary Fund), and the World Trade Organization, as well as other regional intergovernmental organizations. By the late 1990s, many of these movements had coalesced into a global justice movement. Since the war in Afghanistan in 2001 and the beginning of the war in Iraq in 2003, the global justice movement has merged with the global antiwar movement. Though critical of a neoliberal global governance structure, many within the global justice and antiwar movements have been strategically using the UN human rights system to construct antidiscrimination norms, whether pertaining to women, racial and ethnic minorities, the disabled, caste, indigenous peoples, or migrants. These movements try to push for a greater role for global civil society in global governance reforms in order to make existing institutions more transparent, democratic, and equitable.

This development of grassroots globalism has contributed in part to the expansion of internationally linked nongovernmental advocacy networks in Japan. This book is about a continuous pedagogic process by activists in Japan to unlearn the predominant neoliberal, imperialist, and nationalistic meta-narratives in order to reclaim alternative histories. Although significant social, political, and scholarly attention has been paid to the emerging third sector in Japan, most of this research continues to focus on the country's traditional bases of social capital, namely, neighborhood, welfare, and business organizations. Beyond the fact that they exist, little is known about the activists—about their ideas, activism, and transnational connections—who make up a whole range of networks on global governance reforms, sustainable development, labor, food democracy, peace, HIV/AIDS, gender, racism, and youth that have emerged since the late 1980s and early 1990s. Japan's fall from being the world's economic superpower when the bubble economy collapsed in the early 1990s as well as subsequent corporate restructuring have dramatically changed labor relations in Japan. Nikkeiren (the Japan Federation of Employers Associations) has consistently emphasized that mobility, flexibility, specialization, and diversity should be the keys to the Japanese labor market in order for Japan to survive global competition. In addition to revision of the lifelong employment system within large corporations, restructuring has brought about an increase in unemployment and nonregular employment, particularly for women and migrant workers. Neoliberalism in Japan manifests itself not only through labor restructuring, but also in agricultural liberalization and privatization of public services such as the postal system, water, and education. The sense of crisis is not only economic, but also profoundly political. After September 11, 2001, the Japanese government passed a series of emergency legislation to broaden the mandate of the Japanese Self-Defense Forces (SDF), including their dispatch to Iraq in December 2003. The contentious U.S. military bases in Okinawa and elsewhere in Japan, the junior high history textbook controversy, the revision of the Fundamental Law on Education to instill "a sense of love and respect of the country," and above all, the proposed constitutional amendments by the ruling Liberal Democratic Party have galvanized networks of alternative globalization, antiwar, and antidiscriminatory groups in Japan.

This book's portraits of fifty organizations give us some ideas of what is new in these internationally linked advocacy groups. Each focuses on an issue that has both global significance and a local manifestation within Japan, whether it is caste discrimination, the status of migrant workers, genetically modified foods, trafficking in persons, or military bases. In contrast to the majority of groups that constitute Japanese civil society, such as nonprofit service organizations, these networks focus on advocacy and are globally oriented in terms of both movement frames and repertoires. Hence, discrimination against Buraku is couched as a caste issue to be taken up at the UN World Conference Against Racism. The mission of Japanese SDF to Iraq is intimately linked to the illegitimacy of the war in Iraq and is a target of the global peace movement. Finally, like their counterparts elsewhere in the world, these advocacy groups focus on alternatives to current neoliberal, militaristic, and nationalistic trends. The alternatives range from reforms of domestic and international institutions—such as the inclusion of basic human rights standards into free trade agreements, and the recognition of civil society participation in governance—to strategies on empowerment, self-expression, and the construction of people's networks.

An immediate question arises: Why have these kinds of new advocacy networks, which seem to be qualitatively different from the traditional bases of social capital in Japan, developed in the past two decades? Three factors may be at work. The first one is the rise in the socioeconomic level that has fostered overall civil society development. As Inoguchi argues, Japan's social capital has steadily increased in the last fifty years and by the late 1980s NGOs already existed in vibrant forms.[1] A series of articles on two hundred civic groups focusing on the environment, peace, food, gender, and so forth in the *Asahi Journal* in 1989 demonstrates the emergent network style and multinational ties.[2] Second, however, the advocacy nature of these nongovernmental networks could best be explained by the institutionalization of a UN human rights system rather than by socioeconomics. Because the Japanese government is often slow in signing and ratifying international human rights conventions, many nongovernmental networks take on watchdog functions in order to monitor the government's behavior in international society. Third, the quantitative expansion of these kinds of networks—in particular, the expansion of youth participation—could be attributed to the overall visibility and social legitimacy of nonprofit and nongovernmental work after the 1995 Kobe earthquake. The rest of this concluding chapter sums up, in terms of the concept of global citizenship education, some of the key ideas that emerged from the fifty narratives.

Global Citizenship Education:
Participation, Knowledge Production,
and Space Creation

Social movements produce knowledges through their everyday practices of
survival, resistance, organizing, and solidarity. Progressive social movements
produce new and distinct knowledges about the world as it is and as it might/
should be, and how to change it. Movement-based knowledge is largely tacit,
practical, and unsystematized. It is partial, situated, and grounded in activist
practice; fostered by concrete engagement in social struggle; and embedded
in specific times and places. . . . It also implies a pedagogical process . . .
active intentional knowledge production processes in which the intellectual
development of self and others is a central dimension of capacity building for
political struggle. Pedagogy in this sense is a sense of cultural politics—
a purposeful intervention in the shaping of knowledges and identities for a
political project, and constitutive of a permanent process of ongoing cultural
transformation.

Conway 2004, 56–58

Most studies of Japanese social movements have focused on their political
efficacy and ignored their larger civic and educational functions. This book
has looked at new social movement activism in Japan as a pedagogical process centered on participation, knowledge production, and space creation.
The World Social Forum (WSF) process that started in Porto Alegré, Brazil,
in 2001 and that has become polycentric and worldwide, is one example of
global citizenship education that emphasizes participation, new knowledge,
and space. The annual gathering draws approximately one hundred thousand
participants from diverse social movements around the world to participate,
converse, and create a "radical, participatory and living democratic process."[3]
Despite many tensions over issues of representation, organization, and strategies, WSF and its many regional and local extensions have become a public political space where people come to live and re-create their citizenship
through democratic deliberation.[4]

In Japan, advocacy NGOs encourage participation in order to contest the
"black-box" nature of many state policies or to counteract the biased textbooks and the media that they do not necessarily trust. As both Yoshioka
Tatsuya and Sakuma Tomoko attest, direct participation and democracy are

crucial in peace education (see Chapters 47 and 2). Through the participation of five to eight hundred people in each voyage, Peace Boat has become an alternative media; that is, people themselves are observing, experiencing, and then distributing information to Japanese society. Particularly through its onboard exchange programs in which young students and NGO activists from conflict areas share and contextualize their experiences, Peace Boat aims to build peace through participation and mutual understanding. Similarly, the Freedom School of the Pacific Asia Resource Center was created to encourage people to engage directly with the issues and materials. World Peace Now, a new peace coalition, emphasizes individual participation and new ways of expressing peace. Nakamura Keiko of Peace Depot highlights the importance of experience-based learning in her outreach work on disarmament (see Chapter 23). Green activists further point out the important connection to the earth. The Trace and Smile program of BeGood Cafe, for example, by connecting consumers through their mobile phones to the farmers who produce the food they eat, encourages people to think about where and how the food has been grown and to get closer to nature through what they eat. Other youth-oriented groups, such as A SEED Japan and Body and Soul, are conscious of creating opportunities for young people who might not identify with the older social movements to participate. Finally, participation not only is about local, regional, global, and earth connections, but also maintains a past and future relationship. As Kitagawa Yasuhiro of the Japan Campaign to Ban Landmines points out, one of the most urgent tasks is the training of campaign successors (Chapter 22).

Furthermore, new social movements in Japan contribute to global citizenship education through knowledge production. The activists portrayed in this book can be considered "cultural negotiators" and knowledge producers. They negotiate between global human rights frames and local cultural narratives to translate global governance issues into accessible terms and to introduce an international human rights language to the Japanese public. Against each state metanarrative on deregulation, privatization, liberalization, efficiency, "sacrifice for the sake of the world's free trade system," "sense of love and respect for the country," and becoming a "normal country" in order to participate in international cooperation militarily, advocacy NGO networks construct their alternative knowledge on international human rights standards such as decent work, equal treatment, food sovereignty, access for all, and reproductive rights (see Table 5).

TABLE 5. Another Japan Is Possible:
Alternative Knowledges of Japanese Advocacy NGO Networks

Issue Area	Neoliberal, Militaristic, and Nationalistic Ideologies	Alternative Knowledges
Kōzō kaikaku (structural reforms)	Deregulation, privatization of public services, and cuts in public spending	Decent work, equal treatment, and right to public services
Free trade agreements	Liberalization	Transparency, participation, and human rights
Agricultural liberalization within the WTO	"Sacrifice for the sake of the world's free trade system"	Multifunctionality of agriculture and food sovereignty
Service liberalization within the WTO	Efficiency	*kyōyū zaisan* (public commons)
Education	"A sense of love and respect for the country"	Freedom of thought and conscience, guaranteed in the constitution and UN Convention on the Rights of the Child
Dispatch of Japanese Self-Defense Forces to Iraq	Emergency legislation and international cooperation	World peace now; people's security
HIV/AIDS	Treatment access depending on immigration status	Access for all
Gender	Women's "participation" to revive Japanese demography and economy by giving birth and participating in the labor market	Reproductive rights
Buraku	Japanese citizens (not a minority)	Elimination of caste-based discrimination
Indigenous peoples	Cultural promotion	Indigenous peoples' rights
Okinawa	U.S.–Japan Security Treaty	Indigenous peoples' rights
Koreans	Permanent resident aliens	Citizenship rights
Foreign residents	Foreigner crime	Recognition, participation, and human rights
Prisoners	Criminals	Basic human rights
Refugees	Arbitrary detention	International human rights standards
Youth	"Crisis"	Slow life; another work is possible

The narratives of Mori Maya of the Buraku Liberation League, Sakai Mina of the Association of Rera, Taira Satoko of the Association of Indigenous Peoples in the Ryūkyūs, Hwangbo Kangja of Mirine, Tony László of Issho Kikaku, and Hirukawa Ryōko of the Japan National Assembly of Disabled Peoples' International, for example, all challenge the assumptions of Japanese citizens about ethnicity, race, and able-bodiedness (see Chapters 37, 39, 40,

41, 42, and 43). The narrative of Hirayama Motoh of the Grassroots Movement to Remove U.S. Bases from Okinawa and the World also reminds us that, far from having a unitary and linear history, Japan has been constructed through the continuous colonization of Okinawa (see Chapter 17). Further, Kasai Kazuaki of the Shinjuku Homeless Support Center, Sakai Kazuko of Equality Action 21, Ishihara Virgie of the Filipino Migrants Center, Yasuda Yukihiro of Labor Net, and Ohno Kazuoki of the No WTO—Voices from the Grassroots group deconstruct the assumptions of the global abstraction of the market when in reality a neoliberal ideology affects laborers, women, the homeless, migrant workers, and farmers in concrete and locally specific ways (see Chapters 8, 9, 10, 11, and 13).

Despite the diversity of issues across these groups, a key characteristic of the Japanese advocacy NGO networks discussed in this book is the significant amount of time and energy spent on self and public education. As an alter-globalization activist reflects,

As important as winning that battle was realizing that the better part of a decade of grassroots organizing—very tedious, painstaking, district by district, small town by small town, educating rooms of people, fifty at a time—had actually come to critical mass. . . . The time of all times was to see so many Americans educated enough to take time off and come to Seattle on their own dollar, with all of the chaos and confusion of trying to find a place to stay, simply to have their own word.[5]

As a study of a dozen cases of global citizen action concludes, "to be credible, effective, and accountable, global citizen action must pay attention to its own knowledge and learning strategies."[6] Every single NGO or network holds some forms of benkyōkai (study meetings), whether on the Tobin Tax, the Millennium Development Goals, or the International Criminal Court. Public education takes diverse forms, including seminars; local, regional, and international conferences; video documentaries; mock tribunals; and summer schools.

In Japan, the large volume of research publications by NGOs and NPOs, proceedings of benkyōkai (study meetings), and mini-komi (mini communication) in the form of newsletters, magazines, and Web-based materials, such as the Liberalization Impacts Monitor, published by AM-Net, and Tanemaki, published by A SEED Japan, has largely escaped scholarly attention. Many NGOs specifically run popular educational programs. Besides the much-noted example of the Freedom School of the Pacific Asia Resource Center, operating since the 1970s, and Peace Boat, operating since 1983, advocacy NGOs in Japan use education caravans, popular tribunals, agricultural projects, radio programs, Internet courses, video documentaries, and domestic and international art shows to engage the public.[7] Just as feminists have argued that the "women's problem" was believed not to exist because there was no name for it, several activists in Japan have mentioned the importance of new data, language, and knowledge in their struggle against a politics of invisibility, whether that applies to minority women in national politics, indigenous peoples in textbooks, or disabled women who suffer from domestic violence (see Hara, Chapter 29; Taira, Chapter 40; and Hirukawa, Chapter 43).

Further, staging countersummits—for example, against APEC in Osaka in 1995 and against G8 in Okinawa in 2000—has become a common public education and advocacy tool. In particular, more than half of the groups and networks in this collection (including the Convention on the Elimination of All Forms of Discrimination Against Women; the Convention on the Elimination of Racial Discrimination; the Convention Against Torture and Other Cruel, Inhuman, or Degrading Treatment or Punishment; the UN Convention on the Rights of the Child; the International Criminal Court; and the Nuclear Nonproliferation Treaty) lobby or focus their work on the UN and the WTO. While their work and participation have become international, a parallel emphasis on direct local experience—for example, through permaculture and *Peace Kitchen*—and new ways of expression (including art, museums, open talk, alternative media, and multilingual Web sites) has emerged.

If movement-based knowledge helps to construct new subjectivities about who the Japanese are and how they relate to others—locally, regionally, and globally—these new subjectivities nonetheless need space in which to be expressed. To the extent that space ability reflects power struggles, the lack of social, political, and cultural space for advocacy NGOs speaks volumes about the power of the state and the market in Japan.[8] As Sakuma points out, the recent NPO boom in Japan does not necessarily increase the space in which NGOs can function. Given that public interest corporations rarely identify themselves with NGOs, NGOs in Japan represent a very limited sector of the society. Advocacy NGO networks have tried various ways to create new space for "conversability." Peace Boat began in 1983 when major Japanese universities shut off space for dissent and it was realized that "ships had a lot of space" and students were "thirsty for such a space" (Yoshioka). Upon return from the fourth WSF in Mumbai in January 2004, Ogura Toshimaru started the WSF Japan mailing list server so that members of the emerging alterglobalization movement in Japan could connect and organize. Later that year, the Association for Taxation of Transactions to Aid Citizens Kyoto organized the Kyoto Social Forum to create a space in which various resistance movements within Japan could come together. On the Internet, the use of virtual space has been maximized. Issho Kikaku, for example, created a multilingual networking Web site for people interested in diversity issues.

When the Japanese educational system, media, and electoral politics limit the space for civic participation, NGO networks in Japan go abroad to utilize or create the space they need for solidarity meetings, countersummits, world conferences, art exhibitions, and press conferences. Every single group discussed in this book has engaged in cross-border conversations. Both ATTAC Japan and World Peace Now have organized workshops at the World Social Forum. The Shimin Gaikō Centre, the Buraku Liberation League, and Issho Kikaku made several presentations at the NGO Forum during the World Conference Against Racism in Durban in 2001. The most dramatic recent international appearance of Japanese advocacy NGO networks was the petition by the No! GMO Campaign against the imminent approval of genetically modified wheat by the Canadian government. A delegation of Japanese consumers from the No! GMO Campaign network carried the signatures of 1.2 million Japanese to Ottawa in March 2004. The fact that Japanese did not want GM wheat from Canada to be imported to Japan made national news headlines. Two months later, Monsanto cancelled its development of GM wheat. Although there are occasional success stories about such effective use of international space for lobbying, the bulk of spatial politics remains at the local level. Few examples are as illustrative as the struggles in Okinawa. In addition to the subversive activism of the Hitotsubo Antiwar Landowners Association—consisting of three thousand landowners whose land had been confiscated for military purpose and who had been selling one-tsubo plots of land as an act of defiance since 1982—Okinawan *obāsan* (elderly women) have been doing their demonstrations under water to protest the construction of a new offshore military base on the protected coral reefs of Henoko Bay of the city of Nago. The commonality across the alterglobalization, antiwar, and antidiscrimination movements in Japan is the reclaiming of the commons. Because land has been appropriated by the military and the market, these activists are reclaiming their nature, culture, and public space, all of which are important preconditions for expressions of citizenship.

SUCH AN INTRODUCTORY STUDY on new, internationally linked social movements in Japan would not be complete without examining the issues and challenges these movements face. Nongovernmental organizations in Japan remain small. Movement organization faces a lot of practical constraints, from resource mobilization to political and cultural marginalization. Cross-issue networking within and among the alterglobalization, antiwar, and antidiscrimination movements is not devoid of tensions (to name just a few: intellectual versus grassroots focus; the relationship between labor unions and NGOs; class issues, that is, who can afford to go "slow" in the slow-life movement; and gender dynamics within each movement). The members of various movements disagree on tactics, extent of engagement with the Japanese government, and relative emphasis on grassroots empowerment. Internally, these movements face issues of funding, scaling up (professionalization and sustainability), postcampaign follow-up capacity, and innovation. Externally, they strive for recognition, connections with political channels, public interest, and international networking.

Although each issue covered in this book represents an opportunity for future research, three areas—alternative media, the role of academia, and regional social movements—in particular are important in furthering our understanding of the role of civil society in resistance in Japan and Asia. Although some studies have been done on corporate ownership and the close ties between the government and the media, few have looked at the role of the media in Japan in perpetuating neoliberal, militaristic, and nationalistic ideologies; at the emergence of alternative media; and at the relationship between the media and the new social movements.[9] Regarding the role of academia, several activists have commented on the limited role that academics play in social movements in Japan. Some academics are founders of NGO networks. They contribute to social movements through theory building and knowledge dissemination. They serve on government councils as well as on national delegations to world conferences, and in that capacity they function as a bridge between NGOs and the government. But beyond these obvious roles, little is known about the connections between academia and social movements in Japan. In particular, in the current context of university restructuring, the introduction of market forces might further curtail the potential for universities to take on critical functions related to an agenda for alternative globalizations, including the promotion of democratic participation, sustainable development, cultural diversity, and peace.[10] Not only is the university an important public and communal space where ideas of citizenship are debated and expressions of it are encouraged, but academic research—"'a relentless erudition,' scouring alternative sources, exhuming buried documents, reviving forgotten (or abandoned) histories"[11]—plays a crucial role in holding neoliberalism, militarism, and nationalism at bay as only one set of truth claims. Finally, resistance movements have sprung up not only in Japan but also in South Korea, Taiwan, Thailand, Malaysia, the Philippines, Indonesia, and Hong Kong. These movements constitute an understudied part of the "multitude," a global grassroots project of renewing democracy.[12] The post–Asian financial crisis and post–September 11 context, the growing economic power of the region, the expansion of free trade agreements, and increasing opposition to U.S. military presence make Asia a fertile ground for comparative studies of new social movements. In question is not only the articulation of alternatives to corporate-led and imperialist globalization, but also the meaning and future of democracy itself in this important region.

Notes

1. Inoguchi 2002.
2. See the analysis in Inoguchi 1993.
3. Fisher and Ponniah 2003, 13.
4. Mertes 2004; Fisher and Ponniah 2003.
5. Wallach 2000, 32.
6. Gaventa 2001, 283.
7. Maeda 2004.
8. Bih 2001.
9. See, for example, Pharr and Krauss 1996.
10. Peters and Roberts 2000.
11. Said 1994, xviii.
12. Hardt and Negri 2004.

REFERENCE MATTER

ORGANIZATIONS INTERVIEWED

Action for Solidarity, Equality, Environment and Development (A SEED)
 Japan　ア・シード・ジャパン

Advocacy and Monitoring Network on Sustainable Development
 (AM-Net)　AMネット

Africa Japan Forum (AJF)　アフリカ日本協議会

All-Japan Water Supply Workers' Union (Zensuidō)　全日本水道労働組合

Asia Pacific Peace Forum (APPF)　アジア太平洋平和フォーラム

Association for the Taxation of Financial Transactions to Aid Citizens
 (ATTAC)　ATTAC京都

Association of Indigenous Peoples in the Ryūkyūs　琉球弧の先住民族会

Association of Rera　れらの会

BeGood Cafe　ビーグッドカフェ

Body and Soul　ボディアンドソウル

Buraku Liberation League (BLL)　部落解放同盟

Center for Prisoners' Rights (CPR) Japan　監獄人権センター

Equality Action 21　均等待遇アクション21

Feminist Art Action Brigade (FAAB)　フェミニスト・アート・アクション・ブリ
 ゲード

Filipino Migrants Center, Nagoya　フィリピン移住者センター

Food Action 21　ふーどアクション２１

Forum 90 for the Ratification of the Second Optional Protocol to the
 International Covenant on Civil and Political Rights　フォーラム90

Grassroots Movement to Remove U.S. Bases from Okinawa and the
World　沖縄などから米軍基地をなくす草の根運動

International Criminal Bar　国際刑事弁護士会

International Movement Against All Forms of Discrimination and Racism
(IMADR)　反差別国際運動

Issho Kikaku　一緒企画

Japan AIDS and Society Association　AIDS & Society研究会議

Japan Association for Refugees (JAR)　難民支援協会

Japan Campaign to Ban Landmines　地雷廃絶日本キャンペーン

Japan Center for a Sustainable Environment and Society (JACSES)　「環
境・持続社会」研究センター

Japan Civil Liberties Union (JCLU)　自由人権協会

Japan Civil Liberties Union Subcommittee for the Rights of Foreigners　自
由人権協会　外国人の権利小委員会

Japan International Volunteer Centre (JVC)　日本国際ボランティアセンター

Japan National Assembly of Disabled Peoples' International　障害者インタ
ーナショナル日本会議

Japan Network Against Trafficking in Persons (JNATIP)　人身売買禁止ネッ
トワーク

Japan NGO Network for CEDAW (JNNC)　日本女性差別撤廃条約NGOネ
ットワーク

Japan Teachers Union (Nikkyōso)　日本教職員組合／日教組

Japan Trade Union Confederation (RENGO)　日本労働組合総連合会／連合

Labor Net　レイバーネット

Mirine　ミリネ、朝鮮人従軍慰安婦問題を考える会

No to Constitutional Revision! Citizens' Network　許すな！憲法改悪・市民
連絡会

No WTO—Voices from the Grassroots in Japan　脱WTO
草の根キャンペーン

No! GMO Campaign　遺伝子組み換え食品いらない！キャンペーン

Pacific Asia Resource Center (PARC)　アジア太平洋資料センター

Peace Boat　ピースボート

Peace Depot　ピースデポ

People's Plan Study Group (PPSG)　ピープルズ・プラン研究所

Place (Positive Living and Community Empowerment) Tokyo　ぷれいす東京

Regumi Studio Tokyo   れ組スタジオ・東京

Sex Work and Sexual Health (SWASH)   セックス・ワーク&セクシュアル・ヘルス（スウォッシュ）

Shimin Gaikō Centre (Citizens' Diplomatic Centre for the Rights of Indigenous Peoples)   市民外交センター

Shinjuku Homeless Support Center   新宿ホームレス支援機構

Soshiren (Starting from a Female Body)   女（わたし）のからだから

Watch Out for WTO! Japan   WTOを監視せよ！ジャパン

Women's Active Museum on War and Peace   女たちの戦争と平和資料館

World Peace Now   ワールド・ピース・ナウ

APPENDIXES

APPENDIX I: EXAMPLES OF JAPANESE ADVOCACY NGO NETWORKS

A. Members of World Peace Now Organizing Committee (as of 2003)

(SOURCE: World Peace Now, http://www.worldpeacenow.jp)

1. ASIAN SPARK
2. ATTAC Japan
3. All Weapons into Musical Instruments
4. Peacemakers Network
5. Asia Pacific Peace Forum
6. Asian Peace Alliance, Japan
7. BeGood Cafe
8. CHANCE! pono2
9. Campaign for Children of Palestine
10. Christian Peace Network
11. Citizens Association Against Revising the Constitution
12. Citizens Urgent Action for No to War
13. Abolish Security Laws
14. Citizens' Nuclear Information Center
15. Consumers Union of Japan
16. Earth Tree
17. Editing Committee of Fax Information Against War

18. Femin Women's Democratic Club
19. Forum for Peace, Human Rights, and the Environment
20. Global Peace Campaign
21. Group for Let Constitution Alive
22. Group of Citizens 30 Opinions
23. Hatemi
24. LOFT Project NGO
25. No-War Network
26. NO! RAPE NO! BASE Women's Group
27. NO! Security Laws, Go with Barkley, Peace Action
28. National Assembly for Peace and Democracy
29. Network Earth Village
30. No War! Nerima Action Group
31. Nonviolent Peace Force Japan
32. Pacific Asia Resource Center
33. Peace Action 21
34. Peace Boat
35. Peace Cycle Network
36. Rainbow Rogakusha
37. Religious Persons Net for Bringing Peace
38. Save the Dugong Campaign Center
39. STOP! Revision of the Constitution, Citizens Network
40. Sloth Club URIPARAM Utsunomiya Disarmament Research Institute
41. Violence Against Women in War—Network Japan
42. White Ribbon of Peace Campaign Fujisawa
43. Women's Network Against U.S. Bases in Japan

B. Members of Japan NGO Network for CEDAW (as of 2003)

1. Association of Indigenous Peoples Rights in the Ryūkyūs
2. Ainu Association of Hokkaido, Sapporo Branch
3. Anti-Eugenic Network for Women and Disabled People Japan
4. Asia Women's Conference Network
5. Asia-Japan Women's Resource Center
6. Association of Employment Development for Senior Citizens
7. Association of Friendship and Peace

8. Association of Information Society for Women
9. Association of Korean Human Rights in Japan
10. Buraku Liberation League (BLL)
11. Council of Democratic Residents of Korean Women in Japan
12. Disabled Peoples' International (DPI) Disabled Women's Network
13. End Child Prostitution in Asian Tourism (ECPAT) / STOP Japan
14. Equality Action 21
15. Femin Women's Democratic Club
16. House for Women Saalaa
17. International Women's Conference
18. International Movement Against All Forms of Discrimination and Racism (IMADR), Japan Committee
19. International Women's Year Liaison Group
20. Japan Accountability Caucus, Beijing
21. Japan Anti-Prostitution Association
22. Japan Civil Liberties Union (JCLU)
23. Japan Federation of Bar Associations
24. Japan Federation of Women's Organizations
25. Japan Network for Abolishing "Koseki" and Discrimination Against Children Born out of Wedlock
26. Japanese Association of International Women's Rights
27. Japanese Organization for International Cooperation in Family Planning
28. Kanagawa Women's Council
29. Kyōfūkai: Japanese Christian Women's Organization—HELP Asian Women's Shelter
30. Men Thinking About the Role of Men
31. National Network on Domestic Violence Law for the Victims
32. New Japan Women's Association
33. NGO Network of the World Conference on Women, Kansai
34. NPO Dispatched Labor Network
35. Okayama Communication Network of the World Conference on Women
36. Place Tokyo (Positive Living and Community Empowerment Tokyo)
37. Saitama 2000 Women's Network

38. Society for the Study of Working Women
39. Tokyo Women's Union
40. Violence Against Women in War—Network Japan
41. Women Against Sexist-Ageist Remarks by Governor Ishihara
42. Women and Health, Japan
43. Working Women's International Network

C. Members of the Japan Network Against Trafficking in Persons (as of 2004)

1. Japan Women's Council
2. Aizu Mass Choir
3. The Asia Foundation
4. Asia-Japan Women's Resource Center
5. Asian Women's Empowerment Project
6. Asian Women's Center
7. Amnesty International Japan
8. Solidarity Network with Migrants Japan
9. Action Against Child Exploitation
10. Committee to Aid Democracy for Peace Building
11. End Child Prostitution in Asian Tourism (ECPAT) Japan Kansai
12. Center for Asia Pacific Partnership (CAPP) Study Group on Human Security, Human Trafficking and Exploitative Migration
13. Kyoto Young Women's Christian Association "Asian People Together"
14. Clover (Network to Support Non-Japanese Victims of Domestic Violence in Osaka)
15. Japan International Center for the Rights of the Child (JICRC)
16. Committee for Education on Child Sexual Awareness and Well-Being (CESA)
17. Congregation de Notre Dame (CND) Mria Province
18. Fukuoka Empowerment Center for Women
19. House for Women Saalaa
20. Sex Work and Sexual Health (SWASH)
21. Friends of Thai Women
22. Tokyo YWCA

23. International Movement Against All Forms of Discrimination and Racism (IMADR), Japan Committee
24. Japan Accountability Caucus, Beijing
25. Polaris Project

D. Members of the Indigenous Peoples Rights Network, Japan

1. Ainu Shiryo Jōhō Shitsu (Ainu Resource Centre)
2. Okinawa Shimin Joho Senta (Okinawa Citizens' Information Centre)
3. Shimin Gaikō Centre (Citizens' Diplomatic Centre for the Rights of Indigenous Peoples)
4. Senjūminzoku no Jūnen Shimin Renraku Kai (Decade of Indigenous Peoples)
5. Citizens Communication Association
6. Ryūkyū Ko no Senjūminzoku Kai (Association of Indigenous Peoples in the Ryūkyūs)

E. Members of the Japan Disability Forum (as of 2005)

1. Japanese Federation of Organizations of Disabled Persons
2. Japan Council on Disability
3. Japan National Assembly of Disabled Peoples' International
4. Japan Federation of the Blind
5. Japanese Federation of the Deaf
6. Inclusion Japan
7. Japan Federation of Family Organizations for Persons with Psychiatric Disabilities
8. Japanese Society for Rehabilitation of Persons with Disabilities
9. National Council of Social Welfare
10. Japan Deaf-Blind Association (observer)
11. Japan National Group of Mentally Disabled People (observer)

F. Members of the Refugee Council Japan

1. International Social Service Japan
2. Amnesty International Japan
3. Catholic Tokyo International Center

4. Association for Supporting Refugees' Settlement in Kanagawa Prefecture
5. Support21 Social Welfare Foundation
6. Japan Lawyers' Network for Refugees
7. Japan Association for Refugees
8. Catholic Commission of Japan for Migrants, Refugees, and People on the Move, Japan
9. Japan Evangelical Lutheran Association
10. Japan Legal Aid Association

APPENDIX 2: JAPANESE NGOS THAT ATTENDED WTO MINISTERIAL MEETINGS

A. Third Ministerial Meeting, Seattle, 1999

1. Action for Solidarity, Equality, Environment and Development (A SEED) Japan
2. APEC Monitor NGO Network / AM-Net
3. Central Union of Agricultural Cooperatives
4. Friends of the Earth, Japan
5. Fair Trade Center
6. Federation of Japan Tuna Fisheries Cooperative Associations
7. Food, Agriculture, Forestry, Fisheries, and Environment Forum
8. Global Village
9. Japan Fisheries Association
10. Japan Green Coalition
11. Japan Wood-Products Information & Research Center
12. Japan Business Federation (Nippon Keidanren)
13. Japan Institute for Social and Economic Affairs (Keizai Kōhō Center)
14. National Chamber of Agriculture (Zenkoku Nōgyō Kaigisho)
15. National Confederation of Farmers' Movement, Japan (NOUMINREN)
16. National Congress of Workers, Farmers and Citizens for Protection of Food, Forests and Water (Rōnōh Shimin Kaigi)

17. National Council of Agricultural Cooperative Youth Associations (JA Zenseikyō)
18. National Council of Farm Policy Organizations
19. National Federation of Agricultural Co-operative Associations (JA-Zennoh)
20. National Federation of Fisheries Cooperative Associations (ZENGYOREN)
21. National Federation of Trade Unions of Agricultural Cooperative Associations in Japan (Zennōkyōrōren)
22. Pacific Asia Resource Center (PARC)
23. Peoples' Forum 2001
24. Solid Action on Globalization & Environment (SAGE)

B. Fifth Ministerial Meeting and NGO Forum, Cancun, 2003

1. Advocacy and Monitoring Network on Sustainable Development (AM-Net)
2. All Japan Purse Seine Fisheries Association
3. Asian Farmers' Group for Cooperation (AFGC)
4. Beneficiaries of the Sea Coalition
5. Central Union of Agricultural Cooperatives
6. Fair Trade Center
7. Food, Agriculture, Forestry, Fisheries, and Environment Forum
8. General Insurance Association of Japan
9. Global Guardian Trust
10. Global Industrial and Social Progress Research Institute
11. Institute for Global Environmental Strategies
12. Institute for the Development of Agricultural Cooperation in Asia (IDACA)
13. International Cooperative Fisheries Organization of the International Cooperative Alliance (ICFO)
14. National Council of Agricultural Cooperative Women's Associations (JA-Joseikyo)
15. Japan Agricultural Corporations Association
16. Japan Association of WTO Negotiation on Wood Products
17. Japan Center for a Sustainable Environment and Society (JACSES)

18. Japan Deep Sea Trawlers Association
19. Japan Federation of Wood Industry Associations
20. Japan Fisheries Association
21. Japan Services Network
22. Japan Wood-Products Information & Research Center
23. Miyagi Prefectural Federation of Fisheries Cooperative Associations
24. Japan Trade Union Confederation (RENGO)
25. Keizai Kōhō Center (Japan Institute for Social and Economic Affairs)
26. National Chamber of Agriculture
27. National Confederation of Farmers' Movement
28. National Council of Agricultural Cooperative Youth Associations
29. National Council of Farm Policy Organizations
30. National Federation of Fisheries Cooperative Associations
31. National Federation of Medium Trawlers (Zensokoren)
32. National Federation of Trade Unions of Agricultural Cooperative Associations in Japan (Zennōkyōrōren)
33. Japan Business Federation (Nippon Keidanren)
34. Organization for Promotion of Responsible Tuna Fisheries (OPRT)
35. Pacific Asia Resource Center (PARC)
36. Solid Action on Globalization & Environment (SAGE)
37. Water Advocates
38. Japan Mariculture Association (ZEN KAI SUI)
39. Japan Stick-held Dip Net Saury Fishery Cooperative Association (ZEN SAMMA)
40. National Federation of Agricultural Co-operative Associations (ZEN-NOH)
41. National Federation of Forest Owners Cooperative Associations (ZENMORI-REN)

C. Sixth Ministerial Meeting, Hong Kong, 2005

1. Action for Solidarity, Equality, Environment and Development (A SEED) Japan
2. All Japan Purse Seine Fisheries Association
3. All-Japan Federation of Farmers Union (ZEN-NICHINO)

4. Advocacy and Monitoring Network on Sustainable Development (AM-Net)
5. Asian Farmers' Group for Cooperation (AFGC)
6. Beneficiaries of the Sea Coalition
7. Central Union of Agricultural Cooperatives (JA ZENCHU)
8. Consumers Union of Japan
9. Fair Trade Center
10. Federation of Japan Tuna Fisheries Cooperative Associations
11. Food, Agriculture, Forestry, Fisheries and Environment Forum
12. Forum for Peace Rights and Environment
13. Global Guardian Trust
14. Hokkaido Trawl Fisheries Cooperative Federation (KISENREN)
15. International Cooperative Fisheries Organization of the International Cooperative Alliance (ICFO)
16. Ie-no-hikari Association
17. Institute for the Development of Agricultural Cooperation in Asia (IDACA)
18. Japan Center for a Sustainable Environment and Society (JACSES)
19. Japan Chemical Industry Association
20. Japan Deep Sea Trawlers Association
21. Japan Electronics and Information Technology Industries Association
22. Japan Fisheries Association
23. Japan Pharmaceutical Manufacturers Association
24. Japan Trade Union Confederation (RENGO)
25. JF Miyagi-ken GYOREN
26. Japan Services Network (JSN)
27. Keizai Koho Center (Japan Institute for Social and Economic Affairs)
28. National Chamber of Agriculture (Zenkoku Nōgyō Kaigisho)
29. National Confederation of Farmers' Movement, Japan (NOUMINREN)
30. National Congress of Workers, Farmers and Citizens for Protection of Food, Forests and Water
31. National Council of Agricultural Cooperative Women's Associations (JA Joseikyo)

32. National Council of Agricultural Cooperative Youth Associations (JA Zenseikyo)
33. National Council of Farm Policy Organizations
34. National Federation of Fisheries Cooperative Associations (ZENGYOREN)
35. National Federation of Trade Unions of Agricultural Cooperative Associations in Japan (Zennōkyōrōren)
36. National Mutual Insurance Federation of Agricultural Cooperatives (ZENKYOREN)
37. Japan Business Federation (Nippon Keidanren)
38. Organization for Promotion of Responsible Tuna Fisheries (OPRT)
39. Oxfam Japan
40. Pacific Asia Resource Center (PARC)
41. People's Plan Study Group
42. 21st Century Public Policy Institute
43. General Insurance Association of Japan
44. Tokyo Chamber of Commerce and Industry
45. Japan Mariculture Association (ZEN KAI SUI)
46. Japan Stick-held Dip Net Saury Fishery Cooperative Association (ZEN SAMMA)
47. National Federation of Agricultural Cooperative Associations (ZEN-NOH)
48. National Federation Medium Trawlers (Zensokoren)

APPENDIX 3: NGO MEMBERS OF THE JAPAN PLATFORM

(SOURCE: Japan Platform, http://www.japanplatform.org)

1. Adventist Development and Relief Agency (ADRA) Japan
2. Association for Aid and Relief (AAR) Japan
3. Basic Human Needs Association Japan
4. Humanitarian Medical Assistance (HuMA)
5. International Peace Assistance Center (IPAC)
6. Japan Alliance for Humanitarian Demining Support (JAHDS)
7. Japan Mine Action Service (JMAS)

8. Japanese Red Cross Society
9. Japan Rescue Association
10. Japan Emergency NGOs (JEN)
11. Medical Relief Unit, Japan
12. Nippon International Cooperation for Community Development (NICCO)
13. Peace NGOs Hiroshima
14. Peace Winds Japan (PWJ)
15. Save the Children Japan (SCJ)
16. Shanti Volunteer Association (SVA)
17. Institute of Cultural Affairs, Japan (ICA Japan)
18. Japan Asian Association & Asian Friendship Society (JAFS)
19. Japan Center for Conflict Prevention
20. World Vision Japan

REFERENCES

Adachi, Kenki. 2004. *Otawa purosesu: Taijin jirai kinshi rejīmu no keisei* [The Ottawa process: Formation of antipersonnel landmines ban regime]. Tokyo: Yūshindo.

Ainu Association of Hokkaido. 1999. "A Statement of Opinion Regarding the Partial Revision of ILO Convention No. 107." Olympia, WA: Center for World Indigenous Studies. Available at ftp://ftp.halcyon.com/pub/FWDP/Eurasia/ainu.txt

Akao, Nobutoshi. 1994. "Kōshō tantōsha ga kataru Uruguai Raundo seiritsu no butai Ura" [The backstage of completing the Uruguay Round as told by a negotiator]. *Gaikō Forum*, 67.

Akiyama, Emi. 2006. *Keimusho wa kawarunoka: Nagoya keimusho jiken kara 3 nen* [Will a prison change? Three years since the Nagoya jail incident]. Video. OurPlanet TV. Available at http://www.ourplanet-tv.org

Alexander, Nancy, and Kyōko Ishida. 2004. "Driving Forces of Water Privatization: The Multilateral Development Banks (MDBs)/IMF." Tokyo: JACSES. Available at http://www.jacses.org/en/sdap/water/report03.html

Alvarez, Sonia, Evelina Dagnino, and Arturo Escobar, eds. 1998. *Culture of Politics, Politics of Cultures: Re-Visioning Latin American Social Movements*. Boulder, CO: Westview.

Amagasa, Keisuke. 2004. *Sekai shokuryō sensō* [World food war]. Tokyo: Ryokufu.

Amano, Yasukazu. 2000. *Okinawa keiken: Minshū no anzenhoshō e* [The experience of Okinawa: Toward people-based security]. Tokyo: Shakai Hyōronsha.

Amnesty International. 2002a. "Welcome to Japan?" AI Index: ASA 22/002/2002, May. Available at http://web.amnesty.org/library/index/engasa220022002

Amnesty International Japan. 2002b. *Nyūmon kokusai keiji saibansho* [Introduction to the International Criminal Court]. Tokyo: Gendaijinbunsha.

Angst, Linda Isako. 2003. "The Rape of a Schoolgirl: Discourses of Power and

Women's Lives in Okinawa." In *Islands of Discontent: Okinawan Responses to Japanese and American Power*, edited by Laura Hein and Mark Selden. New York: Rowman & Littlefield.

Appiah, K. Anthony. 2003. "Citizens of the World." In *Globalizing Rights*, edited by Matthew Gibney. Oxford, UK: Oxford University Press.

Arasaki, Moriteru. 1996. *Okinawa hansen jinushi* [Okinawan antiwar landlords]. Tokyo: Kōbunken.

Arudou, Debito. 2004. *Japanese Only: The Otaru Onsen Refusals and Racial Discrimination in Japan*. Tokyo: Akashi Shoten.

A SEED Japan. 2004. *Guide to Globalization*. Tokyo: A SEED Japan.

Ashino, Yuriko. 2001. "Reproductive Health/Rights: The Present Situation of Japan and Its Problems." Tokyo: Women's Online Media. Available at http://wom-jp .org/e/JWOMEN/repro.html

Asia Society. 2004. *The Human Security Challenges of HIV/AIDS and Other Communicable Diseases: Exploring Effective Regional and Global Responses*. New York: Asia Society.

Asian Centre for Women's Human Rights. 2000. *From the Depths of Silence: Voices of Women Survivors of War*. Quezon City, the Philippines: Asian Centre for Women's Human Rights.

Asian Development Bank. 2001. "Water for All: The Water Policy of the Asian Development Bank." Manila: ADB. Available at http://www.adb.org/Documents/Policies/Water/water0301.asp?p=policies

Asian Peace Alliance. 2002. "APA Against U.S. Plans to Attack Iraq." Available at http://www.arenaonline.org/details/103816730831637.shtml

Asia-Pacific Human Rights Information Center. 2003. *Shōgaisha no kenri* [Rights of persons with disabilities]. Tokyo: Gendaijinbunsha.

Association of Indigenous Peoples in the Ryūkyūs. 2004. *Kokusai jinkenhō to Ryūkyū, Okinawa* [International Human Rights Law and Ryūkyū, Okinawa]. Tokyo: AIPR.

Barlow, Maude, and Tony Clarke. 2002. *Blue Gold: The Battle Against Corporate Theft of the World's Water*. Toronto: Stoddart.

Bayefsky, Anne. 2002. *How to Complain to the UN Human Rights Treaty System*. New York: Transnational.

Beer, Lawrence W., and John M. Maki. 2002. *From Imperial Myth to Democracy: Japan's Two Constitutions, 1889–2002*. Boulder: University Press of Colorado.

Bello, Walden. 2002. *Deglobalization: Ideas for a New World Economy*. London and New York: Zed Books.

Benhabib, Seyla. 2002 *Claims of Culture: Equality and Diversity in the Global Era*. Princeton, NJ: Princeton University Press.

Berberoglu, Berch. 2002. *Labor and Capital in the Age of Globalization: The Labor*

Process and the Changing Nature of Work in the Global Economy. New York: Rowman & Littlefield.

Berndt, Caroline M. 1997. "Popular Culture as Political Power: Writing the Reality of Sexual Slavery." *Journal of Popular Culture*, 31(2), 177–187.

Bhabha, Homi. 2003. "On Writing Rights." In *Globalizing Rights*, edited by Matthew Gibney. Oxford, UK: Oxford University Press.

Bih, Herng-Dar. 2001. *The Power of Space.* Taipei, Taiwan: Psygarden.

Blondel, Jean, and Takashi Inoguchi. 2002. "Political Cultures Do Matter: Citizens and Politics in Western Europe and East and Southeast Asia." *Japanese Journal of Political Science*, 3(2), 151–171.

Body and Soul. 2004. *Peace Kitchen.* Tokyo: Body and Soul.

Boli, John, and George Thomas. 1997. "World Culture in the World Polity: A Century of International Non-Governmental Organization." *American Sociological Review*, 62, 171–190.

Boling, David. 1995. "Mass Rape, Enforced Prostitution, and the Japanese Imperial Army: Japan Eschews Legal Responsibility?" *Columbia Journal of International Law*, 32, 533–590.

Bove, Jose, and Francois Dufour. 2001. *The World Is Not for Sale: Farmers Against Junk Food.* London: Verso.

Brecher, Jeremy, Tim Costello, and Brendan Smith. 2000. *Globalization from Below: The Power of Solidarity.* Boston: South End Press.

Brinton, Mary. 1994. *Women and the Economic Miracle: Gender and Work in Postwar Japan.* Berkeley: University of California Press.

Broadbent, Kaye. 2003. *Women's Employment in Japan: The Experience of Part-Time Workers.* New York: Routledge Curzon.

Broomhall, Bruce. 2004. *International Justice and the International Criminal Court: Between Sovereignty and the Rule of Law.* Oxford, UK: Oxford University Press.

Brysk, Alison, ed. 2002. *Globalization and Human Rights.* Berkeley: University of California Press.

Buraku Liberation League. 2005. "What Is Buraku Discrimination?" Osaka City, Japan: Buraku Liberation and Human Rights Research Institute. Available at http://blhrri.org/blhrri_e/blhrri/buraku.htm

Butler, Judith. 1999. *Gender Trouble: Feminism and the Subversion of Identity.* New York: Routledge.

Cameron, Max, Robert Lawson, and Brian Tomlin, eds. 1998. *To Walk Without Fear: The Global Movement to Ban Landmines.* New York: Oxford University Press.

Cassen, Bernard. 2003. "On the Attack." *New Left Review*, Jan.–Feb., 41–60.

Cassese, Antonio, Paola Gaeta, and John R.W.D. Jones, eds. 2002. *The Rome Statute of the International Criminal Court: A Commentary.* Oxford, UK: Oxford University Press.

Castells, Manuel. 1997. *The Power of Identity*. Boston: Blackwell.

Cavanagh, John, and Jerry Mander, eds. 2004. *Alternatives to Economic Globalization: A Better World Is Possible*. San Francisco: Berrett-Koehler.

Center for Prisoners' Rights. 2004. *The Latest Situation of Japanese Prisons*. Tokyo: CPR.

Chalmers, Sharon. 2002. *Emerging Lesbian Voices from Japan*. London and New York: Routledge Curzon.

Chan, Jennifer. 2005. "Localiser la société civile au Japon" [Locating civil society in Japan]. In *La Dynamique du Japon* [Japan's transformation], edited by Jean-François Sabouret. Paris: Saint Simon.

Chan, Jennifer. 2007. "The Antiwar Movements in Japan 1990–2005." *Critique Internationale, 36*.

Chan-Tiberghien, Jennifer. 2004a. *Gender and Human Rights Politics in Japan: Global Norms and Domestic Networks*. Stanford, CA: Stanford University Press.

Chan-Tiberghien, Jennifer. 2004b. "La participation féministe au mouvement alter-mondialiste: Une critique de l'Organisation mondiale du commerce" [Feminist participation in the alterglobalization movement: A critique of the World Trade Organization]. *Recherches Féministes, 17*(2), 195–225.

Charter 99. 2000. "A Charter for Global Democracy." London: One World Trust. Accessed February 25, 2005, at http://www.oneworldtrust.org/pages/download.cfm?did=97

Childers, Erskin, and Brian Urquhart. 1994. *Renewing the United Nation System*. Uppsala, Sweden: Dag Hammarskjold Foundation.

Chinen, Hidenori, and Kasumi Izena. 1998. "Education in Okinawa and the Okinawan Languages: A Position Paper on the Rights of the Okinawans to Education and Languages." Tokyo: Shimin Gaikō Centre. Available at http://www005.upp.so-net.ne.jp/peacetax/e5.html

Chinkin, Christine. 1994. "Rape and Sexual Abuse of Women in International Law." *European Journal of International Law, 15*(3). Available at http://www.ejil.org/journal/Vol5/No3/art2.html#TopOfPage

Citizens' Diplomatic Centre for the Rights of Indigenous Peoples. 2001. "Written Statement on the World Conference Against Racism," submitted to UN Commission on Human Rights, January 2001. Available at http://www005.upp.so-net.ne.jp/peacetax/#English

Cho, Sangmie, ed. 2000. *Comfort Women Speak: Testimony by Sex Slaves of the Japanese Military*. New York: Schellstede Hornes and Meir.

Commission on Global Governance. 1995. *Our Global Neighborhood*. Oxford, UK: Oxford University Press.

Consumers Union of Japan. 2002. Newsletter. Tokyo: Consumers Union of Japan.

Consumers Union of Japan, ed. 2005. *Shokuryō shuken* [Food sovereignty]. Tokyo: Ryokufu.

Conway, Janet. 2004. *Identity, Place, and Knowledge: Social Movements Contesting Globalization*. Black Point, Nova Scotia: Fernwood.

Coomaraswamy, Radhika. 1997. "Reinventing International Law: Women's Rights as Human Rights in the International Community." Edward A. Smith Visiting Lecturer Human Rights Program, Harvard Law School, September.

Coomaraswamy, Radhika. 2000. *Integration of the Human Rights of Women and the Gender Perspective: Report of the Special Rapporteur on Violence Against Women*. Available at http://www.unhchr.ch/Huridocda/Huridoca.nsf/0/e29d45a105cd8143802568be0051fcfb/$FILE/G0011334.pdf

Crenshaw, Kimberlé. 2000. "Gender-Related Aspects of Race Discrimination." Paper presented at the Expert Group Meeting on Gender and Racial Discrimination, November 21–24, Zagreb, Croatia.

D'Adesky, Anne-Christine. 2004. *Moving Mountains: The Race to Treat Global AIDS*. London and New York: Verso.

D'Adesky, Anne-Christine. 2005. *Pills, Profits, and Protest*. Video. New York: Outcast Films.

Danaher, Kevin. 1994. *Fifty Years Is Enough: The Case Against the World Bank and the International Monetary Fund*. Boston: South End Press.

Davis, Christina. 2003. *Food Fights over Free Trade*. Princeton, NJ: Princeton University Press.

Denoon, Donald, Gaven McCormack, Mark Hudson, and Tessa Morris-Suzuki, eds. 1996. *Multicultural Japan: Paleolithic to Postmodern*. Melbourne: Cambridge University Press.

Development Action for Women Network. 2003. *Pains and Gains: A Study of Overseas Performing Artists in Japan from Pre-Departure to Reintegration*. Manila: DAWN.

Disabled Peoples' International Japan. 2003. *Sekai no shōgaisha: Warerajishin no koe* [Disabled people of the world: Our own voices]. Tokyo: Gendai Shokan.

Dolgopol, Ustina. 1995. "Women's Voices, Women's Pain." *Human Rights Quarterly*, *17*(1), 127–154. Available at http://muse.jhu.edu/journals/human_rights_quarterly/toc/human_rights_quarterlyv017.html

Dore, Ronald. 1959. *Land Reform in Japan*. London and New York: Oxford University Press.

Douglass, Mike, and Glenda Susan Roberts, eds. 2002. *Japan and Global Migration: Foreign Workers and the Advent of a Multicultural Society*. Honolulu: University of Hawaii Press.

Dudden, Alexis. 2001. "'We Came to Tell the Truth': Reflections on the Tokyo Women's Tribunal." *Critical Asian Studies*, *33*(4), 591–602.

Ebara, Mamoru. 2003. *Minzoku gakkō mondai wo kangaeru* [On the issue of ethnic schools]. Kyoto: Agenda Project.

Eschle, Catherine, and Bice Maiguashca. 2005. *Critical Theories, International Relations and 'the Anti-Globalisation Movement': The Politics of Global Resistance.* London and New York: Routledge.

Ezzat, Heba Raoul. 2005. "Beyond Methodological Modernism: Towards a Multicultural Paradigm Shift in the Social Sciences." In *Global Civil Society 2004/5*, edited by Helmut Anheier, Marlies Glasius, and Mary Kaldor. London: Sage.

Falk, Richard. 1999. *Predatory Globalization: A Critique.* Malden, MA: Polity Press.

Fan, So-jGyon, Moriteru Arasaki, Yuko Tsushima, Naruhiko Ito, Kei Nakazawa, and Keun-Cha Yoon. 2003. "Higashi ajia no minshū rentai wo kataru" [Talk about people's networking in East Asia]. *Associé, 11,* 212–239.

Feldman, A. Eric. 1999. "HIV and Blood in Japan: Transforming Private Conflict into Public Scandal." In *Blood Feuds: AIDS, Blood, and the Politics of Medical Disaster,* edited by A. Eric Feldman and Ronald Bayer. New York: Oxford University Press.

Field, Norma. 1993. *In the Realm of a Dying Emperor: Japan at Century's End.* New York: Vintage Books.

Fisher, William, and Thomas Ponniah, eds. 2003. *Another World Is Possible: Popular Alternatives to Globalization at the World Social Forum.* London and New York: Zed Books.

Focus on the Global South. 2002. "The Struggle for Peace in Asia." Available at http://www.focusweb.org/publications/declarations/APA-declaration-2002.html

Food Action 21. 1995. *Inochi wo tsunagu "shoku to nō": "Shoku no kihonhō" tōron no tame ni* [Connecting life "Food and Agriculture": For the discussion of the draft of the Basic Food Law]. Tokyo: Food Action 21.

Food Action 21. 2003. "WTO Should Respect Survival Equivalent: Voice of the Grassroots in Japan." Unpublished statement at the NGO Forum of the World Trade Organization Ministerial Meeting in Cancun, Mexico, September.

Food Action 21. 2004. Food Action 21 setsuritsu 10 shūnen kinen shūkai [Tenth anniversary symposium: Food, agriculture, region, and environment: What our movement aims at]. Tokyo: Food Action 21, November 12.

Forum 90. 2001. *The Hidden Death Penalty in Japan: The Legal Process and the Legal Challenge in Japan.* Report presented at the First World Congress Against the Death Penalty, Strasbourg, France. Tokyo: Forum 90. Available at http://www.ncadp.org/html/intlreport1.html

Foster, Karen. 2006. "Japan Can't Stop the Tide of People: UNHCR Chief." *Japan Times,* December 7. Available at http://search.japantimes.co.jp/print/nn2006 1207f1.html

Fujimoto, Yukihisa. 2005. *Marines Go Home: Henoko, Mehyang, Yausubetsu.* Video. Mori no Eigasha. Available at http://www.ourplanet-tv.org/main/contents/review.html

Fukuoka, Yasunori. 2000. *Lives of Young Koreans in Japan*. Melbourne: Trans Pacific Press.

Gallagher, Kevin. 2004. *Free Trade and the Environment: Mexico, NAFTA, and Beyond*. Stanford, CA: Stanford University Press.

Garon, Sheldon. 1997. *Molding Japanese Minds: The State in Everyday Life*. Princeton, NJ: Princeton University Press.

Gaventa, John. 2001. "Global Citizen Action: Lessons and Challenges." In *Global Citizen Action*, edited by Michael Edwards and John Gaventa. Boulder, CO: Rienner.

Genda, Yuji. 2005a. *A Nagging Sense of Job Insecurity: The New Reality Facing Japanese Youth*. Tokyo: International House of Japan.

Genda, Yuji. 2005b. "The NEET Problem in Japan." *Social Science Japan* (Newsletter of the Institute of Social Science, University of Tokyo), *32*, 3–5.

Gill, Tom. 2001. *Men of Uncertainty: The Social Organization of Day Laborers in Contemporary Japan*. Albany: State University of New York Press.

Glipo, Arze, Laura Carlsen, Arza Talat Sayeed, Rita Schwentesius de Rindermann, and Jayson Cainglet. 2003. "Agreement on Agriculture and Food Sovereignty." Unpublished paper presented at the World Trade Organization Conference in Cancun, Mexico, September 10–14.

Goodman, Amy. 2004. "Mass Antiwar Protests in Japan, Fate of Iraq Hostages Remains Unclear." Democracy Now! April 12. Available at http://www.democracynow.org/article.pl?sid=04/04/12/1423256

Goodman, Roger, and Ian Neary, eds. 1996. *Case Studies on Human Rights in Japan*. Surrey, UK: Japan Library.

Gordon, Andrew. 1998. *The Wages of Affluence: Labor and Management in Postwar Japan*. Cambridge, MA: Harvard University Press.

Green, Robert. 1999. *Fast Track to Zero Nuclear Weapons: The Middle Powers Initiative*. Christchurch, NZ: Disarmament and Security Center.

Green, Robert. 2000. *The Naked Nuclear Emperor: Debunking Nuclear Deterrence*. Christchurch, NZ: Disarmament and Security Center.

Group of 77. 1997. "Ministerial Declaration." New York: Group of 77. Available at http://www.g77.org/doc/Decl2001.htm

Gucewicz, Tony. 2000. *Tokyo's Homeless: A City in Denial*. New York: Kroshka Books.

Hahei Chekku Henshūiinkai, ed. 1996. *Nichibei ampo "saiteigi" wo yomu* [Reading the "redefinition" of the U.S.-Japan security alliance]. Tokyo: Hahei Chekku Henshūiinkai.

Haken Rodō Nettowāku. 2004. Pamphlet. Tokyo: Haken Rodō Nettowāku.

Halifax Initiative. 2001. "Taxing Currency Transactions: From Feasibility to Implementation." Ottawa, Canada: Halifax Initiative. Available at http://www.halifaxinitiative.org/updir/Conference_Papers.pdf

Hall, David. 2001. *Water in Public Hands*. London: Public Services International Research Unit.

Hall, Peter, and David Soskice, eds. 2001. *Varieties of Capitalism: The Institutional Foundations of Comparative Advantage*. New York: Oxford University Press.

Hardt, Michael, and Antonio Negri. 2004. *Multitude: War and Democracy in the Age of Empire*. New York: Penguin Press.

Hasegawa, Koichi. 2004. *Constructing Civil Society in Japan: Voices of Environmental Movements*. Melbourne: Trans Pacific Press.

Heater, Derek. 2002. *World Citizenship: Cosmopolitan Thinking and Its Opponents*. London and New York: Continuum Press.

Hein, Laura, and Mark Selden, eds. 2003. *Islands of Discontent: Okinawan Responses to Japanese and American Power*. New York: Rowman & Littlefield.

Held, David. 2003. "From Executive to Cosmopolitan Multilateralism." In *Taming Globalization*, edited by David Held and Mathias Koenig-Archibugi, 160–186. Cambridge, UK: Polity Press.

Herbert, Wolfgang. 1996. *Foreign Workers and Law Enforcement in Japan*. London: Kegan Paul International.

Hirakawa, Keiko, ed. 2005. *Onnatachi no orutanatibu: Pāto ni kintō taigū wo!* [The alternatives for women: Equal treatment for part-time workers]. Tokyo: Akashi Shoten.

Holland, Ann-Christian Sjolander. 2005. *The Water Business: Corporations Versus People*. London and New York: Zed Books.

Hood, Roger. 2002. *The Death Penalty: A Worldwide Perspective*. Oxford, UK: Clarendon Press.

Hook, Glenn D., and Gavin McCormack. 2001. *Japan's Contested Constitution: Documents and Analysis*. London and New York: Routledge.

hooks, bell. 2004. *Teaching to Transgress*. New York: Routledge.

Hughes, Christopher W. 2004. *Japan's Security Agenda: Military, Economic, and Environmental Dimensions*. Boulder, CO: Lynne Rienner.

Human Rights Committee, Sixty-Fourth Session. 1998. "Concluding Observations to Japan's Fourth Periodic Report." Available at http://www.unhchr.ch/tbs/doc.nsf/(Symbol)/5a2baa28d433b6ea802566d40041ebbe?Opendocument

Human Rights Forum 21. 1998. *Nihon no jinken hakusho* [White paper on human rights in Japan]. Tokyo: Kaihō Shuppansha.

Human Rights Forum 21. 2002. "Japanese National Human Rights Commission." Available at http://www.hurights.or.jp/asia-pacific/no_28/05japanesehrc.htm

Human Rights Watch. 2001. *Caste Discrimination: A Global Concern*. Report for the UN World Conference Against Racism, Racial Discrimination, Xenophobia and Related Intolerance, Durban, South Africa, September. Available at http://www.hrw.org/reports/2001/globalcaste/index.htm#TopOfPage

Hunter, Susan. 2005. *AIDS in Asia: A Continent in Peril*. New York: Palgrave Macmillan.

Ifunke no kai, ed. 1991. *Ifunke: Aru ainu no shi* [Ifunke: The death of an Ainu]. Tokyo: Sairyūsha.

Iha, Yōichi, and Hiroshi Nagai. 2005. *Okinawa kichi to Iraku sensō: Beigun heli tsuiraku jiko no shinsō* [Military bases in Okinawa and the Iraq war: Deep inside the U.S. military helicopter crash accident]. Tokyo: Iwanami Shoten.

Inaba, Nanako. 2002. "Kokusai jinken kijun to Nihon ni okeru ijūsha no kenri hoshō no genjō" [International human rights standards and the status of human rights protection of migrant workers in Japan]. In *Hanjinshushugi, sabetsu teppai sekaikaigi to Nihon* [World conference against racism, racial discrimination, xenophobia, and Japan], edited by International Movement Against All Forms of Discrimination and Racism. Tokyo: Kaiho Shuppansha.

Inoguchi, Takashi. 1993. Keizai Taikoku No Seiji Unei [Governing an economic power: Japan]. Tokyo: University of Tokyo Press.

Inoguchi, Takashi. 2002. "Broadening the Basis of Social Capital in Japan." In *Democracies in Flux: The Evolution of Social Capital in Contemporary Society*, edited by R. D. Putnam. Oxford, UK, and New York: Oxford University Press.

International Consortium of Investigative Journalists. 2003. *The Water Barons: How a Few Powerful Companies Are Privatizing Your Water*. Washington, DC: Center for Public Integrity.

International Federation of Human Rights. 2002. "Death Penalty in Japan." Paris: FIDH. Available at http://www.fidh.org/article.php3?id_article=1499

International Gender and Trade Network. 2003. *International Gender and Trade Network at Cancun*. Washington, DC: International Gender and Trade Network.

International Human Rights NGO Network. 1999. *Wocchi! Kiyaku jinken iinkai: Doko ga zureteru? Jinken no kokusai kijun to Nihon no genjō* [Watch! Human Rights Committee: Where is the gap? International human rights standards and the situation in Japan]. Tokyo: Nihon Hyōronsha.

International Institute on Sustainable Development. 1995. *Youth Sourcebook on Sustainable Development*. Winnipeg, Canada: IISD. Available at http://www.iisd .org/YOUTH/ysbk000.htm

International March of Women. 2004. "Women's Global Charter for Humanity." São Paulo, Brazil: World March of Women. Available at http://mmf.lecarrefour.org/ publications/charte/en

International Movement Against All Forms of Discrimination and Racism. 2001. *Kokuren kara mita Nihon no jinshu sabetsu* [Racial discrimination in Japan from UN perspectives]. Tokyo: IMADR.

International Movement Against All Forms of Discrimination and Racism, ed. 2002a. *Hanjinshushugi, sabetsu teppai sekaikaigi to Nihon* [World conference against racism, racial discrimination, xenophobia, and related intolerance and Japan]. Tokyo: Kaihō Shuppansha.

International Movement Against All Forms of Discrimination and Racism, ed. 2002b. *Mainoritī josei ga sekai wo kaeru!* [Minority women change the world!]. Tokyo: Kaihō Shuppansha.

International Movement Against All Forms of Discrimination and Racism. 2002c. "Summary of Caste Discrimination: A Global Concern Symposium." Available at http://www.imadr.org/old/project/dalit/smita.html

International Movement Against All Forms of Discrimination and Racism Project Team on Multiple Discrimination Against Minority Women, ed. 2003. *Mainoritī josei no shiten wo seisaku ni! Shakai ni!* [Policy and society from the perspectives of minority women]. Tokyo: IMADR JC.

Irwin, Alexander, Joyce Millen, and Dorothy Fallows. 2003. *Global AIDS: Myths and Facts.* Cambridge, MA: South End Press.

Ishikawa, Eri. 2003. "Nihon ni okeru nanmin hogo no kakuritsu e mukete: Nanmin shinseisha, nanmin no seikatsu jittai chōsa hōkoku yori" [Toward a system of refugee protection in Japan: A survey report on asylum seekers and refugee living conditions]. *Rīgaru eido kenkyū* [Legal aid research], 8, 37–54.

Ishikawa, Yuka. 2001. "Rights Activists and Rights Violations: The Burakumin Case in Japan." Available at http://imadr.org/old/tokyo/ishikawareport.html

Iwamuro, Shin'ya. 1996. *AIDS ima nani wo dō tsutaeru ka* [AIDS: What and how we should convey now]. Tokyo: Taishūkan Shoten.

Iwata, Masami. 2003. "Commonality of Social Policy on Homelessness: Beyond the Different Appearances of Japanese and English Policies." *European Journal of Housing Policy,* 3(2), 173–192.

Izumo, Marou, and Claire Maree. 2001. *Love Upon the Chopping Board.* Melbourne: Spinifex Press.

Jackson, Judy. 2006. *The Ungrateful Dead: In Search of International Justice.* Video. Saltspring Island, BC: Judy Films.

Japan AIDS and Society Association. 2001. *Eizu wo siru* [Learning about HIV/AIDS]. Tokyo: Kadokawa Shoten.

Japan Association for the Lesbian and Gay Movement (OCCUR). 1999. *Eizu yobōshishin: Sono kaisetsu to kadai* [AIDS prevention: Commentary and guidelines]. Tokyo: OCCUR.

Japan Center for International Exchange. 2004. *Japan's Response to the Spread of HIV/AIDS.* Tokyo: JCIE.

Japan Center for International Exchange. 2005. *East Asian Regional Response to HIV/AIDS, Tuberculosis, and Malaria.* Tokyo: JCIE.

Japan Civil Liberties Union. 1997. *Nihon de kurasu gaikokujin no kodomotachi: Teijūka jidai to kodomo no kenri* [Foreign children living in Japan: The era of long-term residency and children's rights]. Tokyo: Akashi Shoten.

Japan Civil Liberties Union. 2005. *Universal Principle, 12*(Spring).

"Japan Discussing, Not Developing, Nukes: Goodbye Nuclear Taboo." 2006. *The Oriental Economist, 74*(11), 1-2.

Japan Federation of Bar Associations. 1992. *Prisons in Japan: The Human Rights Situation in Japanese Prisons.* Tokyo: JFBA.

Japan International Volunteer Centre. 2000. *NGO no jidai: Heiwa, kyōsei, jiritsu* [The NGO era: Peace, coexistence and independence]. Tokyo: Mekon.

Japan International Volunteer Centre. 2003. *Kodomotachi no Iraku* [The children's Iraq]. Tokyo: Iwanami Shoten.

Japan Network Against Trafficking in Persons and Yoko Yoshida, ed. 2004. *Jinshin baibai wo nakusu tame ni: Ukeire taikoku Nihon no kadai* [Toward the elimination of human trafficking: Issues in the big receiving country of Japan]. Tokyo: Akashi Shoten.

Japan NGO Center for International Cooperation. 2004. *Directory of Japanese NGOs Concerned with International Cooperation.* Tokyo: JANIC.

Japan NGO Network for CEDAW. 2004. *Josei sabetsu teppai jōyaku to NGO* [UN Convention on the Elimination of All Forms of Discrimination Against Women and NGO]. Tokyo: Akashi Shoten.

Japan Times. 1997. "Japan and Multiculturalism." Editorial on the Law to Promote Ainu Culture and Disseminate Knowledge of Ainu Traditions. May 13. Available at http://www.hurights.or.jp/asia-pacific/no_9/no9_multi.htm

Jawara, Fatoumata, and Aileen Kwa. 2003. *Behind the Scenes: Power Politics in the WTO.* New York: Zed Books.

Johnson, Chalmers. 1982. *MITI and the Japanese Miracle.* Stanford, CA: Stanford University Press.

Johnson, Chalmers, ed. 1999. *Okinawa: Cold War Island.* Tokyo: Japan Policy Research Institute.

Johnson, David. 2002. *The Japanese Way of Justice: Prosecuting Crime in Japan.* New York: Oxford University Press.

Johnston, Hank, and Bert Klandermans. 1995. *Social Movements and Culture.* Minneapolis: University of Minnesota Press.

JoJo. 2004. *Onnatachi no benrichō* [Directory of women's groups in Japan]. Tokyo: JoJo.

Kageyama, Yuri. 2004. "American Rice Growers Court Japanese." AP Online, March 07. Available at http://lists.iatp.org/listarchive/archive.cfm?id=89718

Kalakasan Migrant Women Empowerment Center and International Movement Against All Forms of Discrimination and Racism Japan Committee, eds. 2006. *Transforming Lives: Abused Migrant Women in Japan Blaze a Trail Towards Empowerment.* Tokyo: Kaiho Shuppansha.

Kanai, Yoshiko. 2004. "Sanka shite teikō wo! Josei sanka, sankaku, dōin taisei wo

mae ni shite" [Participate and resist! Women's participation, planning, and mo-
bilization]. *People's Plan*, Special Issue: NGO, NPO wa ima, doko ni iruka: Teikō
ka sanka ka [Where are the NGOs and NPOs? Resist or participate], *28*.

Kaname, Yukiko. 2003. "Sekkusu wāku to iu mondai teiki: Sekkusu wāku to jink-
en" [From the viewpoint of sex work: Sex work and human rights]. In *Sei wo
saikō suru: Sei no tayōsei gairon* [Rethinking sex: A conceptual analysis of sexual
diversity], edited by Hideo Hashimoto, Hanatate Tsuyoshi, and Shimazu Takeo.
Tokyo: Seikyūsha.

Kaplan, Caren. 1994. "The Politics of Location as Transnational Feminist Critical
Practice." In *Scattered Hegemonies: Postmodernity and Transnational Feminist
Practices*, edited by Inderpal Grewal and Caren Kaplan. Minneapolis: University
of Minnesota Press.

Katō, Masae. 2005. *Women's Right? Social Movements, Abortion, and Eugenics in
Modern Japan*. Leiden, the Netherlands: Leiden University.

Kato, Yoshiteru. 2000. *Kenpō kaikaku no ronten: 21 seiki no kenpō kōsō* [Points of
constitutional revision: A conception of the constitution in the twenty-first
century]. Tokyo: Shinzansha.

Kawakami, Masako, ed. 2005. *Nihon ni okeru hōmuresu no jittai* [The reality of the
homeless in Japan]. Tokyo: Gakubunsha.

Kawamura, Ken'ichi, and Hiroyuki Kokado. 1995. *Sustainable community jizoku
kanō na toshi no arikata wo motomete* [Sustainable community: Searching for
ways of sustaining cities]. Kyoto: Gakugei Shuppansha.

Kawasaki jinken keihatsu suishin kyōgikai [Commission on the Promotion of
Human Rights in Kawasaki]. 2005. *Iken-gusin: Kawasaki-shi no jinken seisaku ni
tsuite* [Report: Opinions on the human rights policy of Kawasaki City]. Kanagawa, Japan: Kawasaki City Government.

Kaya, Yōichi, and Keiichi Yokobori, eds. 1997. *Environment, Energy, and Economy:
Strategies for Sustainable Development*. Tokyo and New York: Nations University
Press.

Kayano, Shigeru. 1994. *Our Land Was a Forest: An Ainu Memoir*. Boulder, CO:
Westview Press.

Keck, Margaret, and Katherine Sikkink. 1998. *Activists Beyond Borders*. Ithaca, NY,
and London: Cornell University Press.

Keiji Rippō Kenkyūkai. 2005. *Keimusho kaikaku no yukue: Kangokuhō kaisei wo
megutte* [On prison reform: Regarding the revision of the prison law]. Tokyo:
Gendaijinbunsha.

Kempadoo, Kamala, and Jo Doezema, eds. 1998. *Global Sex Workers: Rights, Resistance, and Redefinition*. New York: Routledge.

Kennedy, Joy. 2003. "Currency Transaction Tax: Curbing Speculation, Funding
Social Development." In *Civilizing Globalization: A Survival Guide*, edited by

Richard Sanbrook. Albany: State University of New York Press.

Kerr, George. 2000. *Okinawa: The History of an Island People*. Boston: Tuttle.

Khagram, Sanjeev, James Riker, and Kathryn Sikkink. 2002. *Restructuring World Politics: Transnational Social Movements, Networks, and Norms*. Minneapolis: University of Minnesota Press.

Kim, Puja. 1996. "'Jūgun ianfu' mondai: Undō to sono imi" [The question of comfort women: The movement and its meaning]. In *Jendā* [Gender], edited by Hiroko Hara, Mari Osawa, Makoto Maruyama, and Yasushi Yamamoto. Tokyo: Shinseisha.

Kimoto, Kinuko. 2001. "Barriers to Safer Sex Practices Among Commercial Sex Workers in Osaka, Japan: Scope for Prevention of Future HIV Epidemic." Boston: Harvard School of Public Health. Available at http://www.hsph.harvard .edu/takemi/RP181.PDF#search='antiprostitution%20law%20in%20Japan'

Kimura, Takashi. 2002. "Kore ga NGO to iu ikikata da!" [This is the lifestyle of NGOs!]. *Stage, 9*.

Kitahara, Megumi. 1999. *Art Activism*. Tokyo: Impact.

Kitazawa, Yōko. 2003. *Rijun ka jinken ka: gurōbaruka no jittai to atarashii shakai undō* [Profits or humanity? The reality of globalization and new social movements]. Tokyo: Commons.

Kitazawa, Yōko, Reiko Inoue, and Tomoko Sakuma. 2003. *Jiyū bōeki wa naze machigatte iru no ka? Shimin ni totte no WTO* [What is wrong with free trade? WTO for citizens]. Booklet 12. Tokyo: Pacific Asia Resource Center.

Kō, Fua-Jon. 2004. "Bunka to teikō" [Art and resistance]. *Zenya, 1*(Founding Issue).

Kondō, Atsushi. 2001. *Gaikokujin sanseiken to kokuseki* [The right to vote and nationality of foreigners]. Tokyo: Akashi Shoten.

Kumamoto, Hiroyuki. 2005. "'Henoko' kara Henoko e" [From 'Henoko' to Henoko]. In *Gunshuku chikyūshimin* [Global Citizens for Disarmament], Special Issue: Okinawa kara/Okinawa e [From Okinawa/to Okinawa], *2*, 65–71.

Kumazawa, Makoto. 2004. *Josei rōdō to kigyō shakai* [Women's labor and corporate society]. Tokyo: Iwanami Shoten.

Kume, Ikuo. 1998. *Disparaged Success: Labor Politics in Postwar Japan*. Ithaca, NY: Cornell University Press.

Kusunoki, Toshio. 2005. "Rights of Disabled Persons and Japan." *Asia Pacific News*, 29. Available at http://www.hurights.or.jp/asia-pacific/no_29/04rightsdp.htm

Kymlicka, Will. 1996. *Multicultural Citizenship*. New York: Oxford University Press.

Kymlicka, Will. 2000. *The Rights of Minority Cultures*. New York: Oxford University Press.

Kyōiku kihonhō kaiaku sutoppu! Zenkoku shūkai (National forum to stop the revision of the Fundamental Law of Education). 2004. *Kyōiku kihonhō kaisei mondai no ronten* [Debates surrounding the revision of the fundamental law of education]. Tokyo: Advantage Server.

Kyoto YMCA, Asian People Together. 2001. *Jinshin baibai to ukeiretaikoku Nippon: Sono jittai to hōteki kadai* [Trafficking and the big recipient country, Japan: Reality and legal issues]. Tokyo: Akashi Shoten.

Lal Das, Bhagirath. 1999. *The World Trade Organization: A Guide to the Framework for International Trade*. Penang, Malaysia: Third World Network.

Lane, Charles. 2004. "Why Japan Still Has the Death Penalty." *Washington Post*, January 16, B01. http://www.washingtonpost.com/wp-dyn/articles/A11306-2005 Jan15.html

László, Tony. 1998. "Gaikokuseki jūmin wo fukumu atarashii shakai ketsugō" [A new social cohesion inclusive of foreign residents]. In *Gendai Nihon no paburikku firosofi* [Public philosophy of modern Japan], edited by Naoshi Yamawaki, Mari Ōsawa, Wataru Ōmori, and Ryūichirō Matsubara. Tokyo: Shinseisha.

László, Tony. 2002. "Jūminhyō ga kazoku to chiiki wo bundan suru: Kisai sarenai gaikokujin haigūsha" [Resident certificate as divider of families and communities: Non-Japanese spouses go unrecorded]. *Sekai, 7*, 182–189.

Law, Lisa. 2000. *Sex Work in Southeast Asia: The Place of Desire in a Time of AIDS*. London and New York: Routledge.

Lie, John. 2001. *Multiethnic Japan*. Cambridge, MA: Harvard University Press.

Lloyd, Fran, ed. 2002. *Consuming Bodies: Sex and Contemporary Japanese Art*. London: Reaction Press.

Loos, Noel, and Takeshi Osanai, eds. 1993. *Indigenous Minorities and Education: Australian and Japanese Perspectives on Their Indigenous Peoples, the Ainu, Aborigines, and Torres Strait Islanders*. Tokyo: San'yūsha.

Lummis, Douglas. 2005. "Why Are the Japanese Self-Defense Forces in Iraq?" Available at http://www.ppjaponesia.org/modules/tinycontent1/index.php?id=8#cont

Mackie, Vera. 2002. "'Asia' in Everyday Life: Dealing with Difference in Contemporary Japan." In *Gender Politics in the Asia-Pacific Region*, edited by Brenda Yeoh, Peggy Teo, and Shirlena Huang. London: Routledge.

Maeda, Akira. 2004. *Minshū hōtei no shisou* [On the people's tribunal]. Tokyo: Gendai Jinbun Sha.

Makishi, Yoshikazu. 2000. *Okinawa wa mō damasarenai: Kichi shinsetsu-SACO gōi no karakuri wo utsu* [Okinawa won't be cheated anymore: Taking a shot at the SACO agreement]. Tokyo: Kōbunken.

Malarek, Victor. 2003. *The New Global Sex Trade*. Toronto: Viking Canada.

Matsushige, Itsuo, and Suzuko Yasue. 2003. *Shitte imasu ka? Hōmuresu no jinken* [Do you know? The human rights of the homeless]. Osaka: Kaiho shuppansha.

Medoruma, Syun. 2005. *Okinawa "sengo" zero nen* [Okinawa "postwar" year zero]. Tokyo: NHK Shuppan.

Mekata, Motoko. 2000. "Building Partnerships Toward a Common Goal: Experiences of the International Campaign to Ban Landmines." In *The Third Force: The Rise of Transnational Civil Society,* edited by Ann Florini. Washington, DC: Carnegie Endowment for International Peace.

Mekata, Motoko. 2002. *Jirai naki chikyū e: Yume wo genjitsu ni shita hitobito* [Toward an earth without mines: People who made it a reality]. Tokyo: Iwanami shoten.

Melluci, Alberto. 1995. "The Process of Collective Identity." In *Social Movements and Culture,* edited by Hank Johnston and Bert Klandermans. Minneapolis: University of Minnesota Press.

Mendieta, Eduardo. 2006. *Take Care of Freedom and Truth Will Take Care of Itself: Interviews with Richard Rorty.* Stanford, CA: Stanford University Press.

Mertes, Tom, ed. 2004. *A Movement of Movements: Is Another World Really Possible?* London and New York: Verso.

Micollier, Evelyne. 2004. *Sexual Cultures in East Asia: The Social Construction of Sexuality and Sexual Risk in a Time of AIDS.* London and New York: Routledge Curzon.

Migrants Rights International for the Global Campaign on Migrants Rights. 2000. *Achieving Dignity: Campaigner's Handbook for the Migrants Rights Convention.* Geneva: MRI. Available at http://www.migrantwatch.org

Ministry of Health, Labor and Welfare. 2006. Food Sanitation Law. Available at http://www.jetro.go.jp/en/market/regulations/pdf/food-e.pdf

Miyazaki, Shigeki, ed. 1999. *Kokusaika jidai no jinken to dōwa mondai* [Human rights in an era of internationalization and the Buraku issue]. Tokyo: Akashi Shoten.

Morris-Suzuki, Tessa. 1998. *Re-Inventing Japan: Time, Space, Nation.* London: ME Sharpe.

Munakata, Tsunetsugu, Mako Morita, and Kazumi Fujisawa. 1994. *Nihon no AIDS* [AIDS in Japan]. Tokyo: Akashi Shoten.

Munck, Ronaldo. 2002. *Globalization and Labor: The New Great Transformation.* London and New York: Zed Books.

Murphy-Shigematsu, Stephen. 2002. *Multicultural Encounters: Case Narratives.* New York: Teachers College Press.

Mutō, Ichiyō. 2003. *Empire Versus People's Alliance.* Tokyo: Shakai Hyōronsha.

Mutō, Ichiyō. 2004a. "Asian Peace Movements and Empire." Presentation at the Conference on the Question of Asia in the New Global Order, Asia/Pacific Studies Institute, Duke University, October 1–2. Available at http://multitudes.samizdat. net/article1254.html

Mutō, Ichiyō. 2004b. "Upper House Elections Mark the Beginning of the End of the Koizumi Era: A Major Confrontation Is Impending over the Peace Constitution." Available at http://www.europe-solidaire.org/spip.php?article1853

Naim, Moises. 2000. "Lori's War." *Foreign Policy,* Spring, 28–55.

Naito, Ema. 2005. "The Boy Next Door: Preventing HIV/AIDS Among Japanese MSM." Pamphlet of OCCUR, Japan, distributed at the Seventh International Congress on AIDS in the Asia-Pacific, Kobe, July.

Nakamura, Karen. 2002. "Resistance and Co-optation: The Japanese Federation of the Deaf and Its Relations with State Power." *Social Science Japan Journal*, 5, 17–35.

Nakano, Mami. 2004. "Haken, pāto no chingin to shuntō" [Wages of dispatch and part-time workers and spring wage negotiations]. *Rōdōkumiai*, Supplement Issue, June, 14–16.

Nakata, Hiroko. 2006. "Government Had Plants in Five Town Meetings on Education Bill." *Japan Times*, November 10.

Narain, Jai P., ed. 2004. *AIDS in Asia: The Challenge Ahead*. Thousand Oaks, CA: Sage.

National Network in Solidarity with Migrant Workers. 2002. *Protecting Foreigners in Japan: Some Proposals*. Tokyo: National Network in Solidarity with Migrant Workers. Available from http://www.hurights.or.jp/asia-pacific/no_29/03mnet japan.htm

Neary, Ian. 1989. *Political Protest and Social Control in Pre-War Japan: The Origins of Buraku Liberation*. Manchester, UK: Manchester University Press.

Neary, Ian. 1997. "Burakumin in Contemporary Japan." In *Japan's Minorities: The Illusion of Homogeneity*, edited by Michel Weiner. London: Routledge.

Nemoto, Tōru. 2004. "HIV/AIDS Surveillance and Prevention Studies in Japan: Summary and Recommendations." *AIDS Education and Prevention*, 16(Supplement A), 27–42.

Nenpō Shikeihaishi Henshū Iinkai, ed. 1996. *Aum ni shikei wo" ni dō kotaeruka* [How to respond to the voice, "Sentence Aum to death"]. Tokyo: Impakuto Shuppankai.

Nenpō Shikeihaishi Henshū Iinkai, ed. 1997. *Shikei: sonchi to haishi no deai* [The death penalty: Encounter of maintenance and abolition]. Tokyo: Impakuto Shuppankai.

Nenpō Shikeihaishi Henshū Iinkai, ed. 1998. *Hanzai higaisha to shikei seido* [Victims of crime and the death penalty]. Tokyo: Impakuto Shuppankai.

Nenpō Shikeihaishi Henshū Iinkai, ed. 1999. *Shikei to jōhō kōkai* [The death penalty and information disclosure]. Tokyo: Impakuto Shuppankai.

Nenpō Shikeihaishi Henshū Iinkai, ed. 2000–2001. *Shūshinkei wo kangaeru* [Examining the life sentence]. Tokyo: Impakuto Shuppankai.

Nenpō Shikeihaishi Henshū Iinkai, ed. 2002. *Sekai no naka no Nihon no shikei* [The death penalty of Japan in the world]. Tokyo: Impakuto Shuppankai.

Nenpō Shikeihaishi Henshū Iinkai, ed. 2003. *Shikeihaishi hōan* [A bill to abolish the death penalty]. Tokyo: Impakuto Shuppankai.

Nenpō Shikeihaishi Henshū Iinkai, ed. 2004. *Mujitsu no shikeishūtachi* [Innocent death-row convicts]. Tokyo: Impakuto Shuppankai.

Nenpō Shikeihaishi Henshū Iinkai, ed. 2005. *Aum jiken jyūnen* [Ten years since the Aum incident]. Tokyo: Impakuto Shuppankai.

New Japan Women's Association. 2004. *NGO Alternative Report: Comments on the Response of the Government of Japan to the Questionnaire on Implementation of the Beijing Platform for Action (1995) and the Outcome of the Twenty-Third Special Session of the General Assembly (2000).* Tokyo: New Japan Women's Association. Available at http://www.shinfujin.gr.jp/c_4_english/4_resource/files/b+10njwareport.pdf.

Nikkeiren. 1999. *The Current Labor Economy in Japan 1999.* Tokyo: Nikkeiren.

Nikkeiren. 2000. *Toward a Market Economy with a Human Face.* Tokyo: Nikkeiren.

Nikkeiren. 2002. "Promoting Structural Reform to Overcome the Crisis." Tokyo: Nikkeiren. Available at http://www.keikyoweb.gr.jp/nikkeiren/english/Reports.htm

Nishimatsu, Hiroshi. 2004. "Aigamo suitō dōjisaku" [Integrated rice cultivation and duck farming]. *Kyūshū no mura* [Kyushu village], 15.

No! GMO Campaign. 2004. "Canada–U.S. Press Conference Resume." Handout.

Nohno, Chieko. 2004. *Sei dōitsu sei shōgaisha seibetsu toriatsukai tokureihō* [On the Special Law on Sexual Difference Treatment for Gender Identity Disorder]. Tokyo: Kajo.

Nomura, Kōya. 2005. *Muishiki no shokuminchi: Nihonjin no beigun kichi to Okinawajin* [Unconscious colonialism: Japanese U.S. military bases and the Okinawans]. Tokyo: Ochanomizu Shobo.

Norgren, Tiana. 2001. *Abortion Before Birth Control: The Politics of Reproduction in Postwar Japan.* Princeton, NJ: Princeton University Press.

O'Brien, Robert, Anne-Marie Goetz, Jan Art Scholte, and Marc Williams. 2001. *Contesting Global Governance* Cambridge, UK: Cambridge University Press.

Ogata, Sadako. 2005. *The Turbulent Decade: Confronting the Refugee Crises of the 1990s.* New York: Norton.

Ogawa, Akihiro. 2004. "Invited by the State: Institutionalizing Volunteer Subjectivity in Contemporary Japan." *Asian Anthropology*, 3, 71–96.

Ogura, Toshimaru. 2004a. "Making an Issue of the Alternative World." Available at http://www.ppjaponesia.org/modules/tinycontent0/index.php?id=3

Ogura, Toshimaru. 2004b. "Kokka to shihon ni nomikomareru 'shimin shakai'" [Civil society that is swallowed by the state and capital]. *People's Plan*, 28(Special Issue: NGO, NPO wa ima, doko ni iruka: teikō ka sanka ka [Where are the NGOs and NPOs? Resist or participate], 6–15.

Oguri, Saori. 2002. *Dārin wa gaikokujin* [My darling is a foreigner]. Tokyo: Mediafactory.

Ōhashi, Yukako. 1995. "Umu umanai wa watashi ga kimeru" [I decide whether to give birth]. In *Nihon no feminism 5 bosei* [Japanese Feminism 5 Motherhood], edited by Teruko Inoue, Chizuko Ueno, and Ehara Yumiko. Tokyo: Iwanami Shoten.

Ōhashi, Yukako. 1998. "Ekkyōsuru" [Transgressing the border]. In *Gender de manabu shakaigaku* [Learning sociology through gender], edited by Kimio Ito and Kazue Muta. Kyoto: Sekai Shisō Sha.

Ōhashi, Yukako. 2001. *Karada no kimochi wo kīte miyō* [Let's listen to our bodily feelings]. Tokyo: Yukkusha.

Ōhashi, Yukako. 2003. "Umu umanai wa watashi ga kimeru soshite undemo umanakutemo watashi wa watashi" [I decide whether to give birth and I am me even if I give birth or not]. In *Yūseihogohō ga okashita tsumi* [Crimes committed by the Eugenic Protection Law], edited by Yūsei shujutsu ni taisuru shazai wo motomeru kai [Committee asking for apology for eugenic surgery]. Tokyo: Gendai Shokan.

Ohno, Kazuoki. 2004. *Nihon no Nōgyō wo kangaeru* [On Japanese agriculture]. Tokyo: Iwanami Shoten.

Okamoto, Masataka. 1999. "Zainichi korean mainoritī" [Korean resident minority]. In *Wocchi! Kiyaku jinken iinkai: Doko ga zureteru? Jinken no kokusai kijun to Nihon no genjō* [Watch! Human Rights Committee: Where is the gap? International human rights standards and the situation in Japan], edited by International Human Rights NGO Network. Tokyo: Nihon Hyōronsha.

Okamura, Tetsuo. 2004. *Kyōiku kihonhō "kaisei" to wa nani ka* [What is the revision of the Fundamental Law of Education]. Tokyo: Impact.

Olivera, Oscar, and Tom Lewis. 2004. *Cochabamba: Water War in Bolivia*. Boston: South End Press.

Ong, Aihwa. 1999. *Flexible Citizenship: The Cultural Logics of Transnationality*. Durham, NC: Duke University Press.

Onodera, Tadaaki. 2003. *Chiiki union collaboration ron: Orugu kara mita chiiki kyōtō to wa* [Theory of community union collaboration: Community joint struggle seen by an organizer]. Tokyo: Impact Shuppan Kai.

Osborne, Stephen, ed. 2003. *The Voluntary and Non-Profit Sector in Japan: The Challenge of Change*. London and New York: Routledge Curzon.

Ota, Masahide. 1996. *Kyozetsu suru Okinawa: Nihon hukki to Okinawa no kokoro* [Okinawa that resists: Return to Japan and Okinawan heart]. Tokyo: Kindaibungeisha.

Ota, Masahide. 2000a. *Minikui nihonjin: Nihon no Okinawa ishiki* [Ugly Japanese: Japan's consciousness of Okinawa]. Tokyo: Iwanami Shoten.

Ota, Masahide. 2000b. *Okinawa, kichi naki shima eno dōhyō* [Okinawa, a guidepost toward the islands without military bases]. Tokyo: Shūeisha.

Ota, Masahide. 2000c. *Okinawa no ketsudan* [Okinawa's decision]. Tokyo: Asahi Shimbun Sha.

Ōyama, Shirō. 2005. *A Man with No Talents: Memoirs of a Tokyo Day Laborer*, translated from the Japanese by Edward Fowler. Ithaca, NY: Cornell University Press.

Pacific Asia Resource Center. 1969–2000. *Japan Asia Quarterly Review*. CD ROM. Tokyo: Pacific Asia Resource Center.

Pacific Asia Resource Center. 1995. *The Debt Crisis: The Unnatural Disaster*. Video. Tokyo: Pacific Asia Resource Center.

Peace Depot. 2005. *Year Book: Nuclear Disarmament and Nuclear Weapon–Free Local Authorities*. Tokyo: Peace Depot.

Peaceboat, ed. 2003. *Sensō wo okosanai tame no 20 no hōsoku* [Twenty rules for preventing war]. Tokyo: Poplar Sha.

Peaceboat, ed. 2005. *Peaceboat daikōkai jidai: 84 ka kan chikyū isshū cruise 94 ōgon no utatane* [Age of great voyages by Peaceboat: Cruise around the globe for eighty-four days in 1994: The golden siesta]. Tokyo: Dai san shokan.

Pekkanen, Robert. 2006. *Japan's Dual Civil Society: Members Without Advocates*. Stanford, CA: Stanford University Press.

Pesticide Action Network Asia Pacific. 2000a. *Empty Promises . . . Empty Stomachs: Impacts of the Agreement on Agriculture (AoA) and Trade Liberalisation on Food Security*. Penang, Malaysia: Pesticide Action Network Asia Pacific.

Pesticide Action Network Asia Pacific. 2000b. *Past Roots, Future of Foods: Ecological Farming Experiences and Innovations in Four Asian Countries*. Penang, Malaysia: Pesticide Action Network Asia Pacific.

Peters, Michael, and Peter Roberts. 2000. "Universities, Futurology and Education." *Discourse*, *21*(2), 125–139.

Pharr, Susan. 2003. "Conclusion: Targeting by an Activist State: Japan as a Civil Society Model." In *The State of Civil Society in Japan*, edited by Frank Schwartz and Susan Pharr. New York: Cambridge University Press.

Pharr, Susan, and Ellis Krauss. 1996. *Media and Politics in Japan*. Honolulu: University of Hawaii Press.

Pollock, Griselda, ed. 1996. *Generation and Geographies*. New York: Routledge.

Prideaux, Eric, and Akemi Nakamura. 2006. "'Fascist' Power Grab? Education Bill Shifts Power to the State." *Japan Times*, November 18.

Rajagopal, Balakrishnan. 2003. *International Law from Below: Development, Social Movements, and Third World Resistance*. Cambridge, UK: Cambridge University Press.

RENGO and Nikkeiren. 1999. "Joint Declaration on Employment Stabilization." Available at http://www.jtuc-rengo.org/updates/before2003/weekly/1999/week99oct/99oct7.html

RENGO. 2004. "Position paper on FTAs and EPAs." Tokyo: RENGO.

Rorty, Richard. 1997. *Truth Politics and Post-Modernism*. Amsterdam: Van Gorcum.

Rorty, Richard. 2006. "The Quest for Uncertainty: Richard Rorty's Pilgrimage: Interview by James Ryerson" and "After Philosophy, Democracy: Interview by

Giovanna Borradori." In *Take Care of Freedom and Truth Will Take Care of Itself: Interviews with Richard Rorty*, edited by Eduardo Mendieta. Stanford, CA: Stanford University Press.

Rosset, Peter. 2002. "U.S. Opposes Right to Food at World Summit." Oakland, CA: Food First / Institute for Food and Development Policy. Available at http://www.foodfirst.org/media/printformat.php?id=162

Roth, Joshua Hotaka. 2002. *Brokered Homeland: Japanese Brazilian Migrants in Japan*. Ithaca, NY: Cornell University Press.

Ryang, Sonia, ed. 2001. *Koreans in Japan: Critical Voices from the Margin*. London: Routledge.

Said, Edward. 1994. *Representations of the Intellectual*. New York: Vintage Books.

Saito, Yukiko. 2002. *Botai hogohō to watashitachi* [The Mother's Body Protection Law and us]. Tokyo: Akashi Shoten.

Sakai, Kazuko. 2003. "Problems of the Equal Employment Opportunity Law." Women's Online Media. Available at http://wom-jp.org/e/JWOMEN/kinto.html

Sakuma, Tomoko. 2004. "The Third World Water Forum: Concerned Citizen's Perspective on Water Privatization." Tokyo: JACSES. Available at http://www.jacses.org/en/sdap/water/report01.html

Salamon, Lester. 1994. "The Rise of the Nonprofit Sector." *Foreign Affairs*, 73(4), 109–122.

Sallis, John, ed. 1987. *Deconstruction and Philosophy: The Texts of Jacques Derrida*. Chicago: University of Chicago Press.

Salomon, Gavriel, and Baruch Nevo, eds. 2002. *Peace Education: The Concept, Principles, and Practices Around the World*. Mahwah, NJ: Erlbaum.

Samuels, Richard. 2004. "Constitutional Revision in Japan: The Future of Article 9." Roundtable luncheon of the Brookings Institution Center for Northeast Asian Policy Studies. Available at http://www.brookings.edu/fp/cnaps/events/20041215.pdf

Sandbrook, Richard, ed. 2003. *Civilizing Globalization: A Survival Guide*. Albany: State University of New York Press.

Sands, Phillipe. 2003. *From Nuremberg to The Hague: The Future of International Criminal Justice*. Cambridge, UK: Cambridge University Press.

Sano, Hideo, and Makoto Sano. 2005. *Yoku wakaru nyūkan tetsuzuki* [Understanding immigration procedures]. Tokyo: Nihon Kajo Shuppansha.

Sasaki-Uemura, Wesley. 2001. *Organizing the Spontaneous: Citizen Protest in Postwar Japan*. Honolulu: University of Hawaii Press.

Sawa, Takamitsu. 2000. *21 seiki no mondaigun jizoku kanō na hatten e no michi* [Issues in the twenty-first century: A path to sustainable development]. Tokyo: Shinyō sha.

Schabas, William. 2001. *An Introduction to the International Criminal Court*. Cambridge, UK: Cambridge University Press.

Schellstede, Sangmie Choi, ed. 2000. *Comfort Women Speak: Testimony of Sex Slaves of the Japanese Military*. New York: Holmes and Meier.

Schmidt, Petra. 2002. *Capital Punishment in Japan*. Leiden, the Netherlands: Brill.

Scholte, Jan Arte. 2003. "Democratizing the Global Economy: The Role of Civil Society." Coventry, UK: University of Warwick, Center for the Study of Globalisation and Regionalisation.

Schwartz, Frank, and Susan Pharr. 2003. *The State of Civil Society in Japan*. New York: Cambridge University Press.

Sherr, Lorraine, Catherine Hankins, and Lydia Bennett. 1996. *AIDS as a Gender Issue: Psychosocial Perspectives*. London and Bristol, PA: Taylor and Francis.

Shimada, Yoshiko. 2000. "Defining Experiences: Feminist Exhibitions in the 1990s. A Response from Yoshiko Shimada." *N. Paradoxa*, 13. Available at http://web. ukonline.co.uk/n.paradoxa/define.htm

Shimamoto, Yasuko. 2004. *Rupo kaiko: Kono kuni de ima okite iru koto* [Layoff: It is happening in this country]. Tokyo: Iwanami Shoten.

Shimin Gaikō Centre. 2004. "Use of Depleted Uranium Munitions and Related Contamination in and Around Military Training Areas in Okinawa, Japan." Available at http://www005.upp.so-net.ne.jp/peacetax/e6.html

Shipper, Apichai. 2002a. "Political Construction of Foreign Workers in Japan." *Critical Asian Studies* 34(1), 41–68.

Shipper, Apichai. 2002b. "Pragmatism in Activism: Organizing Support for Illegal Foreign Workers in Japan." Cambridge, MA: Harvard University Program on U.S.-Japan Relations.

Shipper, Apichai. 2005. "Criminals or Victims? The Politics of Illegal Foreigners in Japan." *Journal of Japanese Studies*, 31(2), 299–327.

Shirakawa, Masumi. 2002. Special Issue: Sanka: Seido to undō no kyōkai de [Participation: From the angles of system and movement]. *People's Plan*, 19.

Shirakawa, Masumi. 2004. Special Issue: NGO, NPO wa ima, doko ni iruka: Teikō ka sanka ka [Where are the NGOs and NPOs: Resist or participate]. *People's Plan*, 28.

Shiva, Vandana. 2000. *Stolen Harvest*. Boston: South End Press.

Shiva, Vandana. 2001. "Caring in Agriculture: We Need to Move Away from the Violence of Science." *Resurgence*, 208. Available at http://www.resurgence.org/ resurgence/issues/shiva208.htm

Shiva, Vandana. 2002. *Water Wars: Privatization, Pollution, and Profit*. Boston: South End Press.

Siddle, Richard. 1996. *Race, Resistance, and the Ainu of Japan*. London: Routledge.

Sonohara, Toshiaki. 1997. "Toward a Genuine Redress for an Unjust Past: The Nibutani Dam Case." *Murdoch University Electronic Journal of Law*, 4(2). Available at: http://www .murdoch.edu.au/elaw/issues/v4n2/sonoha42.html

South Centre. 1996. *For a Strong and Democratic United Nations: A South Perspective on UN Reform*. Geneva: South Centre.

Soysal, Yasmine. 1994. *Limits of Citizenship: Migrants and Postnational Membership in Europe*. Chicago: University of Chicago Press.

Stetson, Dorothy, and Amy Mazur. 1995. *Comparative State Feminism*. New York: Sage.

Stevens, Georgina. 2001. "The Ainu and Human Rights: Domestic and International Legal Protections." *Japanese Studies*, *21*(2), 181–199.

Stevens, Georgina. 2003. "UN Expert, R. Stavenhagen, Meets with Ainu Indigenous People." Available at http://www.imadr.org/pub/web/r.stavenhagen-ainu.html

Stiglitz, Joseph. 2002. *Globalization and Its Discontents*. New York: Norton.

Stone-Mediatore, Sharon. 2003. *Reading Across Borders: Storytelling and Knowledges of Resistance*. New York: Palgrave Macmillan.

Suzuki, Mari. 2002. An Interview: "Motto shiritai—NGO saishin jōhō" [I want to know more—The newest NGO information]. *Stage*, *9*, 24–27.

Takada, Ken. 2004. *Goken wa kaiken ni katsu* [Constitutional protection will win over constitutional revision]. Tokyo: Gijutsu to ningen.

Takahashi, Tetsuya. 2004. "'Kokumin' kyōiku to gisei poritikusu" [National education and the politics of sacrifice]. *Gendai Shisō / Revue de la pensée d'audourd'hui* [Contemporary thought], Tokushū: Kyōiku no kiki [Special issue: Educational crisis], *32*(4), 70–75.

Takazato, Suzuyo. 1996. *Okinawa no onnatachi: Josei no jinken to kichi, guntai* [Women in Okinawa: Women's rights and military bases, army]. Tokyo: Akashi Shoten.

Takenobu, Mieko. 2004. "Bashing Gender Equality: Establishing a System That Skews the Population on All Sides." Available at http://www.ppjaponesia.org/modules/tinycontent/index.php?id=9

Takeuchi, Junko. 2002. "Hisabetsu buraku shusshin no josei no tachiba kara" [Women of Buraku origins who have experienced discrimination]. In *Mainoritī josei ga sekai wo kaeru!* [Minority women change the world!], edited by International Movement Against All Forms of Discrimination and Racism. Tokyo: Kaihō Shuppansha.

Taran, Patrick. 2000. *Human Rights of Migrants: Challenges of the New Decade*. Geneva: International Labour Organization.

Taylor, Charles. 1992. "Multiculturalism and the Politics of Recognition." In *Multiculturalism*, edited by Amy Gutmann. Princeton, NJ: Princeton University Press.

Teivainen, Teivo. 2002. "The World Social Forum and Global Democratization: Learning from Porto Alegré." In *Third World Quarterly*, *23*(4), 621–632n.

Teruya, Kantoku. 2002. *Okinawa kara yūjihō–sensōhō wo kangaeru* [Thinking about the Emergency Law–War Law from Okinawa]. Uruma, Japan: Yui Shuppan.

Thornberry, Patrick. 2002. *Indigenous Peoples and Human Rights*. Manchester, UK: Juris and Manchester University Press.

Tlou, Sheila. 2002. "Gender and HIV / AIDS." In *AIDS in Africa*, edited by Max Essex, Souleymane Mboup, Phyllis Kanki, Richard Marlink, and Sheila Tlou. New York: Kluwer Academic / Plenum.

Tokyo Kanrishoku Union, ed. 2003. *Tenkanki no Nihon rōdō undō: Neo kaikyū shakai to kinben kakumei* [Japanese labor movement in the transitional era: Neo-class society and industrious revolution]. Tokyo: Ryokufu Shuppan.

Tomonaga, Kenzō. 1999. "Buraku mondai" [Buraku issue]. In *Wocchi! Kiyaku jinken iinkai: Doko ga zureteru? Jinken no kokusai kijun to Nihon no genjō* [Watch! Human Rights Committee: Where is the gap? International human rights standards and the situation in Japan], edited by International Human Rights NGO Network. Tokyo: Nihon Hyōronsha.

Tongeren, Paul van. 2005. *People Building Peace II: 65 Inspiring Stories*. Boulder, CO: Lynne Rienner.

Tsuji, Shin'ichi. 2001. *Sulō izu byūtifuru* [Slow is beautiful]. Tokyo: Heibonsha.

Uemura, Hideaki. 1999. "Ainu minzoku no kenri to okinawa no jinken jōkyō" [Ainu people's rights and the human rights situation of Okinawa]. In *Wocchi! Kiyaku jinken jinkai: Doko ga zureteru? Jinken no kokusai kijun to Nihon no genjō* [Watch! Human Rights Committee: Where is the gap? International human rights standards and the situation in Japan], edited by International Human Rights NGO Network. Tokyo: Nihon Hyōronsha.

Uemura, Hideaki. 2002. "Dāban e no nagai michinori, soshite, sabetsu teppai no mirai e no shiza" [The long road to Durban and the vision toward elimination of discrimination]. In *Hanjinshushugi, sabetsu teppai sekaikaigi to Nihon* [World Conference Against Racism, Racial Discrimination, Xenophobia, and Related Intolerance and Japan], edited by International Movement Against All Forms of Discrimination and Racism. Tokyo: Kaihō Shuppansha.

Uemura, Hideaki. 2003. "The Colonial Annexation of Okinawa and the Logic of International Law: The Formation of an 'Indigenous People' in East Asia." *Japanese Studies*, 23(2), 213–222.

Uemura, Hideaki. 2004. "Escape from Freedom in the Information Age: Insecure Society Generated by Globalization and the Sacrificed Human Rights of Minorities." *Asia Rights Journal*, 1. Available at http://rspas.anu.edu.au/asiarightsjournal /Uemura.html

Uemura, Hideaki, Mieko Fujioka, and Kenji Nakano. 2004. *Gurōbaru jidai no senjūminzoku: "Senjūminzoku no jūnen" to wa nan datta no ka?* [Indigenous peoples in the era of globalization: What was the International Decade of the World's Indigenous People?] Kyoto: Hōritsu Bunkasha.

Ukai, Satoshi. 2000. "Hata no kanata no kaisō: Naze hinomaru wa 'omedetai' no ka" [Reminiscence across the flag: Why is Hinomaru auspicious?]. In *Impaction*, Tokushū: Hinomaru, Kimigayo no kobami kata [Special issue: Ways to refuse the Hinomaru and Kimigayo], *118*, 28–38.

UNAIDS, UNICEF, and WHO. 2004. *Epidemiological Fact Sheets on HIV / AIDS and Sexually Transmitted Infections (Japan)*. Available at http://www.who.int/hiv/pub/epidemiology/pubfacts/en

United Nations Development Programme. 1992. *Human Development Report: Global Dimensions of Human Development*. New York: Human Development Reports. Available at http://hdr.undp.org/reports/global/2002/en

United Nations Development Programme. 1999. *Human Development Report: Globalisation with a Human Face*. New York: Human Development Reports. Available at http://hdr.undp.org/reports/global/2002/en

United Nations Development Programme. 2002. *Human Development Report: Deepening Democracy in a Fragmented World*. New York: Human Development Reports. Available at http://hdr.undp.org/reports/global/2002/en

United Nations High Commissioner for Human Rights (UNHCHR). 2005. "Fact Sheet No. 24: The Rights of Migrant Workers." Geneva: UNHCHR. Available at http://www.ohchr.org/english/about/publications/docs/fs24.htm

Vines, David, and Christopher Gilbert. 2004. "The IMF and International Financial Architecture: Solvency and Liquidity." In *The IMF and Its Critics*, edited by David Vines and Christopher Gilbert. Cambridge, UK: Cambridge University Press.

Wallach, Lori. 2000. Interview. *Foreign Policy*, Spring, 28–57.

Wallach, Lori, and Michelle Sforza. 1999. *The WTO: Five Years of Reasons to Resist Corporate Globalization*. New York: Seven Stories Press.

Watch Out for WTO! Japan. 2001. *Dai 3 kai WTO-NGO senryaku kaigi hōkokusho* [Report on the third WTO-NGO strategic meeting]. Fukuoka: WOW Japan.

Watkins, Kevin. 1996. *Agricultural Trade and Food Security*. London: Oxfam.

Weiner, Michel, ed. 1997. *Japan's Minorities: The Illusion of Homogeneity*. London: Routledge.

Williamson, Hugh. 1995. *Coping with the Miracle: Japan's Unions Explore New International Relations*. London: Pluto Press.

Williamson, John. 1993. "Democracy and the 'Washington Consensus.'" *World Development*, 21(8), 1329.

Wong, Amy. 2001. *The Roots of Japan: International Environmental Policies*. New York: Garland.

World Bank. 1993. *Social and Gender Dimension of the AIDS Epidemic in Asia*. Washington, DC: World Bank.

World Health Organization. 2001. "Macroeconomics and Health: Investing in Health for Economic Development." Available at http://www.un.org/docs/ecosoc/meetings/hl2002/RT.K.MacroeconomicsHealth.pdf

Yamamoto, Mari. 2004a. "Japan's Grassroots Pacifism." Available at http://japanfocus.org/products/details/2102

Yamamoto, Mari. 2004b. *Grassroots Pacifism in Post-War Japan: The Rebirth of a Nation*. London and New York: Routledge Curzon.

Yamamoto, Tadashi. 1999. *Deciding the Public Good*. New York: Japan Center for International Exchange.

Yamamoto, Tadashi, and Satoko Itoh, eds. 2006. *Fighting a Rising Tide: The Response to AIDS in East Asia*. Tokyo: Japan Center for International Exchange.

Yamashita, Sōichi, and Kazuoki Ohno. 2004. *Hyakushō ga jidai wo tsukuru* [The farmers create another world]. Tokyo: Nanatsumori.

Yamazaki, Koshi. 2005. "Proposed Human Rights Commission in Japan: A Critique." *Asia Pacific News*, 39. Available at http://www.hurights.or.jp/asia-pacific/039/04.htm

Yanbe, Yukio. 2001. *Kōzō kaikaku to iu gensō: Keizaikiki kara dō dasshutsu suru ka* [Illusion of structural reform: How to escape from economic crisis]. Tokyo: Iwanami Shoten.

Young, Iris Marion. 2000. *Inclusion and Democracy*. New York: Oxford University Press.

Yui, Akiko. 2005. "The Okinawan Anti-Base Movement Regains Momentum: New U.S. Base Project Off Henoko Beach Met with Effective Non-Violent Resistance on the Sea." Available at http://www.europe-solidaire.org/spip.php?article5147

Yuval-Davis, Nira. 1999. "The Multi-Layered Citizen." *International Journal of Feminist Politics*, 1(1), 119–136.

INDEX

f = figure; t = table